ENERGY AND NATURAL RESOURCES LA

IN A NUTSHELL

by

JAN G. LAITOS
Professor of Law and
Director, Natural Resources Law Program
The University of Denver College of Law

JOSEPH P. TOMAIN
Dean and
Nippert Professor of Law
University of Cincinnati College of Law

WEST GROUP

Bancroft-Whitney • Banks-Baldwin • Clark Boardman Callaghan
Lawyers Cooperative Publishing • WESTLAW® • West Publishing

1992

Nutshell Series, In a Nutshell, the Nutshell Logo and the West Group symbol are registered trademarks used herein under license.

COPYRIGHT © 1992 By WEST PUBLISHING CO.

610 Opperman Drive
P.O. Box 64526
St. Paul, MN 55164–0526
1–800–328–9352

Printed in the United States of America

Library of Congress Cataloging-in-Publication Data
Laitos, Jan.
    Energy and natural resources law in a nutshelll / by Jan G. Laitos and Joseph P. Tomain.
        p.   cm.
    Includes index.
    ISBN 0–314–00118–2
    1. Power resources—Law and legislation—United States.   2. Energy industries—Law and legislation—United States. 3. Conservation of Natural resources—Law and Legislation—United States.
    4. Environmental law—United States. I. Tomain, Joseph P., 1948- .
    II. Title.
    KF2120.Z9L27   1992
    346.7304 '679—dc20
    [347.3064679]   91–39247
                                                                CIP

ISBN 0–314–00118–2

 TEXT IS PRINTED ON 10% POST CONSUMER RECYCLED PAPER

4th Reprint — 2001

"In Memory of
    Peter Paul Viviano"
            J.G.L.

"In Memory of my father
    Joseph P. Tomain"
            J.P.T.

*

PREFACE

This book is an effort to pull together in one place the salient legal issues associated with energy law and natural resources law. The theme of the book is that not only are energy and natural resources law interrelated, but so too are the topics that comprise energy law and natural resources law. Energy law addresses all the component parts of the energy fuel cycle, as well as the market and government policies that oversee this cycle. Natural resources law consists of public lands and resources law, environmental law, environmental assessment, minerals law, timber law, and water law. These subjects should not be learned or studied in isolation. Practitioners, government policy-makers, resources industries, and public interest organizations confront all of the subjects that make up energy and natural resources law, not, for example, just environmental law, or just oil and gas law. This book reflects that reality.

The authors wish to gratefully acknowledge the support provided this project by the Rocky Mountain Mineral Law Foundation. This Foundation has previously helped to bring to publication many important books on natural resources matters. Dean Tomain wishes to thank Lynn Clark and Connie Miller for their assistance in preparing the manuscript for publication. Professor Laitos wishes to thank and recognize the tireless efforts of Jeanne Reynolds, without whose dedication to the book its eventual publication might not have been possible.

> JAN G. LAITOS
> Denver, Colorado
>
> JOSEPH T. TOMAIN
> Cincinnati, Ohio

January, 1992

OUTLINE

OUTLINE

XIV

PART IV. ENERGY RESOURCE DISTRIBUTION AND USE

TABLE OF CASES
References are to Pages

B

C

E

F

G

H

I

J

K

L

M

N

P

Q

R

S

T

U

V

W

Y

Z

*

ENERGY AND NATURAL RESOURCES LAW

IN A NUTSHELL

*

PART I

LAW AND THE RESOURCES MARKET

LAW AS A RESPONSE TO FAILURES OF THE NATURAL RESOURCES MARKET

Chapters One (Economics and Natural Resources Markets) and Two (Law and Government and the Natural Resources Market) examine the interplay between the market that exists for natural resources, and the different types of laws that affect this market. Some of the property interests that comprise the resources market are similar to those in other markets. Some are so dissimilar, involving public goods, common goods, and private goods with significant negative externalities, that the natural resources market is unique in many ways. In fact, it is so unique that a specialized body of law has arisen to address many of the failures of the unregulated resources market. This law of natural resources entails common law doctrine, statutory and administrative regulation, and constitutional law limitations on government action.

CHAPTER ONE

ECONOMICS AND NATURAL RESOURCES MARKETS

Natural resources, and the energy produced from many of these resources, are fundamental to society. Economic analysis is both a policymaking tool, and a means of explaining the distribution and allocation of these resources. Understanding the distribution and allocation of natural resources in turn allows policymakers and decisionmakers, such as lawyers, judges, administrators, and legislators, to formulate laws and policies regarding the use of natural resources and the production of energy.

Economics is the study of the distribution of scarce resources in the face of basic human needs and unlimited wants. The usual economics course starts with the assumption of a workably competitive market, described below in more detail. Too often, however, the property characteristics of items bought or sold in the market are assumed and, consequently, ignored. To ignore the many attributes of "property" can be dangerous for lawyers and policymakers in natural resources economics because natural resources have unique property characteristics. Before one can understand the natural resources market, one must therefore understand the nature of the property interests that make up this market.

I. PROPERTY INTERESTS IN NATURAL RESOURCES

There are three types of "goods," the stuff of economic analysis, relevant to Energy and Natural Resources Law—private goods, public goods, and common goods.

A. PRIVATE GOODS

Private goods fit the usual understanding of property. A ton of coal, a cord of wood, even a thousand cubic feet of natural gas (stored within some container) can each be considered a private good. Such goods can be owned, used, and transferred in the lay and legal senses of those terms. The traditional concept of private goods means that property rights and duties can be defined *completely;* that owners of property can *exclude* others from using that specified property; and that property can be *transferred* easily from one owner to another. Private goods, then, are characterized by completeness, exclusivity, and transferability.

The coal, wood, and, containerized natural gas referred to above have these three attributes. The owner knows the limits and extent of ownership, can exclude others from using these goods, and can transfer these goods for another person's use. Indeed, such goods can be relatively easily priced and exchanged in either a private transaction or in a larger market exchange. Such exchange transactions are relatively easy because both quantity and legal rights and duties incident to the goods are known.

All natural resources do not share these characteristics. Indeed, the natural gas above was qualified as being containerized. Absent containerization, natural gas does not share all of these property attributes. The inability of a particular natural resource from being owned completely, or the inability to exclude others from it, or the inability to easily transfer ownership, requires economic analysts to talk and think differently about some natural resources.

B. PUBLIC GOODS

Air, sunlight, and wind cannot be owned in the same ways that a ton of coal or an acre of timber can be owned. Because ownership, a person's legal rights and duties relative to a particular good, cannot be completely defined, such goods have different economic effects.

First, dominion (control) over these resources is difficult, and in many instances impossible. No one can capture the sun or control the wind, even though energy from these resources can be harnessed. "Rights" to air, sunlight, and wind cannot be defined completely. Second, because dominion or control is difficult or impossible, so too is transfer. No one can sell you the wind, even though someone can sell you a kilowatt of electricity generated by a windmill. Finally, and most perplexing for economic analysis, one person cannot exclude another person from also using some resources. Further, because ownership cannot be completely defined or easily transferred, and because persons cannot be excluded, the products created by public goods are very difficult to price accurately. In fact, public goods are too often undervalued and, consistent with economic theory, overconsumed.

Undervaluation and overconsumption have two interrelated effects—waste and externalities. Waste occurs because, apart from capital costs, public goods do not cost anything; they will therefore be consumed disproportionately to their "real" value. Externalities occur because, even though wind and sunlight have zero costs, the users who construct windmills and solar collectors may obstruct views or use land in ways that generate social costs. These costs are not included in the price of the energy generated from the windmill or solar collector. Social costs are the result of overconsumption of low or zero cost resources. These social costs are called externalities precisely because they are not included in, and are external to, the price of the product.

C. COMMON GOODS

Here, "common goods" refer to a separate category of resources that are frequently migratory. Natural resources such as oil, natural gas, and water do not stay in one place; rather, they migrate in light of geophysical constraints. Common goods need to be "captured" before an owner can exercise dominion or control over such a good. Similarly, since for common, migrating goods a complete definition of property rights is difficult, it is also difficult to transfer these resources, or exclude others from their use.

Two attributes, the need for capture and the inability to exclude others, combine to produce waste and create what is known as "the tragedy of the commons." To understand this phenomenon, consider an underground reservoir of oil. From the surface, the dimensions of the reservoir are not known and, not surprisingly, the reservoir does not honor any legal boundaries established on the surface. In order to obtain economic benefits from the oil, the surface owner will drill into the reservoir.

The legal (and economic) incentive to drill is known as the rule of capture, which holds that whoever "captures" the resource keeps it. Thus, the reward goes not to the frugal interest holder who keeps the oil in the ground, but to the persons who drill and capture it. A landowner is encouraged by the rule of capture to bring the resource to the surface before a neighboring landowner or lessee does. The "tragedy" is that such common natural resources are overconsumed (wasted) rather than used in response to market demand. When there is overconsumption of a resource, the free market in that resource is in disequilibrium and government regulation is usually necessary to correct the defect. State oil and gas conservation laws are the regulatory response to the problem of waste created by the rule of capture. These laws attempt to limit waste by reducing production and conserving supply.

This chapter, and the remainder of the book, use the terms natural resources, property, and goods. While these three terms may be used interchangeably, one should remember that different resources have distinct property attributes that affect economic, policy, and legal analyses.

II. THE FREE MARKET AND NATURAL RESOURCES USE

The United States polity can be described as a state of democratic capitalism. Simply defined, the phrase "democratic capitalism" means that individual rights and liberties can flourish best in a market economy, rather than a highly centralized or socialized one. While debatable, this idea is the starting point for government regulation.

A. THE REGULATORY LIFE CYCLE

As a matter of political philosophy, government policymakers (executives, legislators, administrators, and judges) start from the *laissez-faire* premise that the free market is preferred over government regulation. However, *laissez-faire* is more an ideal than a reality. The reality is that when the market fails, government regulation is often used to correct the defect until the regulation itself fails. The process of government regulation can be seen as a "life cycle," falling into six more or less identifiable stages:

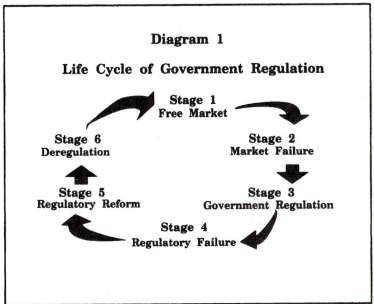

Diagram 1

Life Cycle of Government Regulation

Stage 1
Free Market

Stage 2
Market Failure

Stage 3
Government Regulation

Stage 4
Regulatory Failure

Stage 5
Regulatory Reform

Stage 6
Deregulation

|50A|

Stage 1, the Free Market, is the period when there is no government intervention in an industry or market. Consistent with our political system of democratic capitalism, this stage adopts a version of *laissez-faire*, limited government. If the market is functioning properly or reasonably well, and if the market is efficient and fair, then government intrusion cannot improve the situation. In economic jargon, the absence of government regulation may be seen as Pareto optimal, i.e., the intrusion of government regulation would make at least one person worse off. In the face of a well working (efficient and fair) market, government regulation will, at a minimum, add unnecessary administrative costs, thus reducing allocative efficiency and causing inequitable distributions. Such a market will not improve with government price or quality controls. Rather, these regulations will likely raise prices, reduce supply, and drive some producers from the market, thus reducing competition.

However, achieving or maintaining an ideal free market is difficult. Frequently, a market is in disequilibrium because of the existence of a market failure. Standard examples of Stage 2 market failures are described later in this chapter. Many failures are externalities, such as pollution. Identification of a failure suggests a regulatory response from government. The existence and identification of market failure become the justification for government intervention into private enterprise that moves regulation from Stage 2 into Stage 3.

A justification for government intervention, Stage 3, is a necessary but insufficient condition for government regulation, because government must respond with the correct regulatory tool to the perceived market failure. The consequence of using the wrong regulatory tool, for example, using price supports to correct inadequate information, may worsen a situation rather than improve it. The goal of a government regulation is to improve a particular market situation by making it more efficient, more fair, or both. In the best of circumstances, the introduction of government regulation can be seen as a Pareto superior move, i.e., a change in the status quo that makes at least one person better off without making anyone worse off. According to another economic test, called Kaldor–Hicks efficiency, a government regulation is successful when it increases net benefits.

The wrong regulatory tool may make government intervention into the private market more costly, or impose the costs more unfairly, or both. The use of inadequate or incorrect regulation creates regulatory failure, or Stage 4. Part of the debate about the 1990 Amendments to the Clean Air Act, estimated to cost tens of billions of dollars, emerged because the costs could outweigh the benefits. Such analysis of costs and benefits raises myriad technical, social, and economic questions which ultimately must be resolved through the political process. The question is always the same—do the costs of regulation outweigh the benefits? If clean air regulation "costs" more than the "benefits," then there will be regulatory failure. "Costs" and "benefits" are placed in quotation marks to emphasize that they may include social as well as economic costs and benefits, and that the calculation is not a simple matter.

There are two reactions to regulatory failure. In the last two stages of the regulatory life cycle, either government can respond by correcting the failure through regulatory reform (Stage 5), or, government can extract itself from the market altogether by deregulation (Stage 6), i.e., by eliminating regulations, thus reverting back to Stage 1—the free market.

Not every regulatory effort goes through each of these stages. A program caught in the stage of government failure, for example, need not entertain a package of regulatory reforms, and may instead proceed to deregulation. Still, the life cycle, and its underlying aspirations for efficiency and fairness, highlight the role that the political process plays in our system of government regulation. The underlying ideology of government regulation is to correct inequities in markets, in response to the reality that markets do not always run smoothly.

B. THE MARKET

It is especially important to understand the first stage of the regulatory life cycle, the free market, because this stage forms the base for government regulation. Free market advocates often extol the virtues of the market. These virtues include the efficient use of resources, which means that cheaper resources are used before more costly resources. As a corollary to this virtue, consumer satisfaction is maximized because consumers will buy the cheapest goods first. The free market also sends correct "price signals," in that consumers buy goods at the prices they want, thus "signalling" to producers what goods should be on the market at what prices. This give and take between producers and consumers stimulates innovation as producers attempt to lower costs or improve quality to increase profits. Finally, the medium of market exchange is money, and money is race and gender blind. Voting in the market is done through the pocket book rather than the ballot box. In this way, liberty and equality become hallmarks of the free market. These virtues—efficient prices, fair distribution, wealth creation, innovation, and liberty and equality—follow from the market as defined in micro-economic theory.

According to that theory, the market must have the following attributes:

(1) there must be numerous buyers and sellers;

(2) there must be a large enough quantity of goods so that no single buyer or seller perceives that he or she can affect price by varying either the quantity demanded or supplied;

(3) the product must be homogeneous;

(4) there must be accurate and complete product information for buyers and sellers; and,

(5) there must be freedom of entry into and exit from the marketplace.

Given these characteristics, the market can achieve the virtues earlier listed through certain operations.

1. Demand

The law of demand can be considered the fundamental economic principle driving the market. The law means that if someone wants or needs a given good, that person will be less willing to pay for another unit of the good if the price rises. If unleaded gas could be purchased for $1.25 per gallon, and if it rose to $1.30 per gallon, the law of demand says that less gasoline would be purchased. The law is graphically shown by a downward sloping demand curve (D):

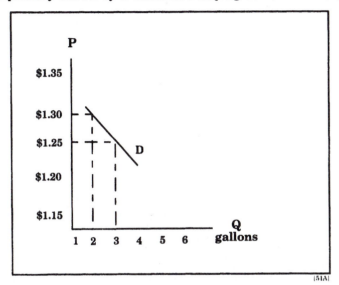

Quite simply, as prices increase, demand decreases. According to the slope of the graph, at $1.25, three gallons of gasoline will be purchased, whereas only two gallons will be purchased at $1.30.

2. Supply

The law of supply is a corollary to the law of demand. As prices increase, producers are encouraged to place more goods on the market. The classic supply curve is upward sloping. The higher the price of a cord of wood, the greater the quantity of timber that will be produced for the market. The graph below demonstrates that four cords of wood will be placed on the market at $50 per cord, whereas only three cords of wood will be placed on the market at $40 per cord.

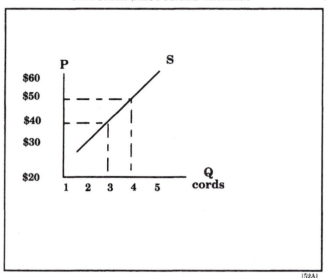

These simple, perhaps obvious, laws of supply and demand are significant for natural resources economics. As the price of a barrel of oil rises on the global oil market, there will be an increase in oil drilling in order to profit from the more lucrative market. Likewise, when the price of interstate natural gas drops below that of intrastate gas, then natural gas producers will try to put their product on the more profitable intrastate market.

The laws of supply and demand determine which goods are produced and, in turn, which resources are used in production. When the price of oil is higher than the price of natural gas, then producers, following the supply curve, are encouraged to produce oil, just as consumers, following the demand curve, are encouraged to purchase natural gas. It would seem that producers' desire for higher prices and consumers' desire for lower prices produce an unresolvable conflict. Not so. Rather, the give and take of producers and consumers push the market toward equilibrium as consumers' demand has an upward effect on prices and producers' supply has a downward effect.

3. Equilibrium

Imagine a market for coal in which the equilibrium price (E) is $23 per ton. The graphic depiction of that market would have the demand and the supply curves intersect at $23 per ton:

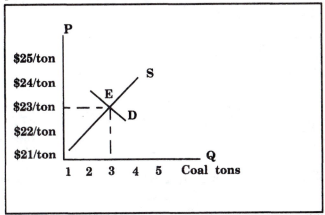

At the equilibrium point *E*, three tons of coal will be sold at $23. Given a competitive market, i.e., buyers and sellers so numerous that no single buyer or seller can affect price, no producer will supply coal at $24 per ton because there will be no buyers. Consumers can purchase all they want at $23. Likewise, no consumer *can* purchase at $22 because no producer can afford to supply at that price; otherwise they will go broke. However, these consequences follow only from a perfectly competitive market. In the absence of such a highly sensitive degree of competition, producers and consumers will experiment with prices, some offering and buying at $24, and others at $22, until the optimum allocation of goods reaches an equilibrium of $23.

Price equilibrium has another effect, particularly as it relates to government price regulation. If a government subsidy reduced the price of coal below the equilibrium point to $22 per ton, there would be a theoretical shortage of coal because consumer demand would be greater than producer supply. Similarly, if the price were raised above the equilibrium point to $24 per ton, for example through a tax, then there would be a "surplus" of coal as producers placed more coal on the market than consumers would want to purchase at the higher price. In both situations, shortage and surplus, the market is in disequilibrium.

4. Costs

Producers place goods on the market when it is profitable for them to do so. Profit is revenue minus costs. When the costs of drilling for oil exceed the revenue gained, then it is no longer profitable to drill and no oil will be produced.

Costs follow a pattern. In the beginning of the production cycle, costs start high. But costs decline as more units are produced. The initial costs of producing the first barrel of oil are extremely high, but fall for the next several thousand barrels. Costs will decline until there are diminishing returns, i.e., until it becomes necessary to drill deeper, or to use enhanced recovery techniques, or to drill another well. Each of these events adds costs. In other words, as output increases, costs for the production of a single unit will decline until they reach the point of diminishing returns. Consequently, cost curves are U-shaped.

It is also important to distinguish between marginal and average costs. Average costs are determined by dividing all costs by the number of units produced, as the cost curve in the next figure demonstrates.

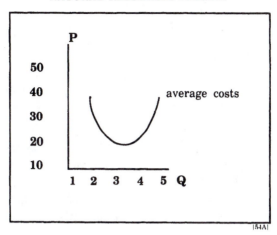

Costs may also be defined as marginal costs—the costs associated with the production of an additional unit:

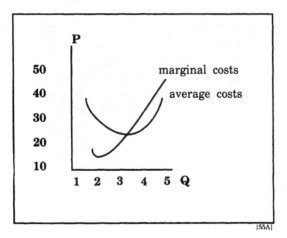

The distinction between average cost and marginal cost is important. If a single oil well, for example, produces 1,000 barrels of oil for a total cost of $20,000, then the average cost is $20 per barrel. If the next barrel of oil costs $25 to produce because of higher drilling costs, then the average cost is approximately $20.005 ($20,025 divided by 1001 barrels) even though the marginal cost is $25 (the cost of producing the 1,001st unit). A producer should charge $25 for the 1,001st unit. A producer should charge $25 for the 1,001st barrel rather than $20.005, because $25 accurately represents production costs. Therefore, for competitive firms, marginal cost is the supply curve.

The distinction between average and marginal costs is also important because average costs will underestimate current costs in an inflationary market. Marginal costs give better information about production costs and profitability. The marginal cost curve is the individual firm's supply curve because it is the better indicator of current costs and profitability.

5. Marginal Revenue

A discussion of marginal revenue demonstrates why the marginal cost of producing the next unit is the more accurate indicator of cost (and profit). Optimum price is based on marginal revenue. Producers want to maximize profits. However, profit maximization does not depend on selling the most units. Rather, profit is maximized when marginal cost equals marginal revenue. The following chart shows the relationship between revenue and profits:

Q	P	TR	TC	TP	MC	MR
1	10	10	8	2		
2	9	18	10	8	2	8
3	8	24	14	10	4	6
4	7	28	16	12	2	4
5	6	30	18	12	2	2
6	5	30	20	10	2	0
7	4	28	22	6	2	-2
8	3	24	24	0	2	-4
9	2	18	26	-8	2	-6
10	1	10	28	-18	2	-8

Q	=	Quantity		TP	=	Total Profit
P	=	Price		MC	=	Marginal Cost
TR	=	Total Revenue		MR	=	Marginal Revenue
TC	=	Total Cost				

[56A]

Notice that total revenue (TR) is maximized at 30, when either 5 or 6 units (Q) are sold. Contrast this level of revenue with the TR of 10, when 10(Q) is the maximum level of units sold. The price must decline as the quantity sold increases in a competitive market where the laws of supply and demand function. To sell more quantity, the producer must lower price, thus running the risk of reducing total revenue. Notice, then, how TR declines as more units are sold after 6(Q). At some point in the production cycle, increasing the number of units sold does not increase total revenue.

From a total revenue standpoint, it makes no difference if 5 or 6 units are sold because TR is the same at 30. However, if one considers total profitability (TP), at 5 units TP is 12, and at 6 units TP is 10. TP is the result of deducting total cost (TC) from total revenue (TR). Therefore, a greater profit is made by selling 5 units than by selling 6 or more units. Notice that profit is maximized when marginal cost (MC) is equal to marginal revenue (MR), i.e., MC = MR = 2.

6. Price Elasticity of Demand

The law of demand requires that for every change in price there will be a change in demand. For every price rise, there will be a decline in demand. The more refined question is: What is the rate of change? If for every 1% price rise there is a 1% decrease in demand, then the price elasticity is said to be unitary. Elastic prices are those that respond with a greater percentage decrease in demand for every percentage increase in price. In a highly competitive market, a firm that sets prices higher than the market risks losing all consumers. Likewise, a firm that can sell at below the market will capture customers.

Some goods, however, are highly valued so that there will be less of a decline in demand for every corresponding price rise. Such a situation is said to be inelastic. When prices are inelastic, producers can raise prices without an exact corresponding decrease in demand. Inelastic demand has the effect of increasing producers' revenues and effecting a greater transfer of resources from consumers to producers. For many years, electricity prices were thought to be so inelastic that electric utilities could raise prices to increase profits (absent close public utility commission oversight). However, in the 1970s, as electricity (and all energy) prices escalated at a rate greater than inflation, consumers did respond to rising electricity prices by reducing consumption. This reduction in demand had the result of forcing electricity prices down.

These six market operations allow the perfectly competitive market to achieve the virtues earlier noted. The operative phrase here, of course, is "perfectly competitive." Markets for ball point pens, video recorders, and hamburgers are examples of at least workably competitive markets. These markets have numerous buyers and sellers, and a great variety of alternatives. Consequently, prices are competitively set as buyers and sellers move into and out of these markets. Natural resources, particularly those used in the production of energy, often do not achieve a state of workable competition because of the existence of market failures. Some resources like oil and natural gas have property characteristics (notably their migratory nature) that prevent proper supplies from reaching the market. Other industries, e.g., electricity and natural gas transportation, are structured in such a way that firms can exercise market power over consumers. And, other resources, such as the use of air and water, entail costs that are not included in the price of the product. When markets are not competing, government may have to intervene in order to move that market toward competition.

III. FAILURES OF THE MARKET

In our political economy, there are two effects of recognizing a market failure. The first effect is descriptive. The identification of the failure points out the inefficiency or unfairness of the market. The second effect is prescriptive. Once a market failure is identified, then this identified defect becomes a justification for government intervention, and helps indicate what sort of regulatory tool is appropriate. The following list of market failures or imperfections is derived from Judge Stephen Breyer's scholarly work, *Regulation and Its Reform* (1982).

A. MONOPOLY

Some industries, e.g., public utilities and railroads, are so structured that only a small number of firms or only one firm may enter the market. The entry costs are high and viable alternatives are not available. These industries tend towards monopoly or oligopoly power. Because there is an absence of competition, firms need not set prices according to the laws of supply and demand, or according to their costs. Rather, firms in a monopoly position can restrict output, increase profits, and consequently, impose a social welfare loss by charging higher than competitive prices. The exercise of such monopoly power has been found to be inconsistent with the public interest. Regulation is therefore needed to set prices at competitive levels. Government-established prices are intended to more closely reflect this kind of producer's costs.

It is often said that the distribution systems for electricity and natural gas utilities are "natural monopolies." According to theory, because of large capital costs of entry (e.g., costs of land acquisition and capital construction), it would be economically wasteful to have two or more utilities attempt to serve the same area. But because even natural monopolies can cause waste through noncompetitive pricing practices, government price setting is necessary.

B. RENT CONTROL

Another justification for regulation is to control or capture windfall profits. These are also referred to as economic rents. They occur when there are sudden increases in the price of a resource. In the regulation of the oil industry in the late 1970s, the rationale behind imposition of the Crude Oil Windfall Profits Tax was that if oil prices were allowed to rise to world levels (levels that were artificially high because of the OPEC cartel), then existing domestic oil stocks, that cost less to produce, would also rise to the world price level. The result would be higher profits for domestic reserves unrelated to domestic producers' costs. These profits were seen as excessive and as a "windfall" to domestic oil companies. These producers' windfall profits were taxed, and the revenues raised from these taxes were transferred for other public purposes in the belief that the profits were not "earned" by producers. Iraq's invasion of Kuwait and its threats to Saudi Arabia also caused the world price of oil to rise to the economic benefit of domestic reserves.

C. EXTERNALITIES

Externalities are costs that are not borne by the actors in a particular transaction. If a manufacturing plant is allowed to pollute and the property of neighboring homeowners is devalued because of the pollution, that devaluation is an externality or spillover cost of the decision to allow the plant to operate. Because polluting firms do not voluntarily incur social costs, regulation appears needed to compensate for the fact that the price of the product does not reflect the costs of production. Environmental laws protecting air and water and land through standard setting are the most pervasive examples of the way government regulation deals with externalities.

D. INFORMATION COSTS

Regulation is also designed to provide consumers with information that may not be made readily available by private industry because of the high cost of acquiring and distributing that information. Further, information itself has value. Frequently, a firm will not voluntarily incur the costs involved with acquiring or distributing information. Nor will firms give away valuable information. Therefore, in order to make information available, government will intervene.

Health warnings on cigarettes, mileage ratings on cars, and ingredients labeling are all examples of government mandated distribution of information. Because the market does not supply this information voluntarily, government intervention serves to provide information with which consumers can make choices. Although consumers as a class may have the interest and wherewithal, economically and politically, to seek this information, individual consumers do not. It is often impractical to aggregate large groups of consumers, because the costs of doing so are so high.

E. EXCESSIVE COMPETITION

Excessive competition is another market defect, occurring when prices are set so low that rival companies go out of business. After enough companies leave the market, the remaining few can then engage in monopoly or oligopoly pricing. Regulation results, setting prices at a level where firms can stay competitive. The airline and trucking industries are often cited as examples of excessive competition. These industries petitioned government for relief from that competition, and for price setting at levels sufficient to maintain reasonable profitability. Curiously, these industries are now undergoing deregulation, and one consequence has been a reduction in competition leading to oligopoly pricing.

F. SCARCE RESOURCE ALLOCATION

Regulation may also be imposed on an industry to alleviate scarcity. In a time of a natural gas shortage, for example, producers could find it more profitable to service one class of consumers over another. This is consonant with a market dominated by a profit principle, but it does not necessarily bring about a fair distribution of resources. Government intervenes to allocate resources where they are needed most, such as to hospitals, schools, and critical manufacturing facilities.

G. UNEQUAL BARGAINING

If the actors in any given market do not have equal bargaining power, then exchange transactions cannot occur smoothly. Producers can take advantage of consumers in a monopoly market, or large consumers can take advantage of producers in a monopsony market (a market made up of very few consumers). An individual residential utility customer, for example, cannot easily or cheaply bargain with a utility. The bargaining costs will often be greater than the value of the transaction. Often, government will facilitate such bargaining through regulatory oversight.

H. RATIONALIZATION

Another word for rationalization is standardization. Efficiencies are realized when light bulbs, even when made by different manufacturers, are a uniform size, and when electricity service is of a uniform power. If one firm, or a small group of firms, control a particular market, then there is less incentive to move to widespread uniformity. Government regulation, however, can facilitate that uniformity by rationalizing an industry.

I. PATERNALISM

Just as the word implies, there are times when government will step into a market because policymakers either want to correct or to preempt behavior. Speed limits, pesticide labeling requirements, and fuel standards each can be seen as a form of paternalist government regulation.

J. MORAL HAZARD

A moral hazard is a situation in which the probability of a loss, as well as the size of the loss, may be increased because a person has less of an incentive to take precautions. Another way of conceptualizing moral hazard is thinking of it as a situation when someone else pays. Expense accounts, insurance, and medical benefits have the effect of encouraging consumers to spend more than they would if the expenses were internalized (paid directly by the consumer). In the energy and natural resources area, historic cost ratemaking for natural gas and electric utilities is an example of a form of moral hazard, because a utility can build more plants with the knowledge that its customers will pay for the plant through higher rates. This form of ratemaking led to historic excess capacity in the 1970s.

IV. COST–BENEFIT ANALYSIS

If a market is in disequilibrium, and if there has been a political choice for government to enter that market, then government policymakers must choose an appropriate regulatory strategy, including non-intervention. To assess the appropriate intervention or non-intervention, policymakers frequently rely on cost-benefit analysis.

Cost-benefit analysis is a methodology used to decide which, among competing public projects, will best maximize social benefits and minimize social costs. Cost-benefit analysis is capable of a simple formulation: "Is the social benefit greater than the social cost?" However, this statement obscures the complexity of its application and can mask hidden assumptions inherent in its use.

A. AN OVERVIEW OF COST-BENEFIT METHODOLOGY

Cost-benefit analysis can be divided into four stages: identification, classification, quantification, and presentation. First, the various effects of a proposed project are identified. These are then classified into economic and social benefits and costs. At this stage, risks are also identified and then translated into costs. Next, the effects are quantified. The easiest and most common to quantify involve economic effects. Obviously, all things cannot be measured in monetary terms. One value of a life from an accounting standpoint is how much a person may earn in a projected lifetime. But surely no one can confidently say that that measure is the sole value of a life. Even between two people similarly situated financially, the value of a dollar differs between the frugal daughter and the prodigal son. So quantification is also a tricky step. The final major stage is the presentation of information. Presentation entails an articulation of assumptions and the implications of assumptions.

The core question of cost-benefit analysis is whether any given action has made society better or worse off. Between two policies, A and B, for example, it may readily be determined that A is superior to B, yet it may not be so easy to determine if A is a useful choice, or whether the better choice is no choice.

B. A CRITIQUE OF COST-BENEFIT ANALYSIS

The methodology has not been without its critics. Although it has value because it encourages the gathering of information and highlights sensitive normative and positive issues, its application may be misplaced or overemphasized by decision-makers. Advocates of cost-benefit analysis see it as a way to deal with large masses of complex and often conflicting data. Critics do not impugn the contributions of cost-benefit, but warn those that attempt to use it to not rely entirely on an equation that focuses only on economic efficiency criteria. Use of the method may obscure the equally delicate moral and social issues that occur within the context of the allocation of scarce resources. This allocation is ultimately a political, not an economic question.

Even the idea of identifying benefits is troublesome. Assume the Environmental Protection Agency and Department of Energy must decide whether or not to require a certain type of anti-pollution device for coal fired electric plants. If the decision is made to enforce the requirement, some plants will never be built because the cost of installation is so high. Is the loss of the electric plant a cost? Or, is it a benefit in that pollution is reduced? Or, is it a benefit to create an anti-pollution industry which, if successful, will produce cleaner air and more coal-fired electric plants?

The identification of costs poses a similar set of problems. Is it a cost, in the above hypothetical, that certain plants never opened? There appears to be a lost opportunity cost, where people will be without employment in that electric plant. Should the equation also include the costs attendant with industry concentration, i.e., those that arise because only the largest firms will be able to install such devices? And should the equation include costs attributable to air pollution immediately around the site, the adverse impact on the health of the workers, and the costs of lost life expectancy?

This latter cost raises another set of identification problems—the identification of risks. While a prediction can be made that some people will suffer health effects from breathing the pollutants from the proposed plant, one does not know how many people will be affected, nor for what period of time.

A cost-benefit analysis may also vary according to the decision-maker being scrutinized. In the above hypothetical

on anti-pollution, will the presentation change if it is made
by the Department of Energy, rather than the EPA?

C. THE LEGAL ROLE OF COST–BENEFIT ANALYSIS

Cost-benefit analysis has become a major methodology in
environmental decisionmaking. Although the National Environmental Policy Act, 42 U.S.C.A. § 4374 (1988), does not
explicitly allow this method, other statutes do. See e.g., The
Flood Control Act of 1936, 33 U.S.C.A. § 701a (1988).

The question of the proper role for cost-benefit analysis in
the law was presented to the Supreme Court in American
Textile Manufacturers Institute, Inc. v. Donovan (1981). The
majority opinion, relying on Justice Marshall's dissent in an
earlier case, Industrial Union Dept., AFL–CIO v. American
Petroleum Institute (1980), held that cost-benefit analysis
could not be used to override the express purpose of legislation. The Court reasoned that the Occupational Safety and
Health Act had already defined the basic relationship between costs and benefits by placing the benefit of workers'
health above all other considerations. Additional cost-benefit analysis would be superfluous or inconsistent with the
statute.

The *American Textile* case wisely recognizes that decisionmaking may be too complex to be left to the dictates of a
mathematical equation. Some administrative reform efforts,
such as Executive Order 12,291, 46 Fed.Reg. 13193–98 (Feb.
19, 1981), have attempted to increase dependence on cost-
benefit analysis. Quantitative methods appeal to our need
for certainty by providing hard, positive data; they yield
answers when asked. Nevertheless, they also deemphasize
normative issues.

Economic analysis and its public decisionmaking counterpart, cost-benefit analysis, are useful tools. Both are capable
of pointing out and highlighting positive and empirical data

that are useful for formulating policy and making policy decisions. Nevertheless, both methods are capable of distortion. Neither method can be the sole decisionmaking method because public policy decisions must also account for broader social issues, the variables of which are difficult if not impossible to quantify.

CHAPTER TWO

LAW AND GOVERNMENT AND THE NATURAL RESOURCES MARKET

Natural resources markets are comprised of parties who discover, own, develop, use, transfer, sell, purchase, or protect economically valuable natural resources. As with other markets, the natural resources market does not operate efficiently in the absence of legally-enforceable rules. If the market were law-free, there would be no principled way to establish ownership, enforce transfers, resolve disputes among market actors, or internalize the external "social" costs of natural resources development.

In the United States, four legal regimes referee, organize, and establish the norms of the natural resources market— the common law, regulations, statutes, and constitutional law. The common law is defined by courts, usually in the context of private party transactions. By contrast, statutory law stems from an organ of elected government, the legislature. State legislatures ordinarily derive their authority to act from the police power, while the United States Congress typically exercises power under the Commerce or Property Clauses of the Constitution (art. I, § 8, cl. 3; art. IV, § 3). State and federal statutes affecting natural resources are implemented through regulations, adopted by administrative agencies specialized in resources law matters. Constitutional law not only establishes the basic structure of government and fundamental rights, it also serves as a limit on the exercise of the statutory law. All four regimes are further interpreted and defined by courts.

I. THE COMMON LAW AND NATURAL RESOURCES

By the end of the Twentieth Century, much of energy and natural resources law was statutory and regulatory. Nonetheless, common law torts, property, and contracts continue to play an important role. These common law doctrines are particularly useful to those in a resources market wishing to establish ownership rights, transfer legal interests in natural resources, or settle controversies arising when one market participant's action affects another. The common law sets a baseline for the market, and without these rules no market could operate. Actors using common law in the natural resources market tend to be private parties—individuals, corporations, and public interest or property owners' organizations. If the natural resource is owned by local government, a state, or the federal government, a government agency may be a plaintiff or defendant in a common law action involving a private party.

A. LIMITATIONS ON THE COMMON LAW

1. Statutory Law

Statutes (and regulations adopted thereunder) may abolish rights recognized at common law. For example, in Hull v. Sun Refining and Marketing Co. (1989), when an oil and gas royalty owner-lessor executes a division order, state statutory law provides that the owner is bound by the provisions of the division order, even though it may abrogate more favorable common law rights arising under the lease. In Cunningham v. Anchor Hocking Corp. (1990), an employees' common law action based on strict liability for an employer's ultra hazardous activity was barred by the state Workers' Compensation Act. Federal statutes may also preempt common law tort claims. See Papas v. Upjohn Co. (1991) (the Federal Insecticide, Fungicide, and Rodenticide Act preempts state common law tort claims for inadequate labeling); Elliot v. United States Fish and Wildlife Serv. (1991) (action against federal agency based on alleged breach of common law fiduciary duty to protect wildlife preempted by federal statutes).

To soften the preemptive potential of statutes, state constitutional provisions may preserve certain common law rights and remedies. The court in Carrow Co. v. Lusby (1989) held that a statute protecting livestock owners from liability for damage caused by animals in open range did not violate the state constitution retaining common law rights of action, because a common law action for negligent grazing of livestock did not pre-exist the constitution.

Common law actions can also survive a statute if the applicable statute provides for common law relief as an alternative basis for recovery. In State of New York v. Shore Realty Corp. (1985), a common law public nuisance claim to compel clean up of a hazardous waste site was brought by a state in conjunction with a suit under federal statutory hazardous waste law. A common law claim can sometimes serve as an exception to statutory law, when the claim is not in conflict with the statute. Cascade Energy and Metals Corp. v. Banks (1990). Even though statutory formalities are taken by resources companies to keep separate corporate and individual property, courts may impose individual liability and disregard the statutory corporate form when it has been used unfairly. Pan Eastern Exploration Co. v. Hufo Oils (1988).

2. Public Rights

Sometimes non-statutory public rights to natural resources are elevated over private ownership rights. This limitation, itself rooted in the common law, provides that private rights may be subject to superior public rights involving (1) use of the surface of certain waterways, (2) ownership of the lands under particular waterbodies, and (3) access to waters across private lands.

a. The Federal Navigational Servitude

If a waterbody is navigable in fact, then it may be subject to the navigational servitude of the United States. A waterbody is navigable in fact when it is used or susceptible of being used in its ordinary condition to transport commerce. United States v. Appalachian Elec. Power Co. (1940). To be navigable, a stream need not be open to navigation at all seasons of the year, nor at all stages of the water. Economy Light & Power Co. v. United States (1921). However, susceptibility of use as a highway for commerce should not be confined to exceptional conditions or short periods of temporary high water. As the Supreme Court has held, "the mere fact that logs, poles, and rafts are floated down a stream occasionally and in times of high water does not make it a navigable river." United States v. Rio Grande Dam & Irr. Co. (1899). Nor is a waterway navigable for purposes of the servitude if it becomes navigable subsequently. Kaiser Aetna v. United States (1979); Boone v. United States (1991).

The navigable waters of the United States are public property, and subject to the control of the federal government under the Commerce Clause. Gibbons v. Ogden (1824). The federal government holds *lands* under navigable waters in trust for future states, to be granted to such states when they enter the Union. Montana v. United States (1981).

If a state chooses not to exercise its sovereign powers over the lands beneath navigable waters, or if the federal government has reserved these lands at the time of statehood, then these lands become subject to the federal navigational servitude. This servitude extends laterally to the bed of a navigable waterbody, and to the entire *surface* of the waterbody, which includes all the lands and waters below the "ordinary high water" mark. United States v. Rands (1967). This servitude is imposed both on private lands submerged by navigable waters, and on lands riparian to (adjacent to) navigable waters. The servitude prohibits riparian landowners and owners of the bed from making uses, such as construction of bridges or the filling of submerged lands, that unreasonably interfere with public navigational rights. Union Bridge Co. v. United States (1907); Grosse Ile Tp. v. Dunbar & Sullivan Dredging Co. (1969). The navigational servitude also means that there is, subject to state law, a right of public access to the waterbody. United States v. Harrell (1991).

The Supreme Court has held that the "bed" of a river subject to the navigational servitude does not include land covered by the "extraordinary freshets of the winter or spring, or the extreme droughts of the summer or autumn." United States v. Chicago, Milwaukee, St. Paul, & Pac. R. Co. (1941). Nor does the bed of a river include lands covered by vegetation, which are temporarily overflowed in exceptional seasons when the river is at flood. Oklahoma v. Texas (1923). The "ordinary high water mark" has been defined as the line where the water stands sufficiently long to destroy vegetation below it. United States v. Cameron (1978). See also Matter of Determination of the Ordinary High Water Mark and Outlet Elevation for Beaver Lake (1991) (even when artificial structures have existed long enough to be considered natural, purely natural factors take precedence in determining the high water mark).

b. *The Public Trust Doctrine*

Another source of public rights in water is the public trust doctrine. This doctrine assumes that at the time of statehood, title to beds beneath navigable waters passed to those states wishing to control the beds, and these submerged lands became subject to a public trust. As a result, in states where the doctrine applies, states may neither convey lands, Illinois Central R. Co. v. Illinois (1892); 101 Ranch v. United States

(1990), nor the surface waters above these lands, Kootenai Environmental Alliance, Inc. v. Panhandle Yacht Club, Inc. (1983), inconsistently with the trust. Owners of fee simple title impressed with the public trust hold the fee subject to a condition subsequent that it be used for a public purpose. Therefore, in State v. Central Vermont Ry., Inc. (1989), filled lands owned by a railroad company subject to the public trust could not be conveyed to a real estate developer unless such lands were used for a public purpose. While the public trust interests are traditionally defined in terms of navigation and commerce, some courts have lately applied the trust concept to preserve the public's interests in fishing, bathing, swimming, and recreation, Marks v. Whitney (1971), as well as water quality. See United States v. State Water Resources Control Board (1986). Even though public trust waters were held by the federal government prior to statehood, after statehood, claims based on the public trust doctrine do not arise under federal law, but rather are governed purely by state law. New York v. DeLyser (1991). See also County of Lake v. Smith (1991) (determination of area below low-water mark, subject to the public trust, is a matter of state law).

c. *Public Rights to Non-navigable Waters*

If waters are otherwise non-navigable, the public may still have rights, to both the surface and lands beneath these waters, that are superior to rights stemming from the common law. There are many clever ways for courts to superimpose public rights on non-navigable waters. A state can simply adopt an expanded definition of navigability. Diana Shooting Club v. Husting (1914). A state court can hold that, notwithstanding private ownership of the bed, the public may use the surface of non-navigable waters. Montana Coalition for Stream Access, Inc. v. Curran (1984); Day v. Armstrong (1961). But see Kansas ex rel. Meek v. Hays (1990); People v. Emmert (1979), which found that the public has no right to the surface use of non-navigable waters overlying private lands for recreational purposes.

The United States Supreme Court has expanded the public trust doctrine to include lands under waters subject to the ebb and flow of the tide, regardless of whether such waters are navigable. Phillips Petroleum Co. v. Mississippi (1988). Some courts have opened non-navigable waters to the public through the common law doctrine of dedication. In such cases a mixture of prescription and estoppel makes irrelevant the owner's non-intent to dedicate.

d. Public Access

In addition to acknowledging a public right to certain waterways, some courts have created an implied right of public access across private lands to beaches and shores. Although the right of a property owner to exclude the public is one of the most protected common law rights, courts have been able to fashion several theories for providing public access rights. Among these are: implied dedication, Gion v. Santa Cruz (1970); easement by prescription, City of Daytona Beach v. Tona—Roma, Inc. (1974); the public trust doctrine, Matthews v. Bay Head Improvement Ass'n (1984); and custom, McDonald v. Halvorson (1988).

B. USES OF THE COMMON LAW

The common law is available to parties who wish to establish a legal relationship with another party or parties through the use of non-regulatory, judge-made law. The primary advantage of the common law is its decentralized nature, permitting parties to initiate and adopt acceptable norms of conduct largely in the absence of agency rules. The common law relationship is typically defined after-the-fact by tort law, and before-the-fact by property and contract law.

1. Tort Law

A common law tort action is brought by an injured plaintiff seeking to hold liable a defendant who caused injury to the plaintiff as a result of a breach of a legal duty. If successful, the plaintiff's injuries are remedied by money damages or injunctive relief. In the natural resources world, a tort cause of action for trespass or property damage is a frequently occurring response. A tort action lies, for example, for a wrongful cutting and removing of timber. See Thomas Creek Lumber & Log Co. v. United States (1990).

Tort actions are even more likely in environmental litigation. See Fletcher v. Rylands (1865). Use of tort law to redress environmental harms is fraught with difficulties. An injured plaintiff may lack incentive or the financial wherewithal to bring suit, but hope that others similarly injured may instead take the initiative, and assume the litigation expenses. If all potential plaintiffs thereby become free riders, no litigation will occur and the environmental harms will continue unabated. Consequently, Congress and state legislatures have adopted a broad array of environmental protection measures that have supplanted common law relief through statutes and regulations.

Common law tort actions also confront problems associated with the nature of environmental harms, which often (1) obscure defendants responsible for the harm, (2) tend to result in adverse health effects long after the harm is done, and (3) are aesthetic or psychological, rather than economic. See English v. General Electric Co. (1990) (intentional infliction of emotional distress); Metropolitan Edison Co. v. P.A.N.E. (1983) (adverse psychological effects of restarting a nuclear power plant); Ayers v. Jackson Tp. (1987) (fear of enhanced risk of illness due to environmental contamination).

Despite these obstacles, the common law continues to play an important role in promoting environmental quality. Use of the common law is especially popular whenever legislative schemes have been unable to provide adequate compensation to environmentally wronged parties. Theories of tort liability for environmental damage include nuisance, Prah v. Maretti (1982), negligence, Philip Morris, Inc. v. Emerson (1988), and strict liability, Sterling v. Velsicol Chemical Corp. (1986).

2. Property Law

The common law of property is of obvious significance to those wishing to use, transfer, or assert ownership interests in natural resources. Common law property rules make possible markets, which are nothing more than structured exchange mechanisms. Property rules identify the legal relationships between persons that make exchanges possible, and these rules back up the exchanges with the enforcement powers of the state.

Because resources are scarce, and economically valuable, several parties may claim a legally protected property interest in the same resource. The common law sorts out these competing claims through traditional property doctrines—quiet title actions, DeWitt v. Balben (1986) (property rights in water spring); adverse possession, Monroe v. Rawlings (1951) (private land used for hunting and fishing); the rule of capture, Trent v. Energy Development Corp. (1990) (neighboring landowner who taps an oil and gas deposit under adjoining land has property interest in it); and the public trust doctrine, Sierra Club v. Department of Interior (1975) (public trust asserted to protect National Park from logging operations on surrounding private lands).

Because resources are often located beneath the land, surface and subsurface estates may be legally distinct. When surface and mineral ownership interests are severed, property law helps to establish the respective rights of the surface and mineral owners. Smith v. Linmar Energy Corp. (1990) (ownership of mineral rights is dominant over surface rights to the extent necessary to extract minerals). When a deed has reserved certain minerals to the surface owner, property law also helps to interpret ambiguous reservation terms. Kunkel v. Meridian Oil, Inc. (1989) (reservation of "certain coal or iron or other minerals" reserves the right to underlying oil and gas). When one party owns both the surface and subsurface interests, that party may create a leasing arrangement whereby the lessor-owner grants a lessee-producer the right to extract and sell the subsurface resource in exchange for a royalty. The common law imposes on such a lessee certain implied duties. Robbins v. Chevron U.S.A., Inc. (1990) (implied duty to market oil and gas). It also grants lessees certain rights. Davis v. Cramer (1990) (right of access to use the surface to extract subsurface minerals).

The common law of property is also used by parties wishing to transfer, sell, or purchase natural resources. Praire Producing Co. v. Schlachter (1990) (oil and gas deed conveyed a mineral rather than a royalty interest); Esplanade Oil & Gas, Inc. v. Templeton Energy Income Corp. (1989) (sale of oil and gas properties can close despite dramatic decline in the price of oil).

3. Contract Law

When parties enter into a contract whose subject is energy or natural resources, traditional contract law principles usually apply. From the point of view of the common law, it is irrelevant that the contract involves oil and gas, coal, minerals, timber, water, or land. To be a legally binding agreement, there must have been an offer and acceptance of unambiguous terms, supported by consideration, that is not contrary to public policy. Heiner v. S.J. Groves & Sons Co. (1990) (general contract law principles apply to documents conveying mineral interests).

As with other contracts, if the agreement concerns a natural resource, the contract vendor has a reasonable time to provide good and merchantable title. Wolken v. Wade (1987) (gold mining operation). If it is a sales contract, the Uniform Commercial Code applies. Lubecki v. Omega Logging, Inc. (1987) (timber sales contract). The parol evidence rule and statute of frauds have effect. Trujillo v. CS Cattle Co. (1990) (water rights contract); Moore v. Adolph (1990) (water contract). The terms of the contract may provide the sole remedy for breach. Transcontinental Gas Pipe Line Corp. v. American Nat. Petroleum Co. (1988) (natural gas contract).

For some natural resources, the particular nature of the resource, and the market for that resource, have created a need for specialized contracts, as well as the resolution of contract issues that are specific to the resource. For example, the natural gas market uses the "take or pay" contract, which guarantees that the purchaser will take a quantity of gas, or pay for failure to do so. Falcon Petroleum Co. v. Panhandle Eastern Pipe Line Co. (1990). The oil and gas market employs a contract called a "farmout agreement," which is an agreement to assign an interest in acreage in return for drilling or testing oil and gas operations on that acreage. W & W Oil Co. v. Capps (1990). In most western states, because water rights may be bought and sold without regard to the real property over which the water flows, Navajo Dev. Co. v. Sanderson (1982), contracts for the sale of land must specify whether the contract also transfers full appurtenant water rights. Sun Vineyards, Inc. v. Luna County Wine Dev. Corp. (1988).

II. GOVERNMENT ACTION AND NATURAL RESOURCES

Although the common law continues to play a role in the natural resources market, by far the more significant organizing legal force is statutory law, enacted by the Congress and state legislatures. All the remaining chapters address the statutory and regulatory schemes surrounding particular resources. This section highlights the administrative law and constitutional law themes common to many resources.

A. ADMINISTRATIVE LAW THEMES

At both the federal and state level, statutes frequently define original ownership rights to natural resources, and provide either for their public regulation and management, or disposition into private hands. Sometimes these statutes are self-executing; more commonly, they delegate to new or existing administrative agencies the job of implementing the general legislative mandate. As a consequence, much of energy and natural resources law involves administrative law, and requires an understanding of the administrative process.

There are several key federal agencies assigned the task of carrying out statutory policy regarding energy and natural resources. These include the Department of Agriculture (primarily the Forest Service), the Department of Interior (usually the Bureau of Land Management (BLM), the Minerals Management Service, National Park Service, and Fish and Wildlife Service), the Department of Energy (DOE), the Nuclear Regulatory Commission (NRC), the Federal Energy Regulatory Commission (FERC), and the Environmental Protection Agency (EPA). Because energy and natural resources occupy such a large portion of the nation's economy, many other federal agencies may become involved with resource regulation. These range from the Securities and Exchange Commission to the Army Corps of Engineers.

These federal agencies promulgate rules and regulations, issue licenses, permits, and orders, and occasionally adjudicate disputes. Their actions are constrained by, and should be consistent with, the language of (1) federal statutes known as "enabling legislation," giving agencies particular duties, and (2) the Federal Administrative Procedure Act (the APA, codified in various parts of Title 5, United States Code Annotated).

The APA is the seminal federal administrative law statute. It sets minimal procedural standards for all agencies to follow. Vermont Yankee Nuclear Power Corp. v. NRDC (1978). In the absence of explicit congressional instructions in an enabling statute, the APA has two functions. It sets out how federal agencies are to operate, and, for those wishing to challenge agency action in court, the APA specifies the nature of the judicial review, the grounds for challenge, the parties who may challenge, and the timing of the challenge.

1. Adjudication and Rulemaking

Agencies have two major modes of decisionmaking, adjudication and rulemaking. Adjudication is basically dispute resolution that attempts to resolve a conflict, usually retrospective, that affects an individual entity or group of entities. It is limited in that the agency's main concern is in ascertaining what happened, or what should happen to those particular disputants. Although adjudication can be formal or informal, it is more like a trial-type hearing than a legislative-type hearing.

Section 554 of the APA sets out the general rules for an adjudication. 5 U.S.C.A. § 554. A § 554 hearing must be provided in every case of adjudication required by statute to be determined "on the record after opportunity for agency hearing," with limited exceptions enumerated in the statute. Persons entitled to such a hearing are given notice and all interested parties have the opportunity to submit evidence to the agency. Parties before an agency are entitled to counsel and agencies may issue subpoenas if authorized by law. 5 U.S.C.A. § 555. Evidence which is presented at adjudicatory hearings required by § 554 is taken under oath and the hearing officer is authorized to issue subpoenas, rule on offers of proof and receive relevant evidence, allow depositions, and otherwise regulate the hearing. A party is entitled to present oral or written evidence and to conduct such cross-examination as may be required for a full disclosure of the facts. A transcript is required to be made and this constitutes the exclusive record. 5 U.S.C.A. § 556. When a hearing is required by § 554, the decision shall include a statement of findings and conclusions and the basis therefore on all the material issues of fact and law and the appropriate relief or denial. 5 U.S.C.A. § 557.

In contrast to this method, agencies also engage in rulemaking, which is a legislative-type hearing. Rulemaking is prospective and affects large numbers of individuals. It is policy oriented rather than a dispute settlement. Hence, a trial-type hearing is ill suited for the needs of rulemaking, formal or informal. Informal rulemaking, also referred to as "notice and comment" rulemaking, consists of notice and the opportunity to participate through the submission of written data with or without the opportunity for oral presentation. 5 U.S.C.A. § 553. Formal rulemaking includes these procedural safeguards, as well as those provided by § 556, which is triggered when a statute requires that rules be made "on the record after an opportunity for an agency hearing." Once a decision is rendered then it is subject to judicial review.

Although the discussion below focuses on judicial review of agency action, one should keep in mind that the day-to-day practice of energy and natural resources law is before administrative agencies, not courts. This is because the underlying natural resources or energy statute often does not have practical effect until its meaning is implemented by agency actions. So, if actors in the resources market wish either to influence policy, or change the way a statute is administered, the proper forum is initially the agency. Courts are the last resort. Only if parties fail before agencies, and have the necessary patience and financial commitment to fight an agency further, will the judiciary become involved. In such a case, several principles of administrative law constrain disputants in court.

2. The Right to Judicial Review

Generally, an interested party affected by agency action has a legal right to have a claim against an agency adjudicated in court. However, some lawsuits will not be heard by a court if they are brought either by the inappropriate party, or at the wrong time (e.g., if initiated too soon, before the agency's action is sufficiently final to have a particularized impact). Other agency actions are not judicially reviewable if (1) Congress has explicitly precluded such review, or (2) the relevant statute is silent concerning judicial review, and courts interpret the challenged action as being committed to the sole discretion of the agency. See 5 U.S.C.A. § 701(a); Assiniboine and Sioux Tribes of Fort Peck Indian Reservation v. Board of Oil and Gas Conservation (1986). Absent a clear signal from Congress to the contrary, however, one may normally presume judicial review is permissible, often under the APA. Abbott Laboratories v. Gardner (1967).

3. Standard of Review

A court reviewing the actions of an administrative agency will not substitute its judgment for the agency's. Rather, courts defer to agency decisions because agencies are specialized bodies, more expert in the matter being challenged than the judiciary. Chevron, U.S.A., Inc. v. NRDC (1984). Deference is particularly likely when a court reviews either decisions within an agency's area of special expertise, New York v. United States EPA (1988), or an agency's interpretation of its own regulations. Udall v. Tallman (1965). While courts give agency decisions substantial deference, they must also carefully review the record and "satisfy themselves that the agency has made a reasoned decision based on its evaluation

of the significance * * * of the * * * information [before it]."
Marsh v. Oregon Natural Resources Council (1989). Also, an
agency's discretion does not include the power to reshape a
policy judgment made by Congress. Louisiana Public Service
Com'n v. F.C.C. (1986).

4. Overturning Agency Actions

The function of judicial review of federal agency action is
for a court to take a "hard look" at the agency decision to
determine whether the agency is (1) in compliance with
appropriate procedural requirements, (2) within the statutory
authority granted the agency, (3) acting constitutionally, or
(4) illegally acting in a way characterized as "arbitrary,
capricious, an abuse of discretion, or otherwise not in accordance with law." 5 U.S.C.A. § 706; Citizens to Preserve
Overton Park, Inc. v. Volpe (1971). This so-called "hard
look" doctrine of judicial review was softened in Vermont
Yankee Nuclear Power Corp. v. NRDC (1978) and Chevron,
U.S.A., Inc. v. NRDC (1984). In *Vermont Yankee,* the Supreme Court decided that a reviewing court should not "impose upon the agency its own notion of which procedures are
'best' or most likely to further some vague, undefined public
good." In *Chevron,* the Court said that the question before
reviewing courts is not whether an agency decision is appropriate in the general context of a statutory program, but
whether the agency's decision "is a reasonable one."

Of the above four possible grounds for challenge, perhaps
the most successful are allegations of *ultra vires* or arbitrary
and capricious agency action. An *ultra vires* action is one
where the agency acts outside its statutory authority. In
Fertilizer Institute v. United States EPA (1991), the Court
found that the EPA had interpreted the reporting requirements of CERCLA (the "superfund" statute) in a way that
was *ultra vires* the statute's express terms. In Acadian Gas
Pipeline System v. F.E.R.C. (1989), FERC was found to have

acted arbitrarily and capriciously by deviating from past agency practice without a sufficiently articulated justification.

5. Standing

The important question of who can bring a lawsuit—"standing"—to attack an agency action turns on whether that person has satisfied certain preconditions found in statutes or the United States Constitution. While the Congress may not alter constitutional standing requirements, it may grant standing to individuals and organizations that might otherwise be foreclosed from initiating suit against an agency. This "statutory" standing comes in two forms. First, Congress may expressly provide for judicial review pursuant to specific authorization in the agency's substantive statute. Defenders of Wildlife, Friends of Animals and Their Environment v. Hodel (1988) (the Endangered Species Act broadly permits "any person" to commence a suit to enjoin violations of the Act). Some major federal environmental statutes liberally permit citizen groups to file court actions designed either to stop persons from violating a statute, or to force agency action consistent with its statutory mission. In Gwaltney of Smithfield, Ltd. v. Chesapeake Bay Foundation (1987), the Supreme Court agreed that the Clean Water Act permitted, in the absence of agency enforcement, private citizens to commence civil actions against persons in violation of their discharge permit.

Second, in the absence of such explicit statutory language, the APA provides for judicial review at the behest of any person "suffering legal wrong because of agency action, or adversely affected or aggrieved by agency action." 5 U.S.C.A. § 702. In this context, the standing doctrine imposes important limitations on the seemingly broad Congressional grant of judicial authority under the APA. The constitutional core of standing is the minimum requirement of injury. This concept is founded on Article III of the Constitution, which limits the power of the federal judiciary to hear "cases" and "controversies." From this simple language a threshold three-pronged test for standing has emerged: (1) actual or threatened injury to a legal right; (2) injury that is traceable to the defendant's activity; and (3) the likelihood that the injury will be redressed by a favorable decision. Valley Forge Christian College v. Americans United for Separation of Church and State, Inc. (1982). In addition, litigants must assert their own rights rather than the rights of third parties.

Prior to the passage of the APA, where statutes involving agencies were silent as to judicial review, standing was construed to permit judicial interference only where the agency exceeded its grant of power, and only to the extent necessary to protect justiciable individual rights. The passage of the APA of 1946 provided for judicial review where a claimant's rights were within those arguably protected by the meaning of the relevant statute, and for a claimant who had been "adversely affected or aggrieved" by the agency action. 5 U.S.C.A. § 702. Standing under the APA seems to enlarge the class of litigants in an administrative agency context, subject to the limitations of the Constitution.

Initially, the basis for interpretation of section 702 of the APA became the prudential "zone of interests" test first articulated in Association of Data Processing Service Organizations, Inc. v. Camp (1970). However, this test, which relates to the merits of the dispute, rarely was invoked to deny standing. The focus of standing analysis under the APA instead concentrated on the constitutional "injury" question. The courts permitted challenges to agency decisions where intangible injury was alleged. Sierra Club v. Morton (1972) (non-economic environmental interests are protected interests); United States v. SCRAP (1973) (non-economic injury could be trifling in nature).

Sierra Club provided the classic model for environmental litigation by which organizations could sue on behalf of their membership but not on behalf of the public at large. An organization could enter the judicial arena on mere proof of "use" of the affected land and injury to a member of the organization as a result of the agency action. Throughout the 1970s and 1980s the standing doctrine was interpreted to open further the court system to public interest groups seeking judicial reversal of agency decisions. Duke Power Co. v. Carolina ESG, Inc. (1978) (fear of daily exposure to radiation and concern for aesthetic value of resources are protected interests); Bryant v. Yellen, 447 U.S. 352 (1980) (statute may be challenged despite uncertainty regarding outcome of statute's application).

In 1990, the United States Supreme Court may have narrowed the number of litigants who may successfully use the APA to invoke standing, by acknowledging additional limitations that apply to section 702 review of agency action. In Lujan v. National Wildlife Federation (1990), members of the National Wildlife Federation submitted three affidavits alleging injury resulting from withdrawal revocations for public lands under the Federal Land Policy Management Act. In a 5–4 decision, the Court ruled that the affidavits were insufficient to withstand summary judgment. The Court reasoned that a party seeking standing carries the burden of establishing that it is actually "adversely affected." General assertions that Federation members had merely used lands "in the vicinity of" the affected lands were insufficient to create a genuine issue of fact as to the Federation's injury under the terms of section 702. The Court declined to intervene absent an actual or immediately threatened effect. But see Sierra Club v. Robertson (1991) (environmental organization has standing where plaintiff's affidavits describe in detail specific parts of forest that affiants enjoy, and the types of harm that might ensue from clearcutting).

The *Lujan* Court disparaged *SCRAP,* a decision that had emphasized the importance of courts keeping widespread, potentially injurious government actions in check. The *Lujan* Court reasoned that the doctrine of standing is an essential element of the separation of powers. In the administrative agency context, courts must exercise judicial restraint to avoid interfering with policy decisions of other branches of the government. Justice Scalia's majority opinion hinted that previous relaxed standing tests may have been used to cause courts to become a forum for "wholesale improvement" of policies concerning federal natural resources. He thought a more appropriate avenue for such change would be through the agency itself, or Congress.

The *Lujan* decision did keep intact the "zone of interest" test. Decisions prior to *Lujan* established that a key inquiry was whether Congress had intended for a particular class of plaintiffs to challenge agency disregard of the law. Clarke v. Securities Industry Ass'n (1987); Hazardous Waste Treatment Council v. Thomas (1989). Subsequent rulings involving administrative agency challenges have relied on the zone of interest test to deny standing. ASIN v. City of Livonia (1991) (citizen group concerned about odors from sewage basin has no standing to sue under the Clean Water Act, whose zone of interests involves water quality); North Shore Gas Co. v. EPA (1991) (laws that are intended for the protection of the environment may not be used to protect persons deemed responsible for the consequences of having polluted the environment; pollutees have standing but polluters do not); Region 8 Forest Service Timber Purchasers Council v. Alcock (1990) (commercial logging company's interest not protected by the National Environmental Policy Act (NEPA) or the Endangered Species Act). But see NRDC v. Lujan (1991) (recreational use and aesthetic enjoyment are within the zone of interests NEPA was meant to protect).

Lujan's requirement that standing entail an actual or immediately threatened injury may not be applicable to attacks on statutes based on purely constitutional grounds. A court has no need to "consider the separate factual scenarios involving the individual members because they have no bearing on the constitutional issues presented." National Solid Waste Management Ass'n v. Voinovich (1991) (trade association challenging solid waste disposal statute has standing where each member is subject to the statute, where organization's purpose is protection of business interests of members, and where statute is challenged as unconstitutional on its face).

6. Timing

A person in the natural resources market seeking judicial recourse against an agency risks bringing suit either too late, or too early. If the former, the dispute with the agency may be dismissed for being moot, unless it is capable of repetition. Honig v. Doe (1988), Fair v. United States EPA (1986). See also Tobyhanna Conserv. Ass'n v. Country Place Waste Facility (1991) (mere showing of postfiling compliance with Clean Water Act (CWA) is not sufficient to render CWA action moot; defendant must also demonstrate that there is no reasonable expectation that wrong will be repeated).

More likely, the litigation is initiated too early. If so, administrative law doctrines demanding ripeness, final agency action, and exhaustion of administrative remedies discourage premature resort to courts.

One claiming to be "adversely affected or aggrieved" under § 702 of the APA must identify some "agency action" that is harming the claimant. Some statutes permit broad regulations to serve as this "agency" action, and these may be directly reviewed in court, even before the specific effects are felt. Absent such a provision, an agency's action is shielded from premature challenges by the ripeness doctrine, which prevents courts from "entangling themselves in abstract disagreements," Abbott Laboratories v. Gardner (1967), that are not adequately "fleshed out." National Ass'n of Regulatory Utility Com'rs v. United States DOE (1988). Ripeness principles are invoked as part of the process establishing the proper relationship between administrative action and judicial review.

Ripeness analysis enters the administrative law domain through the APA's requirement that a party be adversely affected or aggrieved by, or suffering a legal wrong because of, an "agency action." 5 U.S.C.A. § 702. Even the apparently broad language of section 702 demands that a dispute be sufficiently concrete to present a minimal Article III "case." Babbitt v. United Farm Workers Nat. Union (1979). This constitutional precondition limits APA review to controversies involving agency actions that have run the full course of the decision-making process. In addition to APA statutory requirements and constitutional Article III limitations, courts also have recognized various "prudential" factors designed to deny review as a matter of judicial self-limitation.

While the ripeness doctrine may pose a significant potential barrier to some litigants, it was seldom invoked to prevent courts from deciding the merits of disputes involving federal resource allocation decisions. For example, in Rocky Mountain Oil & Gas Ass'n v. Watt (1982), the Tenth Circuit ruled that an association did not have to contest agency denial of mineral exploration permits through administrative review before its claims could be considered by the court. See also Parker v. United States (1971) (claimants may obtain an injunction enjoining timber harvesting on public lands).

The standard for ascertaining whether an "agency action" is seasoned enough for judicial evaluation is that it be final, and that it have a present effect on, or be a present threat to, the interests of the plaintiff. Toilet Goods Ass'n v. Gardner (1967). Courts also consider the hardship to the parties if judicial resolution is withheld. Abbott Laboratories v. Gardner (1967) (agency action resulting in immediate and significant change in plaintiff's conduct of its business, with serious penalties attached, warrants access to the courts).

Abbott Laboratories also formulated a balancing test for ripeness. If the interests of the court and agency in postponing review outweigh the interests of those seeking relief, adjudication should be postponed. National Ass'n of Regulatory Utility Com'rs v. United States DOE (1988). In the natural resources context, courts have been more inclined to review purely legal disputes involving formally promulgated rules than general challenges to broad policies. American Motorcyclist Ass'n v. Watt (1982).

In Lujan v. National Wildlife Federation (1990), the Supreme Court held that an agency's action is not considered sufficiently ripe for judicial review under the APA until there has been a final focused agency decision whose concrete, non-theoretical application causes (or threatens to cause) specific injury to the claimant. General challenges to broad-based agency programs, whose effect on a challenger is diffuse, are less likely to be ripe absent some site-specific application affecting the challenger. The National Wildlife Federation's lawsuit was on behalf of it's 4.5 million members. It sought to overturn portions of the Bureau of Land Management's land withdrawal revocation program. The program proposed freeing hundreds of millions of acres of federal lands for mining of untapped resources. The main claim asserted was that the agency had failed to adhere to the procedures under the Federal Land Policy Management Act (FLPMA) for reporting and public participation.

The springboard for the Court's decision was the conclusion that the entire land withdrawal review program was not an identifiable "final agency action." According to the Court, aspects of the program are not ripe for challenge within the meaning of the APA until the "scope of the controversy has been reduced to more manageable proportions and its factual components fleshed out." This fleshing out occurs when subsequent discretionary agency action takes place involving separate and independent decision-making that "obviously" is divorced from the general withdrawal revocation decisions. Until this process is complete, it is impossible to ascertain where the results of the program (mining) will be experienced, or whether it could potentially cause immediate harm.

After *Lujan*, rules and programs that once were ordinarily considered the type of agency action ripe for judicial review may first have to be applied to a specific set of circumstances. Any broad challenges to executive policies or agency programs may be unripe where there is still room for exercise of agency discretion to resolve the dispute. National Ass'n of Regulatory Utility Com'rs v. DOE (1988) (notice establishing the method for allocating costs of nuclear waste repositories cannot be challenged before its effects and implications can be examined).

Under this case-by-case approach, litigants must wait until an agency activity has ripened into a "commitment" that imposes an obligation, denies a right, or fixes a legal relationship. Compare Ash Creek Mining Co. v. Lujan (1991) (mere announcement of agency's interim decision to withhold tract of land from coal leasing program not a final agency action ripe for review), with Sierra Club v. Robertson (1991) (ripeness present when challenge to Forest Service final plan, where plan makes decisions regarding forest management). At the litigation stage, pleadings must meticulously set out specific facts as to the application of the challenged action and the harm caused thereby.

Lujan suggests that courts should be reluctant to tackle an early broad challenge to a controversial public policy. For example, in Sierra Club v. Yeutter (1990), the Tenth Circuit held that a district court erred in granting a declaratory judgment that the Wilderness Act creates federal reserved water rights. The Sierra Club had alleged that the Forest Service's failure to claim wilderness water rights in ongoing Colorado water rights adjudications violated federal law and the public trust. The Tenth Circuit cited *Lujan* in concluding that the alleged harm that might befall a wilderness water value was too speculative and contingent because there was no assurance that the Forest Service would continue to forgo pursuit of these water rights in the future.

Apart from ripeness, "finality" and "exhaustion" also preclude challenges to agency action brought too early. When review is sought under the general provisions of the APA (and not pursuant to authorization in the agency's enabling statute), the "agency action" must be "final agency action." 5 U.S.C.A. § 704. The relevant consideration in ascertaining finality is whether the process of administrative decisionmaking has reached a stage where judicial review will not disrupt agency determination of rights or obligations, or legal consequences that will flow from the agency action. Massachusetts Public Interest Research Group, Inc. v. United States NRC (1988).

Exhaustion focuses on whether an avenue for relief still remains at the agency level, which would otherwise be bypassed with direct judicial review. A plaintiff will not be required to exhaust administrative remedies when the agency action under challenge has immediate effect (and is therefore "final"), or if there is already an adequate factual record for judicial review. Bowen v. New York City (1986); National Coalition Against the Misuse of Pesticides v. Thomas (1987).

B. CONSTITUTIONAL LAW THEMES

If an agency affecting natural resources interests is procedurally correct, and neither *ultra vires* nor arbitrary and capricious, then one wishing to attack the action in court is usually limited to some constitutional ground. The United States Constitution also erects jurisdictional barriers to those wishing to bring their challenges in federal courts.

1. Federalism

Decisions involving energy and natural resources face assertions of authority by two sovereigns—the state and the federal. Both state and federal law seek to protect the environment; state and federal law may also simultaneously affect mining activity, timber management, water use, and development of energy resources. Several constitutional law principles define the relationship between federal and state power.

The United States Congress has extensive authority to regulate and control natural resources under the Commerce Clause. Preseault v. ICC (1990) (upholding legislation preserving railroad rights-of-way for recreational trails). Congress also has complete authority over public lands through the Property Clause. Kleppe v. New Mexico (1976) ("[congressional] power over the public lands * * * is without limitations"). The Tenth Amendment does not serve as a source of state sovereignty that restricts the exercise of congressional power. Garcia v. San Antonio Metropolitan Transit Authority (1985); Union Oil of California v. United States EPA (1987).

The broad scope given to congressional power, the demise of the Tenth Amendment, and the presence of the Supremacy Clause (art. VI, § 2), combine to permit congressional preemption of a vast variety of state laws. For example, in California v. FERC (1990), the Supreme Court decided that the Federal Power Act preempted state minimum stream flow requirements for rivers on which federally licensed dams were located. If Congress does not explicitly preempt state law, see, e.g., Schneidewind v. ANR Pipeline Co. (1988), the simultaneous existence of federal and state statutes addressing the same natural resources subject does not necessarily invalidate the state law.

Dual federal and state regulation of a natural resource activity is permissible, providing three conditions are *not* present. First, state regulation may not frustrate congressional purposes. Florida Lime & Avocado Growers, Inc. v. Paul (1963). Second, state law may not regulate conduct in a field Congress intended federal law to occupy exclusively. California v. ARC America Corp. (1989). Third, state law may not directly conflict with federal law. Transcontinental Gas Pipe Line Corp. v. State (1986). In the absence of these conditions, states may regulate areas also federally regulated. Wisconsin Public Intervenor v. Mortier (1991) (federal law does not preempt local governmental regulation of pesticide use); English v. General Electric Co. (1990); Pacific Gas & Electric Co. v. State Energy Resources Conservation & Development Com'n (1983) (federal law does not preempt state regulation of nuclear waste storage). Even state regulation of federal land is not always forbidden. California Coastal Com'n v. Granite Rock Co. (1987) (state environmental regulations not preempted by federal land use planning statutes).

In the absence of federal law, the "dormant" Commerce Clause will strike down state statutes that discriminate, for protectionist purposes, against out-of-state residents. In New England Power Co. v. New Hampshire (1982), the Supreme Court held that a state prohibition on the export of locally generated hydropower was unconstitutional for favoring New Hampshire citizens at the expense of out-of-state citizens. See also City of Philadelphia v. New Jersey (1978); Hazardous Waste Treatment Council v. State of S.C. (1991).

Yet, a state may protect its natural resources so long as the incidental effect on interstate commerce does not exceed the putative local benefits. Northwest Central Pipeline Corp. v. State Corp. Com'n of Kansas (1989) (conservation of natural gas); Maine v. Taylor (1986) (baitfish importation ban designed to prevent introduction of parasites). State laws may adversely affect commerce if the law (1) serves a legitimate local purpose, and (2) is not designed to be protectionist in nature. Bill Kettlewell Excavating, Inc. v. Michigan DNR

(1991) (counties may deny importation of solid waste). Even obvious state discrimination involving a local resource may be permitted if the resource is "owned" by the state, Reeves, Inc. v. Stake (1980) (cement), or if the discrimination is expressly allowed by federal law. South–Central Timber Development, Inc. v. Wunnicke (1984) (timber).

2. Limitations on Regulation

Several constitutional provisions serve to protect holders of interests in natural resources from federal or state regulation of that interest. The Takings Clause of the Constitution's Fifth Amendment prohibits the taking of private property for public use without just compensation. It is designed to prevent the government from forcing some individuals to bear public burdens which should be borne by the public as a whole.

In the regulatory context, a land use restriction intended to benefit the public may so intrude upon private property rights in natural resources as to constitute a taking requiring just compensation. Pennsylvania Coal Co. v. Mahon (1922). As a general rule, even if a regulatory agency intends to act pursuant to the police power, the agency's action may nonetheless effect a taking requiring compensation if (1) it denies an owner the economically viable use of property, or (2) it does not substantially advance legitimate government interests. Agins v. City of Tiburon (1980); Penn Central Transp. Co. v. City of New York (1978).

The test for economically viable use of property requires a comparison of the value that has been taken as a result of the regulation, with the value that remains in the property as a whole. In Keystone Bituminous Coal Ass'n v. DeBenedictis (1987), there was no taking when a state mining regulation only deprived coal mine operators of a "support estate" in the properties under which they mined coal, but not the entire remaining coal estate. The economically viable use test also requires a concrete application of the regulation. Pennell v. City of San Jose (1988) (facial challenge to rent control ordinance was premature); Williamson County Regional Planning Com'n v. Hamilton Bank (1985). Without such an application, the claim might not be ripe. Rocky Mountain Materials & Asphalt, Inc. v. Board of County Com'rs (1991).

In Nollan v. California Coastal Com'n (1987), a regulation requiring public access to beaches through private property as a condition to the issuance of a building permit constituted a regulatory taking. The regulation, which resulted in a physical invasion of private property, was found not to "advance legitimate state interests." An exception to this second prong of the takings test is that the government has unquestioned authority to prevent a property owner from using property in such a manner as to cause harm to others. There is no taking where the government merely acts to arrest a perceived, significant threat to the common welfare "akin to a public nuisance." McNulty v. Town of Indialantic (1989).

In addition to this basic two-step analysis, other factors of varying influence may be considered in determining the point at which a regulatory taking occurs. One concern, related to economic viability, is the value of the property before and after the government action. *Keystone,* supra. The loss of value does not have to be permanent. First English Evangelical Lutheran Church of Glendale v. County of Los Angeles (1987) (a temporary taking that denies a property owner all use of property requires compensation for the period during which the taking was effective); Yuba Natural Resources, Inc. v. United States (1990). The degree of interference with the distinct or reasonable "investment-backed expectations" of the property owner also is given weight in assessing the economic viability of the property. Duquesne Light Co. v. Barasch (1989) (statute denying recovery of costs expended on canceled nuclear power plants is not a taking because it does not destroy the financial well-being of utility companies); Western Energy Co. v. United States Dept. of Interior (1991) (adjustments to coal lease did not constitute a taking because lease was issued pursuant to federal law which contemplated possibility that leases might be amended). The "character" of the government action is significant under both tests. A taking of private property may more readily be found when government interference with property is a physical invasion. Loretto v. Teleprompter Manhattan CATV Corp. (1982); Kaiser Aetna v. United States (1979).

Where a landowner seeks to enjoin a government action or declare it unconstitutional, the takings clause is not initially the proper basis for challenge. Where the challenged action is not otherwise precluded by statute and the regulation is within the authority of the governmental unit, suits for compensation by the federal government must be brought under the Tucker Act. Preseault v. ICC (1990). The *Preseault* decision effectively delegated to the Federal Circuit and the Court of Claims substantive determinations of when a taking occurs. These courts have been more willing to interpret the 1987 Supreme Court trilogy of *Keystone, First Evangelical,* and *Nollan* as broadening the circumstances under which a regulatory taking may occur.

In Whitney Benefits, Inc. v. United States (1991), the Federal Circuit found that a land use restriction implemented pursuant to the Surface Mining Control and Reclamation Act of 1977 (SMCRA) had resulted in a taking. The court reasoned that the regulation had rendered valueless the coal estate by precluding all mining, and found irrelevant the continuing value of the surface estate. *Accord* Belville Mining Co. v. United States (1991). Similar reasoning has been applied in the context of challenges to permit denials under section 404 of the Clean Water Act. If property values are reduced to zero for parcels that cannot be developed because of a section 404 permit denial, it is irrelevant that there may still be value in the remaining parcels of land. Loveladies Harbor, Inc. v. United States (1990); Florida Rock Industries, Inc. v. United States (1990). Contra, Ciampitti v. United States (1991).

Other courts have expanded the class of successful takings claims by construing the nuisance exception narrowly. Yancy v. United States (1990). In *Whitney Benefits,* the court found a taking because the purpose of SMCRA was to protect the environment and agricultural productivity of the land, not to abate a public nuisance. Some courts have also found takings by concluding that a subjective expectation of a mining lease approval is "reasonable investment-backed expectation." Regulatory interference with this expectation might mandate compensation. United Nuclear Corp. v. United States (1990). See also NRG Co. v. United States (1991) (cancellation by the United States of mineral prospecting permits a taking where permittees had reasonable investment-backed expectation that the option to later obtain a lease would be honored).

For public natural resources, an unconstitutional taking may be more difficult to establish. First, certain interests created by federal law, such as a grazing permit on federal land, may not amount to a protectable property right. United States v. Fuller (1973). Second, if a claimant establishes a property right of some character, the public interest in regulating the use of public natural resources may weigh heavily in favor of the regulatory scheme. United States v. Locke (1985) (no taking when an individual's reasonable, investment-backed expectations in a mining claim can continue by compliance with retroactively imposed regulatory restrictions); Bolt v. United States Dept. of Interior (1991) (forfeiture of a mining claim for failure to comply with federal statute's retroactively applied recordation requirement not a taking).

The Due Process and Equal Protection Clauses also restrict government regulation by requiring some minimal connec-

tion between the law and the objects sought to be accomplished by the law. Big D. Const. v. Court of Appeals (1990).
The Supreme Court is disinclined to entertain due process challenges to the retroactive operation of a statute affecting natural resource interests for public health or safety purposes. Usery v. Turner Elkhorn Mining Co. (1976). Also, since courts tend to defer to legislative judgments regarding economic property rights, due process and equal protection arguments are not often invoked successfully in defense of natural resources interests. Exxon Corp. v. Eagerton (1983); Texaco, Inc. v. Short (1982); Peterson v. United States Dept. of Interior (1990).

The Contracts Clause (art. I, § 10, cl. 1) is a limitation only on state authority. State of Nevada Employees Assoc. v. Keating (1990). Despite its language preventing the "impairing" of contracts, courts have interpreted it narrowly. No Contracts Clause violation occurs merely because a statute has the effect of restricting, or even barring altogether, the performance of duties created by pre-existing contracts. Energy Reserves Group, Inc. v. Kansas Power & Light Co. (1983).

3. The Cases and Controversies Requirement

One seeking relief in federal court must comply with the constitutional requirement found in Article III, § 2 that federal jurisdiction be limited to "cases and controversies." Courts have construed this phrase to create constitutional restrictions on those who can sue (standing), and on the timing of the lawsuit (ripeness and mootness).

Constitutional standing demands that a party meet three requirements. First, to be a "controversy," the plaintiff must have personally suffered some actual or threatened "injury" as result of illegal conduct of the government-defendant. Cognizable injuries include harm to aesthetic interests and environmental well-being. Sierra Club v. Morton (1972).

Second, the injury must be fairly "traceable" to the challenged action. National Wildlife Federation v. Agricultural Stabilization & Conservational Service (1990). Third, the injury should be "redressed" by the requested relief. Natural Resources Defense Council v. EPA (1990). An association has standing to sue on behalf of its members only when its members would have standing to sue in their own right. Public Interest Research of New Jersey, Inc. v. Powell Duffryn Terminals, Inc. (1990); Competitive Enterprise Institute v. National Highway Traffic Safety Admin. (1990).

The Constitution also requires that government action be final, and not subject to further administrative relief, before it is sufficiently ripe to constitute a "case" for judicial review. MacDonald, Sommer & Frates v. Yolo County (1986). Courts seem to apply ripeness principles most strictly in takings cases. Pennell v. City of San Jose (1988).

An action may be moot (and nonreviewable as a "case") either when there is no reasonable expectation that the defendant's wrong will be repeated, Atlantic States Legal Foundation, Inc. v. Tyson Foods, Inc. (1990), or if a court cannot grant any effective relief. Headwaters, Inc. v. BLM (1989) (injunction seeking to prevent timber sale moot when trees already cut). See also State of Nevada v. Watkins (1991).

*

PART II

RESOURCE MANAGEMENT AND PROTECTION

LAW AS A MEANS OF ADMINISTERING AND PRESERVING "PUBLIC" RESOURCES

Chapters Three (Public Lands and Natural Resources Law), Four (Environmental Law), and Five (Environmental Assessment and NEPA) consider how law is employed to both manage and protect the use of the nation's public resources. Typically, the "law" in these chapters is federal and statutory, implemented by federal agencies specialized either in resource management (e.g., the Department of Interior), or resource protection (e.g., the EPA). The resources that are the subject of these chapters are "public" in that they are either owned by the federal government (e.g., national parks and wilderness areas), or owned in common by all American citizens (e.g., air and water). In the former case, the goal of the applicable law is usually to regulate and plan for the most efficient *use* of the federally-owned resource. In the latter case, when the resource is commonly owned, the law's goal is often to *protect* it from pollution and environmental harm.

CHAPTER THREE

PUBLIC LANDS AND NATURAL RESOURCES LAW

A significant proportion of the nation's energy and natural resources are owned and managed by the federal government. These include economically valuable lands (rangeland) and resources (minerals, water, timber). They also encompass lands (national parks and wilderness) and resources (wildlife) which are protected from economic exploitation or environmental harm. An understanding of the primary legal issues involving these public lands and resources requires an introductory discussion of (1) the nature and extent of this public treasure, (2) the constitutional power of the federal government to manage these lands and resources (sometimes in the face of conflicting state laws), and (3) the history of public lands and resources policy over the past two centuries.

I. FEDERAL POWER OVER PUBLIC LANDS AND RESOURCES

A. NATURE AND EXTENT OF PUBLIC OWNERSHIP

The United States owns about one-third of the country's on-shore surface land (over 730 million acres of a total land area of 2.3 billion acres). Most of this land is in 11 states in the Rocky Mountain West, and in Alaska, whose 350 million acres comprise almost one-half of the total of all federally-owned lands. In addition to fee ownership of onshore surface lands, the federal government owns certain less-than-fee interests, such as easements for wildlife, and subsurface mineral interests underlying nearly 60 million acres in the West. The United States also has sovereignty over the mineral and fishery resources of the off-shore continental shelf.

There are four major resources on these lands: water, timber, minerals, and wildlife. In addition, the land may be valuable as rangeland, or to protect recreational, historic, or aesthetic values. This latter category of "resource preservation" lands includes the National Park System (Parks, Monuments, Archaeological and Historic Preservation Sites, Recreation Areas, Seashores, Trails, and Wild and Scenic Rivers), Wilderness Areas, and the National Wildlife Refuge System.

Apart from resource preservation lands, all public lands and resources are usually managed according to the "multiple use" philosophy. Multiple use seeks to ensure that as many resources as possible are *used* (not preserved) in as many different ways as is compatible with all the other uses of resources otherwise sustained by the land. This philosophy engenders bitterly-fought disputes over land and resource use. Organizations espousing the goals of environmentalism and conservation are often pitted against powerful economic and developmental interests. Recreational users may collide with groups interested in resource extraction. Industrial users may disagree among themselves over the direction of public land policy. It is the job of federal land and resources agencies (typically within the Department of Interior or Agriculture) to somehow reconcile these inevitable conflicts, consistent not only with applicable federal law, but also with an elusive goal called the "public interest."

B. LEGAL AUTHORITY OF FEDERAL GOVERNMENT AND STATES

1. Source of Power

The lands of the United States were originally held by American Indians. In Johnson v. McIntosh (1823), the Supreme Court concluded that "the Indian inhabitants are to be considered merely as occupants, [and therefore] deemed incapable of transferring the absolute title to others." As a result of *McIntosh,* the nation's lands initially became part of the United States, either by purchase from and treaty with foreign nations, or conquest of (and subsequent treaty with) Indian tribes.

Prior to statehood, Congress managed all lands in the territories outside state boundaries. United States v. Gratiot (1840). The source of this federal power is the Property Clause (art. IV, § 3, cl. 2), which permits Congress to "dispose of and make all needful Rules and Regulations respecting the Territory or other Property belonging to the United States." After statehood is achieved (with the consent of Congress through the operation of art. IV, § 3, cl. 1), states' police power provides authority to regulate all non-federal lands within their borders. This state power may be limited by the federal enabling act authorizing statehood. ASARCO, Inc. v. Kadish (1989) (state must comply with enabling act before leasing lands granted from the United States). State power over non-federal lands may also be preempted by federal law. International Paper Co. v. Ouellette (1987) (state nuisance law preempted by federal environmental law).

When states were created out of territories, the federal government retained title to all lands within the state that had not passed into private hands prior to statehood. United States v. Percheman (1833). Title to lands underlying navigable waters passed to states upon statehood, unless there was some federal reservation. Pollard v. Hagan (1845). Title to riverbeds of all non-navigable rivers remained in the United States. State of North Dakota v. United States (1991). Even when the bed or bank of a navigable waterway had passed into state or private hands, there remained a "navigable servitude" on such waters, to ensure a right of way for the public to use the surface of the waterway. Union Bridge Co. v. United States (1907). This navigable servitude of the United States encompasses the entire navigable waterway up to the ordinary high water mark. United States v. Rands (1967); Owen v. United States (1988). A river's "ordinary" high water mark does not include a river's peak flow or flood stages. United States v. Harrell (1991).

States did not come into title of non-submerged public lands within their borders without a grant or a sale to the state by the United States. These public lands within states remain under the regulatory control of the Congress, acting pursuant to several power clauses in the Constitution. Camfield v. United States (1897). These clauses include the Commerce Clause, First Iowa Hydro–Elec. Co. v. FPC (1946), the General Welfare Clause, United States v. Gerlach Live Stock Co. (1950), and the Treaty Power Clause. Missouri v. Holland (1920). But by far the two most significant sources of federal constitutional power over public lands within states are the Property Clause (art. IV, § 3, cl. 2), and Jurisdiction Clause (art. I, § 8, cl. 17).

2. The Reach of the Property and Jurisdiction Clauses

a. *The Property Clause*

In Kleppe v. New Mexico (1976), the Supreme Court interpreted the Property Clause so as to rebut the notion that the federal government was merely a proprietor over public lands. Instead, Congress was deemed to have complete sovereign power over such lands. The Congress is thus vested with full legislative authority over federal property without any implicit limitations. See also California Coastal Com'n v. Granite Rock Co. (1987) ("the Property Clause gives Congress plenary power"). The Property Clause can sometimes reach beyond federal lands to affect (1) certain private activities on adjacent lands, United States v. Alford (1927) (fires); Christy v. Hodel (1988) (killing of wildlife); and (2) private inholdings within federal lands. Minnesota v. Block (1981). Congress may not use the Property Clause to circumvent functional restraints placed on it by the Constitution. Citizens for Abatement of Aircraft Noise, Inc. v. Metropolitan Washington Airports Authority (1990) (separation of powers doctrine limits use of Property Clause).

b. *The Jurisdiction Clause*

The Jurisdiction Clause of art. I, § 8, cl. 17 gives Congress "power to exercise exclusive legislation * * *, and to exercise like authority over all places purchased by the consent of * * * the State * * * for the erection of forts, magazines, arsenals, dock-yards, and other needful buildings." Since "exclusive legislation" has been construed to mean "exclusive jurisdiction," and since lands so acquired are commonly called "federal enclaves," the Clause has become known as the Jurisdiction or Enclave Clause. Over 5% of all public lands are enclaves, consisting primarily of military bases, post offices, and national parks.

If one were to adopt a literal interpretation of the Clause, then, the United States could (1) "purchase" parcels of state land, (2) only with the "consent" of that state's legislature, (3) after which the state would lose jurisdiction, and the United States would gain "exclusive" legislative power over the parcel, (4) in order to construct those "needful buildings" listed in the Clause. But in fact the courts have never restrictively interpreted these terms of the Clause. Thus, the United States can acquire land from states by any legal means without their "consent." Fort Leavenworth R. Co. v. Lowe (1885). The "needful buildings" phrase means, in effect, "for any legitimate federal purpose," including national parks. Collins v. Yosemite Park and Curry Co. (1938). Furthermore, "exclusive legislation" does not forbid all application of state law within the enclave, or create a kind of state-within-a state. Howard v. Commissioners of Sinking Fund (1953).

States may retain some jurisdictional powers at the time of making the initial cession to the federal government. James v. Dravo Contracting Co. (1937). The Congress, by subsequent statute, may assimilate pertinent state law so that it applies within the enclave. United States v. Sharpnack (1958) (Assimilative Crimes Act). States must treat inhabitants of the enclave in the same manner as other state citizens. Evans v. Cornman (1970) (enclave residents cannot be denied right to vote in state elections). However, while the applicable law is state law in effect at the time the state ceded jurisdiction, Arlington Hotel Co. v. Fant (1929), state law adopted after cession is without force in the absence of congressional approval. Black Hills Power & Light Co. v. Weinberger (1987).

3. Federal and State Power

a. Federal Preemption

Kleppe v. New Mexico (1976) not only established the plenary nature of federal power exercised through the Property Clause over public lands and resources, it also declared that state law conflicting with federal public land law is invalid even in the absence of express congressional articulation of preemptive intent. *Kleppe* is the easy preemption case, where the federal-state conflict was obvious (implementation of state law would have permitted the slaughter of federally protected wild burros). Another easy preemption case is where Congress explicitly overrides inconsistent state laws. For example, the Endangered Species Act forbids state law permitting commerce in wildlife otherwise prohibited by the Act. 16 U.S.C.A. § 1535(f). Without such clear-cut expression of intent, or apparent conflict, preemption is far more difficult to predict.

In public lands and resources law, federal preemption of state law varies statute-by-statute, resource-by-resource. Nevertheless, certain generalizations may be made. First, preemption may be by federal statute, or by the actions of a federal regulatory agency. Chrysler Corp. v. Brown (1979). The agency must have properly exercised its delegated authority for its actions to have preemptive effect. City of New York v. FCC (1988). Second, in the absence of express preemption or direct conflict with state law, there may be preemption if (1) Congress so "intends," (2) federal law "occupies" the entire regulatory field, or (3) state law "interferes" with the accomplishment of federal purposes.

Divining congressional "intent" is usually very difficult, in part because most federal statutes acknowledge some interstitial role for state law. When federal law permits "cooperative federalism" (a sharing of federal and state authority sanctioned also by Congress), the task is to interpret the extent to which Congress intends states to play a role as part of a federal regulatory scheme. Compare California v. FERC (1990) (Federal Power Act preempts state minimum stream flow requirements despite language in Act providing that "nothing contained [herein] shall * * * in any way interfere with [state] laws relating to * * * water"), with California v. United States (1978) (no preemption if state allocates water from federal dam, because 1902 Reclamation Act provides that "nothing in the Act shall * * * interfere with [state] laws relating to * * * water").

Federal law "occupies" a field when the field involves important national concerns, and application of state law would be hostile to federal interests. One such field appears to be wildlife management. United States v. Little Lake Misere Land Co. (1973) (federal purchases of state land for wildlife refuges not controlled by state law); North Dakota v. United States (1983) (application of state law may not interfere with federally-acquired waterfowl easements).

A state law becomes an "obstacle" to the accomplishment of federal goals either if the state holds a veto power over a right granted under federal law, or if compliance with state law somehow burdens one seeking to reap the benefits of federal law. For example, if an applicant for a federal oil and gas lease or mining patent could be deprived of that federal interest by denial of a state permit, then the state permit unconstitutionally stands in the way of the federal law. Ventura County v. Gulf Oil Corp. (1979); Brubaker v. Board of County Com'rs (1982). On the other hand, not all state requirements interfere with federal goals. Commonwealth Edison Co. v. Montana (1981) (state severance tax on coal located on federal land does not frustrate purposes of federal minerals statute by reducing federal royalties).

For many years, some state courts adopted a preemption test which permitted reasonable state regulation, while forbidding state laws which absolutely prohibited the federally-sanctioned development. State ex rel. Andrus v. Click (1976); State ex rel. Cox v. Hibbard (1977); Gulf Oil Corp. v. Wyoming Oil & Gas Conservation Com'n (1985). In California Coastal Com'n v. Granite Rock Co. (1987), the Supreme Court impliedly rejected this overly simplistic regulation/prohibition test by announcing a new, but equally unsatisfactory, preemption test. *Granite Rock* seems to hold that federal land planning and management statutes do not preempt state "environmental protection" laws. Preemption occurs only with state laws that affect federal "land use." The line between environmental and land use laws is a fuzzy one (as is the line between regulation and prohibition). It remains to be seen if *Granite Rock* has wider application beyond its immediate facts.

b. *Federal Immunity from State Law*

At one time, the Supreme Court interpreted the Supremacy Clause as forbidding state laws that interfered with federal lands or federal employees. McCulloch v. Maryland (1819) (state tax on national bank); Johnson v. Maryland (1920) (state driver's license requirement for federal employee); Gillespie v. Oklahoma (1922) (tax on lease of federal property).

The Court has more recently adopted a functional approach to claims of federal governmental immunity, accommodating the full range of state regulations. See North Dakota v. United States (1990) (upholding state labeling and reporting requirements as applied to liquor sold on military bases). A state regulation will be invalidated only if it regulates the United States "directly," United States v. County of Fresno (1977), or if it discriminates against federal interests. Davis v. Michigan Dept. of Treasury (1989).

Of course, when federal immunity is present, Congress may waive it. See 43 U.S.C.A. §§ 1068–1068(b) (limited waiver of immunity from state adverse possession laws). Or, where federal lands are immune from direct state taxation, the Congress may reimburse states for taxes thereby lost. Reimbursement is accomplished by providing federal revenues to states and local governments in lieu of taxation. See Payment in Lieu of Taxes Act, 31 U.S.C.A. § 6901 et seq.

The doctrine of intergovernmental immunities may also prevent parties from raising estoppel against the federal government. Utah Power and Light Co. v. United States (1917); United States v. Ruby Co. (1978). However, some lower courts have found estoppel acceptable when there has been affirmative misconduct by federal employees. Tosco Corp. v. Hodel (1985).

4. Congressional and Executive Authority

The two primary sources of constitutional power over public lands and resources—the Commerce and Property Clauses—are powers given to Congress. As a result, exercises of authority involving federal lands and resources must either stem directly from Congress, or be through a delegation to the President or federal administrative agency by Congress. In the vast majority of cases, Congress delegates to the President or agencies the power to make land management or resource use decisions. Only rarely will Congress retain the sole power to act, such as in the creation of national parks, or the withdrawal of certain resources from the operation of a previously-enacted resource disposition statute. See the Mineral Leasing Act of 1920, 30 U.S.C.A. § 181 *et seq.*, withdrawing federally-owned energy minerals (e.g., oil, gas, coal) from the operation of existing federal mining statutes which had permitted private ownership of such minerals.

In the more usual case, when power over federal property is delegated by Congress to the President or a federal agency, there are three primary ways to attack the resulting Executive or agency action. First, one can argue that the delegation is too broad, and lacks sufficient standards to guide any subsequent exercise of discretion. Panama Refining Co. v. Ryan (1935). Courts have universally rejected such challenges by finding acceptable the most vague and general of delegations. United States v. Grimaud (1911). Second, an exercise of delegated authority may be questioned for being *ultra vires* or contrary to the authorizing legislation. For example, in National Wildlife Federation v. Burford (1987), the court found that the BLM had acted inconsistently with a federal land management statute in revoking previous land withdrawals without first preparing plans. However, when statutes delegate authority directly to the President, courts usually defer to any exercise of presidential discretion under the statute. Wyoming v. Franke (1945). Third, an exercise of delegated authority may be overturned for failure to follow proper procedural requirements. Mountain States Legal Foundation v. Hodel (1987).

Some Presidents have claimed an inherent power to make public lands policy without congressional authorization. Although the Supreme Court has never acknowledged such inherent powers, it has upheld certain presidential actions on the theory that congressional acquiescence (inaction) creates a power in the President until Congress directs otherwise. Arizona v. California (1963); United States v. Midwest Oil Co.

(1915) (validating executive land withdrawals in the absence of specific congressional authorization).

B. EXERCISES OF POWER

Congress and the Executive tend to exercise power over federal property in specific ways. The United States originally had to "acquire" all the nation's land from native American Indian tribes, foreign nations, and the 13 colonies. The United States then "disposed" of land and resources by grants to states, farmers, ranchers, homesteaders, and railroad companies. In recent years, the United States has utilized condemnation, purchase, and exchange to "reacquire" land that was once in the public domain. Federal land reacquisition is often for conservation purposes, such as for wildlife habitat or national park inholdings.

There are few legal mechanisms in place for the United States to "sell" federal lands to private or corporate interests. The Federal Property and Administrative Services Act of 1949, 40 U.S.C.A. § 471 *et seq.,* permits the General Services Administration, in some instances, to dispose of surplus federal real estate (but not Forest Service lands). Rhode Island Committee on Energy v. GSA (1977). The Federal Land Policy and Management Act of 1976, 43 U.S.C.A. §§ 1701; 1713(a) (FLPMA), authorizes the Bureau of Land Management (BLM), the federal government's largest land-holder, to sell lands that are (1) difficult to manage, (2) no longer needed by the United States, or (3) better utilized if not federally owned. These sales must be conducted by competitive bidding, and be for fair market value.

"Exchanges" of federal lands for private lands are more common than sales, because the latter type of transfer reduces the amount of federal property. Most exchanges occur either to ensure access, or to eliminate private "islands" within federal property. Each federal land management agency has statutory power to exchange lands, and to thereby consolidate federal land holdings—BLM, 43 U.S.C.A. § 1716; Forest Service, 16 U.S.C.A. § 485; National Parks, 16 U.S.C.A. § 4601–4 *et seq.*; Fish and Wildlife Service, 16 U.S.C.A. § 668dd(b)(3). BLM and Forest Service exchanges are now largely governed by FLPMA, 43 U.S.C.A. § 1716, as amended by the Federal Land Facilitation Act of 1988, Pub.L. No. 100–409. Exchanges of lands in Alaska are subject to the Alaska National Interest Lands Conservation Act of 1980. 16 U.S.C.A. §§ 3103; 3192.

All of these exchange statutes have similar requirements. The private lands acquired through the exchange should be consistent with land uses on surrounding federal property. Exchanges must be in the "public interest." National Audubon Soc. v. Hodel (1984) (exchange of an uninhabited island in Alaska for native holdings within Alaskan refuges not in public interest). Offered lands must be of "equal value" to the federal lands conveyed. Committee of 100 on Federal City v. Hodel (1985). Exchanges have been approved even if they result in a private resource developer gaining a competitive advantage over a rival developer. National Coal Ass'n v. Hodel (1987). Most exchanges must be preceded by some environmental analysis under the National Environmental Policy Act of 1969. Northern Plains Resource Council v. Lujan (1989).

In addition to undertaking acquisition, disposal, reacquisition, sale, and exchange of federal lands, Congress and the Executive may control the uses and purposes of public lands and resources. This control is exercised in four ways. "Planning," an increasingly occurring requirement of federal lands agencies, calls for the development of planning documents to govern subsequent land use and resource management decisions. "Classifications" designate public lands for retention, and sometime segregate the lands from the operation of various land disposal laws. See Classification and Multiple Use Act of 1964, 43 U.S.C.A. § 1411 *et seq.*, now expired. "Withdrawals" prevent designated federal property from being subject to previously-enacted land use or resource disposal statutes (e.g., the Taylor Grazing Act of 1934, 43 U.S.C.A. § 315 *et seq.*, withdrew lands from the operation of then-existing homesteading statutes). "Reservations" dedicate withdrawn land or resources to a specified purpose (e.g., for national parks or national forests).

Of these four land use control decisions, Congress has been most concerned with withdrawals. This is because *Midwest Oil* and subsequent cases acknowledge implied withdrawal powers in the President if there has been congressional acquiescence. To prevent the exercise of such powers, in the 1976 FLPMA, Congress expressly repealed all implied authority under *Midwest Oil*. 43 U.S.C.A. § 1714. Although FLPMA is prospective only, the Act also repealed pre-FLPMA withdrawal statutes so that post-FLPMA withdrawals would be subject to its terms. 43 U.S.C.A. § 1704(a). In National Wildlife Federation v. Burford (1987), the court invalidated a Reagan Administration attempt to "revoke" several pre-FLPMA withdrawals. The court found that such revocations needed to be preceded by FLPMA-mandated land use plans.

FLPMA permits the Secretary of Interior to make withdrawals of less than 5,000 acres without congressional consent. Withdrawals in excess of 5,000 acres are subject to legislative veto, but the Secretary is not subject to this congressional oversight if a withdrawal greater than 5,000 acres is made for "emergency" purposes. 43 U.S.C.A. § 1714. Alaska v. Carter (1978) (upholding emergency withdrawal of land in Alaska while Congress resolved Native title claims). Such emergency withdrawals can be ordered by one of two congressional committees. Any agency decision to exclude a "major use" for more than two years on more than 260,000 acres is also subject to congressional veto, even if the decision is not labeled a withdrawal. 43 U.S.C.A. § 1712.

Two legal questions have arisen regarding these FLPMA withdrawal procedures. First, the Act's legislative veto provisions, as well as the section requiring emergency withdrawals when there is a command from a congressional committee, may be of doubtful constitutionality after Immigration and Naturalization Service v. Chadha (1983). In *Chadha,* the Supreme Court deemed some legislative vetoes invalid if not passed by both houses and presented to the President. If statutes enacted under the Property Clause are subject to *Chadha,* then parts of FLPMA may be similarly invalid. See National Wildlife Federation v. Watt (1983).

Second, two cases from the Wyoming District Court have held that agency inaction regarding applications for development on federal lands might constitute a "de facto" withdrawal, triggering the need to follow FLPMA withdrawal procedures. Mountain States Legal Foundation v. Andrus (1980); Mountain States Legal Foundation v. Hodel (1987). Interestingly, neither case raised the issue of whether the inaction was, in effect, a FLPMA exclusion of a major use, thereby raising the specter of legislative veto.

C. HISTORICAL DEVELOPMENT OF PUBLIC LANDS AND RESOURCES POLICY

One wishing to understand public lands and resources law must be familiar with the history of statutes and policies that shaped this law. Current legal issues involving both private and public lands often stem from governmental or judicial decisions made decades or even centuries ago. The history of public lands and resources law reveals five overlapping eras, each of which is characterized by a particular policy bias.

1. Acquisition

The United States acquired all its land within the North American continent from three sources—native American Indian tribes, the original 13 colonies, and from foreign nations. Today, tribes own only reservation lands, which are held in trust by the United States. All other Indian lands have been ceded to the United States by treaty or conquest. Transfers of original tribal land without approval by Congress are invalid. Oneida County v. Oneida Indian Nation (1985). Title to land in the 13 colonies passed to the original states through the Peace of Versailles Treaty of 1783. When these colonies became states, they did not grant significant amounts of land to the federal government; however, they did cede to the United States most of their claims to western territories east of the Mississippi. The remainder of the public domain was acquired by treaty, purchase, or war with England, France, Spain, Russia, and Mexico. With the purchase of Alaska from Russia in 1867, the original acquisition era had come to an end.

2. Disposition

a. Statehood

All lands acquired were eventually to become parts of states, admitted by the Congress into the United States through the operation of Article IV, Section 3, clause 1. The first state admitted was Ohio, in 1803, and the most recent was Alaska, in 1959. All states enter the United States on an "equal footing" with all previously-admitted states. Coyle v. Smith (1911).

When the 13 colonies became independent from Great Britain, they claimed title to the lands under navigable waters within their boundaries as the sovereign successors to the English Crown. Because all subsequently admitted states enter on an equal footing with the original 13 states, they too hold title to the land under navigable waters within their boundaries upon entry into the United States, absent some federal reservation. Pollard v. Hagan (1845); State of Alaska v. Ahtna, Inc. (1989). The issue of "navigability" is determined by a uniform federal test. United States v. Holt State Bank (1926) (susceptible of being used, in a waterway's ordinary condition, as a "highway for commerce"); United States v. Utah (1931).

Upon admission, states are not only vested with title in the beds of inland navigable streams and lakes, but also to tidelands and shorelands. Caminiti v. Boyle (1987). In Phillips Petroleum Co. v. Mississippi (1988), the Supreme Court acknowledged state ownership of lands under non-navigable waters subject to the ebb and flow of the tide. Although the United States originally held title to offshore lands, United States v. California (1947), the federal government returned title to the states in the Submerged Lands Act of 1953, 43 U.S.C.A. § 1301 *et seq.*

While the federal government may defeat a prospective state's title to land under navigable waters by a pre-statehood reservation or a conveyance to a private party, Shively v. Bowlby (1894), the Supreme Court does not lightly infer a congressional intent to defeat the state's title. Utah Div. of State Lands v. United States (1987) (federal statute did not intend to include the bed of a state lake within a federal reservation, thereby depriving state of title to it).

Lands underlying navigable waters acquired by states at statehood are subject to the public trust doctrine. Ill. Central Railroad Co. v. Illinois, 146 U.S. 387 (1892). The equal footing and public trust doctrines are distinct in their functions. The former grants legal title to the states to lands beneath navigable waters as they existed at the date of admission into statehood; the latter does not grant title, but merely preserves inviolate the public's use of those lands. Idaho Forest Industries, Inc. v. Hayden Lake Watershed Imp. Dist. (1987).

b.   Grants to States

Upon admission, most states were the beneficiaries of federal statutes that granted the new states lands for the support of schools and internal improvements. Although such federal grants do not necessarily create a perpetual trust, with the state as trustee, Papasan v. Allain (1986), courts have found that where the grant is for a specific purpose, states must comply with the original terms. United States v. New Mexico (1976). If these land grants to states are located wholly within federal land, states may have a legal right of access over federal lands. Utah v. Andrus (1979).

When sections designated for the states are unavailable because they have previously been sold or otherwise disposed of (usually by another act of Congress), a line of federal statutes provides for selections of other public lands "in lieu of" the unavailable sections. United States v. Morrison (1916). These indemnity lands must be of roughly equal value to the unavailable lands. Andrus v. Utah (1980). In calculating the state's entitlement to indemnity lands, the federal government may take into account prior lands granted to states, even if the transactions involving these lands are later found to be invalid for having been obtained through fraud. Oregon v. BLM (1989).

c. *Grants to Railroads and Problems of Access*

In order to assist the movement of people westward, and the shipment of resources eastward, Congress granted railroads rights-of-way across the public lands throughout the 19th Century. It also gave many railroads alternate sections of public land, from six to sixty miles on either side of the proposed railroad line, to aid in construction. This congressional grant of rights-of-way and adjacent section-by-section checkerboard pattern raised certain legal questions that continue to have impact.

Rights-of-way passing through Indian land sometimes required tribal consent. Southern Pacific Transp. Co. v. Watt (1983). If the railroad grant was ambiguous about whether it was meant to reserve to the United States subsurface minerals, then the ambiguity had to be resolved by subsequent litigation. See United States v. Union Pacific Railroad Co. (1957). Unclear federal grant reservations have occasionally caused controversy long after assignment or conveyance by the original railroad. Anschutz Land and Livestock Co. v. Union Pacific Railroad Co. (1987). Reversion of the grant to federal ownership occurred if certain conditions were met. Vieux v. East Bay Regional Park Dist. (1990) (cessation of use and occupancy by the railroad). The timber-rich Oregon and California railroad lands were returned to the federal government because of such a forfeiture. If there had been previous reservations or transfers of federal lands within a railroad's grant area, then the railroads (like the states) could select alternative indemnity lands "in lieu of" the grant lands. Santa Fe Pacific R. Co. v. Secretary of Interior (1987).

One of the most enduring legacies of railroad grants involves the checkerboard pattern of private-public land ownership that emerged when Congress granted the railroads over 100 million acres, on both sides of their right-of-way, in alternate, odd-numbered sections. After the end of the disposition era, when the railroads had transferred many of these sections into private lands, often neither the private owner of the odd-numbered section, nor the public owner of the even-numbered section, could access its property without trespassing on the other's property. Over the past century, both Congress and the courts have tried to address the resulting confusion. In so doing they have established a kind of "law of access" which has application beyond the checkerboard railroad sections.

In 1885, Congress passed the Unlawful Inclosures Act, 43 U.S.C.A. § 1061 *et seq.* This Act prohibited private acts, like fence-building, which enclosed public lands. In Camfield v. United States (1897), the Supreme Court found the Act constitutional as applied to a defendant who, in fencing in his own private checkerboard sections, had also enclosed adjacent public sections. Subsequently, in Mackay v. Uinta Dev.

Co. (1914), the Eighth Circuit found that a sheepherder could drive his sheep across private checkerboard lands on the way to public lands because such passage was contemplated by the Act. This trend of guaranteeing access to public lands seemed halted in 1979, in Leo Sheep Co. v. United States (1979). There the Supreme Court held that neither the Act nor notions of implied reservations of easements of access permitted the BLM to relocate a road to a federal reservoir so that it crossed private checkerboard sections. But then, in United States ex rel. Bergen v. Lawrence (1988), the Tenth Circuit resurrected the Act so that it applied to prohibit private fences bordering public lands which permitted human access, but not wildlife access. In light of this subsequent caselaw, it remains to be seen whether *Leo Sheep* is limited to its facts (preventing government road-building across private lands), or whether it has broader implications (private landowners can prevent access over private lands to retained federal lands).

Easements across public lands for access to private inholding within national forests are recognized by Montana Wilderness Ass'n v. United States Forest Service (1981). Access to private inholdings within national wildlife refuges is at the discretion of the Fish and Wildlife Service. Coupland v. Morton (1975). Access across BLM lands is governed by FLPMA, which provides for rights-of-way permits if certain conditions (e.g., environmental protection measures) are met. 43 U.S.C.A. § 1761; Sierra Club v. Hodel (1988) (pre-FLPMA access rights preserved only if existing prior to 1976).

d. Grants to Farmers, Ranchers, and Homesteaders

From the nation's creation, Congress has sought to bring about settlement of western public lands. Early preemption statutes validated the claims of those who had trespassed on public lands, because they had also worked the land to turn it from frontier to civilization. Cash sales of public land helped supply federal revenue before the Civil War. By the time of the Civil War, land sales were largely replaced by the Homestead Act of 1862, which authorized citizens free entry onto 160 acres of land. Settlement of arid land beyond the 100th meridian was encouraged by the Timber Culture Act of 1873 (additional land if trees planted), the Desert Lands Act of 1877 (entry and patent if land irrigated), the Enlarged Homestead Act of 1909 (entry allowed upon 320 instead of 160 acres), and the Stock–Raising Homestead Act of 1916 (entry allowed on 640 acres of semi-arid land designated valuable for livestock grazing). By the time of passage of the Taylor Grazing Act of 1934, 43 U.S.C.A. § 315 *et seq.*, the era of homesteading and uncontrolled grazing on public lands had ended. But by then the settlement of the United States had largely been completed.

3. Withdrawals and Reservations

By the end of the nineteenth century, some far-sighted individuals and lawmakers had begun to question one premise driving the disposition era—that the United States had an inexhaustible supply of land and resources to give away. Others began to recognize the ugly effects of disposal—fraud, greed, and exploitation of the land. Concerns about resource exhaustion and environmental damage led to a decision to halt many of the free grants. The legal mechanisms used for accomplishing this goal were withdrawals and reservations, by both Congress and the President.

While the two terms are sometimes used interchangeably, the technical distinction is that a withdrawal exempts land from the operation of a disposal law, and thereby preserves the status quo, while a reservation dedicates land (typically withdrawn land) to a specific purpose. Public lands and resources withdrawn or reserved during this era were either to be scientifically managed and used, or preserved in a natural state. One important consequence of the withdrawal and reservation era was the creation of six systems of public lands and resources.

Three systems were established for multiple-use, developmental purposes. First, the General Revision Act of 1891 and the Organic Act of 1897 authorized the President to set aside public lands as forest reserves. When the Supreme Court in Light v. United States (1911) decided that Congress could withdraw these lands without state consent, a major obstacle to the creation of a Forest Reservation system, under Forest Service management, had been lifted. Second, because the General Mining Law of 1872 had permitted uncontrolled private ownership (patenting) of federally-owned energy resources, Presidents Roosevelt and Taft decided for resource conservation purposes to withdraw coal and oil from the operation of the 1872 Law. Then the Congress acted to create a system of federal minerals management under the control of the Interior Department. It reserved to the United States all minerals existing under federal land disposition statutes. It also withdrew from patent all the energy minerals of the United States (e.g., coal, gas, and oil), and subjected them to leasing under the Mineral Leasing Act of 1920, 30 U.S.C.A. § 181 *et seq.* See Pathfinder Mines Corp. v. Hodel (1987) (additional lands—game preserve lands—may be withdrawn from mineral entry either by statute or executive proclamation). Third, to prevent overgrazing, the Congress passed the Taylor Grazing Act of 1934, 43 U.S.C.A. § 315. This Act effectively repealed all prior settlement acts by withdrawing most remaining public lands from all forms of entry. The Act also had the practical effect of creating a new class of otherwise unclassified public lands, under the control of the BLM, that were valuable chiefly for grazing, mineral development, and recreation.

The remaining three systems were created strictly for purposes involving recreation, preservation, and conservation. First, the National Park Service is responsible for those lands reserved by Congress for parks, monuments, recreation areas, and wild and scenic rivers. See 16 U.S.C.A. §§ 1, 431, 1271. Second, the 1964 Wilderness Act, 16 U.S.C.A. § 1311, authorized designation of certain roadless lands as wilderness areas, which closes them to all forms of development. The Alaska National Interest Lands Conservation Act of 1980, 16 U.S.C.A. § 3101, created millions of acres of wilderness land in Alaska. A wilderness area is managed by the agency that had jurisdiction over the area prior to wilderness designation. Third, the Fish and Game Sanctuaries Act of 1934, 16 U.S.C.A. § 694, as well as the National Refuge Administration Act of 1966, 16 U.S.C.A. § 668dd, permit withdrawals for the establishment of a national wildlife refuge system. These refuges are administered by the Fish and Wildlife Service.

4. Management

The management era followed from the withdrawals and reservations of public lands and resources. It has continued to the present time. Government management of federal property has reflected five policies: (1) multiple use; (2) preservation; (3) environmental review; (4) planning; and (5) reclamation.

a. *Multiple Use*

The multiple use philosophy encourages scientific management of all the uses theoretically possible within an area. On multiple use lands, a variety of resources (e.g., wildlife, timber, minerals) and land uses (e.g., grazing, watershed, recreation) are to be regulated and managed for the overall public good. The two prongs of the philosophy are "use," not preservation, and equal exploitation of "multiple" uses, not just an area's dominant use.

The two federal agencies that must manage their lands according to the multiple use philosophy are the Forest

Service and BLM. The Forest Service mandate stems from the Multiple–Use, Sustained–Yield Act of 1960, 16 U.S.C.A. § 528, and the National Forest Management Act of 1976 (NFMA), 16 U.S.C.A. § 1601 *et seq.* Statutory authority for BLM's multiple use charge comes from FLPMA, 43 U.S.C.A. §§ 1701(a)(7), 1712(c)(1). Judicial challenges occur when either agency makes decisions that seem to favor one use over others, such as large timber sales that adversely affect recreation. See National Wildlife Federation v. United States Forest Service (1984). Such challenges inevitably fail, usually because of judicial unwillingness to overturn what is an exercise of agency discretion. Perkins v. Bergland (1979); Headwaters, Inc. v. BLM (1988).

b. *Preservation*

Some lands and resources are to be protected from development, and immunized from the multiple use policy. Instead, they are to be preserved in a natural state for various purposes. Wilderness areas and endangered species are afforded the most protection. The former cannot be invaded by humans, except on horseback or on foot. Lyng v. Northwest Indian Cemetery Protective Ass'n (1988). The latter cannot be "taken" or harmed by human or agency actions. TVA v. Hill (1978). "Wetlands" are preserved by section 404 of the Federal Clean Water Act, 33 U.S.C.A. § 1344, which requires a federal permit whenever a wetlands area is threatened with disturbance. United States v. Riverside Bayview Homes, Inc. (1985). The 1906 Antiquities Act, 16 U.S.C.A. § 431, preserves federal lands containing "historic and prehistoric structures, and other objects of historic or scientific interest." The National Wildlife Refuge System is managed primarily for the conservation of wildlife. Recreation is also permitted in the various categories of lands and rivers within the National Park System.

c. Environmental Review

The National Environmental Policy Act of 1969 (NEPA), 42 U.S.C.A. § 4321, has become an important management statute for federal agencies. NEPA requires all federal agencies to consider the environmental consequences of their decisions, *before* making the decisions. Although NEPA will be discussed more fully in Chapter 5 (Environmental Assessment), it deserves mention here because it has been a major ground for judicially attacking the actions of federal lands and resources agencies. See Marsh v. Oregon Natural Resources Council (1989); California v. Block (1982). These agencies have been challenged either for failing to perform some timely NEPA-mandated environmental analysis, Kleppe v. Sierra Club (1976), or for undertaking environmental review alleged to be inadequate. Robertson v. Methow Valley Citizens Council (1989). NEPA cannot prevent an agency from making decisions that ultimately harm the environment. Strycker's Bay Neighborhood Council, Inc. v. Karlen (1980). But a NEPA case can delay the agency action while courts determine if the agency is complying with the statute's terms. NRDC v. Hughes (1977) (halting federal coal leasing pending NEPA compliance). Fear of NEPA litigation has revolutionized agency decisionmaking by making environmental review the most significant condition precedent to the undertaking of a major federal action.

d. Planning

NEPA's emphasis on before-the-fact analysis has continued in a series of planning statutes passed in the 1970s. These statutes require the major federal lands agencies to prepare planning documents, so that subsequent land use management decisions will be in light of an overall plan. See FLPMA of 1976, 43 U.S.C.A. §§ 1712, 1732(a) (BLM); the Forest and Rangeland Renewable Resources Planning Act of 1974, as amended by NFMA of 1976, 16 U.S.C.A. §§ 1600–

1614 (Forest Service); the National Parks and Recreation Act of 1978, 16 U.S.C.A. §§ 1a–1 to 1a–8 (National Park Service).

Judicial review of agency plans, and the planning process, seem to focus on four issues. First, agency action may be challenged for proceeding in the absence of a plan. National Wildlife Federation v. Burford (1987). Second, when plans are prepared, they may be attacked (usually unsuccessfully) for being inadequate. NRDC, Inc. v. Hodel (1985). Third, an agency decision may be questioned for being inconsistent with the plan. Intermountain Forest Industry Ass'n v. Lyng (1988). Fourth, agency action may be voided if the planning process does not comply with NEPA. Northwest Indian Cemetery Protective Ass'n v. Peterson (1985).

e. Reclamation

The final management philosophy involves a specific class of water that was made available for arid private lands by the construction of federal dams and canals under the Reclamation Act of 1902 (the Newlands Act), 43 U.S.C.A. § 371 *et seq.* The Bureau of Reclamation is expected to manage this water to irrigate agricultural lands in water-short regions in the West. Because legal control of water has traditionally been a matter of state law (see Chapter 8—Water Law), the Reclamation Act raises the question of whether, or the extent to which, states may impose conditions on federal reclamation projects. The general rule seems to be that since Congress has traditionally deferred to state water law, state conditions are acceptable, California v. United States (1978) provided they are not expressly precluded by federal law. California v. FERC (1990).

5. Reacquisition and Reclassification

By the end of the 20th century, the federal government had again begun to add to its holdings, much as it had in the first "acquisition" era. Unlike this first era, recent reacquisitions have not been from nations, but from states and individuals. The federal government's reasons for acquiring more land have largely been preservationist in nature. Its means of reacquisition have been by donation, exchange, purchase, or condemnation. See 16 U.S.C.A. §§ 4601–4 (Land and Water Conservation Fund enables federal agencies to purchase land for recreational purposes); 16 U.S.C.A. § 515 (purchase of forested land authorized); United States v. Gettysburg Elec. Ry. Co. (1896); United States v. 16.92 Acres of Land (1982) (condemnation acceptable for broadly defined "public purposes").

A different kind of reacquisition—a major reclassification of federal lands—occurred in Alaska. When Alaska became a state in 1959, the Alaska Statehood Act allowed it to select 103,350,000 acres of land from the United States for the economic and social well-being of the new state. Trustees for Alaska v. State (1987). After Alaskan Natives became dissatisfied with their share of these energy fuel-rich state selections, Congress responded with the Alaska Native Claims Settlement Act of 1971 (ANCSA), 43 U.S.C.A. § 1601. This statute permitted Alaskan Natives to select 44 million acres, allowed state selections to continue, and authorized the Secretary of Interior to withdraw up to 80 million acres of land for inclusion in "national interest" systems (national parks, forests, refuges, and wild rivers). 43 U.S.C.A. § 1616(d)(2). The ANCSA lands were available for selection only if they had not otherwise been appropriated for federal purposes. Lee v. United States (1991) (lands unavailable if previously classified as federal power sites). The withdrawal provisions of ANCSA are "subject to valid existing rights," which include legitimate expectations created by government action. Seldovia Native Ass'n, Inc. v. Lujan (1990); Aleknagik Natives Ltd. v. United States (1986) (valid existing rights not limited to vested rights).

These ANCSA withdrawals expired in 1978. In order to permanently prevent mineral development on proposed national interest lands, President Carter signed into law the Alaska National Interest Lands Conservation Act of 1980 (ANILCA), 16 U.S.C.A. §§ 3101-33. ANILCA added more than 103 million acres to federal preservation systems. In so doing, the Act reclassified lands that otherwise would have been available for mineral exploitation under federal disposition statutes (e.g., the 1920 Mineral Leasing Act). The Act also established a policy of preference for Alaskan Natives' use of ANILCA lands for subsistence. Amoco Production Co. v. Village of Gambell (1987). If America remains dependent on foreign oil, it will be interesting to see whether ANILCA's "lock up" of oil reserves continues in the face of mounting pressures to tap Alaska's energy potential.

II. THE LAW OF PUBLIC LANDS AND RESOURCES

There are two types of special purpose public lands that are managed by federal agencies—rangeland and preservation lands. There are four categories of natural resources that exist on public lands, and that are subject to federal law—wildlife, minerals, timber, and water.

A. MANAGEMENT OF SPECIAL PURPOSE PUBLIC LANDS

1. Rangeland

The middle of the United States, between the Sierras and the Missouri River, is primarily rangeland—vast expanses of grasslands capable of sustaining cattle and sheep grazing. Until 1934, with the passage of the Taylor Grazing Act, most of this land that was under federal ownership was unfenced. The free and unregulated status of these lands encouraged overgrazing, a kind of "tragedy of the commons" where it became in the interest of each rancher to graze as many head as possible before someone else did. The Congress exacerbated this trend when it passed the 1885 Unlawful Inclosures Act. The Supreme Court also sanctioned open grazing when it recognized an implied right of access to, and a right to graze on, unreserved, unregulated federal lands. Buford v. Houtz (1890).

The loss of forage resulting from this open-lands policy was so great that at the turn of the century the Forest Service began prohibiting livestock from grazing on its lands without a permit. The Congress in 1934 sought to impose more sweeping controls on grazing privileges with the passage of the Taylor Grazing Act, 43 U.S.C.A. § 315. As a legal matter, this statute replaced the right-by-custom to public rangeland with a permit and fee system administered by the Interior Department (first the Range Service, and then the BLM). As a practical matter, use of rangeland became largely dictated by ranchers who "captured" the range management process, both through Stockmen's Advisory Boards and through the grazing permit. The advisory boards, comprised of ranchers, largely control BLM range managers. The permit is perceived by the holder to be an inviolate property right, granting the permittee a right to rangeland similar to that enjoyed prior to 1934.

A federal grazing permit may be obtained by a person in the livestock business who is near or adjacent to grazing districts within BLM land. Grazing "leases" can be acquired for isolated tracts. A lease authorizes use of public lands outside of grazing districts. Preference is given to those with "base property"—sufficient private land, water, and forage to serve as a base for livestock operations. By the 1990s, about 20,000 ranchers were grazing livestock on 274 million acres of BLM and Forest Service lands in the 11 western states.

A permittee may graze a fixed number of cattle or sheep on specified public lands during portions of the year. The fee for this privilege is set far below market for use of comparable private grazing lands (approximately $2.00 on BLM lands per animal-unit-month (AUM), which is the amount that can be eaten in one month by one cow/calf unit, compared to $6–$15 per AUM on private lands). Because the fee is so low, and the public grazing lands so large, a federal grazing permit effectively provides a subsidy to permittees, which is certainly among the most valuable possessions of a rancher. In 1991, the General Accounting Office, Congress' investigative agency, concluded that the federal grazing program had become a losing proposition for taxpayers—for each dollar spent on the program, only 20¢ was being returned in the form of grazing fees.

The continued political power of rancher-permittees (particularly the 10% of permittees who control 90% of BLM grazing lands) has meant that largely unregulated grazing has become the dominant rangeland use. Congressional acknowledgement of the resulting deteriorating rangeland came in FLPMA of 1976, 43 U.S.C.A. § 1747(b)(1), and the Public Rangelands Improvement Act of 1978 (PRIA), 43 U.S.C.A. § 1901(a). Although both statutes seek to improve range conditions, tighten management of permittees, and set grazing fees at fair market value, old practices and low fees still predominate.

a. Nature of the Rancher–Permittee's Property Interest

A permit or lease is a less-than-fee interest which normally gives the holder the right to act only in specified ways, where failure to comply with the document's express terms may result in revocation. By contrast, ranchers holding Forest Service or BLM grazing permits and leases have long thought that their legal interest was more in the nature of a vested property right to public rangeland. In fact, the legal rights and duties that flow from a grazing permit depend on whether the rancher-permittee is resisting another competing livestock owner (or some other third party), or the demands of the federal landowner-permittor. In the former case the permittee's legal interest is more protectable than in the latter.

Courts have acknowledged the prerogatives of existing permittees vis-à-vis other potential permittees in Red Canyon Sheep Co. v. Ickes (1938) (land exchange); Oman v. United States (1949) ("lease-jumping"); and McNeil v. Seaton (1960) (reallocation of grazing privileges within a district). In Garcia v. Andrus (1982), statutory preference rights involving control of base property were enforced in deciding priorities between competing permit applicants. Rancher-permittees have been immunized from trespass actions brought by private parties (e.g., miners) and the federal government (e.g., the Forest Service) "invaded" by livestock. Powell v. United States (1956); Chournos v. United States (1952); United States v. Semenza (1987) (no trespass action for livestock straying onto Forest Service lands absent a showing of willfullness). Conversely, a federal mineral lessee may be liable for damages caused to livestock or forage by the lessee's negligent use of the permittee's surface base property. Gilbertz v. United States (1987). Permittees may also transfer grazing rights by private contract between themselves, provided the BLM approves. United States FHA v. Redland (1985).

When the dispute is not with third parties, but with the United States, courts are nearly unanimous in (1) conceding to the federal landowner the superior right, and (2) defining narrowly the property interest held by the permittee. The Interior Department has discretion in determining whether would-be permittees have the requisite qualifications. Sellas v. Kirk (1952). Two cases, Barton v. United States (1979) and LaRue v. Udall (1963), agree that BLM land exchanges are also discretionary acts. As a result, permittees affected by the exchange will likely not succeed in court against the BLM so long as "public interests are served [by the exchange]." A rancher's action against a trespassing mineral claimant will likewise fail if the mineral prospecting rights under the rancher's base property have previously been reserved to the United States. Visintainer Sheep v. Centennial Gold Corp. (1987). If permittees violate applicable statutes, regulations, or the conditions of the permit, the BLM may reduce grazing privileges, Perkins v. Bergland (1979), suspend the permit, Diamond Ring Ranch, Inc. v. Morton (1972), or revoke the permit. Holland Livestock Ranch v. United States (1984); Swim v. Bergland (1983); Osborne v. United States (1944). Forest Service regulations impose criminal liability on ranchers who permit unauthorized livestock to trespass on national forest lands. United States v. Larson (1984).

This consistency in result stems from a single premise: a grazing permit is not a vested, protectable property interest in contexts involving the United States. Rather, it is a revocable license to the use of public lands, which the holder possesses solely at the pleasure and discretion of the federal landlord. See United States v. Fuller (1973) (in a federal condemnation proceeding, the property that is "taken" does not include, for purposes of compensation, the value of adjacent permit lands); Hubbard v. Brown (1989) (grazing permit not an "interest in real property" for purposes of state statute immunizing real property owners from liability arising from recreational use of their property); United States v. Cox (1951) (permits not an interest protected by the 5th Amendment against government takings).

b. Range Management and NEPA

In addition to Taylor Act requirements, the BLM must also comply with the environmental commands of NEPA. In NRDC v. Morton (1974), the court decided that BLM had to prepare environmental impact statements (EISs) for all of its grazing districts. When the BLM was unable to meet the schedule established by this case, the court in 1978 reduced the number of EISs required to 144, and set up a revised schedule calling for the completion of the environmental review by 1988. NRDC v. Andrus (1978).

These NEPA cases forced the BLM to take a hard look at the condition of the rangeland under its control. The resulting environmental evaluations revealed a continuation of overgrazing, a loss of forage, and a crying need for range improvement. However, an EIS only shows the effect on the environment of government action (or inaction); it is not a basis for halting or forcing action if adverse environmental effects are identified. NRDC v. Hodel (1987) (as long as EIS is adequate, a finding of overgrazing is not grounds to challenge BLM rangeland management plans). Other statutes besides NEPA and the Taylor Act would have to be used to protect public rangeland.

c. *FLPMA of 1976 and the Public Rangelands Improvement Act of 1978 (PRIA)*

With the passage of FLPMA and PRIA, Congress has set three goals for public rangeland management. First, range improvement through livestock reduction is to be a management priority. 43 U.S.C.A. § 1903(b). Second, the multiple use philosophy is to guide land use decisions. 43 U.S.C.A. § 1701(a)(7). Third, BLM must prepare land use plans which reflect (1) the multiple use concept, and (2) accompanying EISs. Grazing permits and leases are to be granted, renewed, or conditioned on the basis of these plans. 43 U.S.C.A. § 1712. Subsequent caselaw and BLM practices have made attainment of these goals somewhat doubtful.

Despite congressional recognition of deteriorating range conditions in both FLPMA and PRIA, in 1983 the BLM proposed amendments to its grazing regulations that would have permitted certain ranchers to use public rangeland without BLM control. In NRDC v. Hodel (1985), the Eastern District of California voided this delegation of management responsibility, and required that private grazing on public lands be regulated by permit conditions (e.g., restricting numbers of livestock) that conformed to FLPMA rangeland improvement criteria. 43 U.S.C.A. § 1752. This non-deferential approach to BLM grazing regulations may be an anomaly, particularly in light of the Ninth Circuit's holding in NRDC v. Hodel (1987). There, the court affirmed a decision by a Nevada federal district court upholding a BLM plan which, despite FLPMA and PRIA language to the contrary, seemed to authorize overgrazing.

Although FLPMA and PRIA assume that BLM will manage rangeland consistent with multiple use notions, old habits are hard to change. BLM still believes that a dominant use approach is best, and that use is grazing. Other potential uses of rangeland, such as recreation, wildlife habitat, and watershed, are of secondary importance to BLM managers. The federal judiciary does not seem inclined to hold that failure to act according to multiple use is a legal grounds for stopping BLM. NRDC v. Hodel (1986).

Section 1732(a) of FLPMA is a charge to the BLM to manage public rangelands "in accordance with" land use plans. PRIA contains a similar mandate. However, BLM planning regulations do not indicate whether range management decisions need be consistent with, or even relate to, these plans. As a result, BLM managers have not established a nexus between the planning process and permitting. Although one lower federal court has assumed that these plans must have more than a hortatory effect, NRDC v. Hodel (1985), the Ninth Circuit has concluded to the contrary. See NRDC v. Hodel (1987) (BLM plans need not determine grazing capacity of public rangelands, despite likelihood of continued overgrazing). An EIS under NEPA is usually required both for initial plan drafting, and for plan modifications. Sierra Club v. Clark (1985).

d. Regulation of Non–Grazing Uses of Public Rangeland

(1) FLPMA RIGHTS-OF-WAY

Under FLPMA, both the BLM and Forest Service may grant, renew, or revoke rights-of-way across public lands for transportation, energy transmission, and water pipelines. 43 U.S.C.A. §§ 1761; 1766. A grant of a right-of-way is not a right to use public resources within the corridor. 43 U.S.C.A. § 1764(f). The right may be conditioned—either to protect environmental and wildlife habitat values, 43 U.S.C.A. § 1765(a), or to minimize proliferation by grouping rights-of-way together. See Citizens for a Better Henderson v. Hodel (1985). FLPMA provides that each right-of-way must comply "with State standards for public health and safety, environmental protection, and siting ∗ ∗ ∗ if those standards are more stringent than applicable Federal standards." 43 U.S.C.A. § 1765(a)(iv). This language has been interpreted to impose on federal agencies stricter state substantive standards, Montana v. Johnson (1984), but without the need to obtain state permits. Citizens and Landowners v. Secretary of Energy (1982); Columbia Basin Land Protection Ass'n v. Schlesinger (1981). The scope of pre-FLPMA rights-of-way are determined by state law. Sierra Club v. Hodel (1988). Section 1764(g) of FLPMA allows recovery of "reasonable costs" from private parties granted rights-of-way, Nevada Power Co. v. Watt (1983), but not from state and local governments. Beaver v. Andrus (1980).

(2) RECREATION

It is not clear whether citizens have recreational access rights to BLM lands. Compare United States v. Curtis—Nevada Mines, Inc. (1980) (yes), with Elk Mountain Safari, Inc. v. United States (1986) (no). However, it is clear that under FLPMA, "outdoor recreation" is a legitimate multiple use of these lands. 43 U.S.C.A. § 1702(c). Off-road vehicles

(ORV—snowmobiles, motorcycles, and four-wheel drive vehicles) are a particularly popular form of recreation which cause management difficulties because (1) they are permitted on most BLM lands, and (2) they cause environmental damage. BLM has addressed this dilemma by conforming to Executive Order No. 11,644, which requires that federal agencies assume that public lands are closed to ORV use, unless they are specifically opened pursuant to BLM plans and regulations. See National Wildlife Federation v. Morton (1975). Courts are mixed in their reviews of BLM ORV plans. On the one hand, courts have not only conceded to BLM power to prevent ORV use in certain areas, California Ass'n of 4WD Clubs, Inc. v. Andrus (1982), they have also enjoined BLM approval of ORV use that was environmentally damaging. American Motorcyclist Ass'n v. Watt (1982). On the other hand, the Ninth Circuit sustained a BLM assessment which substantially understated the likely damage from an ORV race—considering damage from the race in light of the entire planning area (12 million acres), not just the corridor used by the ORVs. Sierra Club v. Clark (1985).

(3) Competition with other Animals

Cattle and sheep are permitted limited access to range forage within wildlife refuges, Schwenke v. Secretary (1983), and national forests. 16 U.S.C.A. §§ 580k–580l. But the primary animal forms competing with livestock are "wild" horses and burros, descended from escaped domesticated animals. In the Wild, Free–Roaming Horses and Burros Act of 1971, 16 U.S.C.A. § 1331, Congress sought to check the desire on the part of ranchers to deal with this competition in their own way—wholesale slaughter or roundup for shipment to dog food makers. The Act prevents wild horses and burros from being killed or harmed by private parties. AHPA v. United States Dept. of Interior (1977) (federal agency determines if animals are wild or privately owned). If an area becomes overpopulated, the BLM is authorized either to destroy all old and injured horses or burros, or to remove the healthy ones for adoption "under humane conditions and use." 16 U.S.C.A. § 1333(b); Animal Protection Institute v. Hodel (1988) (ranchers cannot "adopt horses and burros" to resell to dog food manufacturers). The Act does not define what constitutes overpopulation, Dahl v. Clark (1984) (wild horse populations need not be maintained at 1971 lands), and courts have largely deferred to BLM in managing its periodic roundups. AHPA v. Watt (1982); AHPA v. Andrus (1979). The Act also requires that the BLM remove horses and burros that wander onto private land. 16 U.S.C.A. § 1334; Roaring Springs Assoc. v. Andrus (1978). The government's failure to prevent wild horses from grazing on private lands is not a "taking," when the ranchers are not deprived of all "economically viable use" of affected lands. Mountain States Legal Foundation v. Hodel (1986).

2. Preservation Lands

Most United States citizens use public lands not for developmental or economic purposes, but for aesthetic and recreational enjoyment. Federal law reflects this reality in several ways. First, millions of acres have been set aside either so that they remain in an untouched, pristine state, or so that they may be used for recreation. The former—pure preservation lands (e.g., wilderness acres)—are protected from most human intrusions, other than the recreational hiker or rafter. The latter—recreation lands (e.g., national parks)—are similarly preserved so that resource development cannot take place, but these lands are expected to tolerate a greater degree of human interference. These two types of lands will be treated separately below. However, one should realize that recreation lands are often threatened by over-intensive recreational use. Also, there is not always a bright line between preservation and recreation. See Friends of Shawangunks, Inc. v. Clark (1985) (statute authorizing "public outdoor recreation uses" encompasses preservationist values not involving the public's physical presence).

Second, recreation is not only recognized as a primary use in wilderness areas, 16 U.S.C.A. § 1133(d)(5), and national parks, 16 U.S.C.A. § 1, but it is also a statutory component of the multiple use concept in NFMA, 16 U.S.C.A. § 528 (national forests), and FLPMA, 43 U.S.C.A. § 1702(c) (BLM lands). Reconciling recreation with other multiple use activities has been a troublesome task for federal managers that often ends in litigation. See Conservation Law Foundation of New England, Inc. v. Secretary of Interior (1989) (recreational ORV use does not violate Cape Cod National Seashore Act); Otteson v. United States (1980) (Forest Service has no duty to maintain timber supply roads for recreational use).

Third, there appears to be an implied license to visit public lands for recreational purposes. United States v. Curtis—Nevada Mines, Inc. (1980); United States v. Rainbow Family (1988). This license may be limited or revoked by Congress or a relevant land management agency if the "visit" entails a recreational use that threatens other public resources. American Motorcyclist Ass'n v. Watt (1983) (ORV restrictions upheld); Wilderness Public Rights Fund v. Kleppe (1979) (river rafting restrictions sustained). If persons are injured or killed while enjoying this recreational license, an action may be pursued against the United States through the Federal Tort Claims Act, 28 U.S.C.A. §§ 1346(b) and 2671 *et seq.* Ducey v. United States (1987) (tort action against National Park Service for failure to warn of deadly flash flood). But see Cagle v. United States (1991) (in action brought for injury sustained in national park, United States was shielded from liability to same extent as private citizen under applicable state recreation use law).

a. Preservation for Recreation

So-called public "recreation lands" include national parks and monuments, national recreation areas, and national forests. In each of the systems, but particularly in the first, legal and policy questions have arisen over the extent to which federal managers may (or should) encourage recreation at the expense of preservation. Excessive recreational use, or particular recreational uses (e.g., ORVs), may harm lands and their unique resources. In response, the Interior Department may limit access to, and motorized use within, recreation lands. Biderman v. Morton (1974). It may also limit recreational activities. Free Enterprise Canoe Renters Ass'n v. Watt (1983). But it has been reluctant to do so. Conservation Law Foundation of New England, Inc. v. Secretary of Interior (1989); Sierra Club v. Clark (1985). Litigation to force more preservation values on overused recreation lands has usually been unsuccessful. National Wildlife Federation v. National Park Service (1988); Sierra Club v. Watt (1983); Friends of Yosemite v. Frizzell (1976).

(1) NATIONAL PARK AND MONUMENTS

National parks are congressionally created by individualized legislation. 16 U.S.C.A. § 22. The President has been delegated authority to designate national monuments, 16 U.S.C.A. § 431, consistent with the terms of the Antiquities Act of 1906, 16 U.S.C.A. § 431, and the Historic Sites Act of 1935, 16 U.S.C.A. § 461. Both parks and monuments are managed by the National Park Service, 16 U.S.C.A. § 1. National parks are usually established just for their scenic beauty, while monuments may be reserved for their historic or scientific significance as well. This distinction is important in determining whether waters within the reservation may be used for varying purposes pursuant to the federal reserved rights doctrine. Compare Cappaert v. United States (1976) (creation of Devil's Hole National Monument reserved water to sustain scientific value of the reservation), with United States v. Denver (1982) (creation of Dinosaur National Monument did not reserve water for recreational boating purposes). By the 1990s, nearly 300 million visitors were spending time in one of the 357 parks, monuments, historic sites, recreation areas, or seashores run by the Park Service. All these lands encompass 80 million acres of public property.

(a) Concessions, Support Facilities, and Services

Profit-making, privately-owned, concessioner-supplied services are an integral part of the National Park System. Private concessioners may provide food, lodging, and other amenities of civilization. Sierra Club v. Lujan (1989) (proposed hotel on north rim of Grand Canyon). They are licensed by the National Park Service pursuant to the Park System Organic Act of 1916, 16 U.S.C.A. § 3, and the Concessions Policy Act of 1970, 16 U.S.C.A. § 20. Concession activity is big business, increasingly dominated by large corporate concessioners. National Parks and Conservation Ass'n v. Kleppe (1976). The Interior Secretary has broad authority to contract with concessioners. Universal Interpretive Shuttle Corp. v. Washington MATC (1968).

Once granted, a contract affords the concessioner an opportunity to realize a profit, Yachts America, Inc. v. United States (1985), and possibly a monopoly in the supply of services. 16 U.S.C.A. § 20c. Although an existing concessioner has a preferential right of contract renewal, Fort Sumter Tours, Inc. v. Andrus (1977), it has no renewal right on terms identical with the original contract, Canyoneers, Inc. v. Hodel (1985). Rival applicants may obtain review of an adverse decision under the Administrative Procedure Act. Glacier Park Foundation v. Watt (1981). No contractual right of preference exists in awarding concession services to an existing concessioner. Hamilton Stores, Inc. v. Hodel (1991).

(b) Commercial Recreational Activities

Some private outfits provide commercial recreational services, such as rental canoes, or multi-day guided rafting trips. The Park Service has virtually unreviewable discretion to limit the nature and number of recreational activities offered by commercial enterprises. Free Enterprise Canoe Renters Ass'n v. Watt (1983); Wilderness Public Rights Fund v. Kleppe (1979).

(c) Non–Recreational, Commercial Development

Economic development of natural resources (e.g., timber and minerals) is prohibited in most units of the National Park System. 16 U.S.C.A. § 460gg–10. Commercial exploitation of resources (e.g., fish) within Park System lands may be halted or severely limited. Organized Fishermen of Florida v. Andrus (1980). Although mining was originally allowed in some Park System areas, the Mining in Parks Act of 1976 (1) outlawed all future mining activity, and (2) required all pre–1976 claims to be validated, recorded, and closely regulated. 16 U.S.C.A. § 190 *et seq.*; Brown v. United States Dept. of Interior (1982) (lands acquired by the United States in 1972 as part of the Buffalo National River are closed to mining); United States v. Vogler (1988) (placer miner prohibited from operating off-road vehicles in national park system without first obtaining access permit); Northern Alaska Environmental Center v. Lujan (1989) (on-site inspection not needed to verify validity of pre–1976 mining claim in national park). Mining of existing claims within national parks may be barred until proper NEPA analysis is performed in conjunction with mining plan approvals. Northern Alaska Environmental Center v. Hodel (1986).

(d) Threats to Parklands

Even if the internal integrity of parks and monuments is maintained, events and activities occurring outside their boundaries adversely affect them. For example, a federally constructed dam may cause Zion National Park to lose the wild river that carved its most spectacular canyon. Logging has so decimated the hillsides next to Olympic and Mount Rainier National Parks in Washington State, that fish runs are a fraction of what they used to be as erosion has filled the nearby streams with silt. The air in Kings Canyon/Sequoia National Parks, south of Los Angeles, is so polluted that rangers are contemplating posting warning signs that hiking on certain days constitutes a health hazard. Acid rain has stripped high-altitude trees of their foliage in the most popular park in the system, the Great Smoky Mountains. The Everglades of Florida has lost 90 percent of its wading birds since the 1930s, because the park's once extensive wetlands have been drained and polluted by South Florida development. An enormous sight-seeing tower has been constructed on private lands adjacent to the Gettysburg civil war battlefield.

Although power sufficient to abate nuisances on nonfederal land is likely present in both the Property Clause (art. IV, § 3, cl. 2), and in the language of the National Park Act (16 U.S.C.A. §§ 1, 1–1a), courts have been unwilling to protect parklands from external threats. Friends of the Earth v. Armstrong (1973) (impounded waters of Lake Powell may flood Rainbow Bridge National Monument); Commonwealth v. National Gettysburg Battlefield Tower (1973) (tower on private land may be built overlooking Gettysburg Battlefield); Northern Indiana Public Service Co. v. Porter County Chapter of Izaak Walton League of America, Inc. (1975) (nuclear power plant may be built on land abutting Indiana Dunes National Lakeshore); United States v. Arlington County (1979) (office buildings may be built along the Potomac River shoreline even though they affect the green backdrop of various Washington D.C. monuments).

A lower federal court once held that the public trust doctrine gave the Park Service a duty to stop adjacent aesthetic nuisances. Sierra Club v. Department of Interior (1975). This application of the public trust doctrine has been subsequently rejected by one federal court. Sierra Club v. Andrus (1980).

(e) Liability

The United States is not liable under the Federal Torts Claims Act (FTCA) for failure to suppress forest fires originating in federal lands that spread to neighboring private lands. Defrees v. United States (1990) (no liability when federal officials made reasonable effort to contain fire before it damaged private property). The FTCA permits suits against the Park Service for injuries sustained by persons if the United States would, as a private person, "be liable to the claimant in accordance with the law of the place where the [accident] occurred." 28 U.S.C.A. § 1346(b); Miller v. United States Dept. of Interior (1986) (Park Service not liable for failing to remove a rope swing from a tree branch in a national lakeshore park); Cagle v. United States (1991). The FTCA also contains an exception which relieves the United States of liability for any claim based upon the performance of a "discretionary function." 28 U.S.C.A. § 2680(a); Zumwalt v. United States (1991) (alleged negligence of Park Service in marking a trail fell within discretionary function exception to liability).

(2) OTHER FEDERAL RECREATION LANDS
(a) National Recreation Areas

A national recreation area (NRA) is usually created after a federally-authorized dam forms an artificial reservoir. Popular NRAs include Glen Canyon, Lake Mead, Blue Mesa, Flaming George, and Hells Canyon. More development of economic resources is permitted in NRAs than in parks or monuments. Sierra Club v. Watt (1983) (leasing of minerals authorized in Lake Mead NRA). Private concessioners may provide services within NRAs if they first obtain a federal permit. United States v. Hells Canyon Guide Service, Inc. (1981). The negligence of a concessioner's employee may not be imputed to the United States to form the basis of liability under the Federal Torts Claims Act. Ducey v. United States (1983); Ducey v. United States (1987).

(b) Forest Service Lands

The Forest Service must allow recreation as a multiple use of nonwilderness areas in national forests. 16 U.S.C.A. § 528. It regulates private recreational facilities according to twin goals: (1) prevention of overcrowding, Great American Houseboat Co. v. United States (1986); and (2) removal of private docks, houseboats, and lodges. Lake Berryessa Tenant's Council v. United States (1978); Paulina Lake Historic Cabin Owners Ass'n v. USDA Forest Service (1983). The Forest Service is liable under the Federal Tort Claims Act only for gross negligence as defined by state law. Lebeter by Lebeter v. United States (1990) (no federal liability for damages incurred when minor fell off rope swing on tree overhanging river in national forest). Unlike the BLM, the Forest Service controls private ORV use not by regulation, but by site specific ORV plans. Private commercial recreation facilities (e.g., resorts, outfitters) need Forest Service permits. United States v. Richard (1980). Noncompliance with permit terms may result in permit revocation and federal confiscation of the private property. Ness Inv. Corp. v. United States (1979).

One of the most valuable Forest Service use permits is the ski area permit. The permitting process was originally pursuant to the 1897 Organic Act, 16 U.S.C.A. §§ 497, 551; Wilson v. Block (1983). The National Forest Ski Area Act of 1986 (NFSAA), 16 U.S.C.A. § 497b, now governs ski area permits. The NFSAA grandfathers pre–1986 permits, which the Forest Service can nonetheless revoke for cause. NFSAA permits are granted for 40 years, and for the number of acres the "Secretary determines * * * appropriate." They may be canceled if the ski area is needed "for higher public purposes." 16 U.S.C.A. §§ 497(b)(3); (b)(5). The granting of a ski area permit is a "major federal action" under NEPA, requiring Forest Service preparation of an EIS. Robertson v. Methow Valley Citizens Council (1989). While ski area permittees are given several exclusive rights, Sabin v. Berglund (1978) (control over ski instruction), they are not exempt from antitrust laws. Aspen Skiing Co. v. Aspen Highlands Skiing Corp. (1985) (multi-area ski ticket arrangement is an illegal monopolization). Once granted, a permit is treated like a contract for purposes of interpreting its terms. Meadow Green–Wildcat Corp. v. Hathaway (1991).

b. Preservation for Historic, Wilderness, and Ecological Purposes

(1) CULTURAL, HISTORIC AND SCIENTIFIC PRESERVATION

(a) Historic Preservation

Both the Constitution's Property Clause and the states' police power authorize federal and state laws that seek to preserve historic sites and buildings. Penn Central Transp. Co. v. City of New York (1978); Mayes v. Dallas (1984). Congress has established a federal system of historic preservation in three statutes: the Historic Sites Act of 1935, 16 U.S.C.A. § 461; the National Historic Preservation Act of 1966 (NHPA), 16 U.S.C.A. § 470; and the NHPA Amendments of 1980, Pub.L. No. 96–515. The NHPA creates a National Historic Landmark Program whereby "eligible property" may be listed in a National Register of Historic Places. Federal agencies contemplating the expenditure of funds or the undertaking of actions (i.e., licensing) must first consider the effect on any listed property. An Advisory Council on Historic Preservation must also be given the opportunity to comment on such undertakings. 16 U.S.C.A. §§ 470f; 470i. Properties eligible for listing usually have historical or cultural significance, Colorado River Indian Tribes v. Marsh (1985), but do not include entire mountain ranges important to Indian culture. Wilson v. Block (1983). A certified historic structure under the NHPA is entitled to income tax credit under the Internal Revenue Code. Amoco Production Co. v. United States Dept. of Interior (1990).

The "historic impact review" requirement under the NHPA is similar to NEPA's environmental impact review requirement. See United States v. 162.20 Acres of Land (1984) (analysis under NHPA considers same factors as an EIS under NEPA); Walsh v. United States Army Corps of Engineers (1990). Like NEPA, the NHPA sets out procedural, not substantive duties. A federal agency action will be halted only if the effect on a listed site is not considered. Morris County Trust v. Pierce (1983); Warm Springs Dam Task Force v. Gribble (1974). A decision to undertake the action, even in the face of an adverse recommendation of the Advisory Council, is not grounds for attacking the decision if historic impact review has taken place. Hickory Neighborhood Defense League v. Skinner (1990); Paulina Lake Historic Cabin Owners Ass'n v. USDA Forest Service (1983); Pennsylvania v. Morton (1974). Federal actions authorizing inconsequential activities, such as repainting and reroofing historic sites, do not trigger NHPA historic impact review requirements. Vieux Carre Property Owners v. Brown (1989).

(b) Protection of Antiquities and Archaeological Resources

The Antiquities Act of 1906, 16 U.S.C.A. § 431, not only authorizes the withdrawal and reservation of lands containing objects of historic or scientific value, it also prohibits injury to or excavation of "any object of antiquity" without government permission. The 1906 Act proved difficult to enforce because of its tiny penalties (a maximum fine of $500), and the ambiguity of the "objects of antiquity" phrase. United States v. Diaz (1974) (Act void for vagueness); People of State of California ex rel. Younger v. Mead (1980) (6070 pound meteorite is "object of antiquity"). It was supplanted in 1979 by the Archaeological Resources Protection Act (ARPA), 16 U.S.C.A. § 470aa, which prohibits the excavation or alteration of any archaeological resource on public or Indian lands without a permit or exemption. Public lands do not include shipwrecks on the outer continental shelf. Klein v. Unidentified Wrecked and Abandoned Sailing Vessel (1985). The ARPA applies only to purposeful excavation of archaeological resources, not excavations inadvertently uncovering such resources. Attakai v. United States (1990). The Historic Sites Act also contains a provision requiring federal agencies to consider preservation of archaeological resources in licensing or undertaking development projects. 16 U.S.C.A. § 469a–1.

(2) Preservation of Wilderness Values

The wilderness ethic holds that certain lands should be preserved in their natural condition, unaffected by human activities. This is at odds with the multiple use doctrine, by which lands are used, not preserved, and used in multiple ways, not "locked up" in a dormant, wilderness state. Although the wilderness idea may be criticized as being a means of halting valuable resource development for the benefit of a few, privileged, physically-fit backpackers, the wilderness philosophy remains an entrenched and significant component of public land law.

(a) Creation of Wilderness Areas

Federal wilderness areas are established in two ways. The first way is the most direct. Congress designated nearly ten million acres of wilderness areas when it enacted the Wilderness Act of 1964, 16 U.S.C.A. § 1131. In a similar fashion, the Eastern Wilderness Act of 1975, Pub.L. No. 93–622, established as wilderness over 200,000 acres of national forests east of the 100th meridian, and ANILCA designated a whopping 56.4 million acres in Alaska as wilderness, comprising almost ⅔ of the entire federal wilderness system. 16 U.S.C.A. §§ 3101–3233.

Second, Congress has instructed federal land management agencies to make recommendations on certain areas within their jurisdiction for future wilderness designation. The Forest Service was required to study areas "classified * * * as primitive" for wilderness suitability, after which the President may recommend to Congress which lands should be official wilderness, including "contiguous areas." 16 U.S.C.A. § 1132(b). The Department of Interior was to make wilderness recommendations to the President on all "roadless" areas of at least 5,000 or more acres within national parks and wildlife refuges. 16 U.S.C.A. § 1132(c). FLPMA ordered the Interior Secretary to study all roadless parcels of BLM lands of at least 5,000 acres for inclusion as wilderness. 43 U.S.C.A. § 1782(a). If any of these areas eventually becomes wilderness, it will be administered by the same agency that had jurisdiction before wilderness designation. All wilderness recommendations must be accompanied by an acceptable EIS.

These wilderness studies have raised questions regarding the kinds of lands that may qualify as potential wilderness areas. An area is "roadless," despite the presence of old logging roads, if they are overgrown and not in use. An "area" of at least 5,000 acres may exist, even if it is in different watersheds, or if it is bifurcated by a mountain range. An area is "untrammeled by man," 16 U.S.C.A. § 1131(c), if it appears to have wilderness characteristics, and if past human activities there are not inconsistent with wilderness. Parker v. United States (1971). The wilderness review process under FLPMA encompasses all estates in "public lands," including split-estates where the United States owns only mineral interests. Sierra Club v. Watt (1985).

(b) Management of Designated Wilderness Lands

The Wilderness Act requires federal land management agencies to "preserve" designated wilderness areas, primarily for recreation that does not entail motor vehicles. This preservation mandate is "subject to existing private rights." 16 U.S.C.A. §§ 1133(b), (c); United States v. Gregg (1968) (custom of landing airplanes not an existing "right"). Hunting and fishing are permissible, if consistent with state law. O'Brien v. State (1986). Commercial guides and river-runners are allowed in wilderness areas. 16 U.S.C.A. § 1133(d)(5).

Although the preservation rule is intended to forbid roads, motor vehicles, and commercial development, there are exceptions. New mining claims or leases are disallowed. Izaak Walton League v. St. Clair (1973) ("wilderness and mining are incompatible"). But mineral locations and leases validly established before Jan. 1, 1984 may continue, subject to "reasonable regulations." 16 U.S.C.A. § 1133(d)(3); Freese v. United States (1981) (mineral location); Getty Oil v. Clark (1985) (oil and gas leasing). Pre–1984 mineral claims may be challenged under the Endangered Species Act, Cabinet Mountains Wilderness v. Peterson (1982), and the 1977 Clean Air Act Amendments. Chevron U.S.A., Inc. v. United States E.P.A. (1981).

Timber harvesting is forbidden, unless an exception is made for a specific area. Minnesota PIRG v. Butz (1976)

(Boundary Waters Canoe Area). While pre–1964 grazing is allowed, 16 U.S.C.A. § 1133(d)(4), there surely must be a point where cattle and sheep grazing affect wilderness attributes. The President is authorized to develop water resources, such as water storage projects and hydropower facilities, within wilderness areas. 16 U.S.C.A. § 1133(d)(4). Wilderness designations in national forests may impliedly reserve water rights for wilderness purposes that are in addition to the waters impliedly created at the time the national forest was reserved. Sierra Club v. Yeutter (1990); Sierra Club v. Lyng (1987); Sierra Club v. Block (1985).

Interesting questions arise regarding whether human intervention intended to protect wilderness areas from harm is allowed. The Wilderness Act forbids motorized equipment or use of motor vehicles, but the Forest Service may use chain saws and certain vehicles to fight forest fires. 16 U.S.C.A. § 1133(d)(1). Tree cutting to contain insect infestation is acceptable so long as the action protects wilderness values, not commercial timber interests. Sierra Club v. Lyng (1987); Sierra Club v. Lyng (1988). Timber cutting may also be justified for protection of endangered species. Sierra Club v. Block (1985).

(c) Wilderness in National Forests

The 1964 Wilderness Act not only classified many lands in national forests as wilderness, and required the Forest Service to study "primitive" areas for future wilderness inclusion, it also set in motion a voluntary process whereby national forest lands adjacent to designated areas were inventoried to determine if they too should become wilderness. The first of these inventories, known as Roadless Area Review and Evaluation (RARE I), discovered that 56 million acres could qualify as wilderness. When courts enjoined commercial activities (e.g., road building and logging) on RARE I lands because of Forest Service failure to prepare

EISs, Wyoming Outdoor Coordinating Council v. Butz (1973), the Forest Service began again with RARE II, which studied more than 60 million acres of roadless land.

After the Ninth Circuit halted all logging activities on RARE II lands, because the EIS had not discussed the effects of "releasing" 36 million acres of RARE II lands for development, California v. Block (1982), the Forest Service started over again with RARE III in 1983. RARE III opened areas recommended by RARE II as non-wilderness to multiple use management and commercial development. Congress responded to RARE III with uncommon haste, passing individual state wilderness bills in 1984 that added nearly 9 million acres to the wilderness system from national forest lands. By the 1990s, Congress had failed to enact wilderness legislation for just a handful of western states, most notably Colorado and Montana.

The Forest Service's experience with RARE I, II, and III reveals the existence of *de facto* wilderness lands, called wilderness study areas (WSAs), which are created while a federal land management agency reviews and inventories their suitability for potential wilderness designation. After the inventory is complete, some WSAs are designated official wilderness by federal statute. For the remaining WSAs, there can be no release to non-wilderness, multiple use management, without preparation of an adequate EIS. When statewide wilderness bills release nondesignated areas, these lands are typically subject to multiple use management until revision of NFMA forest plans. Road construction on released, nondesignated lands must comply with NEPA. City of Tenakee Springs v. Block (1985).

Prior to designation or release, it is not entirely clear how national forest WSAs are to be managed. Courts are split on whether an EIS must always precede Forest Service actions that might affect wilderness values in WSAs. Compare California v. Block (1982) (yes), with National Wildlife Federation v. Coston (1985) (no). It is equally uncertain whether federal agencies can allow mineral leasing in WSAs without retaining the power to deny the lessee the right to engage in surface disturbing activities. Compare Bob Marshall Alliance v. Hodel (1988) (leasing halted), with Mountain States Legal Foundation v. Hodel (1987) (leasing permitted). Nor is it clear whether, or the extent to which, roadbuilding or commercial construction is permitted in a roadless WSA. Compare Thomas v. Peterson (1985) (road construction enjoined for failure to consider effect on wildlife), with Wilson v. Block (1983) (ski area expansion permissible), and Montana Wilderness Ass'n v. United States Forest Service (1981) (road construction to private inholdings acceptable).

(d) Wilderness in BLM Lands

FLPMA of 1976 requires BLM to evaluate some 174 million acres of land for wilderness potential and to report to the President by 1991 on its findings. 43 U.S.C.A. § 1782(a). Because of the nature of BLM lands, as well as their historic use by grazing and mining interests, only a fraction of the areas studied are to be designated as wilderness. By 1991, only 14% of BLM lands outside of Alaska (24 million acres) were thought to possess wilderness characteristics. The BLM ultimately recommended that just 10.7 million acres be designated as wilderness.

Management of WSAs on BLM lands is pursuant to two statutes—FLPMA and NEPA. Section 1782(c) of FLPMA provides that WSAs should be managed "so as not to impair [their suitability] as wilderness, subject, however, to the continuation of existing [pre–1976] mining and grazing uses and mineral leasing. * * *" This grandfather clause is then qualified by the requirement that BLM "take any action * * * to prevent unnecessary or undue degradation" of WSAs subject to pre–1976 uses. This awkward and somewhat circular language has been judicially construed to grandfather from the non-impairment standard only "actual on-the-ground" mining, mineral leasing, or livestock grazing activities, while still subjecting these to the "undue degradation" standard. Rocky Mountain Oil & Gas Ass'n v. Watt, (1982) (mineral leasing); Utah v. Andrus (1979) (hardrock mining).

The second relevant statute—NEPA—applies to road improvement projects in BLM WSAs. Sierra Club v. Hodel (1988) (BLM has a "duty to prevent unnecessary degradation of the WSAs.") An upgrade of a road from dirt to gravel which passed between two WSAs has been found to have no significant environmental impact under NEPA. Sierra Club v. Hodel (1990).

(e) Wilderness in National Parks and Wildlife Refuges

As a result of the original Wilderness Act's requirement that the National Park Service and Fish and Wildlife Service review their lands for wilderness potential, nearly 60 million acres have been added to the National Wilderness Preservation System (37 million acres from parks, 20 million acres from wildlife refuges). Most of these acres were established by ANILCA in Alaska. Many of these Alaskan wilderness areas may hold large quantities of untapped oil and gas reserves. Pressure to open these areas to oil and gas exploration seems inevitable. See Trustees for Alaska v. State DNR (1990).

(3) PRESERVATION OF WATER RESOURCES

(a) Protection of Free–Flowing Rivers

The Wild and Scenic Rivers Act of 1968 (WSRA), 16 U.S.C.A. §§ 1271–87, creates a nation-wide system of rivers that are protected from various activities, depending upon their classification as "wild, scenic, or recreational." Rivers designated must have "remarkable" scenic or recreational values, be "free-flowing," and be threatened by private activities. 16 U.S.C.A. § 1276(d). Over 100 river segments, encompassing thousands of miles, are part of the Wild and Scenic Rivers System.

The WSRA sets out two methods of adding waters to the system: congressional designation, and by state initiative with federal concurrence. 16 U.S.C.A. § 1273(a). In the former, Congress identifies "potential additions," and then directs the Secretaries of Interior and Agriculture to prepare studies of these, which form the basis of an eventual report to the President, who makes a recommendation to Congress for permanent inclusion in the system. 16 U.S.C.A. §§ 1275(a), 1276(a). Listing a river or river segment as a potential addition prohibits federal licensing of any water development project for a minimum of three years. 16 U.S.C.A. § 1278(b); Town of Summersville v. FERC (1986). Such a listing also withdraws lands within a quarter mile on each side of the river from entry, sale, or non-leasing mineral disposition. 16 U.S.C.A. §§ 1279(b), 1280(b).

State initiatives can add rivers and river segments if the Secretary of Interior concludes that they meet the WSRA's qualifying characteristics, and if the state agrees to administer them. 16 U.S.C.A. § 1273(a). The Secretary's decision is subject to NEPA. Del Norte County v. United States (1984). Although state-proposed rivers are not afforded the same protections as congressionally-designated "potential additions," North Carolina v. FPC, once included in the system by the Secretary they are protected similarly to those initially designated by Congress. Swanson Mining Corp. v. FERC (1986).

Upon designation, river segments must be classified as "wild" (pristine), "scenic" (largely undeveloped), or "recreational" (may contain some developments). For post–1985 designations, management plans must be prepared to guide decisions regarding permissible activities on adjacent lands. 16 U.S.C.A. § 1274(d)(1). For pre–1986 designations, the Act requires only a review of pre-existing plans, rather than preparation of original plans. Wilderness Society v. Tyrrel

(1990). The federal government may, by condemnation or purchase, acquire certain lands on either side of a designated river. 16 U.S.C.A. §§ 1277(a)–(c); 1286(c). Federal condemnation of scenic easements may not affect (1) "any regular use exercised prior to the acquisition," United States v. Hanten (1980), or (2) more stringent local land use zoning laws. Kiernat v. Chicago County (1983).

The WSRA requires that designated rivers and river segments be protected from activities that might interfere with the purposes of the wild, scenic, or recreational classification. Such activities include: timber harvesting and road building, 16 U.S.C.A. § 1283(a); development projects likely to degrade water quality, Wilderness Society v. Tyrrel (1988); and impoundments or diversions that might affect the river's free-flowing condition. Swanson Mining Co. v. FERC (1986); Diack v. City of Portland (1987). Pre-designation mining claims are protected, Skaw v. United States (1984), so long as the mining claimant has a validly-established property right prior to the designation. Skaw v. United States (1988).

(b) Protection of Wetlands and Tidelands

Section 404 of the Federal Clean Water Act extends the federal regulatory jurisdiction of the Army Corps of Engineers beyond the banks of a river or lake to all "navigable waters," which include wetlands. 33 U.S.C.A. § 1344; NRDC v. Callaway (1975). The Corps' regulations define wetlands as "areas that are inundated or saturated by surface or ground water at a frequency and duration sufficient to support * * * a prevalence of vegetation typically adapted for life in saturated soil conditions." Corps' jurisdiction encompasses artificially created wetlands. United States v. Southern Inv. Co. (1989).

The Supreme Court has rejected the argument that flooding is a statutory requirement for the exercise of Section 404 jurisdiction, concluding instead that wetlands adjacent to lakes, rivers, streams, and other waterbodies are subject to Section 404, "even when the moisture creating the wetland does not find its source in the adjacent bodies of water." United States v. Riverside Bayview Homes, Inc. (1985). See also Southern Pines Assoc. v. United States (1990) (wetlands not adjacent to any body of water may be subject to Corps permit); Riverside Irr. Dist. v. Andrews (1985) (Section 404 requires Corps to consider environmental effects of proposed projects many miles downstream of project).

No wetland may be affected ("dredged or filled") without a Corps permit. United States v. M.C.C. of Florida, Inc. (1988); Bersani v. United States EPA (1988); National Wildlife Federation v. Laubscher (1987). The primary exception to this requirement is the statute's exemption for agricultural water use. This exemption has been limited to normal, on-going farming activities, and does not include draining a swamp to put additional land into agricultural production. United States v. Akers (1986); Avoyelles Sportsmen's League, Inc. v. Marsh (1983). A permit application entails full public interest review, Wyoming v. Hoffman (1976), and often triggers NEPA. Sylvester v. United States Army Corps of Engineers (1989). A corps permit may be vetoed by the EPA. 33 U.S.C.A. § 1344(b)–(c).

The Section 404 permit requirement may give rise to a takings challenge. The requirement does not itself "take" the property of a person seeking to alter a wetlands. United States v. Riverside Bayview Homes, Inc. (1985). A 404 permit may be conditioned or denied without compensation if there are other "economically viable uses" of the property affected by the permit. Claridge v. New Hampshire Wetlands Bd. (1984). Economic viability does not mean most profitable. Deltona Corp. v. United States (1981). The federal government usually can successfully defend against a takings claim if it can show that property burdened by a 404 permit condition or denial still has some "fair market value." Jentgen v. United States (1981).

If the permit denial precludes *all* profitable development, then there is more likely to be a taking. Beuré–Co. v. United States (1988). There is also a taking if permit denial precludes economically viable use of the property. Florida Rock Industries, Inc. v. United States (1990) (taking when value of property reduced 95%); Loveladies Harbor, Inc. v. United States (1990).

The nation's tidelands are protected by three federal statutes and one judge-made doctrine. The Coastal Zone Management Act, (CZMA), 16 U.S.C.A. §§ 1451–64, authorizes coastal states to impose controls preserving tidal margins. Secretary of the Interior v. California (1984) (states may require federal agencies to comply with the CZMA when conducting activities affecting a state's coastal zone); California Coastal Com'n v. Granite Rock Co. (1987). The CZMA provides financial assistance to states for the development of coastal zone management programs. The CZMA does not infer a right of action on behalf of a state against a private party who acts without a federal permit. State of New York v. DeLyser (1991).

The Coastal Barrier Resources Act, 16 U.S.C.A. § 3501, makes activities more expensive that might adversely affect the outerbanks. Bostic v. United States (1985) (federal flood insurance denied for improvements to recreational properties). The Estuarine Areas Act of 1968, 15 U.S.C.A. §§ 1221–1226, requires federal agencies to consider the value of estuaries in their planning. Finally, the public trust doctrine has been expanded to include lands under waters subject to the ebb and flow of the tide, regardless of whether such waters are navigable. Phillips Petroleum Co. v. Mississippi (1987).

B. MANAGEMENT OF NATURAL RESOURCES ON PUBLIC LANDS

1. Economically Valuable Resources

Three classes of natural resources that exist on public lands have potentially high economic value to private marketplace actors—minerals, timber, and water. These may be contrasted with the fourth naturally occurring resource, which typically does not have economic value—the wildlife resource. Because they may be considered primarily economic resources, and because they are subject to state and common law in addition to federal law, discussion of these three public resources will be deferred until Chapters Six (Minerals Law), Seven (Timber Law), and Eight (Water Law).

2. The Wildlife Resource

a. *The Legal Framework*

(1) GOVERNMENT "OWNERSHIP" OF WILDLIFE?

At one time it was thought that states owned wildlife within their borders in a trust relationship for state residents. Mayor v. Eslava (1842). Under this theory, states had an interest in wildlife that was superior both to individuals, Leger v. Louisiana Dept. of Wildlife and Fisheries (1975), and to the United States. Geer v. Connecticut (1896). In 1979, in Hughes v. Oklahoma (1979), the Supreme Court overruled *Geer* and held that wildlife in commerce was subject to neither state nor individual ownership. Federal ownership of wildlife has possibly been approved in the context of protection of a species vis-à-vis state action. Palila v. Hawaii Dept. of Land and Natural Resources (1988). Federal ownership theories have been rejected in the context of holding the federal government liable for harm caused by wildlife. Mountain States Legal Foundation v. Hodel (1986); Ashley v. United States (1964).

(2) FEDERAL AUTHORITY OVER WILDLIFE

Federal control over wildlife finds its constitutional basis in three clauses in the Constitution—(1) the Commerce Clause, United States v. Helsley (1979); (2) the Property Clause, Kleppe v. New Mexico (1976); and (3) the Treaty Clause, Missouri v. Holland (1920). Congressional actions taken pursuant to this authority can preempt contrary state wildlife law. Douglas v. Seacoast Products, Inc. (1977).

Federal power over wildlife may affect states in three ways. First, states may be required to close certain areas to hunting if states permit hunting in ways inconsistent with federal law. California Fish & Game Com'n v. Hodel (1987). Second, federal agencies can regulate wildlife on state land if the regulation is aimed at protecting the purposes of nearby federal land. United States v. Brown (1977). Third, federal wildlife managers need not obtain state licenses to kill wildlife on federal land. Hunt v. United States (1928). Such instances of federal preemption are rare. Federal law tends to give states primary responsibility for wildlife management, even on federal lands. Defenders of Wildlife v. Andrus (1980).

(3) LEGAL BOUNDARIES OF STATE WILDLIFE LAW

State law tends to dominate the regulation of hunting, fishing, and trapping of wildlife. State laws may also provide for predator control and habitat protection. City of Aurora v. Commerce Group Corp. (1984) (city condemnation of six miles of stream fishing rights).

(a) Conflicts with Other States

Even in the absence of conflicting federal law, state wildlife law may be unconstitutional if it discriminates either against other states, Hughes v. Oklahoma (1979) (Commerce Clause violated), or the residents of other states. Toomer v. Witsell

(1948) (Privileges and Immunities Clause violated). The two exceptions to the Constitution's aversion to discriminatory state wildlife laws are (1) where the state law relates to recreational, not commercial uses of wildlife, Baldwin v. Fish and Game Com'n of Montana (1978), and (2) where the purpose of the state law is for wildlife conservation. Maine v. Taylor (1986). Occasionally the Supreme Court will allocate wildlife between competing states through use of the equitable apportionment doctrine. Idaho ex rel. Evans v. Oregon (1983) (salmon and trout in the Columbia–Snake River).

(b) State Wildlife Management on Federal Lands

Although Congress may preempt state management of wildlife on federal lands, Kleppe v. New Mexico (1976), it often defers to state law. The extent of state wildlife law permitted on federal lands varies by system. The National Park Service is exempt from state law. New Mexico State Game Com'n v. Udall (1969). The Fish and Wildlife Service follows only state law that is consistent with federal management objectives. 16 U.S.C.A. § 668dd(c). The Forest Service and the BLM are subject to the terms of FLPMA, which provide that "nothing in this Act should be construed * * * as enlarging or diminishing the responsibility and authority of the States for management of fish and resident wildlife." 42 U.S.C.A. § 1732(b). It is unclear whether this language prevents federal agencies from interfering with state wildlife action taken on federal lands. Defenders of Wildlife v. Andrus (1980); Alaska v. Andrus (1979) (Alaskan wolf hunt).

b. Federal Wildlife Management

(1) KILLING, HUNTING, AND FISHING

(a) Taking Wildlife for Business, Recreation, Subsistence, and Predator Control

Although federal wildlife law is often intended to protect animals and their habitat, it also permits and regulates the taking and killing of wildlife on federal lands. The nature of federal regulation depends upon the reason why the wildlife is being killed.

The commercial taking of wildlife is constitutionally protected from discriminatory state laws under the Privileges and Immunities Clause. Toomer v. Witsell (1948). However, commercial fishing can be prohibited in certain sensitive federal lands. Organized Fishermen of Fla. v. Hodel (1985) (Everglades National Park).

"Sport" killing of wildlife in the form of hunting and fishing is permitted in varying degrees on federal lands, usually pursuant to regulations adopted by state fish and game agencies. As a general proposition, while both state wildlife agencies and federal land management agencies tend to condone and accommodate hunting and fishing, courts will uphold these agencies if they ever decide to restrict or ban recreational forms of wildlife killing. Sierra Club v. Clark (1985); National Rifle Ass'n v. Potter (1986); Defenders of Wildlife v. Andrus (1977). Moreover, some federal statutes, such as the Migratory Bird Treaty Act of 1918, 16 U.S.C.A. § 703, impose strict criminal liability standards on hunters who violate their terms. United States v. Chandler (1985); United States v. FMC Corp. (1978).

Hunting or fishing on public lands for subsistence by Indians has been acceptable either if Indians have reserved such rights by treaty, Kimball v. Callahan (1974), or if federal lands statutes, such as ANILCA or the Marine Mammal Protection Act, have codified such rights. 43 U.S.C.A.

§§ 3114, 3120(a); 16 U.S.C.A. § 1371; Kwethluk IRA Council v. State of Alaska (1990); United States v. Clark (1990); Kunaknana v. Clark (1984). Indian treaties do not exempt tribal members from prosecution for taking wildlife specifically protected by federal law. United States v. Dion (1986) (Bald Eagle Protection Act); United States v. Billie (1987) (Endangered Species Act). Despite ANILCA's statutory preference for subsistence uses, injunctive relief may not be the appropriate judicial response to federal agency failure to adequately consider the effects of offshore oil and gas leasing on subsistence uses of Alaskan lands. Amoco Production Co. v. Village of Gambell (1987).

At one time the federal government sanctioned the killing of "predators," such as wolves, bobcats, coyotes, bears, and rodents, that either preyed on livestock or carried infectious diseases. See the Animal Damage Control Act of 1931, 7 U.S.C.A. § 426. These efforts too often resulted in an overpopulation of some species when natural predators were killed. When poisons, like strychnine, were used to kill predators, many non-predator species died as well. See Defenders of Wildlife v. Administrator (1989) (use of strychnine to kill rodents had a prohibited impact on endangered species). Recognition of these harmful consequences of predator control has resulted in more strictly regulated use of poisons. National Cattlemen's Ass'n v. United States E.P.A. (1985). Increased awareness has also led to the imposition of sanctions upon those who harm endangered species, even endangered species that kill livestock. Christy v. Hodel (1988).

(b) Hunting and Fishing within Federal Land Systems

The extent to which hunting and fishing is allowed on federal lands varies according to the federal land system. Hunting and fishing is permitted but restricted in wilderness areas and certain national park system units. 16 U.S.C.A. § 1133(f). The National Park System can prohibit commercial fishing within national parks, Organized Fishermen of Fla. v. Hodel (1985), and ban recreational hunting on state-owned lands within national parks. United States v. Brown (1977). The Fish and Wildlife Service may permit sport hunting and fishing within the National Wildlife Refuge System, Humane Society v. Hodel (1988), in a manner which is "to the extent practicable, consistent with state fish and wildlife laws." 16 U.S.C.A § 668dd(c). The Forest Service and BLM manage wildlife on their lands pursuant to FLPMA, 43 U.S.C.A. § 1732(b). The District of Columbia Circuit Court of Appeals has interpreted this section as giving states primary responsibility for wildlife within their borders, which presumably includes regulation of hunting and fishing. Defenders of Wildlife v. Andrus (1980). FLPMA § 1732(b) nonetheless gives the BLM and Forest Service ambiguous authority to restrict or ban hunting or fishing for "reasons of public safety * * * or compliance with provisions of applicable law."

(2) WILDLIFE IMPACT REVIEW

(a) NEPA

The basic impact review statute is NEPA, which requires federal agencies to consider impacts on wildlife in their decisionmaking. Two issues may arise in litigation involving federal agency compliance with NEPA regarding wildlife—(1) has the agency prepared a timely EIS; and (2) if so, is it adequate?

There is no consensus in the courts regarding the first issue. On the one hand, failure to prepare an EIS has been upheld either when mitigating conditions imposed by the agency were thought likely to avoid harm to wildlife, Cabinet Mountains Wilderness v. Peterson (1982), or when full assessment of the consequences for wildlife could be postponed until there was a more concrete proposal to physically develop federal lands. Village of False Pass v. Clark (1984);

North Slope Borough v. Andrus (1980). Federal actions affecting wildlife have been allowed to continue (1) pending completion of an EIS, Defenders of Wildlife v. Administrator (1989), and (2) following completion of a regional EIS that adequately discussed the threat to an endangered species. Headwaters, Inc. v. BLM (1990). Also, federal *in*action in the face of activities threatening wildlife has been found not to trigger the EIS requirement. Defenders of Wildlife v. Andrus (1980).

On the other hand, several other decisions have not permitted federal agency projects without preparation of a full EIS at an earlier time. Thomas v. Peterson (1985), required the Forest Service to consider the cumulative impacts on wildlife of road construction before approval of the road. Conner v. Burford (1988) and Bob Marshall Alliance v. Hodel (1988), found that an EIS must be prepared at the time the Forest Service issues oil and gas leases, and not at a later time, when permission to drill is sought. Unlike *Cabinet Mountains,* the court in Foundation for North American Wild Sheep v. United States Dept. of Agriculture (1982), rejected the argument that mitigation measures ensured no adverse effects on wildlife, and required the Forest Service to prepare a full EIS when evidence showed that reopening an old access road could affect breeding conditions.

Once an EIS has been prepared, courts have been very deferential when challenges to its adequacy have been raised. In Robertson v. Methow Valley Citizens Council (1989), the Supreme Court concluded that NEPA requires neither a fully developed mitigation plan in the EIS explaining how wildlife will be protected, nor a "worst case analysis." The Ninth Circuit similarly found to be adequate an EIS prepared for offshore oil and gas leasing, despite allegations that it was not based on the best available scientific methodology. Tribal Village of Akutan v. Hodel (1988) (regarding the effect of seasonal changes in the weather on the movement of fish and wildlife).

(b) Other Wildlife Impact Review Statutes

Besides NEPA, a number of federal statutes require federal agencies to take wildlife into account in their decisions. The Endangered Species Act of 1973, 16 U.S.C.A. §§ 1531–1543, discussed more fully below, provides courts with grounds to enjoin any federal action likely to harm a threatened or endangered species. Sierra Club v. Lyng (1988). The Fish and Wildlife Coordination Act of 1958, 16 U.S.C.A. § 661, requires federal agencies to consult with the Fish and Wildlife Service so that mitigation measures are integrated into all agency project plans. Texas Committee on National Resources v. Marsh (1984). The Federal Clean Water Act, 33 U.S.C.A. § 1251 *et seq.*, is intended to ensure that the waters of the United States are "fishable," and that activities be controlled that affect fish by degrading water quality. Northwest Indiana Cemetery Protective Ass'n v. Peterson (1985) (anadromous fish species protected from effects of timber harvesting). Section 404 of the Clean Water Act requires the Corps of Engineers to consider the effects of proposed projects on downstream endangered species before issuing a permit. 33 U.S.C.A. § 1344; Riverside Irr. Dist. v. Andrews (1985) (whooping crane protected from dam). Both FLPMA, 43 U.S.C.A. § 1732(a), and the Multiple–Use Act, 16 U.S.C.A. § 528, require BLM and the Forest Service to balance desirability of wildlife protection with demands for other land uses.

(3) Habitat Acquisition and Protection

(a) The National Wildlife Refuge System

Federal wildlife refuges are managed by the Fish and Wildlife Service (FWS) pursuant to the National Wildlife System Administration Act of 1966, 16 U.S.C.A. § 668dd. This Act consolidated all existing refuges into one land management system. Since some of these were originally established for grazing of domestic livestock, certain refuges are managed both for the protection of wildlife habitat and livestock grazing. Schwenke v. Secretary of Interior (1983).

The 1966 Act authorizes the Interior Secretary to allow uses within refuges "for any purpose * * * whenever he determines that such uses are compatible with the major purposes for which such areas were established." 16 U.S.C.A. § 668dd(d)(1). The Secretary may also exchange lands for wildlife refuges if the federal lands are "suitable for disposition" and of "approximately equal" value. 16 U.S.C.A. § 668dd(b)(3). While exchanges involving refuges are largely unreviewable in court, Sierra Club v. Hickel (1972), exchanges of refuge land in Alaska are reviewable under a "public interest" standard. National Audubon Society v. Hodel (1984).

(b) Habitat Acquisition

In several federal statutes, the Congress has provided financial support for state wildlife programs and state acquisition of wildlife habitat. See the Lacey Act Amendments of 1981, 16 U.S.C.A. § 3371 (upheld in United States v. Bryant (1983)); and the Land and Water Conservation Fund Act of 1964, 16 U.S.C.A. §§ 4601–4. Federal habitat acquisition may occur by condemnation, United States v. Timmons (1982), or pursuant to a more specialized wildlife refuge acquisition law, such as the Migratory Bird Conservation Act of 1929, 16 U.S.C.A. § 715. To fund the 1929 Act, Congress passed the Migratory Bird Hunting and Conservation Stamp Act of 1934 (the Stamp Act), 16 U.S.C.A. § 718. The Wetlands Act of 1961, Pub.L. No. 87–383, appropriates additional money for acquisition of easements over wetland areas for waterfowl breeding and nesting. While no land may be acquired with money from the Stamp Act–Wetlands Act without state consent, 16 U.S.C.A. § 715f, states cannot revoke their consent after acquisitions have been made. North Dakota v. United States (1983). Anyone draining wetlands on federal waterfowl easements is subject to criminal prosecution. United States v. Vesterso (1987).

(c) Management of National Wildlife Refuges

Although the national wildlife refuge system is to be managed primarily to provide habitat for wildlife, the FWS is authorized to permit uses in refuges for "any purpose" which is "compatible with" this primary purpose. Hunting is permitted, if found to be "beneficial." For example, the FWS may permit limited public deer hunting on a refuge established as a sanctuary for an endangered species, in order to control the refuge's deer population. Humane Soc. v. Lujan (1991). 16 U.S.C.A. § 668dd(d)(1)(A); Humane Society v. Hodel (1988). Mineral exploration and development is also permitted, Watt v. Alaska (1981), so long as the wildlife habitat in the refuges is protected. Trustees for Alaska v. State DNR (1990); Trustees for Alaska v. Watt (1981). Private access to refuges may be restricted if wildlife species (particularly endangered species) are adversely affected by the proximity to humans. New England Naturist Ass'n, Inc. v. Larsen (1988); Coupland v. Morton (1975). Recreational uses, like powerboating, may be enjoined if inconsistent with a refuge's primary purpose. Defenders of Wildlife v. Andrus (1978).

(4) SPECIES PROTECTION—THE ENDANGERED SPECIES ACT

The Endangered Species Act of 1973 (ESA), 16 U.S.C.A. §§ 1531–1543, requires the listing of species or threatened species of flora or fauna. By the early 1990s, there were a total of 885 endangered or threatened species worldwide, consisting of birds, reptiles, amphibians, fish, snails, clams, crustaceans, insects, and spiders. There were over 225 endangered plants. Wilson v. Block (1983). Slightly less than 100 of these species exist on federal lands, primarily in the

West. The presence of a listed species on federal lands dramatically affects the nature of activities that can take place on these lands. The ESA sets up an elaborate process by which federal agencies contemplating action near listed species must consult with the FWS, and ensure that no harm comes to the species or its habitat. Failure to comply with the ESA is grounds to enjoin a wide range of proposed agency projects. See Portland Audubon Society v. Lujan (1989) (timber harvesting); Save the Yaak Comm. v. Block (1988) (road paving); Bob Marshall Alliance v. Hodel (1988) (oil and gas leasing); Palila v. Hawaii Dept. of Land and Natural Resources (1986) (livestock grazing); Thomas v. Peterson (1985) (road construction); Defenders of Wildlife v. Andrus (1977) (hunting); TVA v. Hill (1978) (dam building).

The ESA is triggered after a wildlife or plant species is either proposed for listing, or is officially listed by the FWS as endangered or threatened. 16 U.S.C.A. § 1533. An endangered species is defined as one "in danger of extinction throughout all or a significant portion of its range." 16 U.S.C.A. § 1532(a). If a species is only proposed for listing, agencies contemplating action must "confer" with the FWS, but are not prohibited from taking some action. 16 U.S.C.A. § 1536(a)(4); Enos v. Marsh (1985). The ESA does not preempt state regulation of threatened species that are not officially listed. H.J. Justin & Sons, Inc. v. Deukmejian (1983).

If a species is eventually listed, agencies cannot make an "irreversible or irretrievable commitment of resources" until after completion of a more detailed "consultation" with the FWS. 16 U.S.C.A. § 1536(d). In case of an "emergency posing a significant risk to the well-being of any species of fish or wildlife or plants," the Interior Secretary may list the species immediately. 16 U.S.C.A. § 1533(b)(7); City of Las Vegas v. Lujan (1989) (emergency listing of desert tortoise upheld). Critical designations are to occur simultaneously with species listing. 16 U.S.C.A. §§ 1532(5), 1533(a)(3)(A). If a species is listed after an agency has prepared an EIS for an area which includes the species, the agency need not prepare a supplemental impact statement if the original EIS conformed with NEPA. Headwaters, Inc. v. Bureau of Land Management (1991).

Designation of species and habitat under the ESA may be initiated in one of three ways. The FWS can designate based on its own information. Other federal agencies can activate the designation process if it is discovered that proposed projects may impact a suspect species. Private citizens or environmental organizations may also begin the designation process. 16 U.S.C.A. § 1533(b)(3); Northern Spotted Owl v. Hodel (1988). Attempts to "delist" a species usually fail. Las Vegas v. Lujan (1989); Pacific Legal Foundation v. Andrus (1981).

Once a species is listed and its habitat designated, the ESA forbids (1) all actions that "take" an endangered or threatened species, and (2) federal agency actions that "jeopardize" the continued existence of listed species, that result in "destruction or adverse modification" of habitat of such species, or that are inconsistent with the "conservation" of listed species. The ESA also establishes a process by which federal agencies must provide "biological assessments" of actions potentially affecting listed species or their habitat. This step may be followed by a "consultation" with the FWS and the preparation of a "biological opinion" that assesses whether the action can occur in light of harm to the species or its habitat.

(a) The "Taking" Prohibition

The ESA prohibits any entity, public or private, from taking any listed species. 16 U.S.C.A. § 1538(a)(1)(B) & (C). The term "take" is broadly defined to mean "harass, harm, pursue, hunt, shoot, wound, kill, trap, capture, or collect." 16 U.S.C.A. § 1531(19). The FWS has further interpreted "harass" and "harm" to include indirect injury through habitat alteration or destruction. The taking prohibition has supported injunctive relief against proposed federal, state, and private actions: Federal—Sierra Club v. Yeutter (1991); Defenders of Wildlife v. Administrator (1988); State—Palila v. Hawaii Dept. of Land and Natural Resources (1986); Sierra Club v. Clark (1985); Fund for Animals, Inc. v. Florida Game & Fresh Water Fish Com'n (1982); Private—Christy v. Hodel (1988). A private person illegally possessing a listed species may be criminally liable, regardless of whether the person knew that the animal (or plant) was a species protected under the ESA. United States v. Nguyen (1990).

Some courts have been unwilling to enforce the taking prohibition. In State of Louisiana ex rel. Guste v. Verity (1988), the Fifth Circuit conceded that an estimated 2381 threatened or endangered turtles were being killed by shrimp nets each year off the coast of Louisiana, but failed to consider whether this killing violated the ESA. Contra, United States v. Nuesca (1990). In National Wildlife Federation v. National Park Service (1987), the court rejected a taking claim in the absence of proof of harm to protected species.

Two 1982 amendments to the ESA give the FWS and National Marine Fisheries Service (NMFS) discretion to fashion exceptions to the taking prohibition. The first of these permits "incidental" takings resulting from federal action, if the action is not likely to jeopardize the species, and if the FWS or NMFS provide a "written statement" specifying that everything is being done to "reasonably" and "prudently" protect the species. 16 U.S.C.A. §§ 1536(b)(4) & (o)(2); Defenders of Wildlife v. Administrator (1989) (the incidental take statement cannot operate retroactively); National Wildlife Federation v. National Park Service (1987) (a "statement" is not needed when no taking anticipated). The second exception allows non-federal entities to get permits for "incidental takings." 16 U.S.C.A. § 1539(a); Friends of Endangered Species, Inc. v. Jantzen (1984) (permit allowed when county action still permanently protected 86% of listed species' habitat).

(b) The Prohibition Against Federal Actions That Jeopardize Species or Harm Habitat

The ESA forbids all federal actions that may jeopardize a listed species or result in adverse modification of habitat. 16 U.S.C.A. § 1536(a). Courts have interpreted this prohibition broadly. Species have been found to be "jeopardized," and habitat "adversely modified," when proposed federal action might result in (1) species extinction, TVA v. Hill (1978); (2) a decline in species population, Sierra Club v. Lyng (1988); Roosevelt Campobello Intern. Park Com'n v. United States EPA (1982); or (3) harm to habitat. Riverside Irr. Dist. v. Andrews (1985). If the agency proposes mitigation that prevents the harm, then the project may proceed. Cabinet Mountain Wilderness v. Peterson (1982). If mitigation is inadequate, or problematic, then the proposed action will be enjoined. Sierra Club v. Marsh (1987).

(c) The Duty to "Conserve"

Federal agencies are also under a statutory obligation to "conserve" listed species. 16 U.S.C.A. § 1536(a)(1). This duty is supplemental to the prohibitions against jeopardizing species or harming habitat.

Courts have given teeth to the duty to conserve, making it a non-hortatory, substantive standard. The conservation of species was one reason why the Eighth Circuit enjoined a sport hunt of threatened wolves in Minnesota. Sierra Club v. Clark (1985). Failure to abide by the duty to conserve has also resulted in the remand of FWS bird hunting regulations. Defenders of Wildlife v. Andrus (1977). Conversely, the duty has sustained agency decisions designed to protect listed species. See Carson–Truckee Water Conservancy Dist. v. Clark (1984) (fish habitat protected); New England Naturist Ass'n, Inc. v. Larsen (1988) (bird breeding protected).

(d) The Duty to "Consult"

The ESA sets up a two part process for federal agencies contemplating actions that might affect wildlife. The first requirement is for the agency to prepare a "biological assessment" that considers whether listed species may be present in the area of the proposed action. 16 U.S.C.A. § 1536(c); Thomas v. Peterson (1985) (failure to prepare a biological assessment is grounds for enjoining construction of timber road). If the action may impact a listed species or its habitat, the agency must then consult with the FWS, which prepares a biological opinion detailing whether the action may jeopardize the species or harm its habitat. 16 U.S.C.A. § 1536(b).

Consultation extends to all agency actions affecting listed species, whether within the United States or abroad. Defenders of Wildlife v. Lujan (1990). During consultation, the agency may not make "irreversible or irretrievable commitments of resources." After completion of consultation and preparation of the biological opinion, the action may (1) proceed without mitigation (if the action is not likely to jeopardize the species), (2) proceed only with mitigation, Cabinet Mountains Wilderness v. Peterson (1982), or (3) not proceed at all if mitigation is needed but infeasible. Consultation may need to be reinitiated if anticipated mitigation efforts are shown to be inadequate. Sierra Club v. Marsh (1987).

The federal courts have not been able to agree on the scope and timing of the biological opinion, particularly in relation to federal oil and gas leasing decisions. One line of cases seems to hold that the biological opinion for a lease sale need not consider the consequences of post-leasing actions, such as exploration or drilling. According to these cases, additional ESA consultations and further biological opinions are required only if subsequent exploration or development proposals are forthcoming. Park County Resource Council v. United States Dept. of Agriculture (1987); Village of False Pass v.

Clark (1984); Cabinet Mountains Wilderness v. Peterson (1982); North Slope Borough v. Andrus (1980). This result is similar to "segmentation" of agency actions under NEPA, which permits agencies to consider the environmental effects only of actions taken (e.g., lease sale), not actions that might be taken (e.g., approval of post-lease sale drilling operations). Secretary of the Interior v. California (1984). A contrary line of cases holds that the biological opinion for an oil and gas lease sale must, at the time of the sale, consider "all phases of the agency action, which includes post-leasing activities." Conner v. Burford (1988); Bob Marshall Alliance v. Hodel (1988).

(e) Effect of the Endangered Species Act

Frequently, disputes over protected wildlife have moved to the courtroom, resulting in altered federal agency decisions. For example, federal dams on the Columbia River have had to draw down their water in the spring to help save endangered salmon, which need a strong current to help them migrate. The Forest Service's timber selling program has been most affected by the ESA. In 1990, there were nearly 550 legal challenges to federal timber sales, more than doubling the previous year's 230 appeals. Most of these challenges sought court injunctions on behalf of owls, grizzly bears, fish, or woodpeckers. See, e.g., Sierra Club v. Yeutter (1991) (Forest Service clearcutting policy halted for having adverse effect on red-cockaded woodpecker). Timber harvesting in the Pacific Northwest was largely paralyzed by the northern spotted owl. After a federal court forced the Fish and Wildlife Service (FWS) to designate old growth forests in Washington as critical habitat for the owl, Northern Spotted Owl v. Lujan (1991), the FWS proposed logging restrictions for 11.6 million acres of Northwest forests, to ensure protection of the owl's critical habitat. This proposal would cost the Pacific Northwest region about 40,000 jobs in timbering and related industries, roughly three jobs out of every four expected to exist otherwise.

(5) OTHER FEDERAL SPECIES PROTECTION LAWS

(a) Horses and Burros

Wild horses and burros living on federal lands are protected by the Wild, Free–Roaming Horses and Burros Act of 1971, 16 U.S.C.A. § 1331. This Act prohibits the wanton killing or capturing of wild horses and burros, even if they wander onto private land. Although federal marshalls are required to remove horses and burros that stray from public to private lands, 16 U.S.C.A. § 1334, failure to do so is not an unconstitutional taking. Mountain States Legal Foundation v. Clark (1986). Because the animals have no natural predators, and because they are now federally protected, their numbers have risen dramatically. To cope with escalating populations of wild horses and burros, federal managers may either destroy those that are old or sick, 16 U.S.C.A. § 1333(b)(2), or place for adoption healthy animals. If the latter course of action is taken, federal officials have an obligation to ensure that the "adoptions" are not to make commercial use (i.e., dog food) of the adoptees. Animal Protection Institute v. Hodel (1988).

(b) Bald Eagles

The Nation's emblem, the bald eagle, is protected both by the ESA and the Bald and Golden Eagle Protection Act of 1940, 16 U.S.C.A. § 668. The 1940 Act prevents bald eagles from being taken, sold, or transported "at any time or in any manner," except if specific permission is obtained for scientific reasons or religious purposes of Indian tribes. 16 U.S.C.A. § 668a. Without explicit permission, an Indian treaty does not insulate tribal members from prosecution. United States v. Dion (1986); United States v. Fryberg (1980).

Implementing regulations forbidding the commercial sale of bald eagle feathers do not constitute a taking. Andrus v. Allard (1979).

(c) Migratory Birds

The Migratory Bird Treaty Act of 1918, 16 U.S.C.A. §§ 703–11, prohibits the killing of migratory birds "by any means in any manner," unless specifically authorized by federal regulation. Since the Act imposes a strict liability standard, United States v. Chandler (1985), its criminal penalties may be imposed on those who intentionally and accidentally kill migratory birds. United States v. Catlett (1984) (Act violated by use of baited field); United States v. FMC Corp. (1978) (Act violated by accidental release of toxins into a lagoon used by migratory birds). The Act prevents federal actions designed to kill predators, if migratory birds are poisoned after eating the predators. Defenders of Wildlife v. Administrator (1989) (use of strychnine enjoined).

(d) Marine Mammals

The Marine Mammal Protection Act, 16 U.S.C.A. § 1361, seeks to halt the "taking" of marine mammals—whales, porpoises, and seals. Incidental taking of these animals in connection with commercial fishing is subject to regulation and permitting by the Secretary of Commerce. Issuance of permits to foreign commercial fishing operations may be invalidated if the Secretary fails to determine the extent to which marine mammals may be incidentally, but not intentionally, affected by the fishing. Kokechik Fishermen's Ass'n v. Secretary of Commerce (1988). The Act has particular applicability to the tuna industry, whose nets often trap porpoises that accompany schools of tuna fish. See American Tunaboat Ass'n v. Baldrige (1984).

(e) International Protection of Wildlife Species

Certain international agreements govern and restrict trade in protected species. The International Convention for Regulation of Whaling sets whaling quotas. See Japan Whaling Ass'n v. American Cetacean Society (1986). The Convention on International Trade in Endangered Species, 27 U.S.T. 1087, T.I.A.S. No. 8249, authorizes exports of protected animals only if each nation's "Scientific Authority" determines that "such export will not be detrimental" to the species' survival. The FWS is the scientific authority which makes "no detriment" determinations in the United States. Defenders of Wildlife, Inc. v. Endangered Species Scientific Authority (1984).

CHAPTER FOUR

ENVIRONMENTAL LAW

The relationship between human beings and natural resources is captured by the word "use." Natural resources have three primary uses. First, some are used because they are economically valuable. These would include the energy resources (oil, gas, coal, uranium), hard rock minerals, timber, water, and rangeland. Second, some natural resources are used by humans for recreational and aesthetic pleasure, and by wildlife for habitat. These include lands preserved as national forests, wilderness areas, national parks, rivers protected by the 1968 Wild and Scenic Rivers Act, and areas designated as wildlife refuges. Third, other natural resources are used as dumping grounds for the waste products of an industrial world. These include the atmosphere, rivers and lakes, ground waters, oceans, and the earth itself.

This chapter addresses this third use of natural resources—when the resources of air, water, and land become convenient (and supposedly free) disposal sites for pollution and discarded waste. This chapter also discusses how law and government have responded to the inclination of humans to use air, water, and land in this way. This legal response has evolved to be a separate body of law called Environmental Law.

I. NATURAL RESOURCES, ENVIRONMENTALISM, AND ENVIRONMENTAL LAW

Natural resources have always played an important role in the growth of the United States. Initially, the country's wealth of resources, particularly land, water, timber, and minerals, served to spur on westward expansion and settlement. Federal and state law encouraged the development and commercial exploitation of these resources. When we changed from an agrarian to an industrial nation, land, air, and water became garbage dumps for the inevitable pollution that followed from industrialization. Law and government then responded to prevent the depletion of economic resources, and to regulate the environmental degradation of commonly-held resources, such as air and water.

Government responded to the realization that resources were being consumed without consideration of the future consequences of such consumption. This response took two inconsistent forms, both of which are discussed in Chapter Three. "Preservationism" called for the preservation of lands in their natural state. Public land law reflected this philosophy in wilderness acts and in the creation of national parks. By contrast, "conservationism" encouraged the use of valuable stock resources, so long as this use was consistent with scientific principles of resource management. Public land law reflected this approach when it demanded that many federal lands and resources (e.g., rangeland and timber) be managed according to a multiple-use theory, in light of a comprehensive planning process.

Preservationism and conservationism were well established by the beginning of the twentieth century. Environmentalism did not emerge as a fundamental value and legal force until the early 1970s. Its basic tenets were, and are: (1) pollution should be prevented; (2) contaminated air, water, and land should be cleaned up; and (3) overall environmental quality should be protected and preserved.

Environmental pollution, and the law's eventual response to it, reflect certain basic economic principles noted earlier in Chapter One. Pollution most frequently affects natural resources known as "common property." The atmosphere, the oceans, and the fresh water rivers and lakes are held in common by the public. This is either because they are not capable of private ownership (e.g., the air), or because any private ownership interest that may exist (as in the case of river water) does not usually include the right to be free from pollution, only the right to use the resource.

Common property resources lack protection from overutilization, pollution, and depletion normally provided by an exclusive owner. Instead, resource users of common goods assume they are free (i.e., costless to use) and abundant. As a result, users of such goods do not take into account the unfavorable effects of their activities upon others who share the common property. For example, air is a common property resource which everyone consumes, but which no individual owns or has the ability, alone, to protect. Because no one holds the right to exclude others from destructive use of this resource, and because exclusion can only be achieved with difficulty and expense, there is an economic incentive to use the air as a garbage dump. Emissions from automobiles and manufacturing enterprises constitute that garbage.

In an ideal market system, the effects of a market transaction are confined to its participants, and the costs of pollution are "internalized"—reflected in the price of the product of the activity causing the pollution. When there is a common property, there is a failure of the market. In the case of pollution, the costs of pollution are "externalized"—not reflected in the marginal cost or the price of the product. A "negative" externality is present because the costs of pollution are borne by third parties not involved in a market exchange. In the case of pollution, this third party is often society as a whole.

The ideal market could correct the problems associated with negative externalities if there were no impediments to bargaining. Individuals could enter into agreements with those causing the externalities to refrain from producing pollution. Unfortunately, in the real world, such bargains are usually impossible, because of the large number of victims of pollution, and, at least in the case of automobile-caused air pollution, the large number of pollution producers.

Also, bargaining itself entails costs, such as the costs of discovering with whom to deal, informing that person of the desire to transact, data collection and analysis, and negotiating the exchange. Such transaction and information costs may be greater than the benefits to be gained from the exchange.

When the market fails to internalize external costs because of substantial transaction costs in negotiating a solution, there are three recourses remaining. First, internalization may be forced through the stigma of public opinion and notions of responsibility—hardly effective means of overcoming the enormous incentives to pollute common property. Second, the common law may attempt to define legal rights to pollute under theories of nuisance, negligence, trespass, and strict liability. Third, government itself may intervene.

The most brutal form of government intervention is a flat prohibition on polluting activities. A more common approach is through centralized "command and control" regulation, by prescribing standards that the polluter must meet. Such standards may be established for the applicable (1) environment (ambient standards), (2) pollution source (emission or effluent standards), or (3) pollution control device (design or specification standards). Activities that meet these standards are permissible.

A more sophisticated government response uses economic incentives and disincentives to bring about pollution reduction. Subsidies pay for the nonexercise of the right to pollute. Pollution taxes or charges discourage the emission of pollutants, while allowing the producer to choose which technology to use. Another alternative is for government to establish a pollution ceiling, and to permit dischargers to bargain among themselves on the allocation of their pollution up to that ceiling.

From the early 1970s to the 1990s, this nation's growing concern for the environment has manifested itself in two major ways. First, environmental regulation has become centralized as the federal government has adopted laws addressing air quality, water quality, drinking water, solid wastes, hazardous wastes, toxic substances, and pesticides. The federal Environmental Protection Agency (EPA) has been created to implement these laws. States have also had to establish their own environmental control programs, usually pursuant to or based upon federal laws.

Second, in part as a result of these laws, and in part because of the new ethic of environmentalism, there has been significant progress made in enhancing environmental quality and reducing pollution. For example, the enactment of the National Environmental Policy Act has caused environmental considerations to be incorporated into planning processes throughout the federal government. And, despite an increase in the U.S. gross national product from $2.42 trillion in 1970, to $4.17 trillion in 1990 (measured in 1982 dollars), annual national emissions for prevalent air pollutants have dropped. Between 1970 and 1987, there have been reductions of 28% for sulfur dioxide, 61% for particulate emissions, 28% for hydrocarbons, and 38% for carbon monoxide. Twentieth Annual Report of the Council on Environmental Quality 7–13 (1990). The task of cleaning up the nation's air is far from completed, however. In 1991, EPA estimated that air pollution from particulates claimed 60,000 deaths.

II. PRIVATE AND STATE ENVIRONMENTAL LAW

A. COMMON LAW

1. Grounds for Common Law Relief

Although Congress and state legislatures have created a far flung system of regulatory rules for preventing and cleaning up environmental hazards, there is still room for privately-initiated tort actions seeking damages or injunctions for injuries caused by polluting activities. Several common law causes of action are available, including (1) nuisance; (2) strict liability; (3) negligence; (4) intentional infliction of emotional distress; and (5) trespass. See City of Bloomington v. Westinghouse Elec. Corp. (1989); Branch v. Western Petroleum (1982).

Government plaintiffs may challenge pollution sources as "public" nuisances. Village of Wilsonville v. SCA Services, Inc. (1981) (prospective nuisance must be abated). In private nuisance actions, brought by non-governmental parties, courts will usually balance the equities before enjoining an industrial defendant's polluting activities. Boomer v. Atlantic Cement Co. (1970). Hypersensitive plaintiffs may be denied protection by nuisance law. DeBorde v. St. Michael & All Angels Episcopal Church (1979). A damages remedy may be available if plaintiffs can show infringement on their "quality of life." Ayers v. Jackson Township (1987). Successors-in-interest may be held liable for abating nuisances caused by their predecessors. Friends of the Sakonnet v. Dutra (1990).

A *federal* common law of nuisance applies in cases of interstate air and water pollution, Georgia v. Tennessee Copper Co. (1907), so long as no federal environmental statute has preempted federal common law. Milwaukee v. Illinois and Michigan (1981). Federal courts may hear nuisance suits arising under state law, by application of the nuisance law of the discharger's state. International Paper Co. v. Ouellette (1987).

Another theory of liability is based on the premise that some pollutants (e.g., toxins) are so abnormally dangerous that strict liability should apply. State v. Ventron Corp. (1983). The Restatement (Second) of Torts § 520 (1977) still includes fault as a factor in determining if an activity is abnormally dangerous. Some courts have further reduced the number of activities qualifying as "ultrahazardous" by denying strict liability when the risk can be eliminated through the exercise of "reasonable care." Edwards v. Post Transp. Co. (1991).

Other common law theories of liability for environmental harm include: trespass, Folmar v. Elliot Coal Mining Co. (1971), negligence, Philip Morris, Inc. v. Emerson (1988); products liability, Purvis v. PPG Ind., Inc. (1987), intentional infliction of mental distress, Woyke v. Tonka Corp. (1988), and contracts void as against public policy. Branch v. Mobil Oil Corp. (1991).

2. Defenses to Common Law Relief

The issue of causation is certainly one of the most difficult obstacles to overcome when bringing a common law environmental lawsuit. There are three causation problems. First, the plaintiff must establish some nexus between the defendant and the release of the contaminant thought to produce the plaintiff's injury. See Sindell v. Abbott Laboratories (1980) (defendants' liability varies according to their share of the relevant market). Second, the plaintiff must demonstrate that the defendant's pollution causes the type of harm suffered by the plaintiff. See Layton v. Yankee Caithness Joint Venture (1991); Graham v. Canadian Nat. Ry. Co. (1990). Third, it must be shown that the plaintiff's harm was caused by exposure to the substance released by the defendant, and not by some other factor (e.g., smoking, an independent illness). In re Paoli R.R. Yard PCB Litigation (1990); Renaud v. Martin Marietta Corp. (1990).

One relying on the common law to abate an environmental injury may be confronted by an array of affirmative defenses. If the polluting activity is a "public" nuisance, private plaintiffs have no standing to bring suit without a showing of special damage. Statutes of limitations can bar actions filed too late after plaintiffs' contact with or exposure to the defendant's harmful substances. Torrance Redevelopment Agency v. Solvent Coating Co. (1991). Compliance by a licensee with federal licensing requirements may establish under state law that the licensee was not negligent. Coley v. Commonwealth Edison (1991). The actions of an injured party may foreclose relief if a court finds that a plaintiff "came to the nuisance," Spur Industries, Inc. v. Del E. Webb Development Co. (1972), or "assumed the risk." United States v. Hooker Chemicals & Plastics Corp. (1989). But see Fischer v. Atlantic Richfield Co. (1989) ("coming to nuisance" defense inapplicable to public nuisances). Even if affirmative defenses do not stand in the way of liability, courts may be reluctant to grant injunctive relief. See Maxedon v. Texaco Producing, Inc. (1989) (no injunction for past or completed acts).

B. STATE STATUTORY ENVIRONMENTAL LAW

State statutes seek to bring about environmental quality in three ways. First, states are urged by federal legislation to adopt laws which meet or are a means of implementing federally-established environmental standards. This form of cooperative federalism is the traditional way states and the federal government have jointly sought to control air and water pollution. See Part IV, below.

Second, many states have enacted environmental review legislation modeled after the federal National Environmental Policy Act of 1969 (NEPA). These state environmental policy acts (SEPAs) (require state agencies to consider the environmental consequences of their actions in an environmental impact statement *before* taking action. Sacramento County Bd. of Supervisors v. LAFCO (1991). Impact reports prepared pursuant to SEPAs may be attacked for being inadequate. Compare Lewis v. Hughes Helicopter, Inc. (1988) (impact review inadequate for failure to discuss foreseeable consequences of action), with Citizens for Clean Air v. Spokane (1990) (impact statement adequate despite failure to supplement it in light of minor siting change for solid waste incinerator). Unlike federal NEPA, SEPAs may require consideration of socio-economic effects. Chinese Staff & Workers Ass'n v. City of New York (1986). Also, unlike federal NEPA, some SEPAs may have a substantive effect. Polygon Corp. v. City of Seattle (1978) (negative environmental effects revealed in impact statement justify refusal to issue building permit).

Third, many states have enacted their own counterparts to federal hazardous waste statutes. These state laws typically regulate both the removal and transport of hazardous waste, and the siting of hazardous waste facilities. See General Elec. Environmental Services, Inc. v. Envirotech Corp. (1991) (construing the Pennsylvania Hazardous Sites Cleanup Act). Various legal consequences flow from these state laws. Many impose a strict liability standard for the discharge of hazardous wastes. State v. Wisser Co. (1991). As a substantive matter, laws like those in effect in New Jersey may prevent the sale of industrial property if there is no official assurance that the property is free from contamination. Cooper Dev. Co. v. First Nat. Bank of Boston (1991). A state hazardous waste statute may preempt local waste regulations. Envirosafe Services of Idaho, Inc. v. Owyhee County (1987). Conversely, state hazardous waste laws may run afoul of the United States Constitution if the law is (1) preempted by some federal statutory scheme, such as the federal Hazardous Materials Transportation Act, 49 U.S.C.A. §§ 1801–1812; (2) inconsistent with the dormant commerce clause, Philadelphia v. New Jersey (1978); National Solid Wastes Management Ass'n v. Alabama Dept. of Environmental Management (1990); or (3) arbitrary and capricious under the due process clause. Geo–Tech Reclamation Industries, Inc. v. Hamrick (1989).

III. CONTROLLING ENVIRONMENTAL DECISIONMAKING OF FEDERAL AGENCIES

There are two ways to check the environmental decisions of federal agencies. First, one can challenge the agency for improperly interpreting or implementing an environmental statute, such as the Clean Air or Clean Water Acts. This first kind of challenge seeks judicial review of the agency action. Judicial review raises the twin issues of who may sue, and the nature of the oversight relationship that exists between a reviewing court and an agency. Second, one can attack an agency (at the agency and judicial levels) for not having adequately considered the environmental consequences of the agency action. This kind of challenge seeks to ensure agency compliance with the National Environmental Policy Act (NEPA), and is the topic of Chapter Five.

A. PRIVATE ENFORCEMENT OF FEDERAL STATUTORY VIOLATIONS

Federal regulatory agencies, such as the EPA, are responsible for implementing federal environmental statutes. Private citizens are also authorized under several federal statutes to sue either environmental violators directly, or regulatory agencies for failure to perform their legal responsibilities. In such a citizen suit, the plaintiff is often an environmental organization. A citizen suit plaintiff may obtain either an injunction against further actions of the defendant, Public Interest Research Group v. Rice (1991), or penalties paid by the defendant to the United States Treasury. Civil penalties against federal agencies are permitted if suit is brought under the federal Clean Water Act (CWA), Sierra Club v. Lujan (1991), or under a federal hazardous waste law, such as the Resource Conservation and Recovery Act. Proof of a violation of a federal or state environmental standard is sufficient to win court relief. Citizen suit plaintiffs need not prove harm because of the violation, if the plaintiffs are suing only to stop the violation. Naturally, no damages will be awarded to plaintiffs who prove a violation but no harm.

About two-thirds of citizen suits filed involve CWA violations. See Public Interest Research Group v. GAF (1991).

The remainder are suits under the Clean Air Act, Maryland Waste Coalition v. SCM Corp. (1985), and federal hazardous waste statutes. Twentieth Annual Report of the Council on Environmental Quality 211 (1990). Section 505 of the CWA, 33 U.S.C.A. § 1365, permits citizen suits against both polluters and the EPA to compel performance of "any act or duty under this Act that is not discretionary." The Supreme Court has construed this language to limit suits to continuous or intermittent violations. Gwaltney of Smithfield, Ltd. v. Chesapeake Bay Foundation, Inc. (1987). Plaintiffs basing their actions on section 505 must either allege that there is an ongoing violation, or that there is a likelihood that past violations will continue. Sierra Club v. Union Oil Co. (1988); Allen County Citizens for the Environment, Inc. v. BP Oil Co. (1991) (citizen plaintiffs must allege a reasonable likelihood that a past polluter will continue to pollute in the future). Res judicata precludes citizen suits under the CWA after EPA has negotiated a consent decree. United States EPA v. City of Green Forest (1990).

Courts lack the power to fashion common law remedies for specific statutory violations unless Congress specifically grants that power. Middlesex County Sewerage Authority v. National Sea Clammers Assoc. (1981).

B. JUDICIAL REVIEW OF AGENCY ENVIRONMENTAL DECISIONMAKING

One wishing to use courts to overturn agency action must ascertain (1) whether judicial review is available, (2) the extent of judicial review obtainable, and (3) the nature of relief possible.

1. Reviewability

The federal Administrative Procedure Act (APA), 5 U.S.C.A. § 701(a), provides that courts must review challenged federal agency decisions "except to the extent that (1) statutes preclude judicial review; or (2) agency action is committed to agency discretion by law." The first exception is rarely applicable. To trigger it, a court must find clear and convincing evidence that Congress, by express statutory language, intended to restrict access to judicial review.

The "committed to agency discretion" exception was found by the Supreme Court to be very narrow in Citizens to Preserve Overton Park, Inc. v. Volpe (1971). The Court concluded that the exception is applicable only where a statute gives an agency such broad powers that "there is no law to apply." See also Abbott Laboratories v. Gardner (1967) (there is a presumption favoring judicial review). The only time the presumption of reviewability is reversed is when a plaintiff demands that an agency bring an enforcement action. Heckler v. Chaney (1985). For example, a federal agency refusal to establish a tolerance level for dioxin in sports fish was found to be a nonreviewable "enforcement action" in National Wildlife Federation v. Secretary of Health & Human Services (1986).

2. Scope of Review

The extent of judicial review available has waxed and waned over the years, depending in large part on how courts interpret the following ambiguous language of the APA: "The reviewing court shall hold unlawful and set aside agency action * * * found to be arbitrary, capricious, an abuse of discretion, or otherwise not in accordance with law." 5 U.S.C.A. § 706(2)(A).

Initially, courts gave great deference to agency interpretation of statutes, and even greater deference to agency interpretation of its own regulations or orders. Udall v. Tallman (1965). Then, in 1971, the *Overton Park* case construed the APA to require reviewing courts to make a "searching inquiry" into whether agency decisions were "based on a consideration of the relevant factors." This gave birth to the "hard look" doctrine of judicial review, permitting judges to give much closer scrutiny to the substantive and procedural grounds for federal agency decisions. Ethyl Corp. v. EPA (1976); Greater Boston Television Corp. v. FCC (1970). The hard look doctrine was later considerably softened by Vermont Yankee Nuclear Power Corp. v. NRDC (1978), where the Supreme Court emphasized that "administrative decisions should be set aside * * * only for substantial procedural or substantive reasons * * *, not simply because the court is unhappy with result reached."

Given the absence of clear guidance either in the APA or by the Supreme Court, the appropriate scope of review is difficult to predict. As a general matter, less deference is given when an agency is challenged for violating statutory procedural requirements, or for incorrectly implementing clear and unambiguous statutory language. Chevron U.S.A., Inc. v. NRDC (1984). More deference is afforded when one alleges improper agency implementation of either a discretionary or ambiguous statute. Sierra Club v. Clark (1986).

3. Remedies

Substantive environmental injuries in violation of a statute may be judicially enjoined. TVA v. Hill (1978); 5 U.S.C.A. § 703. However, injunctive relief may be denied if the only "irreparable harm" shown is a violation of a federal pollution control statute. NRDC v. Texaco Refining and Marketing, Inc. (1990) (violation of federal Clean Water Act cannot be presumed to cause "irreparable harm"). Procedural violations, such as failure to prepare an environmental impact statement, or failure to obtain a permit under the Clean Water Act, are subject to injunctive relief only if this is deemed the proper remedy after a balancing of the equities. Amoco Production Co. v. Village of Gambell (1986); Weinberger v. Romero–Barcelo (1982); Kleppe v. Sierra Club (1976).

IV. POLLUTION CONTROL
A. AIR POLLUTION

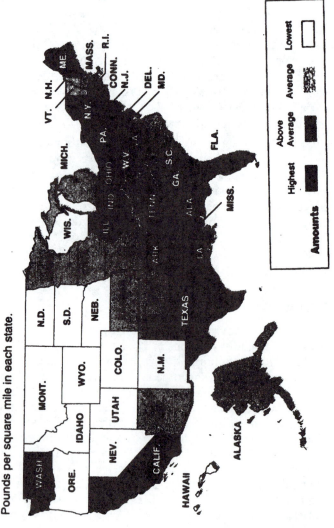

Where the Air Is Bad
Pounds per square mile in each state.

FPA1

The Top 10 Air Polluters

Total amount of toxic chemicals: 2,427,695,968 lbs.

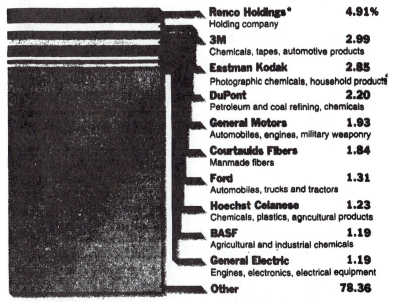

Renco Holdings* Holding company	**4.91%**
3M Chemicals, tapes, automotive products	**2.99**
Eastman Kodak Photographic chemicals, household products	**2.85**
DuPont Petroleum and coal refining, chemicals	**2.20**
General Motors Automobiles, engines, military weaponry	**1.93**
Courtaulds Fibers Manmade fibers	**1.84**
Ford Automobiles, trucks and tractors	**1.31**
Hoechst Celanese Chemicals, plastics, agricultural products	**1.23**
BASF Agricultural and industrial chemicals	**1.19**
General Electric Engines, electronics, electrical equipment	**1.19**
Other	**78.36**

*Part of the Renco Group, which is an iron and steel processing business.

Source: New York Times analysis of Environmental Protection Agency data.
Data was compiled by Citizens Fund.

Ty Ahmad-Taylor/The New York Times

The federal Clean Air Act was originally enacted in 1970, and then was extensively amended in 1977 and again in 1990. 42 U.S.C.A. §§ 7401–7626; Pub.L. No. 95–95 (1977 Amendments); Pub.L. No. 101–549 (1990 Amendments). Under its provisions, every stationary and mobile pollution source must comply with emission standards as a means of cleaning up the ambient air quality in the area. The discussion that follows focuses on the Act's effect on stationary sources.

Federal air pollution regulation, and especially the 1990 Amendments, will impact the oil and gas and minerals industries throughout the 1990s. These industries will face new EPA regulations governing hazardous air pollutant emissions. United States v. Buckley (1991) (defendant convicted for violating Clean Air Act provisions regulating release of asbestos). They may also be required to secure operating permits under the 1990 Amendments' new Title V provisions. Existing oil and natural gas production operations, particularly those located near urbanized ozone nonattainment areas in California and Texas, may be required to install new controls to reduce emissions of volatile organic compounds and nitrogen oxides. Mining operations may have to install control equipment to capture "fine particulates" that cause nonattainment of the ambient air quality standard for particulates.

1. Ambient Air Quality Standards

One key goal of the Clean Air Act is attainment of National Ambient Air Quality Standards (NAAQS) for certain pollutants which endanger public health or welfare. The NAAQS establish ceilings for individual pollutant concentrations that may not be exceeded anywhere in the United States. For each listed pollutant, there are two types of standards: (1) "primary" standards are to protect health (with an "adequate margin of safety"); (2) "secondary" standards are to protect the public welfare from "any known or anticipated adverse effect." In setting primary standards, EPA must seek to protect even the most sensitive persons, such as those with pre-existing illnesses. Cost and technological feasibility may not be considered in setting the NAAQS. American Petroleum Institute v. Costle (1981); Lead Industries Ass'n, Inc. v. EPA (1980).

NAAQS exist for six "criteria pollutants": sulfur dioxide (SO_2); particulate matter smaller than 10 microns in size (PM_{10}); nitrogen oxides (NOx); carbon monoxide (CO); ozone (O_3) and lead (Pb). The NAAQS for these pollutants are not directly enforceable. The Clean Air Act instead requires the EPA and the states to adopt a range of strategies designed to ensure that the ambient standards are met and maintained.

2. Permitting

Before 1990, the Clean Air Act did not have a generally applicable permit program. As a result of the 1990 Amendments, virtually all sources of air pollution will be required to obtain operating permits ensuring compliance with all applicable requirements of the Clean Air Act. This permit program is modeled after the federal Clean Water Act permit program.

After 1991, states must develop programs consistent with EPA permit regulations. Sources have one year from the date EPA approves a state program to submit a permit application. To meet permit requirements, sources must install emission control devices, as well as systems to measure and monitor emissions. Permit fees are to be charged, at a rate of no less than $25/ton/year of each regulated pollutant emitted by all sources owned by a person. EPA may object to permits that violate the Clean Air Act.

Compliance with an issued permit is deemed compliance with the requirements of the permit program, and with all those provisions of the Clean Air Act specified in the permit. Facilities may change operations without a permit revision if the changes are not "modifications" as defined in the Act, and if they will not result in emissions being exceeded under the permit.

3. State Implementation Plans (SIPs)

a. *Purpose and Content*

The SIP is the primary regulatory mechanism for stationary sources. Its purpose is to encourage states to meet NAAQS by employing an array of controls on sources of pollution. These controls include emission standards, permits, monitoring and siting requirements. States may select any mix of control strategies, so long as NAAQS will be achieved.

The Clean Air Act provides that a SIP must cause attainment of primary NAAQS "as expeditiously as practicable but * * * in no case later than three years from the date of the [SIP] approval." Secondary standards are to be met within "a reasonable time." A SIP is to include timetables for compliance with all emissions limitations, as well as the necessary legal authority to enforce the plan. Once approved by EPA, a SIP is enforceable both as a state and federal law. The state agency charged with implementing the SIP must interpret it consistent with the overall goal of the Clean Air Act—to discourage, not encourage, air pollution. United States v. General Dynamics Corp. (1991).

b. Inadequate SIPs

States and local governments constantly strive to obtain EPA approval of SIPs or SIP components. If negotiations fail, and the SIP is found by the EPA to be inadequate to attain any NAAQS, then EPA may either take over the state program or issue SIP amendments that are binding on the state. Coalition for Clean Air v. EPA (1991); Commonwealth of Pa. v. United States EPA (1991) (EPA may require state to show that its attained reductions were maintainable, and may withhold SIP approval if maintenance of standard could not be assured). A court may also order injunctive measures to deter future failures of SIP commitments. Coalition Against Columbus Ctr. v. City of New York (1991).

By 1977, it became clear that a large number of states had failed to achieve the NAAQS, and that their SIPs were inadequate. Rather than have EPA take over all these state programs, Congress in the 1977 Amendments reinvigorated the SIP requirements of the Clean Air Act. The 1977

Amendments mandated that EPA identify the areas that had not attained the NAAQS on schedule, and for these "nonattainment" areas states had to submit additional rounds of SIPs. These SIPs had to bring about compliance with primary standards by 1982, or 1987 for oxidants and carbon monoxide. In all nonattainment areas, SIPs had to require existing sources to install "reasonably available control technology." States must also show "reasonable further progress" toward achievement of the NAAQS, defined as an "annual incremental reduction in emissions." The main sanction for nonattainment of primary NAAQS by the statutory deadlines is a moratorium on construction of "new" or "modified" "major" stationary sources. States can also lose federal highway construction funds, and sewage treatment plant funding under the Clean Water Act.

After the statutory deadlines passed in 1987, EPA employed delaying tactics. It granted "conditional approval" of some SIPs, subject to requirements that they be revised to assure attainment. It also sought and received extensions of the deadlines from Congress. When states still were unable to meet NAAQS by 1990, the Congress amended the Clean Air Act again, subjecting all stationary sources to a new permit requirement (described above), and revising the statutory deadlines for nonattainment areas (described below).

c. Technological and Economic Feasibility

The Supreme Court read the Clean Air Act to test SIPs against one standard—their likelihood of attaining NAAQS. Union Electric Co. v. EPA (1976). When EPA decides whether to approve a SIP, it need not consider technological and economic feasibility of the measures in the plan. Claims of infeasibility are better made at the state level, through state administrative and judicial review.

The *Union Electric* case is significant because it ratifies the strategy of "technology-forcing," which imposes standards so stringent that polluters must either invent new technology to meet the standards or shut down. The case is also significant because it permits states to select a range of controls for existing stationary sources, so long as NAAQS will be met. ASARCO, Inc. v. Puget Sound Air Pollution Control Agency (1989) (smoke opacity regulations may be enforced by state). SIP requirements may be even more strict than necessary to achieve NAAQS. Her Majesty the Queen v. City of Detroit (1989).

d. Use of Tall Stacks and Dispersion Techniques

In implementing SIPs, states had to consider whether polluters could achieve NAAQS through dispersion (building tall stacks), rather than by installing pollution controls. Tall stacks may be a primary cause of acid rain. Both case law and the 1977 Amendments outlaw tall stacks unless all available continuous emission controls at the source (e.g., scrubbers for coal-burning facilities) are somehow infeasible. Kennecott Copper Corp. v. Train (1975). Stack height is relevant in calculating the emissions flow permitted from the stack. Emissions limitations are to be based on the lower of (1) actual stack height, or (2) the "good engineering practice" stack height (that height necessary to ensure that emissions will not cause local "excessive concentration" due to atmospheric downwash in the immediate vicinity of the source). NRDC v. Thomas (1988); Sierra Club v. EPA (1983).

e. Relief Provisions

If a stationary source is unable to meet statutory deadlines for compliance with emission limitations, it may be able to obtain a hardship variance from the SIP. Train v. NRDC (1975). If denied a variance, and if unable to comply with a SIP requirement, the source may apply for a delayed compliance order (DCO). Any DCO must provide for final compliance "as expeditiously as practicable," and warn any source emitting more than 100 tons/year/pollutant that a "noncompliance penalty" will be assessed if the DCO deadline is not met.

If a source is denied a variance and a DCO, it may still assert a claim of infeasibility in state courts. Wells Mfg. Co. v. Pollution Control Bd. (1978). However, even if a state court has invalidated part of a SIP under state law, EPA may still obtain a federal court order enforcing it under federal law. United States v. Ford Motor Co. (1987). The 1990 Amendments strengthen EPA enforcement authority regarding violations of SIPs and permits.

4. New Source Performance Standards (NSPS)

The 1970 Clean Air Act requires nationally uniform performance standards for various categories of "new" or "modified" stationary sources of emissions. The NSPS provisions have two purposes: (1) to require the same degree of control on all similar new pollution sources, regardless of location, so that states may not lure industry with the promise of lax standards; and (2) to place the burden of installing the most costly and effective pollution control technology on the plants best able to incorporate the technology—new plants. ASARCO, Inc. v. EPA (1978).

a. *"New" or "Modified" Sources*

EPA is to promulgate "standards of performance" for air pollutants emitted by "new" stationary sources (constructed or modified after the effective date of NSPS regulations), or sources where there has been a "modification" (a change which either increases the amount of any air pollutant emitted, or causes the emission of a new pollutant). Courts have liberally construed the word "modification." Wisconsin Elec. Power Co. v. Reilly (1990) (renovations are a "physical change" constituting a "modification" subjecting the plant to

NSPS); National–Southwire Aluminum Co. v. United States E.P.A. (1988) (a proposal to turn off wet scrubbers is a "modification" if it would result in an increase of 1174 tons/year of fluoride emissions).

b. Standards

The NSPS require "application of the best system of emissions reduction which (taking into account the cost of achieving such reductions) the [EPA] determines has been adequately demonstrated."   42 U.S.C.A. § 7411(a)(1)(C).   See Portland Cement Ass'n v. Ruckelshaus (1973) (EPA need not prepare quantified cost-benefit analysis to consider "cost of achieving" reductions).

The 1977 Amendments required EPA to set NSPS for fossil-fuel burning sources that would require the standard to include a percentage reduction requirement, so that industry changes from high to low sulfur coal would still require a reduction in emissions below what would be present without control devices.   This was meant to discourage sources from simply switching to low sulfur Western coals from high sulfur Eastern and Midwestern coals.   The EPA tempered this requirement with a "sliding scale" regulation, which permitted the degree of emission control to vary with the pollutant content of the fuel.   Sierra Club v. Costle (1981). The acid rain provisions of the 1990 Amendments repeal the "percentage reduction" requirement for coal when a national cap on sulfur dioxide emissions goes into effect in the year 2000.

5. Prevention of Significant Deterioration (PSD)

If ambient air quality is better than NAAQS, the SIPS must "prevent the significant deterioration" of the air quality in these areas.   42 U.S.C.A. § 7470(4).   Under a statutory designation process, all clean air areas of the country are placed in one of three PSD classes. The maximum allowable increases in ambient concentrations of air pollutants (increments), above original baseline concentrations, vary by class. In Class I areas (national parks and wilderness areas), the increments are very small. All other areas of the country were originally designated Class II, where the increments were designed to allow moderate, controlled economic growth. A Class II area may be redesignated a Class III area, for which increases in pollutants are allowed closer to the NAAQS. The larger increments in a Class III area permit industrial development, so long as NAAQS are not reached or exceeded.

In a PSD area, no construction of a major "new" source, or a "modification" of an existing source, may proceed without a permit. A new source is one that has the "potential to emit" more than 100 tons of *any* pollutant regulated by the Clean Air Act. But see NRDC v. United States EPA (1991) (surface coal mines are not "major emitting facilities" for PSD purposes because the socioeconomic costs of regulating the mines outweigh any environmental benefits). A modification is a change in a major stationary source which, after application of pollution controls, creates a "significant net increase" in emissions of *any* regulated pollutant. The important case of Alabama Power Co. v. Costle (1979) establishes that any modification that increases emissions to any extent requires PSD review. See also United States v. Chevron U.S.A., Inc. (1985) (shut off of pollution control system is a PSD modification). But see Wisconsin Elec. Power Co. v. Reilly (1990) (in determining whether renovation of a facility is a modification, EPA may not simply "presume" that after the modification it will operate continuously). The *Alabama Power* case also determined that PSD review applies only when there is a net increase in emissions from the source; if emissions can be reduced at other locations within the source (treating the source like a "bubble"), then PSD review is not necessary.

Once a new source or modification has been identified, a PSD permit may be issued only if emissions will not exceed the allowable increment, and if the facility installs the "best available control technology" (BACT) for *all* pollutants, not just for those that otherwise might exceed the allowable increment. BACT is defined as the "maximum degree of [emission] reduction * * * which the permitting authority * * * taking into account * * * economic impacts and other costs, determines is achievable for such facility." 42 U.S.C.A. § 7479(3). The determination that emissions will not exceed applicable increments may be based on modeling techniques. Northern Plains Resource Council v. United States EPA (1981).

6. Visibility

The 1977 Amendments directed EPA to protect visibility in certain national parklands and wilderness areas designated as Class I PSD areas. 42 U.S.C.A. § 7491(a). Visibility is to be protected in several ways. First, states must deny PSD permits to new sources, even though Class I increments are not exceeded, if the source will have an "adverse impact" on "air quality-related values." Second, states must identify existing "major stationary sources" that affect visibility, and these must install "best available retrofit technology." Third, states must adopt long-term strategies for making "reasonable progress" toward a goal of preventing impairment of visibility.

EPA regulations implement these statutory demands by requiring states with Class I areas to revise their SIPs to assure reasonable progress toward the visibility goal. Revised SIPs are to consider the impact of proposed major stationary sources on "integral vistas" (views looking out from a Class I area deemed to be an important part of the visitor experience). SIPs are also to remedy two distinct types of visibility impairment: (1) plume blight, and (2) regional haze. See Vermont v. Thomas (1988) (one state impacted by other upwind states' regional haze may not demand that EPA disapprove the SIPs of these states).

7. Nonattainment Areas

In areas where air is worse than NAAQS, the "nonattainment" provisions of the 1977 Amendments call for new and modified sources to meet strict technology-based and air quality-based requirements that are in addition to NSPS. 42 U.S.C.A. §§ 7501–7503. Nonattainment and PSD areas are pollutant-specific, which means that the same location may be nonattainment for one pollutant, and PSD for another.

a. Deadlines

The 1977 Amendments assumed that the presence of nonattainment areas signified inadequate SIPs. States and localities had until either 1982 or 1987 to receive EPA approval of revised SIPs. A SIP unable to obtain EPA approval after failing to attain NAAQS by the statutory deadlines had to meet NAAQS "as soon as possible with every available control measure" after eventual plan approval. Delaney v. EPA (1990).

The nonattainment provisions of the 1990 Amendments focus on the many areas of the country that were not able to meet primary health standards for ozone, carbon monoxide, and particulate matter. In determining whether an area is nonattainment with NAAQS, the EPA may not aggregate all exceedances at all monitoring sites in the air quality control region. Navistar Intern. Transp. Corp. v. United States EPA (1991). Depending on the severity of the pollution problem, nonattainment areas for these pollutants must attain the health standard by 1995, unless another date is specified for a particular pollutant at a particular location (e.g., Los Angeles has until the year 2010 to achieve NAAQS for ozone).

Steady increments of progress towards attainment are required, as are a number of emission-limiting steps. If an area fails to attain NAAQS within the specified time, one of three consequences may follow: (1) limitations are imposed on use of federal highway funds; (2) new industries must offset emissions at a 2 to 1 ratio; or (3) EPA will promulgate federal implementation plans.

b. Standards

Existing stationary sources in nonattainment areas must use "reasonably available control technology." Major new or modified sources must obtain a permit requiring that the source meet an emission standard defined by the "lowest achievable emissions rate" (LAER). The LAER standard was intended to be the strictest of the Clean Air Act's technology-based standards (even more so than BACT applicable in PSD areas).

c. Intra–Source Bubbles and Inter–Source Offsets

A "source" in a nonattainment area includes the entire plant, not individual emission sources within the plant. Since all the emission components of a plant are treated as a single source for regulatory purposes, plant owners can experiment with increases and decreases in emissions from these different components so long as the net effect is not to increase total emissions from the "bubble" (the aggregate of all plant sources). The Supreme Court upheld use of the bubble concept in nonattainment areas in Chevron, U.S.A., Inc. v. NRDC (1984).

The 1977 Amendments contemplate that permits may be issued for construction or operation of new or modified sources only if "total allowable emissions from existing sources in the region" are reduced. EPA regulations have interpreted this language to require an overall net emissions reduction, as a result of action by *any* stationary source, not just the new or modified source seeking a nonattainment permit. A new or modified source may therefore receive such a permit if its emission addition is "offset" by a reduction in emissions elsewhere. See Citizens Against Refinery's Effects, Inc. v. United States EPA (1981) (decreased usage of asphalt reduces hydrocarbon pollution by more than enough to offset expected pollution from a proposed refinery).

The practical effect of this offset policy is to create a private market in emissions rights. Emissions "trading" may occur when a new source secures, from currently emitting sources, sufficient surplus emission reductions to more than offset the new emissions from the proposed facility. United States v. National Steel Corp. (1985). Emissions "banking" is possible when localities acquire and save emission reductions (e.g., from polluters leaving the state), which may later be sold or auctioned off to new firms.

8. Air Toxics

The original Clean Air Act addressed dangerous air pollutants not given an NAAQS with a "national emission standards for hazardous pollutants" (NESHAPs). The pollutants covered were those which may "result in an increase in mortality, or * * * illness." 42 U.S.C.A. § 7412. EPA was to establish emission standards with "an ample margin of safety to protect public health," but the statute did not authorize consideration of cost or technological feasibility. NRDC v. United States EPA (1987) ("ample margin of safety" does not permit EPA to consider cost and technology in determining what is safe, but neither does it require a zero emission standard). Failure to follow work practices requirements under NESHAP results in polluter liability. United States v. MPM Contractors (1990). By the late 1980s, EPA had adopted NESHAPs for only a handful of toxic pollutants (e.g., arsenic, asbestos, vinyl chloride, mercury).

The 1990 Amendments abandon the chemical-by-chemical approach of the NESHAPs and instead declare 189 substances to be hazardous air pollutants (HAPs). EPA is to (1) establish a list of major source categories of these HAPs (e.g., chemical plants, oil refineries), and (2) prescribe "maximum achievable control technology" (MACT) which each category must install and operate. MACT is a technology-based emission standard which takes cost into account. To be a "major" source subject to MACT, a facility need only emit 10 tons/year of a single HAP. New sources must comply immediately with MACT; existing sources must comply within four years of promulgation of the MACT standard. All MACT standards must be established by the year 2000.

9. Interstate Pollution

a. *The Clean Air Act Provisions*

Two sections of the Clean Air Act directly address interstate pollution. Section 110(a)(2)(E) requires that SIPs in upwind states prohibit emissions from stationary sources that prevent attainment of NAAQS in other downwind states. 42 U.S.C.A. § 7410(a)(2)(E). Section 126 requires a state to notify other states of sources that may contribute to the downwind state's air pollution problems, and authorizes these downwind states to petition EPA to determine a violation of section 110(a)(2)(E), and to take steps to abate emissions in the upwind state. 42 U.S.C.A. § 7426. In New York v. United States EPA (1988), the District of Columbia Appeals Court rejected the argument that a section 126 petition immediately obliged EPA to take investigatory steps necessary to determine whether SIPs in all upwind states complied with section 110(a)(2)(E). Accord, Connecticut v. EPA (1982) (EPA may approve New York SIP without responding to Connecticut's section 126 petition). EPA may reject a section 126 petition if the downwind state's air quality standard is more stringent than the NAAQS. Air Pollution Control Dist. of Jefferson County v. United States EPA (1984).

b. The Acid Rain Provisions of the 1990 Amendments

So-called "acid rain," the result of burning coal with sulfates, has been found to ride the winds for hundreds of miles, and devastate foliage, aquatic life, and visibility when dropped to earth. In some parts of the United States, particularly in Ohio, Pennsylvania, and West Virginia, up to 31 pounds of sulfate are thought to fall each year per acre.

The 1990 Amendments call for the reduction of sulfur dioxide (SO_2) emissions by ten million tons per year, and provide a cap on annual sulfur dioxide emissions beginning the year 2000. Emissions of oxides of nitrogen, another contributor to acid rain, are to be reduced by approximately two million tons per year.

Emissions of SO_2 from utility power plants will be capped at various levels, and plants will receive emission "allowances" up to the cap. Plants that are able to control emissions will be able to sell allowances, while plants unable to do so will have to buy allowances so that they may emit SO_2 above their caps. These marketable allowances will favor users (and producers) of western, low-sulfur coal. Plant users of this type of coal may more easily be able to emit SO_2 at levels below their cap, and therefore be in the lucrative position of selling their allowances to those who exceed their cap.

In 1991, the United States and Canada signed a bilateral accord building on the 1990 Amendments whereby each country agreed to sharp reductions in sulfur dioxide emissions.

B. WATER POLLUTION

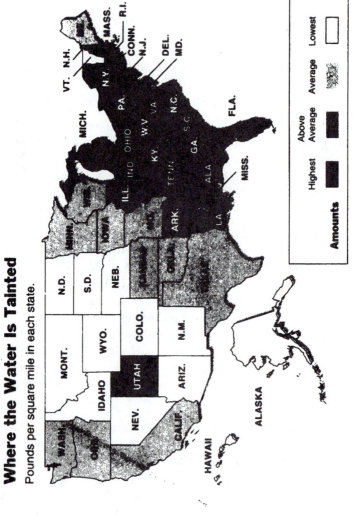

The Top 10 Water Polluters

Total amount of toxic chemicals: 188,994,123 lbs.

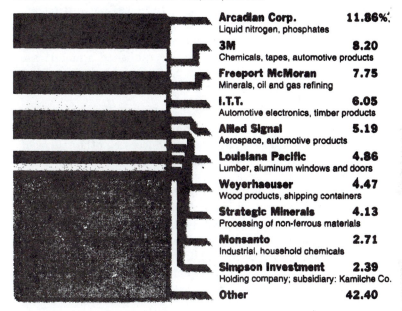

Arcadian Corp. Liquid nitrogen, phosphates	**11.86%**
3M Chemicals, tapes, automotive products	**8.20**
Freeport McMoran Minerals, oil and gas refining	**7.75**
I.T.T. Automotive electronics, timber products	**6.05**
Allied Signal Aerospace, automotive products	**5.19**
Louisiana Pacific Lumber, aluminum windows and doors	**4.86**
Weyerhaeuser Wood products, shipping containers	**4.47**
Strategic Minerals Processing of non-ferrous materials	**4.13**
Monsanto Industrial, household chemicals	**2.71**
Simpson Investment Holding company; subsidiary: Kamilche Co.	**2.39**
Other	**42.40**

The federal Clean Water Act (CWA) was originally enacted in 1972, and then amended in 1977 and 1987. 33 U.S.C.A. §§ 1251–1387; Pub.L. No. 95–217 (1977 Amendments); Pub.L. No. 100–4 (1987 Amendments). The CWA sets out three goals: (1) the elimination of the "discharge of pollutants into navigable waters" by 1985; (2) the establishment of waters with quality sufficiently high to be both "fishable and swimmable" by 1983; and (3) the end of "discharges of toxic pollutants in toxic amounts." 33 U.S.C.A. § 1251(a).

The CWA seeks to accomplish these goals through a variety of regulatory strategies. The EPA is charged with setting effluent limits for a range of pollutants, including toxic pollutants, which are to be met at the mouth of the waste pipe. States are to set ambient water quality standards to be met within the receiving waters (rivers, streams, and lakes). Dischargers must obtain a federal permit, from either EPA, or states which have been delegated federal permitting authority. The permit may not be granted if the discharger cannot, at the point of discharge, satisfy both federally-established effluent limits and state-established ambient water quality standards. The CWA permits citizen suits. New York Coastal Fishermen's Ass'n v. Department of Sanitation (1991).

In addition to this system for controlling point sources, the CWA provides legal mechanisms for addressing other types of waste discharges. These include: (1) pollution from non-point sources; (2) plant site runoff and storm water discharges; (3) oil and hazardous substance spills; (4) thermal pollution, and (5) ground water pollution. The CWA makes it a criminal offense to knowingly discharge into a municipal sewer, any industrial wastewater containing excessively high concentrations of toxics in violation of federal pretreatment standards. 33 U.S.C.A. § 1319(c); United States v. Boldt (1991).

1. Effluent Limitations

The CWA required that EPA establish national effluent limitations on the basis of what is technologically and economically achievable for hundreds of different pollutants for particular categories of dischargers. These technology based effluent limits set the minimum treatment required by direct industrial dischargers, and publicly owned sewage treatment works. Both "conventional" and "toxic" pollutants are to be subject to effluent limitations. American Petroleum Institute v. United States EPA (1988) (EPA may classify an otherwise conventional pollutant, such as grease and oil, as toxic, if it has the ability to carry toxic pollutants).

The effluent limitations are to be established on an industry-by-industry basis, in light of availability and costs of applicable control technologies. In considering technological availability and cost, EPA may base its effluent regulations on the "average of the best existing performance" among discharging industries, not just on the performance of the best plant. Hooker Chemicals & Plastics Corp. v. Train (1976); EPA v. National Crushed Stone Ass'n (1980). See also Chemical Mfrs. Ass'n v. United States EPA (1989) (suitable pollution control technology for the organic chemical, plastics, and synthetic fiber industry could be based on the practice of 71 out of 304 plants, considered the "average of the best"). A particular pollution control technology is not necessarily unavailable simply because it is not yet in use in any plant. American Frozen Food Institute v. Train (1976).

In E.I. du Pont de Nemours & Co. v. Train (1977), the Supreme Court authorized EPA to establish effluent limitations according to classes of plants, as contrasted with a limitation tailored to each individual plant. EPA may also set effluent limitations on the basis of single number, as opposed to a range of numbers. American Petroleum Institute v. EPA (1976). Effluent limits must be met at the mouth of the waste pipe; EPA need not consider the quality or assimilative capacity of receiving waters. NRDC v. United States EPA (1988); Weyerhaeuser Co. v. Costle (1978) (irrelevant that pulp and paper makers discharged effluents into the Pacific Ocean).

a. Levels of Treatment—Types of Pollutants

The CWA requirements for effluent limitations call for industries to adopt different levels of treatment for different categories of pollutants by various statutory deadlines. The original 1972 Act provided that effluent limitations for all point sources were to reflect "best practicable control technology currently available" (BPT) by 1977, and the more stringent standard of "best available technology economically achievable" (BAT) by 1983. For toxic substances, EPA was to establish separate limitations based on protection of public health and water quality, not technological feasibility. "New" sources are to meet effluent limitations equivalent to the 1983 BAT standards.

The 1977 Amendments modified the requirements for toxics by codifying a consent decree previously ordered in a lawsuit between EPA and the NRDC. EPA was to issue effluent limitations for 21 industries and scores of toxic pollutants, requiring the use of BAT by 1984. NRDC v. United States EPA (1991) (the consent decree does not establish that the CWA mandates numerical criteria for toxics). In 1987, the Congress directed that all dischargers of toxic pollutants for which effluent limitations had been established to be in compliance by 1989. 33 U.S.C.A. § 1311(b)(2)(C)–(F). The 1987 Amendments also required states to identify point sources which were exceeding ambient water quality standards for toxics, despite implementation of BAT. States must establish individual control strategies for each such source so that water quality standards are achieved within three years after the date of the establishment of the category.

The 1977 Amendments imposed a new standard, "best conventional pollutant control technology" (BCT), which was to be achieved by 1984 for conventional pollutants. For "nonconventional nontoxic" pollutants, the BAT standard was to be achieved by 1984. The 1987 Amendments extended this compliance deadline to 1989.

(1) BEST PRACTICABLE TECHNOLOGY (BPT)

Since the deadline for BPT achievement is past, its primary relevance is that the post–1977 BCT limitations for conventional pollutants must be at least as stringent as the BPT limits. See Chemical Mfrs. Ass'n v. U.S. E.P.A. (1989) (although BPT limitations may double costs for removal of certain conventional pollutants, the costs are not sufficiently high to void the limitations). In establishing BPT, EPA may consider in-plant "process" changes, in addition to end-of-pipe treatment. 33 U.S.C.A. § 1314(b)(1)(B). Factors relevant in determining BPT include total cost of technology in relation to effluent reduction benefits. American Meat Institute v. EPA (1975).

(2) Best Available Technology (BAT)

The BAT level of effluent control is required for toxic and conventional pollutants. It is the most rigorous of all the effluent control standards. In setting a BAT limitation, EPA is required only to "consider" the cost of achieving the required effluent reduction; no formal balancing of costs and benefits is necessary. Reynolds Metals v. United States EPA (1985). See also Kennecott v. United States EPA (1985) (zero discharge BAT standard upheld); EPA v. National Crushed Stone Ass'n (1980) (BAT should represent "a commitment of the maximum resources economically possible for the ultimate goal of eliminating all polluting discharges"). BAT is a technology-based limitation, and to be technologically "available," it is sufficient that the best operating facilities be capable of achieving the limitation. NRDC v. United States EPA (1988).

(3) Best Conventional Technology (BCT)

The BCT limitations include within the definition of "conventional" pollutants: (1) biochemical oxygen-demanding substances; (2) total suspended solids; (3) fecal coliform bacteria, (4) pH, and (5) oil and grease. These pollutants are discharged by or are characteristics of municipal sewage plants, food processing plants, and pulp and paper mills. In establishing BCT standards, EPA is to consider the economic "reasonableness" of attaining a reduction in effluents. 33 U.S.C.A. § 1314(b)(4)(B). EPA's initial BCT standards were invalidated in API v. United States EPA (1981). The revised effluent limits make BCT equivalent to BPT, except when the cost for an industrial source to remove an additional pound of pollutant above the BPT level is less than the cost for a municipal sewage facility to remove an additional pound above the same level. In such a case, more stringent BAT levels are appropriate.

(4) Nonconventional Nontoxic Pollutants

All pollutants not otherwise classified as conventional or toxic are to achieve the BAT standard by 1984. EPA may modify these requirements up to 1989, if the modification does not interfere with state water quality standards or pose a health risk. 33 U.S.C.A. § 1311(g).

(5) Toxic Pollutants

The 1972 Act required that EPA maintain a list of toxic substances, and establish separate limitations for them based on public health and water quality, not technological feasibility. When this original section proved impractical to implement, EPA entered into a consent decree with the NRDC. Pursuant to the decree, EPA was to develop a program to regulate the discharge of 65 categories of "priority pollutants," including at least 129 specific toxic chemical substances. For each listed substance, BAT level of treatment was required. The 1977 Amendments largely ratified the consent decree. 33 U.S.C.A. §§ 1311(b)(2)(A); 1317(a). See also Citizens for a Better Environment v. Gorsuch (1983).

In establishing BAT regulations for toxics, EPA need not consider economic or technological feasibility. Hercules, Inc. v. EPA (1978). EPA's BAT regulations for toxics take the long-term average of toxics discharged by the best plants, and multiply it by a variability factor to account for variation among all plants. Chemical Mfrs. Ass'n v. United States EPA (1989).

The 1987 Amendments require states to identify (by 1989) toxic "hot spots," segments of water bodies where application of BAT does not achieve state-established ambient water quality standards. For each segment, states must devise an individual control strategy which will produce a reduction in the discharge of toxic pollutants from point sources. 33 U.S.C.A. § 1314(1). This will include identification of many mining and energy dischargers. NRDC v. United States EPA (1990) (EPA must require states to identify all sources discharging any pollutant believed to be impairing water quality of a listed body of water). The 1987 Amendments also require states to adopt numerical water quality standards for toxic pollutants. 33 U.S.C.A. § 1313(c)(2)(B). If numerical standards are impractical, states must employ biological monitoring methods, whereby the effluent is tested to see if it is toxic to a certain percentage of a particular type of marine life in a specified time period. See NRDC v. United States EPA (1988).

b. *Effluent Limitations for New Sources*

The CWA directs EPA to "establish federal standards of performance for new sources" for various listed categories of industries. A new source is "any source, the construction of which is commenced after publication of proposed regulations prescribing a standard of performance." A standard of performance is "a standard for the control of the discharge of pollutants which reflects the greatest degree of effluent reduction * * * achievable through application of best available demonstrated control technology [BDT] * * * or other alternatives." 33 U.S.C.A. § 1316.

While the EPA must consider "the cost of achieving such effluent reduction" in setting the BDT standards, these standards may also reflect "alternative" production processes. Such alternatives include effluent reduction techniques brought about by facility design alteration, not end-of-the-pipe treatment. The issuance of a permit for the discharge of a pollutant by a new source is a "major federal action" triggering NEPA review. 33 U.S.C.A. § 1371(c)(1).

c. Variances

In the 1970s, EPA created a variance mechanism which permits a discharger to be exempt from effluent limitations when the dischargers' plant is "fundamentally different" from the industry norm. To obtain a fundamentally different factors (FDF) variance from EPA, a discharger must show something different or unique about the facility. Fundamentally different factors include the nature, quality, or volume of the effluent, non-water quality environmental impacts of treatment, or energy requirements of the treatment technology.

While FDF variances from BPT standards are available, E.I. du Pont de Nemours & Co. v. Train (1977), they may not be based solely on a plant's economic inability to comply. EPA v. National Crushed Stone Ass'n (1980). Nor is receiving water quality a factor sufficiently "different" to be considered by EPA in granting a BPT variance. Crown Simpson Pulp Co. v. Costle (1981). The 1987 Amendments provide for FDF variances from BAT and BCT. 33 U.S.C.A. § 1311(n). FDF variances are also available for toxic pollutants. Chemical Mfrs. Ass'n v. NRDC (1985).

Nonconventional nontoxic pollutants may receive non-FDF variances from BAT based either on water quality or economic considerations. 33 U.S.C.A. § 1311(c), (g). FDF variances and any of the Act's other variance provisions are not available to "new" sources. E.I. du Pont de Nemours v. Train, *supra.*

2. Water Quality Standards

Dischargers must meet effluent limitations more stringent than the above EPA-derived technology-based standards when the latter fail to achieve ambient water quality standards. 33 U.S.C.A. § 1311(b)(1)(C). Such water quality standards are to be established pursuant to state law, or, if state law is absent or unacceptable, EPA regulation. Water quality standards and the resulting water quality-related effluent limitations often result in levels of treatment higher than BAT, BCT, or BDT for dischargers to certain types of water bodies: (1) where the quality of receiving waters needs to be especially protected due to recreational uses, the presence of sensitive aquatic life (e.g., trout), or exceptional high quality (very clean) water; (2) where there are high numbers of industrial dischargers along a short stretch of shoreline; or (3) where the dilution flows of the water body have been diminished by hydrologic modifications, such as dams or diversions.

a. Setting Standards

Section 302 of the CWA authorizes EPA directly to establish water-quality based effluent restrictions whenever technology-based limits are inadequate to protect a particular water body. 33 U.S.C.A. § 1312. EPA usually relies on states to set water quality standards pursuant to section 303. 33 U.S.C.A. § 1313. EPA will substitute its own standard for a state standard if the state's is found to be inadequate. Mississippi Com'n on Natural Resources v. Costle (1980).

The pollutants addressed by state water quality standards are the "toxic" primary pollutants under the consent decree, conventional pollutants, and listed nonconventional nontoxic pollutants. To establish water quality standards, states first inventory all state waters and identify those whose quality is not being adequately protected by technology-based end-of-pipe effluent limits. Then state standards must be promulgated which (1) divide the waters of each state into segments, (2) determine the present and attainable uses for each segment (e.g., recreation, aquatic life, agriculture, domestic use), and (3) set numeric ambient limits for pollutants low enough to maintain or make possible these uses.

Waters not being adequately protected by technology-based controls for limiting discharges are to be designated by states as being "water quality limited." The states are then to establish a priority ranking for these waters, and in accordance with that ranking, set more stringent pollution limits called "total maximum daily loads" or "TMDLs." 33 U.S.C.A. § 1313(d)(1)(A), (C). TMDLs are the greatest amount of pollutants the water body can receive daily without violating a state's water quality standard. The TMDL calculations help ensure that the cumulative impacts of multiple point and nonpoint discharges are accounted for. Alaska Center for the Environment v. Reilly (1991).

If existing water quality is better than water quality standards, then the 1987 Amendments prohibit effluent discharges which degrade the water up to the standards. 33 U.S.C.A. §§ 1313(d)(4)(B); 1251(a). This is known as an "antidegradation" requirement. States must maintain the uses designated in the standards, unless certain physical or biological aspects of the water body make the designated use unattainable.

b. Conflicts

The CWA sets only *minimum* requirements for water pollution control; states may devise more stringent measures. 33 U.S.C.A. § 1370. However, the ability to set more restrictive standards only "preserves the authority of a state," but "does not preclude pre-emption" of state law. International Paper Co. v. Ouellette (1987) (the CWA preempts a common law nuisance suit filed in Vermont court under Vermont law against a New York discharger causing the injury in Vermont).

Does the CWA require a point source of pollution to comply with the water quality standards of an affected downstream state? In Oklahoma v. EPA (1990), the Tenth Circuit concluded that dischargers must meet applicable EPA-approved water quality standards of other downstream states, as well as those of the source state. This holding was based on language in the CWA providing that "there shall be achieved * * * any more stringent limitation, including those necessary to meet water quality standards * * * established pursuant to any state law." 33 U.S.C.A. § 1311(b)(1)(C). Another section of the CWA authorizes the governor of a state to sue EPA to enforce an "effluent standard or limitation under this chapter," the violation of which is occurring in another state, and is "causing a violation of any water quality requirement in his state." 33 U.S.C.A. § 1365(h).

3. The National Pollutant Discharge Elimination System (NPDES)

At the heart of the CWA is the NPDES permit program. Dischargers must comply with limitations in a permit, which in turn must reflect applicable effluent limitations incorporating both technology-based and water quality-based standards. Homestake Mining Co. v. United States EPA (1979) (as between technological and water quality standards, the discharger-permittee must meet the stricter of the two). Discharge permits may be granted by EPA, or by states with EPA-approved programs. In addition to establishing specific levels of performance, an NPDES permit includes enforceable schedules of compliance to meet various statutory deadlines, and requires dischargers to report failures to meet those levels by the deadlines.

a. Definitions

The CWA contemplates issuance of a permit "for the discharge of any pollutant." 33 U.S.C.A. § 1342(a). The term "discharge of pollutants" is defined as "any addition of any pollutant to navigable waters from any point source."

33 U.S.C.A. § 1362(12)(A). The federal District of Columbia Appeals Court has held that for NPDES requirements to apply, a "pollutant" must be "added" to "navigable waters" from a "point source." NWF v. Gorsuch (1982).

(1) "POLLUTANT"

The CWA broadly defines "pollutant" as "dredged spoil, solid waste, incinerator residue, sewage, garbage, sewage sludge, munitions, chemical wastes, biological materials, radioactive materials, heat, wrecked or discarded equipment, rock, sand, cellar dirt, and industrial, municipal, and agricultural waste." 33 U.S.C.A. § 1362(a). See Weinberger v. Romero—Barcelo (1982) (dropped bombs are pollutants); Association of Pacific Fisheries v. EPA (1980) (fish remains are pollutants).

(2) "ADDED"

The term "added" means the introduction of a pollutant to water from the outside world. Therefore, even though pollutants (e.g., nutrients, heat, sediment) may be created by a facility, such as a storage dam, these pollutants are not added when water is released into surrounding water. NWF v. Gorsuch; Missouri ex rel. Ashcroft v. Department of Army (1982). See also NWF v. Consumers Power Co. (1988) (discharge of dead fish killed by the turbines of a pumped storage plant not an "addition" of a pollutant). A hydrologic modification like a diversion canal likewise does not add pollutants, even though its operation may reduce dilution flows and concentrate existing pollutants.

(3) "NAVIGABLE WATERS"

The CWA defines "navigable waters" as "the waters of the United States, including the territorial seas." 33 U.S.C.A. § 1362(7). EPA has interpreted "waters of the United

States" to encompass intrastate lakes, rivers, streams (including intermittent streams), mudflats, impoundments of waters, tributaries of navigable waters, and wetlands. See United States v. Zanger (1991). The definition is expansive, and courts have given it the broadest possible reach. United States v. Riverside Bayview Homes, Inc. (1985); Quivira Mining Co. v. United States EPA (1985). Even internal waste streams within a waste treatment system are "waters of the United States." Texas Municipal Power Agency v. Administrator (1988).

(4) "POINT SOURCES"

A "point source" is "any discernible, confined and discrete conveyance, including but not limited to any pipe, ditch, channel, tunnel, conduit, well * * * from which pollutants are or may be discharged." 33 U.S.C.A. § 1362(14). Surface waste impoundments are point sources because, even though a discharge from them is not normally expected, a discharge "may be" possible if there is excessive precipitation that falls on them. See Sierra Club v. Abston Const. Co. (1980) (mine operator liable for spoil piles that caused pollution after rainfall).

Congress exempted irrigation return flows from the definition of a point source (33 U.S.C.A. § 1362(14)), and sewage from vessels is regulated under a separate, non-NPDES provision. 33 U.S.C.A. § 1362(6). Agricultural and silvicultural activities, most mining activities, construction, and changes in water flow are specifically labeled as "non-point" sources. 33 U.S.C.A. § 1314(f). Compare United States v. Frezzo Bros., Inc. (1983) (mushroom composting operation not an exempt "agricultural" activity), with NWF v. Gorsuch (dam a non-point source).

When mining activities release pollutants from a discernible conveyance, they are point sources subject to NPDES regulation. United States v. Earth Sciences, Inc. (1979) (5 gallon/minute discharge of sodium cyanide solution from overflowing sumps used in gold leaching operations is from a point source); Trustees for Alaska v. EPA (1984) (gold placer mining operations using sluice boxes are point sources). The 1987 Amendments exempt from the NPDES permit requirement "discharges of storm water runoff from mining operations or oil and gas exploration * * * composed entirely of flows which are from conveyances * * * used for collecting and conveying precipitation runoff, and which are not contaminated by overburden." 33 U.S.C.A. § 1342(*l*)(2).

b. The NPDES Permit

A permit reflecting technology-based and water quality-based standards must ensure that (1) the discharger's effluent does not exceed these standards; (2) sufficient monitoring and reporting of failures takes place; and (3) statutory deadlines for compliance are met. Permits are generally authorized for up to five years, and may be revoked for "cause." 33 U.S.C.A. § 1342(b)(1)(B). The EPA is the issuing authority for all NPDES permits until a state establishes its own EPA-approved program, in which case federal permitting authority is delegated to the state. A previously approved state NPDES program can later be disapproved and the program returned to federal authority if the state permit program does not meet CWA requirements or applicable EPA regulations. 33 U.S.C.A. § 1342(c).

The 1987 Amendments contain an "anti-backsliding" policy which provides that permits may not be "modified on the basis of effluent guidelines promulgated * * * subsequent to the original issuance of the permit, to contain effluent limitations which are less stringent than * * * in the previous permit." The prohibition has primary applicability where a permit is issued on the basis of "best professional judgment" (BPJ) prior to promulgation of effluent limits for a pollutant (e.g., a toxic pollutant). If the BPJ limits prove to be more stringent than the subsequently adopted national effluent limit, the discharger may not be able to relax the more stringent BPJ conditions. NRDC v. United States, EPA (1988).

c. *Section 401 Certification*

Whenever a federal agency is the issuing authority for a license or permit (including an NPDES permit), section 401 requires that the state "certify" that any resulting discharge into navigable waters will comply with the effluent and water quality standards of the CWA. 33 U.S.C.A. § 1341. No federal license or permit may be granted without the requisite 401 certification, thus ensuring that states will have an effective veto over federally authorized projects (e.g., dams) which may impact water quality. City of Fredericksburg v. FERC (1989); (a federal power licensee must file a 401 application); Monongahela Power Co. v. Marsh (1987) (401 certification is a precondition to issuance of a section 404 permit under the CWA). A "discharge" for purposes of 401 certification is construed more broadly than the "discharge of pollutants" phrase that triggers NPDES permitting. Compare 33 U.S.C.A. 1362(12)(A) ("discharge of pollutants" requires an addition of a pollutant from a point source), with Power Authority v. Williams (1984) (a section 401 "discharge" is present when there is a transfer of water between reservoirs with a corresponding water temperature change).

4. Regulation of Other Waste Discharges

a. *Non-point Source Pollution*

Run-off from agricultural and urban areas, silvicultural practices, and abandoned mines constitute the primary sources of non-point pollution. The original CWA's mechanism for controlling non-point sources was section 208, 33 U.S.C.A. § 1288. Under section 208, each state is divided into planning areas, and in those areas having substantial non-point water quality problems, the state's governor is to select a regional planning agency (e.g., a Council of Governments), which is to develop a management strategy (a "208 plan") for controlling the pollution sources. NRDC v. Costle (1977) (state may serve as the planning agency for nondesignated areas). Section 208 was doomed to fail because these plans themselves are without legal effect, and they are not binding on the local governments which have the police power to implement them.

The 1987 Amendments added section 319 to address the failure of section 208. New section 319 requires states to identify waters which, without additional action to control non-point sources of pollution, cannot meet applicable water quality standards. 33 U.S.C.A. § 1329(a)(1)(A). Each state must then submit to EPA a program which sets out "best management practices" and regulatory actions that will control non-point sources. Section 319 seems likely to fail as well, since it neither directly requires states to adopt regulatory controls, nor provides sufficient federal financial grants to implement state management programs.

b. Runoff and Stormwater

The 1987 Amendments require that various categories of industrial stormwaters be regulated as NPDES discharges. These include discharges "associated with industrial activity," and discharges that "contribute to a violation of a water quality standard." 33 U.S.C.A. § 1342(p)(2). For discharges associated with industrial activities, NPDES permits must meet applicable effluent limitations imposed upon the industry, as well as water quality standards. The phrase "associated with industrial activity" has been interpreted by EPA to include active and inactive mining operations, as well as oil and gas exploration and production activities.

Section 304(e), added by the 1977 Amendments, authorizes EPA to require permittees to adopt "best management practices" to regulate plant site runoff where toxic pollutants are involved. 33 U.S.C.A. § 1314(e); Rybachek v. United States EPA, (1990).

c. *Hazardous Waste and Oil Spills*

Section 311 of the CWA declares that there shall be no discharges of oil or hazardous substances into the navigable waters of the United States. Onshore facility operators and offshore vessel owners are liable without fault for the costs of cleanups, and for civil and criminal penalties. 33 U.S.C.A. § 1321; In re Lloyd's Leasing Ltd. (1990); United States v. West of England Ship Owner's Mut. Protection & Indem. Ass'n (1989); United States v. Texas Pipe Line Co. (1979).

Section 311 preempts the United States from recovering cleanup costs under a public nuisance theory, United States v. Dixie Carriers, Inc. (1980), or under a maritime tort theory, Conner v. Aerovox, Inc. (1984), or under common law negligence. Kyoei Kaiun Kaisha, Ltd. v. M/V Bering Trader (1991). Although the United States is limited to seeking relief under section 311, there is no preemption of state legislation providing for strict liability in private actions for damages resulting from an oil or hazardous substance spill. Askew v. American Waterways Operators, Inc. (1973).

There are several defenses available to the strict liability provisions of section 311. Discharges made in compliance with an NPDES permit are immunized. Liability may not exceed $150 per gross ton of the vessel. United States v. Dixie Carriers, Inc. (1984). A discharger may escape liability altogether if the discharge is caused by an act or omission of a third party. 33 U.S.C.A. § 1321(f)(1); Cities Service Pipe Line Co. v. United States (1984).

d. *Thermal Pollution*

The discharge of heated water may alter the biological development of aquatic life, decrease dissolved oxygen, and impede fish migration. Thermal pollution is caused either by steam electric power plants or nuclear power plants. The CWA defines heat as a "pollutant," and thus the technology-based BPT and BAT standards apply. Section 316, 33 U.S.C.A. § 1326(b) presumes that both BPT and BAT may be achieved by closed-cycle cooling. In developing BAT standards for thermal pollution, EPA must balance the cost of achieving a level of heat reduction against the expected environmental benefits. Appalachian Power Co. v. United States EPA (1982). Section 316 allows an exception "for the thermal component of any discharge" if the standard is "more stringent than necessary" to protect indigenous fish and wildlife. Seacoast Anti–Pollution League v. Costle (1979).

e. Groundwater Pollution

(1) Regulation Under the Clean Water Act

The problem of groundwater contamination is not explicitly addressed by the CWA. As a result, most groundwater pollution control laws are state, not federal. When the EPA sought to regulate underground discharges pursuant to the CWA, it had to rely on the Act's broad definition of navigable waters, and section 402(b)(1)(D), which prohibits EPA from approving a state NPDES permit program if the state does not have authority to control the disposal of pollutants into wells. 33 U.S.C.A. § 1342(b)(1)(D). The federal appeals courts initially split on the question of whether EPA had authority under the CWA to regulate disposal of wastes into deep wells unconnected to surface waters. Compare Exxon Corp. v. Train (1977) (no authority), with United States Steel Corp. v. Train (1977) (authority). EPA now relies on two other federal statutes to regulate discharges to groundwater—the Safe Drinking Water Act, and the Resource Conservation and Recovery Act of 1976 (RCRA). See Inland Steel Co. v. EPA (1990) (deep injection wells used for disposal of hazardous chemicals subject to RCRA); Federal–Hoffman, Inc. v. United States EPA (1990) (RCRA requires impermeable liner under landfill to prevent migration of liquid waste to ground water).

(2) REGULATION UNDER THE SAFE DRINKING WATER ACT (SDWA)

The SDWA, 42 U.S.C.A. §§ 300f to 300j–9, directs the EPA to prescribe both primary and secondary maximum levels for contaminants in public drinking water systems. Primary regulations specify federally enforceable maximum levels for contaminants (MCLs) which may have adverse health effects. Secondary regulations are to protect the public welfare. To establish primary regulations, EPA has set "recommended" MCLs (RMCLs), followed by MCLs. RMCLs are at levels at which "no known or anticipated adverse effects on the health of persons occur and which allow an adequate margin of safety." 42 U.S.C.A. § 300g–1(b)(1)(B). RMCLs are non-enforceable goals, and do not take feasibility into account. MCLs are enforceable, and must be set as close to RMCLs as is feasible, taking cost into consideration. EPA primary standards have been upheld by the courts. NRDC v. EPA (1987) (volatile organic compounds may have an RMCL of zero); NRDC v. EPA (1987) (fluoride standard).

There are two regulatory regimes within the SDWA designed to protect usable aquifers from contamination. States must submit to EPA underground injection control (UIC) programs which authorize underground injection only by permit, and only where drinking water will not be endangered. 42 U.S.C.A. § 300h. If injection is permitted, the state must ensure that there will be no migration of fluids from the injection zone into underground sources of drinking water. Phillips Petroleum Co. v. United States EPA (1986). States may, subject to EPA review, classify aquifers as not being underground sources of drinking water. Western Nebraska Resources Council v. EPA (1986). States may, with

EPA approval, exempt portions of aquifers from UIC requirements. Western Nebraska Resources Council v. United States EPA (1991) (exemption to permit injection-process mining of uranium in aquifer). Apart from the UIC program, the EPA also has authority to provide special protection where "an area has an aquifer which is the sole or principal drinking water source for the area." 42 U.S.C.A. § 300h–3(e). When a sole source aquifer (SSA) is designated, local governments qualify for special planning grants. EPA has substantial discretion in setting boundaries for SSAs. Montgomery County v. United States EPA (1981).

5. Section 404 Permitting for Dredged or Fill Material

Section 404(a) of the CWA authorizes the Army Corps of Engineers to issue permits for the discharge of dredged or fill materials into navigable waters at particular sites. 33 U.S.C.A. 1344(a). Monongahela Power Co. v. Marsh (1987) (a 404 permit is required to discharge fill material into waters during construction of hydroelectric facility licensed by FERC). A "discharge of a pollutant" triggering section 404 includes changing the bottom elevations of a stream, United States v. Zanger (1991), and the redeposit of indigenous materials into waters of the United States. United States v. Sinclair Oil (1990).

The Corps may deny the permit if its granting would not be in the "public interest." Compare Van Abbema v. Fornell (1986) (public interest review inadequate), with Mall Properties, Inc. v. Marsh (1988) (404 permit for a shopping center may not be denied on the theory that public interest is furthered by protecting the competitive advantage of existing businesses). Even if the Corps issues a permit, EPA may veto any permit that will have an unreasonable effect upon water supplies, fish, wildlife, or recreation areas. But see James City County, Virginia v. United States EPA (1990)

(EPA may not "presume" that county had available alternatives to proposed reservoir when it vetoed a Corps of Engineers decision). The section 404 process normally triggers NEPA. Audubon Soc. of Central Arkansas v. Dailey (1991) (construction of bridge over creek pursuant to 404 permit enjoined for failure to prepare EIS); People ex rel. Van deKamp v. Marsh (1988).

Section 404 jurisdiction has been construed to extend to all waters of the United States, including wetlands. In United States v. Riverside Bayview Homes, Inc. (1985), the Supreme Court rejected the notion that land must be frequently inundated to be considered wetlands. See also United States v. Larkins (1988) (the presence of vegetation that requires saturated soil conditions is sufficient to consider the lands as wetlands). In Leslie Salt Co. v. United States (1990), section 404 jurisdiction was extended to human-created wetlands. Before the Corps issues a 404 permit involving wetlands, it must determine if an "alternative" site is available that would cause less harm to wetlands. Bersani v. United States EPA (1988).

The stringent approval criteria for section 404 are not applicable for "general" permits, which may be granted where the area affected is small and the need for full review of the proposal activity is slight. Shelton v. Marsh (1990). Nor is section 404 permitting necessary for ongoing or established farming and silviculture operations. 33 U.S.C.A. § 1344(f)(1)(A). The farming and timber harvesting exception applies only to "normal" activities, not to (1) farming practices that put the altered area to a new use or impair the flow of navigable waters, United States v. Larkins (1988); United States v. Akers (1986), nor to (2) clearing timber to permanently change the area to a tract for row crop cultivation. Avoyelles Sportsmen's League, Inc. v. Marsh (1983).

V. TOXIC AND HAZARDOUS
SUBSTANCE CONTROL

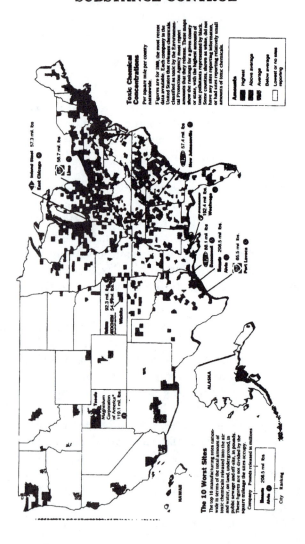

The 10 Biggest Polluters

Total amount of toxic chemicals: 5,710,282,027 lbs.
Includes air, water, land, underground,
public sewage and off-site
releases nationwide.

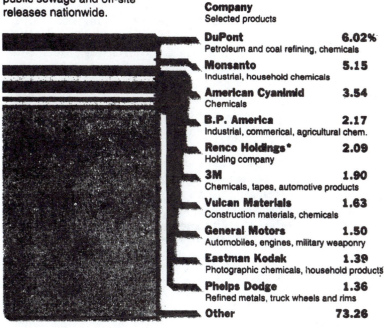

Company Selected products	
DuPont Petroleum and coal refining, chemicals	**6.02%**
Monsanto Industrial, household chemicals	**5.15**
American Cyanimid Chemicals	**3.54**
B.P. America Industrial, commerical, agricultural chem.	**2.17**
Renco Holdings* Holding company	**2.09**
3M Chemicals, tapes, automotive products	**1.90**
Vulcan Materials Construction materials, chemicals	**1.63**
General Motors Automobiles, engines, military weaponry	**1.50**
Eastman Kodak Photographic chemicals, household products	**1.39**
Phelps Dodge Refined metals, truck wheels and rims	**1.36**
Other	**73.26**

The problem of toxic and hazardous wastes typically involves the disposal of poisonous chemicals. While many energy and natural resources activities do not generate or use toxic chemicals, they are linked along a fuel or resource extraction cycle whose end product is often hazardous waste. Hazardous waste control presents two notable issues. First, because the relationship between hazardous substances and harm is still somewhat speculative, how should law and government deal with this uncertainty when it regulates and controls these substances? Second, when government does respond, usually in the form of federal statutes, what is the content of the response?

The first of these issues—how to proceed in the face of scientific uncertainty—was considered in two influential cases decided in the mid–1970s, Reserve Mining Co. v. EPA (1975), and Ethyl Corp. v. EPA (1976). These two leading cases have provided a rationale for courts, regulators, and legislators attempting to be "proactive," protecting public health and the environment in advance of harm, not after-the-fact. Both cases involved courts seeking to ascertain whether certain activities constituted a health hazard grave enough to justify judicial invention under a federal pollution control statute. In both cases the court was hampered by a lack of hard scientific data connecting the activity to a tangible harm. The *Reserve Mining* case concerned whether the ingestion of asbestos fibers in drinking water created a health risk under the Clean Water Act. The *Ethyl* case considered whether the incremental increase of lead in the environment from automobile emissions endangered the public health under the Clean Air Act.

In *Reserve Mining,* the Eighth Circuit directly interpreted the Clean Water Act, while in *Ethyl,* the D.C. Court of Appeals reviewed EPA's decision under the Clean Air Act. Despite these differences, both courts agreed that when government confronts uncertain proof of cause-and-effect (when the evidence is "on the frontiers of scientific knowledge"), the public health may be protected by regulations that take into account the proper relationship between two variables—(1) the likelihood of harm occurring, and (2) the severity of the harm should it occur. The recognized elements of risk and harm, or probability and severity, permit government to conclude that health is endangered both by a lesser risk of a greater harm, and by a greater risk of a lesser harm.

Subsequent cases have further defined the parameters of regulations based on this type of risk assessment. In EDF v.

EPA (1978) and Hercules, Inc. v. EPA (1978), the EPA was permitted virtually to prohibit the discharge of certain substances (PCBs, pesticides) alleged to be carcinogenic. In Lead Industries Ass'n, Inc. v. EPA (1980), the D.C. Circuit held that when a federal pollution statute requires a health-based standard to be set with an "adequate margin of safety," technical feasibility and cost are irrelevant. The D.C. Circuit later refused to interpret "ample margin of safety" to require a "risk-free" state which could be accomplished only with a zero-emission standard. See NRDC v. United States EPA (1987) ("safe" means a level of emissions that would result in only an "acceptable" risk to health).

The second issue—the content of the federal responses to toxic and hazardous wastes—is exemplified by two important statutes, the Resource Conservation and Recovery Act, and the Comprehensive Environmental Response, Compensation, and Liability Act (CERCLA). Both have applicability to energy and natural resources activities.

A. THE RESOURCE CONSERVATION AND RECOVERY ACT (RCRA)

Every year, more than 170 million tons of hazardous waste are produced in the United States, mostly from chemical industries. To deal with the enormous problem of properly disposing of these wastes, Congress passed RCRA of 1976. 42 U.S.C.A. § 6901 et seq., as amended by the Hazardous and Solid Waste Amendments of 1984, Pub.L. No. 98–616.

RCRA is a comprehensive regulatory statute that creates a "cradle to grave" system of controlling the entire hazardous waste lifecycle. Standards protecting public health and the environment are required for generators, transporters, and treatment, storage, and disposal (TSD) facilities. RCRA is prospective in nature, and is aimed at preventing harm from active and new waste handlers. Inactive or abandoned waste sites are addressed primarily by the Comprehensive Environmental Response, Compensation, and Liability Act (CERCLA).

Any person who knowingly violates RCRA is subject to severe criminal penalties. United States v. Hoflin (1989). Even federal employees working at federal facilities are "persons" subject to the statute's criminal provisions. United States v. Dee (1990). Operators of facilities releasing hazardous materials may be required to conduct monitoring, testing, and analysis of the facility. Wyckoff Co. v. EPA (1986). EPA may enter and inspect such facilities. National–Standard Co. v. Adamkus (1989).

The 1984 Amendments strengthen the original 1976 Act in four significant ways. First, EPA must regulate the hundreds of thousands of companies that produce only small quantities of hazardous waste (less than 1000 kilograms/month). Second, underground storage tanks are regulated by requiring inspections and repairs of leaks. Third, all generators of wastes must reduce the volume, quantity, or toxicity of wastes "to the degree determined by the generator to be economically practicable." 42 U.S.C.A. § 6922(b)(1). Fourth, to protect ground water, the 1984 Amendments prohibit the placement of liquid hazardous waste in landfills, as well as the land disposal of most other common hazardous waste. All new landfills, and all new or existing surface impoundments, must have double liners and leachate collection systems. 42 U.S.C.A. § 6924. To ensure that municipal landfills do not leak, regulations adopted in 1991 require that all landfills monitor ground water for possible contamination.

1. Identification and Listing of Hazardous Wastes

EPA's regulatory authority under RCRA extends only to "hazardous waste," which in turn is defined as a subset of "solid waste." 42 U.S.C.A. § 6903(5). Solid waste is broadly defined as any "garbage, refuse, sludge * * * and other discarded material." See United States v. White (1991) (solid waste definition in RCRA not unconstitutionally vague). Wastes that are "discarded" are those that become part of the waste disposal problem, and which are not part of an ongoing industrial process. American Mining Congress v. United States EPA (1990). Solid or dissolved material in domestic sewage is not RCRA "solid waste." Comite Pro Rescate De la Salud v. Puerto Rico Aqueduct & Sewer Authority (1989).

RCRA solid waste may be RCRA "hazardous waste" if it is (1) not otherwise exempt by regulation, and (2) "listed" by EPA for being carcinogenic, mutagenic, or toxic. The EPA has three hazardous waste lists: those from nonspecific sources; specific sources; and discarded or spilled chemical products. Even if a substance is not listed as hazardous, RCRA still applies if it possesses one of four hazardous waste characteristics: ignitability, corrosivity, reactivity, or toxicity. Certain solid wastes resulting from energy and natural resources operations are by regulation exempt from being considered hazardous wastes. These include: mining overburden returned to the mine site; oil and gas exploration drilling waste; wastes from the extraction and processing of ores, coal and other minerals; and arsenical-treated wood wastes generated by end users of such wood. If a substance is not exempt, a company may seek a "delisting" if it can prove either that its particular waste does not have constituents that would cause it to be hazardous, or that its plant processes somehow make the waste not hazardous.

Under EPA rule, a "mixture" of a listed hazardous waste and a solid waste must be considered a hazardous waste. Also, a waste that is "derived from" the treatment, storage, or disposal of a hazardous waste is considered a hazardous waste. Chemical Waste Management, Inc. v. United States EPA (1989) (leachate generated from hazardous waste is presumed hazardous).

2. Cradle to Grave Regulation

RCRA provides that after wastes are identified as hazardous, EPA-adopted performance standards are to bring about their safe generation, transportation, and disposal. A permit system is the key enforcement provision for treatment and disposal sites. As with other federal pollution control statutes, states may carry out their own hazardous waste programs if they are at least as stringent as federal requirements. Hazardous Waste Treatment Council v. Reilly (1991). Otherwise, state laws that do not satisfy minimum EPA prerequisites are preempted. ENSCO, Inc. v. Dumas (1986).

a. Generators of Waste

Those who produce hazardous wastes must properly prepare the waste for transportation off-site. Such waste generators must comply with RCRA standards regarding recordkeeping, labeling, and use of containers, as well as regulations under the Hazardous Materials Transportation Act, 490 U.S.C.A. § 1801 et seq. NL Industries, Inc. v. Department of Transportation (1990). If the waste is processed on site, the generator must demonstrate that its method of treatment, storage, or disposal is "that practicable method currently available * * * which minimizes the present and future threat to human health." 42 U.S.C.A. § 6922(b)(2). Generators may store wastes on site for a period of up to one year. Hazardous Waste Treatment Council v. United States EPA (1989).

b. Transportation of Wastes

Transporters must meet strict standards and requirements for the movement of wastes to disposal facilities. A transporter may be subject to criminal sanctions if wastes are deposited at a hazardous waste facility that does not have a permit that is appropriate for the type of waste being deposited. United States v. MacDonald & Watson Waste Oil Co. (1991). Unauthorized "dumping" exposes the transporter to criminal liability. United States v. Greer (1988). Under RCRA, foreign generated hazardous wastes may be imported into the United States. Once this waste is in the United States, it is subject to RCRA transportation and disposal requirements. Chem. Waste Management, Inc. v. Templet (1991).

c. Treatment, Storage, and Disposal (TSD) Facilities

The 1976 RCRA required TSD facilities to comply with regulations addressing landfills, site location, ground water monitoring, and pretreatment of toxic chemical wastes. The primary goal of the original TSD regulations was to protect ground water by preventing waste releases for the life of the facility, and for 30 years thereafter. The 1984 Amendments went much further, and banned most land disposal of hazardous wastes. The main exception to this prohibition is that if waste is first treated to the "Best Demonstrated Available Technologies" (BDAT) standard, then the treatment residue can be land disposed. American Petroleum Institute v. United States EPA (1990). EPA also banned the land disposal of specified hazardous wastes, such as heavy metals, unless the wastes were pretreated (since California had already banned them, they are known as "California list" wastes). See NRDC v. United States EPA (1990). The 1990 Clean Air Act Amendments do not preclude enforcement of RCRA regulations as they relate to disposal of incinerator ash. EDF v. Wheelabrator Technologies, Inc. (1991).

(1) PERMITS

RCRA requires every TSD facility to obtain a permit ensuring that it is in compliance with applicable technical standards for TSD facilities. Federally owned TSD facilities are subject to RCRA permitting requirements. Sierra Club v.

United States Dept. of Energy (1991). Lack of knowledge that absence of a permit violates RCRA is no defense to RCRA liability. United States v. Laughlin (1991).

The 1984 Amendments demand that a TSD facility take "corrective action" for all releases of hazardous waste, regardless of when the waste was put in the unit. 42 U.S.C.A. § 6924(u)–(v); United Technologies Corp. v. United States EPA (1987) (upholding a broad definition of "facilities" that must take corrective action); In re Consolidated Land Disposal Reg. Lit. (1991) (all TSD facilities that received wastes after 1982, or certified closure after 1983, must obtain a post-closure permit). NEPA does not apply to permits issued under RCRA. State of Ala. ex rel. Siegelman v. United States EPA (1990). A RCRA permit is not required for the treatment, storage, or disposal of hazardous wastes that occurred prior to November, 1980. 42 U.S.C.A. § 6925(a); McClellan Ecological Seepage Situation v. Cheney (1989).

(2) ASSURANCES OF FINANCIAL RESPONSIBILITY

RCRA provides that TSD operators demonstrate "financial responsibility as may be necessary or desirable." 42 U.S.C.A. § 6924(a)(b). Financial responsibility may be established by insurance, guarantee, surety bond, or self-insurance. This provision was included in RCRA to ensure that TSD operators will be financially able to satisfy liability claims resulting from facility operations or closure. Failure to meet these requirements has caused many TSD facilities to close. United States EPA v. Environmental Waste Control, Inc. (1990). But see United States v. Production Plated Plastics, Inc. (1991) (permanent injunctive relief not issued for inability to comply with financial assurance requirement when to do so would conflict with approved closure plan).

3. Imminent and Substantial Endangerment

EPA may seek immediate injunctive relief if the handling, storage, treatment, or disposal of hazardous waste presents an imminent and substantial endangerment to health or the environment. Citizens may also commence a civil action against parties whose past or present hazardous waste activities constitute an imminent hazard. Dague v. City of Burlington (1991). Proof of actual harm is not a requirement. United States v. Vertac Chemical Corp. (1980). One need only show a risk of harm. United States v. Price (1982) (but even if imminent harm is shown, a court may not award injunctive relief if to do so would be "impractical and unfair"). The "imminent endangerment" standard has been interpreted to impose strict liability, and to apply to persons who in the past "contributed to" the handling, storage, treatment, or disposal of hazardous waste. United States v. Aceto Agr. Chemicals Corp. (1989); United States v. Northeastern Pharmaceutical & Chemical Co. (1986).

4. Regulation of Mine Waste

Mining wastes containing hazardous substances are subject to cleanup authority under four federal statutes: RCRA (and the 1984 Amendments); the Solid Waste Disposal Act as amended by RCRA; the Comprehensive Environmental Response, Compensation, and Liability Act (discussed below, in Part B); and the Uranium Mill Tailings Radiation Control Act of 1978 (UMTRA), 42 U.S.C.A. § 7901 et seq.

a. Uranium Mill Tailings

UMTRCA is the most specialized of these statutes, focusing on radiological and nonradiological hazards associated with uranium tailings from active and inactive mill sites. Under UMTRCA, regulatory authority is divided among three federal agencies: EPA (standards of general application); the

Department of Energy (decommissioning of all inactive sites); and the Nuclear Regulatory Commission (ensuring that management of by-product material at new or active sites conforms to applicable EPA standards). See American Mining Congress v. United States NRC (1990); Quivira Mining Co. v. United States Congress NRC (1989). If the Secretary of Energy designates an inactive mill site as a "processing site," the federal government funds ninety percent of the cleanup, while the states pay the remaining ten percent. Hecla Mining Co. v. United States (1990). States may also place restrictions on property subject to UMTRCA. Colorado v. The Mill (1991).

b.   *"Bevill" Wastes under RCRA*

As originally enacted, RCRA excluded from the definition of "hazardous waste" all solid wastes generated in the extraction of ores and minerals, and wastes from oil and gas exploration or production. When EPA proposed listing mine and mineral "processing" wastes as hazardous wastes, Congress responded to this threat to the mining industry in the Solid Waste Disposal Act Amendments of 1980. As part of these 1980 Amendments, the Bevill amendment exempted particular mining industry wastes—known as Bevill wastes—from the hazardous waste controls in RCRA, pending further study by EPA as to their environmental and health effects. 42 U.S.C.A. 6921(b)(3). The Bentsen Amendment gave a similar exemption to oil, gas, and geothermal production wastes—Bentsen wastes—except that if EPA determined that RCRA hazardous waste controls were warranted, it was to transmit this recommendation to Congress for possible adoption. 42 U.S.C.A. §§ 6921(b)(2)(A), (C), 6982(m).

EPA spent the entire 1980s attempting to define the scope of the Bevill amendment. EPA initially determined that "extraction" wastes should not be regulated as hazardous wastes, and this decision was upheld in EDF v. United States

EPA (1988). Another case, also styled EDF v. EPA (1988), ordered EPA to treat "processing" wastes differently than extraction wastes. In its final rule implementing the Bevill amendment, issued in 1990, EPA concluded that only those mineral processing wastes meeting the agency's criteria of both "low hazard" and "high volume" will be excluded from the RCRA hazardous waste regulations.

c. *Additional Federal Environmental Regulation of Mining Wastes*

In the late 1980s, a combination of EPA rule and judicial decision resulted in an unprecedented degree of federal regulation of mine waste from active and inactive mining operations. First, the EPA narrowly interpreted the Simpson amendment to apply only to wastes ultimately retained within the scope of the Bevill amendment. The Simpson amendment, part of the 1984 amendments to RCRA, provided that RCRA requirements applicable to mine wastes may be modified by EPA to take into account special waste characteristics. 42 U.S.C.A. § 6924(x). Second, the EPA concluded that RCRA's "mixture rule" (a mixture of hazardous and solid waste is hazardous) should apply to Bevill and non-Bevill mixed waste streams. Third, EPA proposed a regulatory program under the solid waste provisions of RCRA, governing treatment, storage, and disposal of mine wastes otherwise excluded from regulation as hazardous wastes. This proposal, characterized as the "Strawman II" proposal, would have states take the lead role in managing solid mine wastes that have the potential to accumulate hazardous constituents.

In American Iron and Steel Inst. v. United States EPA (1989), the D.C. Circuit Court of Appeals narrowly construed the Bevill and Bentsen amendments in holding that release of wastes from mining and oil and gas activities are subject to RCRA "corrective action." 42 U.S.C.A. § 6924(u). Prior to 1984, RCRA did not require operators to take remedial action to correct past management of hazardous waste. The RCRA 1984 Amendments decisively changed that focus by permitting EPA to require corrective action, even for pre–1984 releases. The *American Iron and Steel* decision holds that these corrective action requirements can be triggered if otherwise exempt mining and oil and gas wastes cause the release of hazardous "constituents."

Used oil that is mixed with hazardous waste and burned for energy recovery is subject to regulation as hazardous waste fuel under RCRA. Hazardous Waste Treatment Council v. United States EPA (1988); United States v. Eastern of N.J. (1991).

B.　THE COMPREHENSIVE ENVIRONMENTAL RESPONSE, COMPENSATION, AND LIABILITY ACT (CERCLA)

Unlike RCRA, which established a cradle to grave regulatory program for present hazardous waste activities, CERCLA's primary purpose is the cleanup of past (and usually leaking) hazardous waste disposal sites. CERCLA was substantially amended by the Superfund Amendments and Reauthorization Act (SARA) in 1986. Pub.L. No. 99–499. Both Acts are collectively known as "CERCLA," 42 U.S.C.A. §§ 9601–9675. After a hazardous waste site is identified, CERCLA places ultimate cleanup responsibility on those who used the site. Parties responsible for a waste dump are liable for the cost of waste removal and other remedial action. They may be sued by the EPA, states, or citizens; if responsible parties are not available to bear the cost of cleanup, CERCLA creates a federal trust fund (Superfund) to pay for government responses.

1.　CERCLA and RCRA

While there are important differences between the two Acts, there are also important intersections and similarities.

RCRA is a prospective regulatory program that establishes nationally applicable standards that are designed to prevent future contamination from ongoing facilities. CERCLA creates a retroactive response program, implemented on a site-specific basis, intended to clean up inactive hazardous waste disposal sites. RCRA assumes that treatment of such wastes requires a permit; CERCLA specifically provides that no permit shall be required for any CERCLA remedial action. See United States v. Shell Oil Co. (1985). The scope and kinds of materials subject to RCRA are also narrower than those subject to CERCLA. RCRA is triggered by the presence of a pre-determined quantity of "wastes" deemed to be "hazardous." CERCLA jurisdiction attaches to virtually any concentration of more broadly defined "hazardous substances." Thus, a waste may be non-hazardous under RCRA and still be within CERCLA. B.F. Goodrich Co. v. Murtha (1991).

Despite the dissimilarities, the two Acts also interconnect at several points. A facility may not receive wastes from a CERCLA site unless it is in compliance with RCRA standards. 42 U.S.C.A. § 9621(d)(3). A state may pursue a RCRA suit against the United States seeking enforcement of state hazardous waste cleanup laws at a federal facility, at the same time other pending actions instituted under CERCLA are addressing the same site. Colorado v. United States Dept. of the Army (1989). The citizen suit provisions in RCRA and CERCLA both permit actions against anyone who has accepted hazardous materials. 42 U.S.C.A. § 6972(a)(1)(B); 42 U.S.C.A. § 9607(a)(4). See Tanglewood East Homeowners v. Charles–Thomas, Inc. (1988). Also, both RCRA and CERCLA permit EPA to take action against sites that present an "imminent and substantial endangerment." 42 U.S.C.A. § 6973; 42 U.S.C.A. § 9606.

2. Scope of CERCLA

CERCLA's liability provisions are activated if there is a "release or a threatened release," or some "disposal" of, "hazardous substances" at any "facility." 42 U.S.C.A. § 9607(a).

a. *"Release"*

There is a release when there is any spilling, pumping, pouring, emitting, or discharging into the environment. 42 U.S.C.A. 9601(22); State of Vermont v. Staco, Inc. (1988). One can make out a prima facie liability claim under CERCLA without alleging the particular manner of the release. Ascon Properties, Inc. v. Mobil Oil Co. (1989). It is not a release to place a hazardous substance in an unenclosed containment structure (i.e., one that has an open side exposed to the environment). Fertilizer Institute v. United States EPA (1991).

b. *"Disposal"*

Congress adopted in CERCLA the definition of disposal set out in the Solid Waste Disposal Act, 42 U.S.C.A. § 6903(3): "the discharge, deposit, injection, dumping, spilling, or leaking of any solid waste or hazardous waste." 42 U.S.C.A. § 9601(29). The term refers only to the affirmative act of discarding substance as waste, and not to either the productive *use* or the *sale* of the substance (e.g., asbestos). 3550 Stevens Creek Assoc. v. Barclays Bank (1990) (use of asbestos insulation not a CERCLA disposal); Dayton Independent School Dist. v. United States Mineral Products Co. (1990) (sale of building materials containing asbestos not a CERCLA disposal); Anthony v. Blech (1991) (lessee has no CERCLA cause of action against lessor to recover costs incurred in removing asbestos).

c. *"Hazardous Substances" and the Petroleum Exclusion*

A hazardous substance is anything already considered toxic or hazardous under the Clean Water Act, the Clean Air Act, the Toxic Substances Control Act, 15 U.S.C.A. § 2601 et seq., or RCRA. EPA may also designate a substance as hazardous if it presents a substantial danger. 42 U.S.C.A. § 9601(14). There is no quantitative requirement that a material must meet to be hazardous. State of Ariz. v. Motorola, Inc. (1991). A particular substance need not be in a specific chemical form to be hazardous. United States v. Alcan Aluminum Corp. (1991). However, if a chemical reaction would be required to cause a party's nonhazardous waste to generate a hazardous substance, CERCLA may not apply. United States v. New Castle County (1991).

CERCLA excepts from the definition of "hazardous substance" all "petroleum, including crude oil or any fraction thereof which is not otherwise listed as a hazardous substance." 42 U.S.C.A. § 9601(14). Both EPA and the courts have concluded that the exclusion does not cease to apply merely because some petroleum products (e.g., gasoline) contain substances already listed as hazardous. See Wilshire Westwood Assoc. v. Atlantic Richfield Corp. (1989) (petroleum exclusion applies to releases of leaded gasoline). On the other hand, the exclusion does *not* apply to substances that are merely added to petroleum products. City of New York v. Exxon Corp. (1991) (used waste oil does not qualify for exclusion). The exclusion also does not apply to (1) hazardous substances contained in petroleum waste products, Mid Valley Bank v. North Valley Bank (1991); United States v. Hardage (1990), or (2) sludge consisting of petroleum residue from petroleum storage tanks. United States v. Western Processing Co. (1991).

d. *"Facility"*

CERCLA includes in the term "facility" any "site or area where a hazardous substance has * * * come to be located." 42 U.S.C.A. § 9601(9)(B). The courts have construed this definition broadly, so that it encompasses not only waste disposal facilities, United States v. Conservation Chemical Co. (1985), but also roadsides, United States v. Ward (1985), and real estate subdivisions. United States v. Metate Asbestos Corp. (1984). While the term "facility" includes "buildings," it does not include any "consumer product" in consumer use in a building. Anthony v. Blech (1991) (asbestos); Vernon Village, Inc. v. Gottier (1990) (drinking water). But see CP Holdings v. Goldberg–Zoino & Assoc. (1991) (demolished hotel building containing asbestos satisfies CERCLA's "facility" requirement).

3. CERCLA Response Procedures

a. *Removal or Remedial Action*

When there is a hazardous substance release, or a threat of one, EPA may take "removal" or "remedial" action. The former are short-term, limited responses, and the latter entail more permanent solutions. All remedial action requires cooperative agreements with states, which ultimately take responsibility for cleanup operations. 42 U.S.C.A. § 9604. Prior to undertaking remedial action, EPA must prepare a National Contingency Plan (NCP) for determining priorities among CERCLA sites. These priorities are established in a National Priority List (NPL), which by the 1990s ranked over 1200 sites by hazard. Listing and ranking on the NPL is essentially non-reviewable. Eagle–Picher Industries, Inc. v. United States EPA (1987). NPL listing is a precondition to the use of Superfund money, but not to a state that wishes to find the operator liable for its short-term removal costs. Cadillac Fairview v. Dow Chemical Co. (1988); State of New York v. Shore Realty Corp. (1985).

Once on the NPL, a site is first subject to a Remedial Investigation/Feasibility Study which assesses conditions at the site, and then presents alternatives for cleaning it up. EPA's preferred remedy is contained in a Record of Decision. Pre-implementation judicial review of EPA's proposed remedial actions is foreclosed except for citizen suits. 42 U.S.C.A. § 9613(h).

b. *Who Pays?*

CERCLA presumes that removal and remedial actions will be paid for from two sources. If "potentially responsible parties" (PRPs) can be identified, then they can be held liable for either cleanup costs incurred, or for replenishment of the Superfund. Once liability attaches, PRPs are responsible for all conceivable costs, including health assessments and enforcement expenses. A PRP will often seek to be indemnified by its insurance company. Hecla Mining Co. v. New Hampshire Ins. Co. (1991); State of New York v. AMRO Realty Corp. (1991); Hudson Ins. Co. v. Double D Management (1991) (CERCLA does not preempt state law governing construction and interpretation of insurance contracts alleged to cover CERCLA). If there are no PRPs, then the Superfund may be tapped. As amended by SARA, the Superfund is authorized at $8.5 billion, to be raised by various taxes on businesses, petroleum, and chemical feedstocks. 42 U.S.C.A. § 9611.

c. *How Clean Is Clean?*

The extent of cleanup is determined by several factors. Any remedy should seek to remove contaminants added by humans, not by naturally-occurring sources (e.g., heavy metals concentrations). United States v. Ottati & Goss, Inc. (1990). On-site treatment is preferred over offsite disposal. 42 U.S.C.A. § 9621(b)(1). Most important, cleanup strategies must conform to and attain legally "applicable or relevant and appropriate * * * requirements (ARARs)."   42 U.S.C.A. 9621(d)(2)(A).

ARARs are standards adopted under other federal and state environmental laws. CERCLA does not define which federal or state standards are "legally applicable" or "relevant and appropriate," and EPA has discretion to choose among existing standards. "Applicable" requirements are those cleanup standards and criteria under federal or state law that specifically address a hazardous substance at a CERCLA site. "Relevant and appropriate" requirements address problems or situations sufficiently similar to those encountered at the site that their use is well suited to the particular site. States and the EPA first determine if a given requirement is applicable; if it is not, a determination is made of whether it is nevertheless both relevant and appropriate. Such requirements may be either applicable, or relevant and appropriate, but not both. One difference between these two types of ARARs is that for a standard to be "applicable," the entire statute must be identified as an ARAR. On the other hand, if a standard is "relevant and appropriate," portions of a statute may be identified as an ARAR. Also, on-site actions must comply with the substantive parts of an ARAR, while off-site actions must comply only with legally "applicable" requirements. Off-site actions must also comply fully with both substantive and administrative requirements. EPA may waive a state-derived ARAR, such as when the state has not consistently applied it.

4. Liability of Potentially Responsible Parties (PRPs)

CERCLA provides that PRPs associated with hazardous substance releases may be liable for cleanup and restitution costs. CERCLA liability is joint and several, O'Neil v. Picillo (1989), retroactive, United States v. R.W. Meyer, Inc. (1989); United States v. Northeastern Pharmaceutical & Chemical Co. (1986), and strict. State of New York v. Shore Realty

Corp. (1985). So profound has been the impact of CERCLA liability that, by the 1990s, transactions involving the sale or transfer of property usually include investigation into or disclosure of the possible existence of hazardous waste. See Johnson v. Davis (1985). Insurers often exclude liability coverage for claims against insured persons under CERCLA. USF & G v. George W. Whitesides Co. (1991). CERCLA does not allow suit to recover cleanup costs against the insurer of a PRP. Port Allen Marine Serv., Inc. v. Chotin (1991).

a. Costs and Damages Recoverable

PRPs are liable for releases or threatened releases which cause the incurrence of "response costs." A response cost entails all costs of "removal and remedial action," any other "necessary costs" consistent with the National Contingency Plan, and the costs of any health assessment or effects study. 42 U.S.C.A. 9607(a)(4). See Piccolini v. Simon's Wrecking (1988) (diminution in property value and lost income are not recoverable response costs). CERCLA also provides for punitive damages. United States v. Parsons (1991) (United States may recover up to four times response costs). CERCLA does not provide for recovery of costs of postjudgment studies. Cook v. Rockwell Intern. Corp. (1991).

PRPs may also be held liable for damages to or loss of "natural resources." The term natural resources encompasses land, fish, wildlife, biota, air, and water. 42 U.S.C.A. § 9601(16). CERCLA provides for the designation of federal and state "trustees" who are authorized to assess natural resources damages, and press claims for the recovery of such damages. 42 U.S.C.A. § 9607(f). The measure of natural resources damages may not be based exclusively on lost use values. Colorado v. United States Dept. of Interior (1989); Ohio v. United States Dept. of Interior (1989).

b. CERCLA Plaintiffs

The federal government may sue to compel cleanup, or for remedial costs. 42 U.S.C.A. §§ 9606(a), 9607, 9622. In addition, "any person" may sue to recover response costs "not inconsistent with" the NCP. States, municipalities, interstate agencies, and private citizens are persons who can recover. 42 U.S.C.A. §§ 9601(21), 9607(a)(4)(B). Neither NPL listing nor federal approval is a pre-condition to a CERCLA action. New York v. Shore Realty Corp. (1985) (state plaintiff); Richland–Lexington Airport Dist. v. Atlas Properties, Inc. (1990) (private plaintiff). On the other hand, courts have consistently adhered to the view that injunctions are not available to states or private plaintiffs. Colorado v. Idarado Min. Co. (1990); Cadillac Fairview v. Dow Chemical Co. (1988). In a privately-initiated CERCLA suit, the plaintiffs may allege pendent claims based on state law (e.g., negligence and strict liability for ultrahazardous activity). Bolin v. Cessna Aircraft Co. (1991).

c. CERCLA Defendants

Those who may be liable as PRPs under CERCLA include "owners and operators" of waste sites, persons who accepted hazardous substances for transport or disposal, persons who "arranged with a transporter for transport" of wastes, and any person who "arranged for disposal or treatment" of hazardous substances. 42 U.S.C.A. § 9607(a); Weyerhaeuser Corp. v. Koppers Co. (1991) (lessee liable as operator if release of chemicals occurred when lessee was operating plant). Compare Lincoln v. Republic Ecology Corp. (1991) (city's regulatory conduct with respect to removal of abandoned vehicles did not give rise to "arranger" liability); with Sanford Street Local Dev. v. Textron, Inc. (1991) (seller of foundry liable under CERCLA when it was sold for $25,000, but appraised for $200,000, suggesting that decision to sell was for disposal of hazardous materials).

No liability is intended to be imposed on an "owner and operator of a * * * facility" at which hazardous substances were not disposed, but at which such substances were used as building materials (i.e., asbestos)." Anthony v. Blech (1991). Transporters of hazardous waste can be liable only where they have selected the site for delivery of the hazardous waste. United States v. Western Processing Co. (1991). CERCLA actions against dissolved corporations are permissible. Traverse Bay Area Intermediate School Dist. v. Hitco, Inc. (1991).

If one is an owner or operator, liability may attach even if some other party in the past placed the hazardous wastes there. State of New York v. Shore Realty Corp. (1985). A parent company may be considered an owner, despite the formation of a subsidiary with day-to-day control over operations involving wastes. Mobay Corp. v. Allied–Signal, Inc. (1991). A vendor is not an "owner" if it did not own the property at the time of toxic discharge from the facility. Snediker Developers Ltd. Partnership v. Evans (1991).

States and units of local government also fall within the definition of "owner." Pennsylvania v. Union Gas Co. (1989) (state's Eleventh Amendment immunity abrogated by CERCLA); B.F. Goodrich Co. v. Murtha (1991) (municipalities liable even if they did not physically transport or generate waste). A state agency may qualify as an "operator" if it broke open barrels containing hazardous waste, regardless of whether it was moving them in response to an emergency situation. Stilloe v. Almy Bros., Inc. (1991). EPA's regulatory activities do not render it an owner/operator. United States v. Western Processing Co. (1991); United States v. Azrael (1991).

CERCLA excludes as owners those persons who hold "indicia of ownership primarily to protect [a] security interest." 42 U.S.C.A. § 9601(20)(A). This exception has been interpreted to protect shareholders and secured creditors who do not participate in management decisions. Riverside Market Development Corp. v. International Bldg. Products, Inc. (1991); In re Bergsoe Metal Corp. (1990). Both lenders and secured creditors are liable if they actively participate in decisions involving either waste treatment, United States v. Fleet Factors Corp. (1990), or site development. Tanglewood East Homeowners v. Charles–Thomas, Inc. (1988).

PRPs liable because they "arranged for disposal" include: a state agency involved in sale of site causing groundwater contamination, CPC Intern., Inc. v. Aerojet–General Corp. (1991); shareholders, United States v. Conservation Chemical Co. (1985); plant managers who personally participate in the wrongful conduct, United States v. Northeastern Pharmaceutical & Chemical Co. (1986); and suppliers of products later reformulated by another party into a hazardous substance. United States v. Aceto Agr. Chemicals Corp. (1989). "Arranger" liability can apply to parties who simply sell off their hazardous substances in a transaction that is followed by contamination.

"Arranger" liability is not imposed where a "useful" substance is sold to another party, who then incorporates it into a product, which is later discarded. A state is not liable for "arranging" the disposal of hazardous waste at a landfill when the state never possessed or owned the waste, and where the state's contact with the waste is regulatory. Hassayampa Steering Comm. v. State of Ariz. (1991).

d. Nature of Liability—Opportunity for Contribution

Liability under CERCLA is strict, and joint and several, particularly where the harm is not readily divisible. O'Neil v. Picillo (1989); United States v. Monsanto Co. (1988); United States v. Chem–Dyne Corp. (1983). A company that purchases the assets of a company which is primarily liable under CERCLA may be subject to successor liability. United States v. Mexico Feed and Seed Co. (1991). An owner, employer, or waste generator may be liable for the harmful consequences of disposal practices undertaken by third parties in a contractual relationship with it. Lessors, United States v. Northernaire Plating Co. (1987).

Once liability attaches and response costs are recovered from one or more PRPs, those found liable, and those who have incurred response costs, are permitted the opportunity to seek contribution from other PRPs in a separate action. 42 U.S.C.A. § 9613(f); United States v. R.W. Meyer, Inc. (1991); Quadion Corp. v. Mache (1990). Liability for contribution depends upon the relative fault of the parties. Environmental Transp. Systems, Inc. v. ENSCO, Inc. (1991). Sometimes the contribution claims may be decided at the same time the government's cost recovery is determined. Allied Corp. v. Acme Solvents Reclaiming, Inc. (1988). A party with no legally protected interest in the property affected by CERCLA lacks standing to seek contribution for incurred response costs. Alloy Briquetting Corp. v. Niagara Vest, Inc. (1991) (evicted lessee denied standing). A new owner's failure to comply with the NCP bars any contribution against previous owners. County Line Investment Co. v. Tinney (1991).

e. Defenses

CERCLA offers PRPs limited defenses to liability. One section of the Act provides three affirmative defenses when the release is "caused solely by an act of God, an act of war, or a third party [other than one in a contractual relationship with the defendant]." 42 U.S.C.A. § 9607(b). Reviewing courts have construed these defenses narrowly. See United States v. Stringfellow (1987) (heavy rainfall not "exceptional" natural phenomena to which the act of God defense applies). But see Westwood Pharmaceuticals v. Nat. Fuel Gas Dist. (1991) (sale of site did not establish contractual relationship between parties that would defeat seller's "third party" defense to CERCLA liability, provided acts causing release of hazardous substances did not occur "in connection with" deed between parties).

The 1986 Superfund Amendments and Reauthorization Act (SARA) added two other affirmative defenses. One exempts from the definition of "owner or operator" state or local governments which acquired ownership involuntarily (e.g., through tax delinquencies). 42 U.S.C.A. § 9601(20)(D). The other, commonly known as the "innocent landowner" defense, exempts subsequent site owners from liability if at the time of site acquisition the owner "did not know and had no reason to know" that hazardous substance disposal had taken place there. 42 U.S.C.A. § 9601(35)(a)(i); United States v. Pacific Hide and Fur Depot, Inc. (1989). The innocent landowner defense was added to CERCLA after pre–1986 case law had found site owners strictly liable even though they did not contribute to or in any way cause the release of hazardous substances. State of New York v. Shore Realty Corp. (1985).

If a PRP does not fall within the innocent landowners defense, it appears that an absence of a causal nexus between the defendant and the wastes is not enough to defeat CERCLA liability. In Dedham Water Co. v. Cumberland Farms Dairy, Inc. (1989), a PRP was liable even without proof that a release of hazardous waste from its facility had physically migrated to the plaintiff's property. See also United States v. Hardage (1990) (waste generator liable regardless of whether waste found at site may be traced to wastes deposited by generator); United States v. Monsanto Co. (1988) (liability established by existence of chemicals at the site that were similar to those that the defendant had deposited). Nor it is a sufficient defense that a third party was the "proximate cause," or that acts or omissions were committed by persons over whom the defendant had "no control." United States v. Kramer (1991).

Other defenses normally available to defendants in tort actions, but unavailable to CERCLA defendants, include: (1) generator's lack of knowledge that a transporter would deposit wastes at a particular site, United States v. Hardage (1990); (2) the plaintiff's "unclean hands," General Elec. Co. v. Litton Indus. Automation Systems, Inc. (1990); (3) an "as is" provision in a deed transferring contaminated land, Wiegmann & Rose Intern Corp. v. NL Industries (1990); (4) lack of foreseeability, United States v. Fairchild Ind. (1991); and (5) the doctrine of caveat emptor. Smith Land & Imp. Corp. v. Celotex Corp. (1988).

As a last resort, may a PRP avoid liability by seeking refuge in bankruptcy? A bankruptcy usually permits the debtor to discharge all debts that arose before the bankruptcy. In Ohio v. Kovacs (1985), the Supreme Court held that an injunction ordering a cleanup of hazardous waste site was a "debt," and therefore subject to discharge under the bankruptcy laws. See also In re Chateaugay Corp. (1991) (response costs incurred by the EPA under CERCLA are prepetition "claims" dischargeable in bankruptcy). *Kovacs* was narrowed in the following year, when the Court refused to allow a trustee in bankruptcy to abandon a hazardous waste facility. Midlantic Nat. Bank v. New Jersey (1986). Governmental actions under CERCLA to recover costs expended in response to completed environmental violations are not stayed by the violator filing for bankruptcy. City of New York v. Exxon Corp. (1991).

f. Abandoned or Inactive Mining Activities

Many sites listed on the NPL have draining tunnels or tailings from closed down mining operations. In most of these sites, toxic heavy metals escape from the mine and contaminate surface water supplies. If a past or present owner is identifiable, then CERCLA liability may accrue for creation of hazardous wastes. Idaho v. Hanna Mining Co. (1989). If the owners of these mines have long since disappeared, no PRPs may be available to foot the cleanup cost. The Superfund was created in large part to address the problem of these abandoned mine sites.

Ever since passage of CERCLA's strict liability provisions, neither individual volunteers nor local or state governments have been willing to assist in the cleanup of such mine sites. This reluctance have been due to the potential of future CERCLA liability. In order to correct this inadvertent consequence, the 1986 SARA Amendments added a "Good Samaritan Clause," which exempts from liability all persons who "render care, assistance, or advice in accordance with the NCP, or at the direction of an onscene coordinator appointed under such a plan." 42 U.S.C.A. § 9607(d). In 1991, the Congress provided an even broader exemption from liability when it amended the Surface Mining Control and Reclamation Act to ensure that "no state shall be liable under any provision of Federal law for * * * action taken or omitted in the course of carrying out a state abandoned mine reclamation plan." 30 U.S.C.A. § 1235(1).

5. Settlement Agreements

The 1986 SARA Amendments encourage EPA to negotiate settlement agreements to minimize litigation. When there is a multi-party site, there will rarely be a separate settlement with a single party. In order to facilitate agreements among PRPs, EPA has discretion to introduce a Non–Binding Preliminary Allocation of Responsibility (NBAR), whose purpose is to allocate shares of total response costs among PRPs. 42 U.S.C.A. § 9622(e)(3)(c). Although waste volume is the factor that seems most influential, some courts have questioned whether volume alone should serve as the basis for allocating costs. United States v. Monsanto Co. (1988). The 1986 Amendments also authorize EPA to enter into a "covenant not to sue" when settling with parties, which is subject to a "reopener" for conditions unknown at the time of the settlement. 42 U.S.C.A. §§ 9622(c)(1), (f). Before approving a CERCLA settlement, courts must be convinced it is fair and consistent with the Act's objectives. United States v. Vertac

Chemical Corp. (1991).   A settlement extinguishes a cross claim against a settling party.   Comerica Bank–Detroit v. Allen Ind. (1991).

CERCLA does not ban settlement agreements to indemnify parties for CERCLA liability.   The only restriction the statute places on such agreements is that they may not be used to transfer liability.   In other words, liable parties can contractually shift responsibility for their response costs among each other, but they may not thereby escape their underlying liability to the Government or another third party.   Purolator Products Corp. v. Allied–Signal, Inc. (1991);   42 U.S.C.A. § 9607(e)(1).

CHAPTER FIVE

ENVIRONMENTAL ASSESSMENT
AND NEPA

The National Environmental Policy Act of 1969 (NEPA), 42 U.S.C.A. §§ 4321–4370a, adds a component of environmental awareness to much federal agency decisionmaking. It does so by requiring that agencies *consider* specified environmental factors in their decisionmaking process before they act. As such, NEPA's mandate to agencies is essentially procedural. Vermont Yankee Nuclear Power Corp. v. NRDC (1978). It creates no new substantive rights, and does not require that a federal agency make a particular decision in light of the likely environmental consequences of a proposed action. Strycker's Bay Neighborhood Council, Inc. v. Karlen (1980). As the Supreme Court stated in Robertson v. Methow Valley Citizens Council (1989), NEPA procedures do "not mandate particular results, but simply prescribe the necessary process."

One should not assume that NEPA's emphasis upon procedural consideration of environmental consequences somehow diminishes its stature. To the contrary, NEPA is the key environmental statute to be reckoned with in natural resources law. This is because courts have been quite receptive to lawsuits challenging agency action on NEPA grounds. As a result of the popularity of NEPA in court, federal agencies have become extremely sensitive to NEPA's procedural commands. They have not only sought to articulate the environmental impacts of their decisions before-the-fact, they have also either abandoned projects or mitigated their adverse environmental consequences after performing NEPA studies.

218

NEPA remains a significant limitation on federal agency discretion.

If a federal agency does not comply with NEPA, or if some disgruntled person merely believes that it has not complied with NEPA, then the agency faces the prospect of time-consuming, expensive litigation. NEPA has become, to environmentalists and to those opposed to proposed agency action, the primary statutory basis to force judicial review of federal decisions affecting the environment. NEPA lawsuits are particularly common when the federal agency does not have distinct environmental responsibilities.

NEPA litigation has had a major influence on nearly every subject of energy and natural resources law. Lawsuits under NEPA have affected federal timber sales, Sierra Club v. United States Forest Service (1988); nuclear power regulation, Calvert Cliffs' Coordinating Committee, Inc. v. United States AEC (1971); federal oil and gas leasing, Conner v. Burford (1988); federal hardrock mining law, Sierra Club v. Penfold (1988); federal coal leasing, NRDC v. Hughes (1977); federal geothermal leasing, Sierra Club v. Hathaway (1978); federal livestock grazing regulation, NRDC v. Morton (1974); federal wilderness law, California v. Block (1982); federal wildlife law, Foundation for North American Wild Sheep v. United States Dept. of Agriculture (1982); and federal issuance of dredge-and-fill permits. Sierra Club v. United States Army Corps of Engineers (1985). Such litigation may significantly affect private activities, either by causing substantial delays, or by altering the nature of the underlying regulatory program.

I. ADMINISTRATION AND ENFORCEMENT

A. THE COUNCIL ON ENVIRONMENTAL QUALITY

NEPA creates the Council on Environmental Quality (CEQ), an advisory body charged with providing the President with information about environmental matters. The CEQ also has the duty to provide guidance to federal agencies regarding compliance with NEPA. It promulgated regulations in 1979, amended in 1986, which had the effect of standardizing NEPA compliance practices throughout the federal government. The Supreme Court has held that the CEQ regulations are entitled to "substantial deference." Andrus v. Sierra Club (1979). See also Robertson v. Methow Valley Citizens Council (1989) (deferring to CEQ's revocation of its worst case analysis regulation).

B. PROCEDURAL OBLIGATIONS

Section 102 of NEPA contains the statute's primary "action-forcing" mechanism. Agencies must prepare an environmental impact statement (EIS) to accompany "every recommendation or report on proposals * * * and other major federal actions significantly affecting the quality of the human environment." 42 U.S.C.A. § 4332(2)(c). This deceptively simple language raises three questions that must be addressed by agencies contemplating action: (1) is NEPA applicable?; (2) if so, must the agency prepare a full EIS, or something less?; and (3) if a full EIS is needed, what must it contain? These questions are answered by reference to case law and applicable CEQ regulations.

NEPA applicability is determined according to whether statutory threshold requirements have been satisfied. These requirements track the language of section 102. There must be an agency "proposal" to take "action." This proposed action must be "federal," and qualify as being "major." Its impacts must be sufficiently serious to be considered "significant," and the nature of the impacts must be "environmental." The meaning of these triggering requirements is discussed in the next section below.

If NEPA seems applicable, CEQ regulations next require agencies to undertake an environmental assessment (EA), whose purpose is to determine if preparation of an EIS is necessary. The EA is a kind of mini-EIS, usually no more than 20 pages in length. It contains a discussion of the need for the proposal, the alternatives considered, and the likely environmental impacts. If the EA concludes that no EIS is needed, that determination is formalized in a "finding of no significant impact" (a FONSI). A FONSI can avoid the lengthy EIS process if properly substantiated. However, it is not uncommon for judicial challenges to be mounted if an agency decides to forgo a full EIS. See Kleppe v. Sierra Club (1976).

If the agency determines that an EIS is necessary, then it must follow certain procedures for its preparation. Should a single action require approval of or participation by more than one agency, CEQ regulations permit one "lead agency" to prepare an EIS covering the entire action. National Wildlife Federation v. Benn (1980). The next step is "scoping," intended (1) to foster participation by other agencies and the public, (2) to determine the scope of the EIS, and (3) to identify the significant issues to be discussed in the EIS. NEPA also requires comments prior to any detailed impact statement from "any Federal agency which has jurisdiction by law or special expertise with respect to any environmental impact" involved. Commenting agencies do not hold a veto over the EIS. Sierra Club v. Callaway (1974).

Once the scoping process is completed, the agency prepares the EIS. The final EIS must address the environmental impacts of the action, including direct, indirect, and cumulative impacts. The EIS must discuss unavoidable adverse environmental impacts, and possible means of mitigating adverse impacts. Most importantly, the EIS must list alternatives to the proposed action, including the no action alternative.

C. JUDICIAL REVIEW AND INTERVENTION

A different standard of judicial review is used when the case involves whether an EIS is needed, as contrasted with whether the EIS is adequate. An agency may decide to forego an EIS either if it concludes without an EA that certain threshold requirements are missing (e.g., the action is not "major" or "federal"), or if an EA results in a finding that there is no federal action which will have a significant effect upon the environment. In the case of a FONSI, the lower federal courts are divided over the appropriate standard of review. Some have applied the highly deferential "arbitrary and capricious" standard. Wisconsin v. Weinberger (1984); Cabinet Mountains Wilderness v. Peterson (1982). Others have used the more rigorous "reasonableness" standard of review. Enos v. Marsh (1985); Sierra Club v. Froehlke (1987); National Wildlife Federation v. Marsh (1983).

The Supreme Court has been particularly unhelpful in resolving the split in the circuits. In 1989 it rejected the reasonableness standard in favor of the arbitrary and capricious standard in the narrow context of determining whether a supplemental EIS was required. Marsh v. Oregon Natural Resources Council (1989). Although the Court in *Marsh* did not seek to address the broader question, in a footnote it did suggest that "the difference between the [two standards] is not of great pragmatic consequence." See also Baltimore Gas & Electric Co. v. NRDC (1983).

When a challenge is to the adequacy of an EIS, the courts are more uniformly deferential. See National Trust for Historic Preservation v. Dole (1987) (arbitrary and capricious standard applies); Warm Springs Dam Task Force v. Gribble (1977) (test is whether there has been a good faith attempt to discuss foreseeable environmental consequences). Such judicial deference is justified because the adequacy of an EIS typically involves questions of fact, not law. City of Tenakee Springs v. Clough (1990).

Although judicial review is available, NEPA makes no reference to judicial enforcement. It was the decision in Calvert Cliffs' Coordinating Committee v. United States

A.E.C. (1971) that established the principle that agency duties under NEPA are judicially enforceable. Judicial intervention usually takes the form of a court-ordered injunction halting the agency proposal pending NEPA compliance. Since the Supreme Court's holding in Amoco Production Co. v. Village of Gambell (1987), courts have had to "balance the equities" before enjoining agency action inconsistent with NEPA. Northern Cheyenne Tribe v. Hodel (1988).

Often, agencies are challenged under NEPA by citizen organizations. To establish standing for such challenges, plaintiff groups must show not only direct causal connection between their asserted injury and the agency action, but also that they are within the zone of interests protected by NEPA. NRDC v. Lujan (1991). If an environmental organization claims NEPA injury because its mission is to provide information to the public about environmental matters, the organization lacks standing to challenge the absence of an EIS, without a showing that the agency action is the source of the organization's informational injury. Foundation on Economic Trends v. Lyng (1991).

II. THRESHOLD REQUIREMENTS
A. IS THERE A "PROPOSAL" TO UNDERTAKE A "MAJOR FEDERAL ACTION"?

NEPA is not triggered if there is not a "proposal" for some kind of "major federal action." The Supreme Court early on warned that an agency is under no EIS obligation until it officially proposes a particular course of action. Kleppe v. Sierra Club (1976); Aberdeen & Rockfish Railroad Co. v. SCRAP (1975). There is a proposal if (1) the agency itself proposes to take action, (2) the agency permits action by other parties which may affect the environment, or (3) the agency approves a lease, grants licenses or permits, or approves and funds activities that may affect the environment. Scientists' Institution for Public Information, Inc. v. AEC (1973).

There is no proposal if a request has been made for agency action, but the agency has not yet acted. B.R.S. Land Investors v. United States (1979). Nor is the mere contemplation of certain action a proposal, such as a preliminary study document or a plan that may later be used for making a specific proposal. Fritiofson v. Alexander (1985); Sabine River Authority v. United States Dept. of Interior (1990). Where a proposed federal action would not change the status quo, such as the operation of a dam adjusting the release of water in amounts similar to previous years, there is not an action triggering the need for an EIS. Upper Snake River v. Hodel (1990). However, if an ongoing project undergoes changes which constitute "expansion or revision of ongoing programs," these changes may themselves amount to major federal actions necessitating an EIS. Andrus v. Sierra Club (1979).

Apart from the absence of a proposal or action, there are two other conditions which excuse the need for an EIS. First, if an agency does not have an affirmative statutory duty to act, the failure to act does not trigger NEPA. Defenders of Wildlife v. Andrus (1980), State of Alaska v. Andrus (1979). However, if an agency's duty to avoid environmental harm is mandatory, then agency inaction constitutes action for purposes of NEPA. Sierra Club v. Hodel (1988); Bunch v. Hodel (1986). Second, if an agency mitigates the adverse effects of an action, an EIS may be avoided. Roanoke River Basin Ass'n v. Hudson (1991); Friends of the Earth v. Hintz (1986); Cabinet Mountains Wilderness v. Peterson (1982).

B. IS THE FEDERAL ACTION "MAJOR"?

CEQ regulations state that the word "major" only "reinforces, but does not have meaning independent of significant[ly affecting the quality of the human environment]." As a result, any action not likely to have a significant environmental impact will likely not be deemed a major federal action. See Cronin v. United States Dept. of Agriculture (1990) (Forest Service sale of 26 acres of trees not a "major" act because it will not have a "significant" impact on the environment).

C. IS THE ACTION "FEDERAL"?

This requirement raises the issue of the nature and degree of federal participation necessary to invoke NEPA. Federal action within the meaning of NEPA includes not only action by the agency itself, but also action permitted or approved by the agency. This permission can take the form of a dredge and fill permit issued to private parties under section 404 of the Clean Water Act, Riverside Irr. Dist. v. Andrews (1985), a federal decision to hold a timber sale, National Wildlife Federation v. United States Forest Service (1984), or a letter of concurrence from one federal agency to another. Progressive Animal Welfare Soc. v. Department of Navy (1989).

CEQ regulations note that a federal action encompasses "actions which are potentially subject to Federal control and responsibility." The need for some kind of federal control has been the basis for rejecting NEPA applicability when the federal nexus is primarily financial. See Village of Los Ranchos de Albuquerque v. Barnhart (1990) (eligibility of state agency constructing highway for federal funds insufficient to trigger NEPA); Atlanta Coalition on Transp. Crisis, Inc. v. Atlanta Regional Com'n (1979) (no EIS required when federal funds used to prepare regional transportation plan); Carolina Action v. Simon (1975) (no EIS required for general revenue sharing).

For private projects requiring federal approval, the federal link must be more than a simple "but-for" relationship. Thus, NEPA does not apply to an entire privately constructed transmission line, merely because the line could not be built but for a river crossing permit from the Army Corps of

Engineers. Winnebago Tribe v. Ray (1980). Nor is an EIS required for a plan by a bank to demolish an historic structure entered on the National Register of Historical Places, when the federal agency which had authority over the bank did not have control over the demolition decision. Edwards v. First Bank of Dundee (1976). See also Central Arizona Irr. and Drainage Dist. v. Lujan (1991) (ground water recharge by subcontractors using Central Arizona Project water not a major "federal" action); Friends of Yosemite v. Frizzell, (1976) (no EIS required for decision by private concessioner to conduct an advertising campaign meant to increase tourist traffic to Yosemite National Park).

Government decisions at a state or local level may trigger NEPA if the decision affects federal interests. In Sierra Club v. Hodel (1988), a county's road construction project on its right-of-way across public lands adjacent to wilderness study areas was sufficiently federal to require an EIS. However, if the federal-state nexus is financial, courts are more leery of NEPA's applicability. Many federal statutes condition receipt of federal funds on state adoption of federal standards. An EIS may be required for state permits issued pursuant to such a state program funded in part with federal money. See Save Our Dunes v. Pegues (1985).

D. IS THE ACTION AFFECTING THE "ENVIRONMENT"?

An EIS is necessary only for federal actions that have an impact on the environment. This "environment" obviously encompasses the natural and physical environment. It may also include aesthetic and socio-economic environments. Hanly v. Mitchell (1972) [*Hanly I*]. But see Lockhart v. Kenops (1991) (Forest Service not required to consider the sociological and community effects of a proposed land exchange).

The meaning of "environmental impact" was considered by the Supreme Court in Metropolitan Edison Co. v. People

Against Nuclear Energy (1983). The question before the Court was whether the risk of psychological stress caused by reopening the Three Mile Island nuclear plant would have such a significant health effect on the residents of the surrounding communities as to warrant an EIS. While the Court conceded that human health effects, including psychological health, are cognizable under NEPA, such effects are deemed "environmental" only if they have a "reasonable close causal relation" to a change in the physical environment. The causal relationship was missing because the risk of psychological health damage was remote and "unrealized," unlike harm from some physical event or change in the physical environment.

E. WHEN IS THE ENVIRONMENTAL IMPACT "SIGNIFICANT"?

A federal action will not qualify under NEPA if it does not significantly affect the environment. The "significance" requirement is frequently contested, but difficult to articulate as a predictable standard. One leading case has devised a two-part test involving the degree of change from the status quo, and the severity of the impact. Hanly v. Kleindienst (1972) [*Hanly II*]; United States v. 27.09 Acres of Land (1991) (a finding of no significant impact was inappropriate where agency failed to consider cumulative impacts, and where the finding was premised on inclusion of extensive mitigation). In the Ninth Circuit, the standard is not whether significant effects will in fact occur, but whether the proposed project "*may* significantly degrade some human environmental factor." Sierra Club v. United States Forest Service (1988). CEQ regulations also require consideration of "context," defined as short-term and long-term effects on subjects impacted, and "intensity," defined as the absolute magnitude of the impact. See Audubon Society of Central Arkansas v. Dailey (1991). A condemnation action is a decision to put land to a certain public use which may have a significant effect on the environment.   United States v. 0.95 Acres of Land (1991).

III. SCOPE

The question of scope usually arises after the agency decides that an EIS is necessary.   Scope entails placing some borders on the federal action whose environmental consequences are the subject of the EIS.   Difficulties in defining scope emerge in one of three contexts—(1) when there is uncertainty over whether a "proposal" to take action exists at all; (2) when the action consists of both federal and nonfederal decisions; and (3) when an action is part of a larger program or series of actions.

A. THE NEED FOR A PROPOSAL

In Aberdeen & Rockfish Railroad Co. v. Students Challenging Regulatory Agency Procedures (1975) [*SCRAP II*], the Supreme Court noted that "the time at which the agency must prepare the [EIS] is the time at which it makes a recommendation on a proposal for federal action."   The scope of the EIS is defined by the scope of the proposal, and the question of scope is not ripe until there is a proposal.

The Court reiterated this requirement the next year in Kleppe v. Sierra Club (1976).   In rejecting the argument that an EIS was needed for individual coal leasing proposals in an area labeled as the "Northern Great Plains Region," the Court noted that there was no federal proposal for regional coal leasing; there were only proposals for actions of local or national scope.   An EIS was therefore needed for local leasing and for the national coal-leasing program, but not for the region.

The Court's fixation on a "proposal" which can serve as the basis for determining scope was evidenced again in Weinberger v. Catholic Action of Hawaii (1981).   The Court decided that because any proposal to establish storage facilities for nuclear weapons would be classified for security reasons, there was in effect no proposal for which an EIS was required.

The *SCRAP II–Kleppe–Weinberger* reasoning suggests that agencies may be able to avoid EIS preparation (and consideration of scope) until there is an agency decision to formalize plans in the form of a concrete proposal. See Texas Committee on Natural Resources v. Bergland (1978) (sustaining agency decision not to file EIS on a timber management program). Mere contemplation of an action is not a proposal for purposes of NEPA, because NEPA does not expect agencies to delve into the possible effects of hypothetical projects. National Wildlife Federation v. FERC (1990).

B. ACTIONS ENTAILING FEDERAL AND NON–FEDERAL PARTICIPATION

Sometimes a proposal by a private entity or state agency needs some kind of federal permission before it can proceed. This permission usually takes the form of a federal license or permit, for which there must be an EIS. The issue for the agency preparing the EIS is whether its scope should be limited to the permission granted, or broad enough to cover the overall non-federal project. Most courts have adopted a narrow view of NEPA's intended coverage, holding that the EIS need not consider the environmental consequences of the larger action. Save the Bay, Inc. v. United States Corps of Engineers (1980); Winnebago Tribe v. Ray (1980).

C. PARTICULAR ACTIONS AS PART OF A BROADER PROGRAM

A federal proposal may have various parts, each of which may impact the environment. For example, a federal agency may authorize oil and gas leasing throughout public lands in the United States. NEPA does not expressly state whether the leasing agency must prepare an EIS on each lease separately, whether one EIS for the national leasing program will suffice, or whether EISs must be prepared for each lease issued *and* for the national leasing program. Both case law and the CEQ regulations have sought to provide guidance to agencies contemplating specific, focused actions in the context of a larger federal program.

1. Programmatic EISs

One way to avoid preparation of EISs for every site-specific action is to require one "programmatic" impact statement covering all interrelated projects. See Scientists' Institute for Public Information v. AEC (1973) (EIS needed for the entire breeder reactor program). A programmatic impact statement is not warranted when a program's component parts are too discrete or diversified to constitute sufficiently "connected" actions under CEQ regulations. Foundation on Economic Trends v. Lyng (1987).

The courts are split on whether preparation of a programmatic impact statement eliminates the need to prepare an EIS on a specific action included within the program. The Tenth and Seventh Circuits have concluded as a general rule that once an EIS has been issued for a general program, the program may be carried out without the agency having to issue a new statement for every stage of the program. Otherwise the projects within the program could never be completed. "It would be an application of the law of Zeno's Paradox (how can one cross a finite interval in a finite amount of time, when any interval can be divided into an infinite number of segments, each of which must be crossed in turn in order to traverse the entire interval?)." Cronin v. United States Dept. of Agriculture (1990); EDF v. Andrus (1980).

On the other hand, the Ninth Circuit has in several cases found programmatic impact statements to be not sufficiently detailed to cover the environmental aspects of the site-specific actions. In these cases, individual EISs have been needed. Save the Yaak Committee v. Block (1988); California v. Block (1982).

2. CEQ Regulations

The CEQ regulations approach the problem of scope by providing that an EIS should consider all closely related "connected actions," actions which may have a "cumulative effect" with the proposed action, and all "interdependent parts of a larger action," which depend on the larger action for their justification. This scheme is consistent with the admonition articulated in Kleppe v. Sierra Club, that agencies should consider other "reasonably foreseeable" actions, even in the absence of proposals for such actions. See also Save the Yaak Committee v. Block (1988).

Related, connected actions are to be considered in a single EIS, because otherwise agencies might divide one project into multiple individual actions, each of which individually has an insignificant environmental impact, but which collectively have a substantial impact. National Wildlife Federation v. FERC (1990); NRDC v. Hodel (1988). For example, in Thomas v. Peterson (1985), the Forest Service concluded that an EIS was necessary neither for a road in a national forest, nor for proposed timber sales that would use the new road. The *Peterson* court rejected this approach and found that since the road and timber sales were interconnected, a single EIS was required.

3. Segmentation, Independent Utility, and Tiering

Ascertaining the proper scope of an EIS becomes particularly difficult when an agency proposes to undertake a major project in stages. Consider a federal decision to sell oil and gas leases in environmentally sensitive areas. The initial decision to lease is arguably an action affecting the environment. But so too is the subsequent issuance of each individual lease, and the lessee's eventual (but no means certain) decision to drill an oil and gas well. Must the agency prepare an EIS at each of these stages?

Or consider a federal decision to build a road linking an interstate highway to a ski resort located on Forest Service lands. The decision to build the road is an expansion of the interstate highway system, having a national impact. The subsequent road construction will have some environmental impact on the surrounding terrain. The eventual completed road will impact the ski area and surrounding Forest Service lands. Should one EIS consider national impacts (on the interstate highway system), local impacts (on the transportation corridor), and secondary impacts (on the ski resort)? Or should the applicable agency prepare several EISs for each impact?

In both examples, the agency is left with a Hobson's choice. If the overall project is broken down into its component parts, the resulting "piecemealing" might allow the agency to avoid discussion of the cumulative impacts of the entire project. Friends of the Earth v. Armstrong (1973). On the other hand, broadening the scope of the impact statement to include all related and subsequent actions may force the agency to consider the speculative "hypothetical" impacts of actions only being contemplated. County of Suffolk v. Secretary of Interior (1977). Case law and CEQ regulations provide only rough guidance to agencies struggling with this choice.

"Segmentation" of a project into its component parts for NEPA purposes is permitted if each segment is characterized as having "independent utility." Sierra Club v. Stamm (1974); Hudson River Sloop Clearwater, Inc. v. Department of Navy (1988). Segmentation issues are especially common with highway construction proposals. Coalition on Sensible Transp., Inc. v. Dole (1987). Alternatively, an agency wishing to avoid duplicative EISs for all the parts of a larger program may wish to engage in a CEQ-approved process called "tiering." This option consists of a programmatic impact statement, as well as subsequent impact statements on specific actions that "tier to" (refer back to) applicable discussion contained in the earlier program impact statement. See Park County Resources Council, Inc. v. United States Dept. of Agriculture (1987).

IV. TIMING

Both the Supreme Court and the CEQ regulations require an EIS at the time at which there is a "proposal" for federal action. The *SCRAP II* decision states that an EIS is not due before an agency "has a goal and is actively preparing to make a decision on one or more means of accomplishing that goal, and the effects can be meaningfully evaluated." CEQ regulations urge agencies to prepare the EIS "early enough so that it can serve practically as an important contribution to the decisionmaking process," rather than merely justifying "decisions already made."

These generalities regarding the timing of an EIS have proven to be maddeningly difficult to apply. The most troublesome NEPA issue facing agencies and the courts occurs when some federal program authorizes subsequent actions, whose environmental consequences are largely unknown at the time of the decision to proceed with the program. In such a case, the question is whether the agency should at the program stage try to evaluate the environmental impacts of the specific actions that may or may not take place, or whether the agency should wait for these subsequent actions to occur before preparing EISs considering their impacts.

For example, should an EIS be prepared for the programmatic decision to sell offshore or onshore oil and gas leases? Or should EIS preparation be delayed until a lease has been issued, or until a lessee decides to drill at a specific site?

Federal agencies initially assumed either that an EIS was not necessary at the lease sale stage, or that any EIS at that early point did not need to consider the environmental effects of post-lease sale drilling. This assumption was founded on the reality of oil and gas leasing: (1) at the lease sale stage, it is exceedingly difficult to predict where discoveries might occur; (2) very few lessees ever drill exploratory wells; (3) even fewer who do ever discover oil and gas of sufficient quantity to justify full field development; and (4) environmental mitigation can occur at the lease issuance stage by including in the lease a variety of conditions or stipulations aimed at reducing the negative impacts of subsequent drilling and development activities.

For offshore oil and gas leasing, the courts have consistently interpreted the Outer Continental Shelf Lands Act, 43 U.S.C.A. §§ 1801–1866, as exempting initial lease sales from detailed EIS requirements. This is in part because, at lease sale, there is no right granted the lessee to drill, and because the lessee's property interest may be heavily conditioned to incorporate environmental mitigation measures. Secretary of Interior v. California (1984). An EIS at the lease sale stage is also thought premature, since environmental impacts may not be evaluated until drilling is commenced and oil is found. Village of False Pass v. Clark (1984); North Slope Borough v. Andrus (1980); Suffolk County v. Secretary of Interior (1977).

The onshore leasing cases arise under the Mineral Leasing Act of 1920 (MLA), 30 U.S.C.A. §§ 181–287. This statute differs from the Outer Continental Shelf Lands Act in one critical way—one obtaining an onshore lease under the MLA cannot be denied the permit to drill. At best, the leasing agency (usually the Department of Interior) can only impose reasonable conditions designed to mitigate the environmental impacts of the drilling operations.

Despite the agency's legal inability to prevent post-lease drilling, neither the BLM nor the Forest Service believed that an EIS was necessary at the lease sale stage for onshore leases. The reasoning of these two leasing agencies was similar to that used for offshore leasing: (1) few onshore leases were ever developed; (2) environmental impacts could not be evaluated at lease sale, and instead required a site-specific drilling plan (or an actual discovery) to assess the consequences of drilling; (3) an EIS was therefore timely at the drilling permit stage, not the lease sale stage; and (4) lease conditions and stipulations, particularly the "no-surface occupancy" (NSO) stipulation, offered adequate environmental protection when leases were issued.

Both the District of Columbia and Ninth Circuits have rejected these arguments. See Sierra Club v. Peterson (1983); Conner v. Burford (1988); Bob Marshall Alliance v. Hodel (1988). According to these circuits, an EIS is needed at the lease sale stage, not just the drilling permit stage, because under the MLA the leasing agency does not have the absolute power to halt operations after lease issuance. The only exception to this EIS requirement at lease sale is when a lease is issued with an NSO stipulation.

The Tenth Circuit seems to exempt federal agencies from EIS preparation at the lease sale stage. Park County Resource Council, Inc. v. United States Dept. of Agriculture (1987). The *Park County* court was satisfied with a less comprehensive EA at the time of lease sale. The point of "irreversible and irretrievable commitment of resources" triggering an EIS was at the drilling permit stage, because it was only then that an agency could more accurately forecast the environmental impacts of drilling.

V. ADEQUACY OF THE IMPACT STATEMENT

The EIS must be a "detailed" statement that addresses (1) the environmental impacts of the proposed action, (2) unavoidable adverse environmental affects, (3) secondary and cumulative environmental impacts, (4) alternatives to the action, and (5) any mitigation measures designed to minimize or eliminate negative consequences of the action. An EIS may be hundreds or thousands of pages long, and be set out in many volumes. Its preparation may cost hundreds of thousands of dollars, and require years to complete.

One wishing to challenge the adequacy of an EIS may do so on several grounds. Among the most common are: (1) failure to include sufficient information on the environmental impact of alternatives; (2) inadequate, cursory treatment of the likely impacts of the proposed action; (3) overuse of sweeping general conclusions unsupported by documented facts; and (4) failure to consider mitigation as a way of reducing the severity of adverse impacts.

When considering the sufficiency of an EIS, most courts use a "rule of reason" standard of review. Pursuant to this standard, an EIS will be upheld as adequate if it has been "compiled in good faith and sets forth sufficient information to enable the decision-maker to consider fully the environmental factors involved and * * * to make a reasoned choice between alternatives." Town of Huntington v. Marsh (1988); Oregon Environmental Council v. Kunzman (1987).

The burden of proof is on the challenger to show that the EIS is inadequate. Sierra Club v. Morton (1975). Plaintiffs may introduce extra-record evidence to supplement an agency's administrative record only when this record is incomplete. Citizens to Preserve Overton Park, Inc. v. Volpe (1971); Van Abbema v. Fornell (1986).

A. ALTERNATIVES AND MITIGATION

NEPA requires that the EIS discuss "alternatives to the proposed action." 42 U.S.C.A. § 4332(2)(C)(iii), 2(E). The CEQ regulations call for a discussion of two alternatives—other reasonable courses of action for the agency to take, and the no action alternative. NEPA also requires that the EIS discuss the extent to which adverse effects can be avoided through mitigation. It is, however, the alternatives requirement that is the heart of the impact statement process.

In theory, there is an unlimited range of alternatives that must be included in an EIS. To provide some check on the list of alternatives that must be discussed, most courts use a "rule of reason." Northwest Coalition for Alternatives to Pesticides v. Lyng (1988). Using the rule of reason, courts have required agencies to discuss all reasonable alternatives within the jurisdiction of any part of the federal government, as well as the environmental effects of all reasonable alternatives. Citizens Against Burlington v. Busey (1991); NRDC v. Morton (1972). On the other hand, the Supreme Court has underscored the need for reason in considering alternatives: "Common sense teaches us that the 'detailed statement of alternatives' cannot be found wanting simply because the agency failed to include every alternative device and thought conceivable by the mind of man." Vermont Yankee Nuclear Power Corp. v. NRDC (1978). See also Norfolk & Walpole v. United States Army Corps of Engineers (1991) (an alternatives analysis for a proposed landfill may be limited to effects on the surface aquatic ecosystem, and not to groundwater effects); City of New York v. United States Dept. of Transp. (1983) (range of relevant alternatives limited to the agency's statutory objectives).

Failure to discuss the "no action" alternative is usually fatal. Without consideration of this alternative, the very reason for the proposed action is called into question. Town of Norfolk v. United States EPA (1991); City of Tenakee Springs v. Clough (1990); Van Abbema v. Fornell (1986). *But see* NRDC v. Hodel (1985) (EIS adequate despite failure of the BLM to consider the "no grazing" alternative for a grazing district).

Even if an agency considers alternatives, the EIS may fail if the range of alternatives is improperly limited. In California v. Block (1982), the Forest Service never seriously considered an alternative that allocated more than a third of 62 million acres of roadless national forest land to wilderness. Since the alternative of "more than one third" was never comprehensively addressed in the EIS, it was deemed inadequate.

In addition to alternatives, both NEPA and the CEQ regulations require a discussion of steps that can be taken to mitigate adverse environmental consequences. While mitigation must be discussed, the agency need not include in every EIS a fully developed mitigation plan. Robertson v. Methow Valley Citizens Council (1989).

B. IMPACT ANALYSIS

Agencies preparing an EIS are faced with several questions when seeking to comply with NEPA's mandate that they discuss "the environmental impact of the proposal action." Among the most important are: (1) Must impacts be analyzed if there is uncertainty or lack of information about their nature or likelihood? (2) What kinds of impacts need to be discussed? (3) When is impact analysis (and the need for an EIS) unnecessary? (4) How should the agency proceed when new information about impacts becomes available after completion of an EIS?

1. Uncertainty and Lack of Information

As a general rule, purely speculative impacts need not be discussed in the EIS. Carolina Environmental Study Group v. United States (1975) (possibility of a nuclear reactor accident so remote that this impact may be excluded). If an agency chooses to speculate on impacts, this exercise is acceptable so long as the agency identifies all the gaps in its information. North Slope Borough v. Andrus (1980).

In the early 1980s, a CEQ regulation required that if an agency lacked information about the probability of some environmental harm, it must predict the consequences of a "worst case" scenario. Save Our Ecosystems v. Clark (1984). In 1986, the CEQ backed away from this strict worst case analysis requirement in an amended regulation giving agencies the less onerous duty "to describe the consequences of a remote, but potentially severe impact, [if grounded] in evaluation of scientific opinion." In 1989, the Supreme Court rejected the argument that the earlier, more stringent worst case analysis rule was a requirement that flowed directly from NEPA, not from CEQ regulations. Robertson v. Methow Valley Citizens Council (1989).

Where there is incomplete or unavailable information concerning reasonably foreseeable "significant effects" of a proposal, or an alternative to a proposal, the agency must disclose this lack of information. When an agency concludes, despite uncertainties and lack of information, that no adverse environmental impacts will occur, this conclusion will be deferentially reviewed under the "arbitrary and capricious" standard of judicial review. Baltimore Gas & Electric Co. v. NRDC (1983) (determination by the Nuclear Regulatory Commission that permanent storage of nuclear wastes would have no significant environmental effects can be based upon an uncertain "zero-release" assumption).

2. Kinds of Impacts

A discussion of impacts in an EIS must include direct, indirect, and cumulative impacts. A "direct" impact on the environment is one that inevitably follows from the proposed action. For example, failure of the Forest Service to discuss the impact of a timber sale on a biological corridor within the sale area is grounds for invalidating the adequacy of the EIS, because the road building and logging accompanying the sale will have a direct impact on the avenues of travel for wildlife found in biological corridors. Marble Mountain Audubon Society v. Rice (1990). However, full disclosure of such direct impacts, even adverse impacts, largely immunizes the agency from a judicial ruling that the EIS is inadequate. National Wildlife Federation v. Adams (1980).

"Indirect" impacts encompass secondary consequences of a proposal action. Timber sales cause trees to be cut, which increases runoff from precipitation, which increases sedimentation in downslope streams, which may violate water quality standards. Therefore, failure to discuss possible violation of water quality standards stemming indirectly from timber sales is inconsistent with NEPA requirements. Sierra Club v. United States Forest Service (1988).

Not all indirect impacts need to be considered in an EIS. The nexus between the proposed project and the impact cannot be too attenuated. See No GWEN Alliance v. Aldridge (1988) (no linkage between construction of radio towers as part of system for sending war messages and nuclear war). Psychological and socio-economic impacts may also be too indirect to warrant inclusion in an EIS. See Metropolitan Edison Co. v. People Against Nuclear Energy (1983); Olmsted Citizens for a Better Community v. United States (1986).

CEQ regulations require consideration of "cumulative impacts," defined as "the impact on the environment which results from the incremental impact of the action when added to other past, present, and reasonably foreseeable future actions." Several courts have broadly construed this requirement to demand discussion in the EIS of all other developments possible in the area impacted by the proposal, even though they themselves may not be proposals needing an impact statement. NRDC v. Hodel (1988); Town of Huntington v. Marsh (1988); Fritiofson v. Alexander (1985).

3. Impact Analysis Not Necessary

Neither an impact statement nor an impact analysis is necessary if agency mitigation measures have eliminated any adverse environmental effects of the agency action. Cabinet Mountains Wilderness v. Peterson (1982) (threshold NEPA requirement of "significant effects" not met if mitigation "compensates completely" for adverse impacts). It is not enough for an agency to merely conclude that mitigation will make insignificant the environmental impact; the agency must explain *how* measures will mitigate the project's impact. LaFlamme v. FERC (1988).

An EIS also might not be necessary when a project is consistent with local land use regulations. Isle of Hope Historical Ass'n v. United States Army Corps of Engineers (1981); Maryland–National Capital Parks & Planning Com'n v. United States Postal Service (1973).

4. New Information and Supplemental EISs

Although the subject of post-decision supplemental EISs is not expressly addressed in NEPA, CEQ regulations impose a duty on federal agencies to prepare supplements if there "are significant new circumstances or information relevant to environmental concerns and bearing on the proposed action or its impacts." Cases interpreting this requirement make clear that an agency need not supplement an EIS every time new information comes to light after the EIS is finalized. Headwaters, Inc. v. BLM (1991) (designation of spotted owl as endangered species does not warrant a supplemental EIS for a timber sales program); Havasupai Tribe v. Robertson (1991); Friends of the River v. FERC (1983). Other cases have established the principle that where there is a regional EIS, its site-specific effects do not constitute "significant new circumstances" requiring a supplemental EIS. Headwaters, Inc. v. BLM, Medford Dist. (1990); Oregon Natural Resources Council v. Lyng (1989). But see NRDC v. Lujan (1991) (Department of Interior's updated report to Congress, reflecting increased estimate of recoverable oil from Alaska wildlife refuge, requires supplemental EIS).

From the perspective of federal agencies, the decision whether to prepare a supplemental EIS is similar to the decision whether to prepare an EIS in the first instance—

they must take a "hard look" at the environmental effects of their planned action, even after a proposal has received initial approval. If a court is asked to review an agency's decision not to prepare a supplemental EIS, the standard is that the decision not to supplement will be set aside only if it is "arbitrary and capricious." Marsh v. Oregon Natural Resources Council (1989).

If an agency prepares a supplemental EIS, its adequacy may be challenged on the same grounds as the adequacy of the original EIS. Compare Town of Norfolk v. United States EPA (1991) (supplemental EIS for sewage landfill adequate), with City of Tenakee Springs v. Clough (1990) (supplemental EIS inadequate for failure to include cumulative impact analysis of proposed timber harvesting).

VI. NEPA IN SPECIAL CONTEXTS

A. RELATIONSHIP BETWEEN NEPA AND OTHER FEDERAL STATUTES

The language of NEPA provides that nothing in it changes the "specific statutory obligations" of federal agencies to comply with other laws protecting the environment, and that the policies of NEPA are "supplementary" to the existing statutory authorizations of federal agencies. 42 U.S.C.A. §§ 4334, 4335. The Supreme Court has construed these provisions to exempt federal agencies from NEPA when there is a direct statutory conflict with their enabling legislation. Flint Ridge Development Co. v. Scenic Rivers Assoc. (1976) (NEPA not applicable to Department of Housing and Urban Development when that agency's 30–day disclosure statement deadline for real estate developers was too short to permit preparation of an EIS).

When there is no direct conflict, courts will exempt agencies from NEPA if agency action pursuant to an environmental statute is the "functional equivalent" of NEPA review. Portland Cement Ass'n v. Ruckelshaus (1973). The functional equivalency test has particular applicability to the EPA. Most of EPA's regulatory activities under the federal Clean Air Act, Clean Water Act, and Resource Conservation and Recovery Act have been deemed so similar to NEPA that separate EIS review is unnecessary. Even if the functional equivalence exemption is not applicable, courts may excuse agencies from EIS preparation if the agency's statutory duties further NEPA's purposes. Pacific Legal Foundation v. Andrus (1981) (an EIS need not be filed on the listing of an endangered species because listing is consistent with NEPA's goals).

A related but largely unresolved issue is whether an agency which lacks statutory authority to impose conditions on its approvals, can nonetheless impose conditions based on NEPA. For example, if the EPA has no independent statutory authority to require a locality to adopt a comprehensive land use plan, it may wish to approve a grant of federal dollars for a sewage treatment facility on the condition, based upon NEPA, that such a plan be completed. See generally Oregon Natural Resources Council v. Marsh (1987).

B. PROPOSALS FOR LEGISLATION

NEPA provides that any "proposal for legislation" must be accompanied by an EIS. 42 U.S.C.A. § 4332(2)(C). When agencies request legislation to initiate, or halt, a substantive program, NEPA therefore demands that an EIS be prepared on the program. The EIS requirement may be triggered even if the agency is submitting to Congress a statutorily-mandated report. Trustees for Alaska v. Hodel (1986) (EIS needed for report on the mineral reserves in an Alaskan wildlife refuge). One important exception to the "proposal for legislation" requirement was articulated in Andrus v. Sierra Club (1979), holding that appropriations requests are not covered by NEPA. As a result of *Andrus,* no EIS is needed for appropriations bills, even those evidencing a funding reduction in programs designed to protect the environment.

C. EXTRATERRITORIAL RELEVANCE OF NEPA

Congress left open the question of whether NEPA applies to the environmental impacts of federal action abroad. Prior to 1979, case law suggested, but did not hold, that NEPA requirements could be triggered by federal actions taking place outside the borders of the United States. NORML v. United States (1978) (United States support of the Mexican herbicide spraying program designed to eradicate marijuana); Sierra Club v. Adams (1978) (Federal Highway Administration construction of Darien Gap Highway through Panama).

In 1979, President Carter signed Executive Order 12,114, which requires (1) that federal decisionmakers consider the environmental impacts of their actions having effects outside the geographical boundaries of the United States, and (2) that an EIS be prepared for "major Federal actions significantly affecting the environment of the global commons outside the jurisdiction of any nation (e.g., the oceans on Antarctica)." This executive charge to federal agencies has been judicially limited to exempt from the EIS requirement those actions whose environmental impacts fall exclusively within a foreign jurisdiction, particularly a foreign sovereign whose own regulations might conflict with United States regulatory laws. NRDC v. NRC (1981); Greenpeace USA v. Stone (1990).

PART III

RESOURCE PRODUCTION AND USE

Law as an Incentive to Promote Private Development of Energy and Natural Resources

The chapters in Part III focus on particular energy and natural resources that are used or developed by individuals and organizations as raw materials for some economic enterprise. For three such resources, minerals, timber, and water, law and government provide a basis for private ownership, and set parameters for acceptable use. The former function—the establishment of ownership—allocates these resources among those who wish to develop them for economic reasons. The latter function—regulation—limits ownership rights for various public policy reasons. By articulating the rules of permissible behavior, both functions clarify the nature of the legal relationship between persons and these resources, and thereby serve as an incentive for their transformation from a state of nature to an economic product.

CHAPTER SIX

MINERALS LAW

Minerals ownership and development are governed by state and federal law. State mining law has relevance on federal lands and on state lands. On federal lands, state law may supplement federal procedural requirements for perfecting a valid claim to hard rock minerals. 30 U.S.C.A. § 28. State requirements include: posting of location notices on-site, establishing boundaries, performing discovery work, and the recording of certificates of location with the appropriate local body. See Kenney v. Greer (1983) (on-site monumenting, along with a properly filed location certificate, provide notice to junior claimants of a prior claim). State law may also regulate mining operations on federal lands as long as the regulation is characterized as environmental, and not land use planning. California Coastal Com'n v. Granite Rock Co. (1987).

On state lands, state statutory law defines (1) the kinds of minerals subject to private ownership, Tanner Co. v. Arizona State Land Dept. (1984) (clay excluded from private appropriation), (2) the procedures that must be followed to establish a valid mining claim, Wilson v. Kartes (1988) (claim invalid for failure to mark boundaries on ground), and (3) the steps required to protect the environment from mining operations. Oro Fino Gold Mining Corp. v. County of El Dorado (1990). State statutes may also extinguish a mineral estate and merge it with the surface estate if minerals have not been developed during a set period of time. Texaco, Inc. v. Short (1982).

State case law plays an important interpretative role when miners are in conflict. There are three recurring mining law issues that tend to call for judicial resolution. First, when the surface and mineral interests are split, courts often sort out the respective rights and duties of the surface and mineral owners. Mixon v. One Newco, Inc. (1989) (surface owner did not have to show any affirmative acts of dominion over surface estate to recover mineral rights from mineral owners who failed to preserve interest by working the claim). Second, when a mineral owner enters into a leasing arrangement with another party to develop the mineral resource, courts must determine if the lease contains an unwritten "implied covenant" obligating the lessee to perform certain acts. Sundheim v. Reef Oil Corp. (1991) (oil and gas lessee has implied duty to drill offset well to prevent drainage caused by neighboring wells); Davis v. Cramer (1991) (oil and gas lease may have contained an implied covenant to market). Third, when there is a conveyance of a mineral interest, courts frequently are asked to decipher what exactly was conveyed. International Salt Co. v. Geostow, 878 F.2d 570 (2d Cir.1989) (a deed conveying "all mines, veins, seams and beds of salt" did not give grantee an interest in the mine's excavation cavity); Miller Land & Mineral Co. v. State Highway Com'n (1988) (deed reserving to grantor all "minerals and mineral rights" did not reserve gravel).

The remainder of this chapter will address the minerals law applicable to mineral resources on federal lands. There are no less than three separate federal legal systems that govern minerals ownership, use, and regulation. So-called "hard rock" minerals are subject to the location system of the General Mining Law of 1872, 30 U.S.C.A. §§ 22–47. Under this statute, a prospector may enter the public domain at will, search for minerals, "locate" a claim, and upon discovery of a valuable mineral deposit, be entitled to remove all like minerals throughout the claim. The right to remove and sell valuable minerals is conferred even though the miner does not own title in fee to the minerals. By following certain other procedures, the miner may (but is not required to) obtain a "patent" (fee title) to the minerals and the land within the mining claim.

A second system creates a mechanism for leasing the mineral development rights from the United States. If a mineral is subject to lease, the private party lessee obtains no permanent rights from the United States. The lessee is instead granted the right to explore for and mine the specific minerals covered by the lease, upon (1) payment of annual rentals, (2) payment of royalties on all minerals removed, and (3) compliance with all lease conditions and relevant statutes. Minerals subject to lease include onshore fossil fuel minerals (oil, gas, coal, oil shale), offshore oil and gas, geothermal resources, tar sands, fertilizers (phosphate and potash), certain chemicals (sulfur and sodium), and minerals on "acquired lands." Many of these minerals were removed from the location system by the 1920 Mineral Leasing Act, 30 U.S.C.A. §§ 181–287.

A third system has been created for ordinary and commonly occurring minerals (e.g., clay, sand, gravel). For such "common variety" minerals, Congress has authorized their disposal by sale. These minerals were removed from the location system by the Materials Act of 1947, 30 U.S.C.A. §§ 601–602, and the Common Varieties Act of 1955, 30 U.S.C.A. § 611. After 1955, they may be located under the 1872 Mining Law only if they have such distinct and special value as to make them uncommon.

Apart from these three systems regulating mineral ownership and use on public lands, the United States also owns or controls hard rock, leasable, and common variety minerals under privately-owned lands. These subsurface federal mineral interests were created by federal disposition statutes (e.g., the Stock–Raising Homestead Act described in Chapter 3) that gave private parties a patent to the surface estate while reserving minerals to the United States. Because the

United States retains ownership rights to the minerals, they in turn may be subject to location, lease, or sale, depending on the nature of the subsurface mineral. The presence of a federal reserved mineral right beneath privately-owned surface land raises questions regarding (1) the nature of the minerals reserved to the United States, and (2) the legal relationship between one extracting the minerals pursuant to one of the three federal minerals systems, and a private surface owner who previously acquired title to the surface estate from the United States.

I. THE LAW OF LOCATABLE, HARD ROCK MINERALS

In order to obtain a legal interest in most hard rock minerals found on federal lands, a person must comply with the requirements of the 1872 Mining Law. This venerable (archaic?) federal statute has remained largely unchanged since its passage well over a century ago. As a result, the statute has coped with changing times and issues through judicial construction and reinterpretation of its terms. The body of case law that has emerged constitutes a kind of common law of hard rock mining, similar to the common law of NEPA that has grown up around court review of that important environmental statute (see Chapter 5).

At its most basic, the 1872 Mining Law has two requirements that must be fulfilled before one has a legally protectable interest in minerals—location and discovery. The "order of time in which these acts occur is not essential" to acquiring a legal right good against other prospectors and the United States. Union Oil Co. v. Smith (1919). A claim "location" involves qualified prospectors entering available federal lands in search of specified locatable minerals. If a prospector believes a mineral deposit is present, that prospector can establish a mining claim by following certain federal and state location procedures. A "discovery" occurs when the would-be miner physically encounters a locatable mineral deposit that is deemed to be valuable. Prior to a discovery, prospectors in search of minerals are entitled to the exclusive rights of surface occupation. Anyone who satisfies the test of location and discovery is entitled to an "unpatented mining claim." This is a legally protected property right to the minerals, to the claim's surface, and to some form of access to the claim. One holding an unpatented mining claim does not have title to the minerals or the surface (that comes with a patent). Nevertheless, an unpatented mining claim permits the claim holder either to remove and sell the minerals without payment to the United States, or to just sit on the unworked claim indefinitely (so long as $100 worth of assessment work is performed annually). A miner may receive a patent to the mineral and surface estates at the incredibly low fee of between $5 to $2.50/acre, if the BLM is satisfied that all the location and discovery requirements have been met.

The unpatented mining claim has been subject to two major criticisms. First, it permits miners to extract and sell federally-owned minerals without charge. Second, it encourages claim holders to appropriate federal land for other than mineral development (e.g., for residences), as long as a token annual assessment fee is paid. Only rarely are bogus claim holders identified and their location invalidated. United States v. Zweifel (1975) (several million mining claims invalidated because not located in good faith for mining purposes); Cameron v. United States (1920) (claim invalidated when motivation for location was to charge access fees into Grand Canyon). Virtually every survey of unpatented mining claims concludes that only a tiny fraction are producing minerals in commercial quantities.

Although the 1872 Mining Law has served its purpose well over time (i.e., it has encouraged mineral development on federal land), it is likely that the Congress will respond to the above two problems by significantly amending the statute sometime in the 1990s. When the change occurs, it will probably amend the 1872 Law in the following ways: (1) termination of the opportunity to patent mineral claims; (2) payment of a production royalty to the federal government; (3) elimination of the "discovery" concept; (4) abolishment of extralateral rights, by which miners may follow a vein underground beyond the boundaries of the claim; (5) end the right to locate common variety deposits having "distinct and special value"; (6) requirement of plans of operation for all mining activities; and (7) imposition of additional reclamation and bonding requirements.

A. LOCATION

1. Lands Open to Location

The 1872 Mining Law provides that mineral deposits "in lands belonging to the United States * * * shall be free and open to exploration and purchase." 30 U.S.C.A. § 22. Federal mining law thus applies to the "public domain," consisting of western states over which the United States acquired not only title before any private rights attached, but also sovereign jurisdiction prior to the creation of states. Within the public domain, federal mining law applies only to federal lands that have not been appropriated, reserved for nonmining purposes, or withdrawn from the location system. The 1872 Mining Law does apply to locatable minerals reserved to the United States at the time Congress granted patents to the surface under various disposition statutes. See the Taylor Grazing Act of 1934, 43 U.S.C.A. § 315(d) & (e).

"Appropriated" public lands include those subject to prior mining claims, or lands that have previously passed into private hands by grant, sale, exchange, or in lieu land settlement. See Chapter 3. Lands "reserved" for special nonmining purposes include national parks, wildlife refuges, wild and scenic rivers, and wilderness areas.

A "withdrawal" from location can take two forms. Specified lands have been withdrawn from location and mineral entry by executive order. United States v. Midwest Oil Co. (1915) (sustaining President Taft's 1909 withdrawal of oil-bearing lands). The Federal Lands Policy Management Act of 1976 (FLPMA) sharply limited executive withdrawal power, vesting future exercises of this power in Congress. 43 U.S.C.A. § 1714(b). Mining claims cannot be located on lands previously withdrawn. Shiny Rock Mining Corp. v. United States (1987). Mining claims that fail to comply with applicable requirements prior to the withdrawal are void. Kile v. Belisle (1988) (mining claims divested by withdrawal order where there was failure to comply with annual assessment requirements). Valid existing rights are grandfathered. Northern Alaska Environmental Center v. Lujan (1989). Valid grandfathered claims on withdrawn land may be restricted by subsequently-imposed regulations. United States v. Vogler (1988) (placer miner must apply for permit and submit mining plan in order to transport off-road vehicles through Alaskan preserve).

Congress may also effect a withdrawal of a class of minerals from the location system. Onshore energy minerals were withdrawn from location in 1920; offshore oil and gas deposits were withdrawn in 1953; common variety materials were withdrawn in 1955. These withdrawals made the mineral subject to a different disposition system, such as leasing or sale.

2. Locatable Minerals

The 1872 Law provides that "all valuable mineral deposits" may be located. 30 U.S.C.A. § 22. This sweeping phrase has been considerably narrowed by subsequent statutes and case law. Valuable non-mineral substances, such as peat moss, are not locatable. United States v. Toole (1963). Not all minerals that are "valuable" are locatable. Andrus v.

Charlestone Stone Products Co., Inc. (1978) (water, though valuable, and a mineral, is not locatable). Not all substances that have been deemed "minerals" reserved to the United States by federal statutes disposing of the surface estate are locatable minerals. For example, the geothermal resource is a mineral reserved by the Stock–Raising Homestead Act of 1916, United States v. Union Oil Co. (1977), but it is not subject to location because by later statute it has become subject to lease. See the Geothermal Steam Act of 1970, 30 U.S.C.A. § 1101. Some valuable minerals, such as coal, were never locatable. (The Coal Act of 1864, 13 Stat. 205, made coal a salable mineral until it became leasable under the 1920 Mineral Leasing Act.) Other minerals, once locatable, have been withdrawn from the location system by subsequent statute. The 1920 Mineral Leasing Act removed from location onshore oil, gas, coal, and oil shale discovered after 1920. The Materials Act of 1947, as amended by the Common Varieties Act of 1955, removed from location designated commonly-occurring minerals, such as stone, sand, and gravel, discovered after 1955. The Acquired Lands Act of 1947 removed from location all minerals on "acquired" lands (lands the United States acquired from private or state owners by gift, purchase, exchange, or condemnation). 30 U.S.C.A. §§ 351–359.

What minerals then remain locatable? The 1872 Law specifically lists "veins or lodes of quartz or other rock in place bearing gold, silver, cinnabar [mercury], lead, tin, or copper." 30 U.S.C.A. § 23. As a result of this listing, one may assume that all valuable metallic minerals not otherwise withdrawn are locatable. Valuable non-metallic minerals, such as gemstones and diamonds, are also locatable, Rodgers v. Watt (1984). Common varieties that have "distinct and special value" are locatable. 30 U.S.C.A. § 601. Minerals removed from the location system are locatable if there was a valid discovery prior to the statutory removal date. Marathon Oil Co. v. Lujan (1990) (oil shale locatable if discovered two years before passage of the 1920 Mineral Leasing Act).

3. Qualified Locators

The benefits of the 1872 Law are available only to citizens and aliens who have declared their intention to become citizens. Ginaca v. Peterson (1920); Herrington v. Martinez (1942). Locations may be made by agents, and because there are no limits on the number of mining claims held by one locator, multiple agents may be employed to secure multiple mining claims. Baker v. United States (1980).

4. Types of Locations

The 1872 Law authorized several types of mining claims. The two primary types are "lodes" and "placers." A lode claim is an easily identifiable vein of minerals embedded in solid rock. Mills v. Royse (1975). A placer claim encompasses mineral deposits not in place, such as gold placer composed of alluvial material within and along streambeds. United States v. Ohio Oil Co. (1916). Some types of deposits do not fall cleanly into either category, necessitating classification by courts. Globe Mining Co. v. Anderson (1957) (widespread horizontal deposit containing mineralized zones of uranium, carved into the formation by some solution after the host rock was formed, is a lode).

It is imperative that a locator correctly identify the claim as being lode or placer because a placer discovery will not sustain a lode location, and vice versa. Cole v. Ralph (1920). However, if a miner has erred in locating a placer deposit as a lode, courts will strain to validate the claim if the dispute is with a later-in-time locator, and the earlier-in-time locator has acted reasonably. Iron Silver Mining Co. v. Mike & Starr Gold & Silver Mining Co. (1892). A lode claim may not exceed a rectangle that is 1,500 feet in length and 300 feet on the sides, where these side "end lines" must be parallel. 30 U.S.C.A. § 23. There are no requirements governing the shape of placer claims, other than that they conform "as near as practicable" to pre-existing survey lines. 30 U.S.C.A. § 35. For placer claims, the locator must show that each ten-acre tract is "mineral in character." McCall v. Andrus (1980).

Federal mining law permits lodes located in placer claims to become the property of the placer patentee if the lode deposit was *not* known at the time of the placer patent application. 30 U.S.C.A. § 37; Clipper Mining Co. v. Eli Mining & Land Co. (1904). Under the "tunnel site" provisions of the 1872 Law, a tunnel owner has the right to all veins or lodes encountered by a tunnel excavation for a distance of 3,000 feet from the mouth of the tunnel. 30 U.S.C.A. § 27; Enterprise Mining Co. v. Rico–Aspen (1897) (tunnel site rights have priority over surface locations made by others after commencement of the tunnel).

5. Location Procedures

A location is perfected when there is a mineral discovery and compliance with location procedures. Discovery need not precede location, and satisfaction of federal and state location procedures is primarily important because the locator then has a superior right to adverse claimants. Atherley v. Bullion Monarch Uranium Co. (1959). Also, failure to follow proper location procedures may invalidate a claim after discovery has occurred. United States v. Consolidated Mines & Smelting Co. (1971).

The 1872 Law permits state location procedures that supplement, but which are not inconsistent with, federal law. Butte City Water Co. v. Baker (1905). State laws may require a federal locator to (1) post notice of the claim at the mining site, (2) establish the boundaries by staking, and (3) record a location certificate. Kenney v. Greer, (1983). There are two important federal requirements. Under the 1872 Law, the claim must be distinctly marked on the ground so its boundaries can be traced. 30 U.S.C.A. § 28. Under FLPMA, the owner of an unpatented mining claim must record the claim with the local BLM office or "be deemed conclusively to [have] abandon[ed] the mining claim." 43 U.S.C.A. § 1744; United States v. Locke (1985). See also Bolt v. United States (1991) (mining claims within national parks void if not annually recorded). Federal courts have construed the FLPMA recordation requirements quite strictly. Red Top Mercury Mines, Inc. v. United States (1989) (substantial compliance not sufficient); Last Chance Mining Co. v. United States (1987) (claim may be invalidated even if failure to file is due to BLM negligence).

B. DISCOVERY

1. Prospector's Rights Prior to Discovery: Pedis Possessio

The prospector on the public domain prior to discovery is treated like a licensee or tenant at will of the United States. Cole v. Ralph (1920). This status is conferred by the doctrine of pedis possessio, which gives prospectors an exclusive right of possession, as long as "such possession [is] maintained only by continued actual occupancy by a qualified locator * * * engaged in persistent and diligent prosecution of [exploration] work." Union Oil Co. v. Smith (1919). The purpose of the doctrine is to grant prospectors protection against rival claimants. The United States may still withdraw the land prior to discovery. A valid pedis possessio right is also not relevant to the issue of whether the claim has been perfected against the United States. American Colloid Co. v. Hodel (1988). Nonetheless, pedis possessio rights are protected legal rights, which may be sold and leased. United Western Minerals Co. v. Hannsen (1961).

The pedis possessio doctrine has three requirements. First, there must be actual physical occupation of the ground.

Despite a hint in one Tenth Circuit case that the doctrine may be applied on an area basis, Continental Oil Co. v. Natrona Service, Inc. (1978), the better view is that each separate claim must be physically occupied. Geomet Exploration, Ltd. v. Lucky MC Uranium Corp. (1979). Second, there must be diligent, good faith, bona fide work directed toward making a discovery. Ranchers Exploration & Dev. Co. v. Anaconda Co. (1965). Third, the prospector must exclude rival claimants, either by force or legal redress.

2. Discovery of a Valuable Mineral

While the 1872 Law requires a "discovery," it does not define the term. At its most basic, there is a discovery when someone establishes the physical presence of mineralization on a particular claim. Union Oil Co. v. Smith (1919) (discovery on one claim suggesting minerals on a contiguous claim not a discovery on the contiguous claim). The courts and the Department of Interior have developed a more sophisticated two-part test for a discovery. The first part is the "prudent person" test, which requires evidence that the deposit is of a character that a person "of ordinary prudence would be justified in the further expenditure of his labor and means, with a reasonable prospect of success, in developing a valuable mine." Chrisman v. Miller (1905). The second part of the discovery test was ratified in 1968, when the Supreme Court added the "marketability" refinement of the prudent person test. United States v. Coleman (1968). Under *Coleman,* a prudent person is deemed to be willing to only develop mines whose minerals can be extracted and sold in an existing market at a profit.

This two-part test requires objective evidence that the mineral can be sold in a "presently" existing market at a profit; however, it does not require that a claimant show actual profitable mining. Rodgers v. Watt (1984). An applicable "present" market is one existing at the time that the claim is challenged, or the date the land is withdrawn from location. Best v. Humboldt Placer Mining Co. (1963). A claimant may not rely on future contingencies involving either the relevant market, or later-discovered concentrations of minerals. Skaw v. United States (1988); Barrows v. Hickel (1971).

a. The Discovery Test for Controversies Involving the United States

The United States will challenge a discovery in one of three contexts: (1) when a miner applies for a patent; (2) when the United States wishes to invalidate an unpatented mining claim; and (3) when land is withdrawn from location, and the Interior Department asserts that no perfected mining claim preceded the withdrawal. While the government must make a prima facie showing of no discovery, the burden of proving a discovery falls on the miner. Difficult issues of fact are resolved first by the Interior Department (typically against the miner), and on appeal this determination enjoys great deference by the courts. This limited scope of review deters judicial appeals. Indeed, in the 22 years between the *Coleman* decision in 1968 and 1990, there were less than 40 appeals to courts.

In fleshing out the marketability refinement of the prudent person test, the courts have considered five key variables. First, a discovery requires minerals in sufficient quantity and quality that may be marketed for a *profit*. Hallenbeck v. Kleppe (1979). Second, there must be a *market* for the mineral. Foster v. Seaton, 271 F.2d 836 (D.C.Cir.1959). The courts are divided on the question of whether a discovery may be invalidated when a claim contains so much of the mineral that the relevant market may be unable to absorb further sales. Compare Rodgers v. Watt (1984) (local market saturation not dispositive), with Skaw v. United States (1988) (claim rejected when market could not absorb additional minerals). Third, the *costs* of extraction, processing, and transportation must not be excessive. Lara v. Secretary of Interior (1987). The cost of compliance with environmental regulations may be considered. United States v. Kosanke Sand Corp. (1973). Fourth, the evidence required to prove a discovery for an inherently valuable metallic mineral (e.g., gold), will be less demanding than that required for either a common variety mineral alleged to have "distinct and special value" (and therefore locatable), or a leasable mineral thought to be locatable because of discovery prior to 1920. See Dredge Corp. v. Conn. (1984) (sand and gravel); Andrus v. Shell Oil (1980) (oil shale). Fifth, because national forest lands were set aside for timber purposes, not mining, a claimant may have more of a burden to prove a discovery on national forest lands, as contrasted with BLM public lands. Converse v. Udall (1968).

b. *The Discovery Test for Controversies Involving Rival Claimants*

In disputes between private mining claimants, a more liberal discovery standard is applied. Berto v. Wilson (1958). The evidence need only support the conclusion that a person of ordinary prudence would have a reasonable expectation of developing a valuable mine. Boscarino v. Gibson (1983).

C. THE UNPATENTED MINING CLAIM

When acts of location are completed and a valid discovery has been made, the miner acquires a perfected unpatented mining claim. This claim is a property right, carrying with it ownership to all the minerals that may be extracted from within the claim, and equitable ownership to the land surrounding the claim. United States v. North American Transp. & Trading Co. (1920) (claim is "property" which may not be taken without just compensation). Because the holder of the claim receives these valuable rights without payment of rent or royalty, few ever seek to obtain a patent (deed) from the government.

1. Rights Granted

a. *Exclusive Right of Possession*

A perfected unpatented mining claim is removed from the unappropriated public domain. A locator holding a valid unpatented mining claim has a right of present and exclusive possession that protects the claim against rival claimants, so long as the locator satisfies applicable federal and state requirements (e.g., performance of annual assessment work; timely filing of appropriate affidavits). Wilbur v. United States (1930). However, the holder of this claim only has a possessory right, which is subject to the primary title and paramount ownership rights of the United States. Roy v. Lancaster (1991).

Upon abandonment, or failure to comply with conditions upon which the continuing right of possession depends, the entire claim reverts to the federal government. United States v. Rizzinelli (1910). If the claim has never been perfected (e.g., if there has been no discovery), the United States may withdraw the land and minerals from the location system. Skaw v. United States (1988). If the claim has been perfected, but if there is failure to comply with continued obligations, the land may be withdrawn and the claimant divested of mineral rights. Kile v. Belisle (1988).

The Congress may also condition the retention of preexisting unpatented mining claims on the performance of certain tasks. United States v. Locke (1985) (recordation of claim and annual assessment work). A perfected claim is not immunized from the imposition of subsequently-imposed regulations, such as reasonable environmental controls. Trustees for Alaska v. EPA (1984). See also Boesche v. Udall (1963). Congress may prevent the holder of an unpatented claim from applying for a patent. Freese v. United States (1981).

b. Surface Rights

A valid unpatented mining claim encompasses the resources on the surface. Del Monte Mining & Milling Co. v. Last Chance Mining & Milling Co. (1898). Prior to 1955, case law limited the right of exclusive possession of the surface for mining purposes only. Shiver v. United States (1895) (claimant may not cut timber for sale to third party); United States v. Etcheverry (1956) (claimant may not lease surface for grazing). After 1955, the Surface Resources Act provides that the owner is entitled to use the surface only as necessary for the mining operation. 30 U.S.C.A. § 612. For claims perfected prior to 1955, the claimant is precluded from exploiting any surface resources reserved to the United States. 30 U.S.C.A. § 615; Barnes v. Hodel (1987) (mineral claim may not embrace the right to sell timber previously reserved). The Mining Claims Occupancy Act of 1962 permits persons to maintain their residence on the claim if it was their principal residence for at least seven years prior to 1962. 30 U.S.C.A. § 701.

The 1872 Mining Law provides for surface access by owners of unpatented mining claims onto the public domain. FLPMA reaffirms access rights, subject to regulations "to prevent unnecessary or undue degradation of the lands." 43 U.S.C.A. § 1732(b). Such access rights are not exclusive to the owner of the unpatented mining claim; the public has a right of free access to the surface of a mining claim for recreational use or access to adjacent land. Silbrico Corp. v. Ortiz (1989); United States v. Fahey (1985).

c. Extralateral Rights

Once a claimant establishes the "apex" of a lode vein (the leading edge of the vein) within the surface boundaries of a claim, the vein may be followed on its downward subsurface course outside of the claim's side lines. 30 U.S.C.A. § 26. The right to mine the mineral deposit after it is outside and under the side lines is the owner's extralateral right. Extralateral rights do not attach to placer claims, or to lode deposits mistakenly located as placer.

In a rectangular lode claim, the "side lines" generally define the rectangle's longest sides; they may not exceed 1,500 feet in length. 30 U.S.C.A. § 23. The "end lines" are the two shortest sides of the claim, defining its width. The end lines must be parallel to each other, while the side lines may be nonparallel without affecting extralateral rights. Jim Butler Tonopah Mining Co. v. West End Consolidated Mining Co. (1918). The "apex" may or may not be the portion of the vein nearest to the surface. If some of the vein is exposed to the surface, while the remainder of the vein rises above the exposed portion in a mountain within the claim, the exposed vein would not be the apex. A vein not surfacing at the surface is a blind apex.

If the mineral deposit located is a vein or lode, and if the apex of the lode is within the surface of lines of the claim extended downward vertically, the locator may follow the vein on its downward course outside the side lines so long as the locator stays within the extension of the end lines. Swoboda v. Pala Mining, Inc. (1988). The extralateral rights claimant must prove continuity of the vein in order to follow its downward progress outside the side lines. Silver Surprize, Inc. v. Sunshine Mining Co. (1976). The claimant must also be able to prove that the apex of the vein is located within the claim's boundaries. Sunshine Mining Co. v. Metropolitan Mines Corp. (1986). End lines may not be moved to take advantage of underground discoveries. Iron Silver Mining Co. v. Elgin Mining & Smelting Co. (1886). Extralateral rights do not extend to neighboring lands that were patented under non-mining statutes (e.g., agricultural) prior to location of the mining claim. Burke v. Southern Pacific Railroad Co. (1914).

d. The Right to Amend or Relocate Claims

A claim may be "amended" to correct a defect on an otherwise valid claim. Such an amended location may change boundaries, or include within the claim an abandoned claim. Shoshone Mining Co. v. Rutter (1898). An amended claim is not allowed if adverse rights have intervened before the amendment date. Atherley v. Bullion Monarch Uranium Co. (1959). An amended location relates back to the date of the original location; an amended location cannot relate back if the original location is void. Silbrico Corp. v. Ortiz (1989); Brown v. Gurney (1906).

A void location is where the land was withdrawn from mineral location at the time the claim was originally located, or one where the locator failed to comply with a material statutory requirement (e.g., failure to perform annual assessment work). Burke v. Southern Pac. Railroad Co. (1914). Such void claims cannot be amended; they must be relocated. 30 U.S.C.A. § 28.

2. Limitations and Requirements

a. Assessment Requirements

The only diligence requirement contained in the 1872 Law for unpatented mining claims is that "not less than $100 worth of labor shall be performed or improvements made during each year." 30 U.S.C.A. § 28. The purpose of this assessment requirement is to prevent miners from holding several valuable claims, while working only some of them. If assessment work is not performed, or not performed on time, the claim is "forfeited" by the original locator and becomes subject to other claimants. Belk v. Meagher (1881).

(1) Acts that Qualify for Assessment Work

The general rule is that the work must be of a character as to develop and protect the claim, and to facilitate extraction of minerals. If some work is performed in good faith, and if something is accomplished consistent with mining purposes, the courts will defer to the judgment of the miner. The following acts have been found to constitute acceptable assessment work: (1) clearing growth on a path to a mine shaft, Silver Jet Mines, Inc. v. Schwark (1984); (2) work done off site, Chambers v. Harrington (1884); (3) employing a watchman, James v. Krook (1933); and (4) repairing access roads. Pinkerton v. Moore (1959).

(2) Effect of Failure to Perform Annual Assessment Work

Failure to do assessment work results in reversion of full title to the United States when either the mineral or the land is subsequently withdrawn from location. Hickel v. The Oil Shale Corp. (1970) (mineral withdrawn); Kile v. Belisle (1988) (land withdrawn). FLPMA provides that failure to file an affidavit of assessment work "shall be deemed conclusively to constitute an abandonment of the mining claim." 43 U.S.C.A. § 1744(c); United States v. Locke (1985). The Ninth Circuit strictly construed the FLPMA filing requirements in Red Top Mercury Mines, Inc. v. United States (1989) (claimant's affidavit insufficient when it only stated, without other written evidence, that "I believe I submitted another copy of my * * * assessment year notice to the BLM"), and in NL Industries, Inc. v. Secretary of Interior (1985) (the word "thereafter" in FLPMA governing filing requirements, refers to each year following initial filing, regardless of when claim was initially recorded).

When there is neither a withdrawal nor a failure to file under FLPMA, but simply a lack of assessment work, the original locator may retain the otherwise forfeited unpatented claim by resuming the annual labor before a subsequent location is made. There are three instances when the original locator cannot revive the original claim by resuming assessment work: (1) when there has been an intervening valid relocation by a rival claimant, Golden Condor, Inc. v. Bell (1984); (2) when the original locator has truly abandoned the claim, Sawyer–Adecor Intern., Inc. v. Anglin (1982); and (3) when the claim has been validly relocated by a rival, but then abandoned. Public Service Co. v. Bleak (1982).

b. Surface Use and Environmental Limitations

The traditional view was that a miner satisfying all the prerequisites of a valid unpatented mining claim had an absolute right to extract discovered minerals regardless of the effect of the mining operation on others. However, a series of new statutes and regulations promulgated under old and new statutes have limited this "absolute" right. These laws require a consideration of land use and environmental values, and they have particular impact on surface uses.

(1) STATUTORY RESTRICTIONS

The 1872 Law states that federal mining claims are subject to "regulations prescribed by law." 30 U.S.C.A. § 22. When this provision seemed inadequate authority to control the environmental abuses of mining, Congress responded with the 1955 Surface Resources Act. 30 U.S.C.A. § 612. This Act applies to all federal land, and contains three important provisions: (1) no mining claim located after July, 1955, may be used, prior to patent, for any non-mining purposes; (2) unpatented claims are subject to the right of the United States to manage all "vegetative" and other surface resources; and (3) licensees of the United States have access rights across unpatented claims. The Act does not restrict surface uses after patent.

The statutory mandates of the Act have been construed to authorize the Forest Service to bar the use of a backhoe and bulldozer on a valid claim. United States v. Richardson (1979) (such uses are "unreasonably * * * damaging to the environment"). In United States v. Curtis–Nevada Mines, Inc. (1980), the Ninth Circuit upheld the public's right to use the surface of a mining claim for recreation without special permission.

Unlike the Surface Resources Act, the Wilderness Act of 1964 applies post-patent. If a valid location is made before 1984, a patent may issue. But a patent in a wilderness area reserves to the United States title to both the surface and the products of surface lands. A pre–1984 unpatented claim that does not go to patent is grandfathered, as long as the mining location is used "solely for mining." 16 U.S.C.A. § 1133(d).

NEPA's applicability to hard rock mining varies by the nature of the federal involvement and by the federal land agency. If either the Forest Service or BLM propose mining regulations, NEPA applies to this action. Sierra Club v. Penfold (1988). On Forest Service lands, an EIS is required for approval of a miner's Plan of Operation, Friends of the Earth, Inc. v. Butz (1975), and an EA is needed prior to mineral exploration. Jette v. Bergland (1978). On BLM lands, compliance with NEPA depends on the category of mining operation. Neither an EIS nor an EA is expected for "casual use" mines (only negligible disturbance of federal lands) or "notice" mines (cumulative surface disturbance of five acres or less/year). However, NEPA fully applies to "plan" mines (where there is cumulative surface disturbance of more than five acres/year).

No EIS is necessary prior to awarding a patent. South Dakota v. Andrus (1980) (patent grant is a nondiscretionary act).

Following on the heels of NEPA, the Mining and Minerals Policy Act of 1970 encourages the "development of methods for the disposal, control, and reclamation of mineral waste products and * * * mined land, so as to lessen any adverse impact * * * upon the physical environment." 30 U.S.C.A. § 21a. Statutory authority with teeth was provided in 1976 by FLPMA, which requires the Interior Secretary to "take action necessary to prevent unnecessary or undue degradation of the public lands." 43 U.S.C.A. § 1732(b). CERCLA of 1980 exposes the mining industry to liability for creation of hazardous waste sites. Idaho v. Hanna Mining Co. (1989).

(2) REGULATORY RESTRICTIONS

(a) Forest Service Regulations

In 1974, the Forest Service relied on the Organic Act of 1897 to adopt regulations governing methods of mining development and operation. These regulations provide for reclamation and mitigation of adverse environmental impacts. 16 U.S.C.A. § 478. All mining "operations" on national forest lands are subject to the regulations, including maintenance of structures. United States v. Burnett (1990). Under these regulations, a miner must first file a notice of intention to operate. If it is determined that there is likely to be "significant disturbance of surface resources," the operator must then submit a proposed Plan of Operations providing for environmental protection. Failure to file a plan may subject the operator to criminal liability. United States v. Goldfield Deep Mines Co. (1981); United States v. Nordwick (1987).

The validity of the Forest Service regulations was upheld in United States v. Weiss (1981). In Havasupai Tribe v. United States (1990), plan approval was found not to violate an Indian tribe's right to free exercise of religion. The courts have been reluctant to definitively decide whether the Forest Service may disapprove proposed mining plans, and thereby foreclose mining operations. See United States v. Brunskill (1986). It seems likely that courts will sustain most any reasonable regulatory restriction on a mining activity so long as the regulation is not deemed to completely prohibit mining. United States v. Doremus (1989).

(b) BLM Regulations

Pursuant to FLPMA, BLM in 1980 adopted surface management regulations for mining operations. These regulations, based on the Forest Service regulations, seek to prevent "undue degradation" depending on the size and location of the mine, and the level of mining activity. "Plan" mines (surface disturbance of more than five acres/year) require a plan of operation. Northern Alaska Environmental Center v. Lujan (1989) (BLM need not inspect site before approving a plan of operations). "Notice" mines (less than five acres of surface disturbance) do not require BLM approval, but the operator must notify BLM of the activities proposed. Sierra Club v. Penfold, supra. "Casual Use" mines (negligible disturbance) require neither notification to nor approval by BLM. Bales v. Ruch (1981) (a mobile home and use of vehicles do not constitute "casual use").

D. THE PATENTED CLAIM

There are several reasons why the holder of an unpatented mining claim might seek a patent. Without a patent, the claim must be maintained (i.e., annual assessment work performed), and the locator must be vigilant lest an adverse claimant locate an overlapping claim. An unpatented claimholder also risks challenge by the United States that the claim should be invalidated for: (1) locating on land withdrawn from mineral location; (2) failure to comply with required location procedures; (3) lack of discovery; (4) failure to perform assessment work; or (5) failure to record with the BLM. Also, claims located after 1955 are subject to the Surface Resources Act, while patented claims are not. Moreover, if the lands of a valid unpatented claim are withdrawn prior to patent, Congress can cut off the opportunity to patent. Freese v. United States (1981).

There are several conditions that must be met before a patent will be issued, and the applicant bears the burden of proving that they have been satisfied. Foster v. Seaton (1959). The two most important requirements are proof of the applicant's general eligibility, and proof of discovery. The former demands proof that the claim was made on lands open to location, and not on lands otherwise withdrawn or reserved. Claims on lands withdrawn from mineral entry before location are *void ab initio*. Claims on land withdrawn from mineral entry after location are invalid either if there has been no discovery before withdrawal, or if there has been noncompliance with annual assessment requirements. Kile v. Belisle (1988). Some withdrawals and reservations limit the time period in which a claimant may apply for a patent. Alaska Miners v. Andrus (1981) (Alaska Native Claims Settlement Act requires that application for patent must occur within five years after the Act's enactment). The discovery test is applied as of the date of the application for patent (or the date of a challenge to an unpatented claim), not the date of the initial discovery. Best v. Humboldt Placer Mining Co. (1963).

If the claimant has met all applicable requirements, then the claimant usually has an absolute right to a patent from the United States. Wilbur v. United States ex rel. Krushnic (1929); Marathon Oil Co. v. Lujan (1990). Because patent issuance is non-discretionary, patent approval is not an "action" under NEPA. South Dakota v. Andrus (1980).

A patent grants a fee simple to the minerals, as well as an exclusive right and ownership to all the surface and surface resources within the claim (except in wilderness areas, where patents include only the minerals). After patent, the surface and minerals on the claim are private property subject to local property taxation.

II. THE LAW OF LEASABLE, ENERGY MINERALS

The federal mineral leasing system is the product of the 1920 Mineral Leasing Act (MLA), and other, mineral-specific leasing statutes (e.g., the Federal Coal Leasing Amendments Act of 1976). Although each leasable mineral is subject to specialized statutory and regulatory leasing requirements, some generalizations may be made about the entire leasing system. Most importantly, those seeking to develop leasable minerals are subject to extensive federal control. The lessor-federal government may exclude enormous tracts from development; it may restrict the mineral lease period and acreage available under the lease; it may require the lessee to pay rent and royalties; it may condition the lease to protect the environment; it may cancel the lease for violations. Whether and how the federal government exercises these powers is generally left to its discretion, limited only by statute and judicial opinion.

The federal leasing system is particularly significant because it governs development of energy fuels on federal lands. The primary fuel minerals subject to lease include: (1) oil and gas; (2) coal; (3) oil shale; and (4) geothermal resources. In addition, leasable minerals encompass potassium, sodium, phosphate, chlorides, sulphates, carbonates, borates, silicates, and minerals found on acquired lands.

A. OIL AND GAS

Domestically produced oil and gas comprises almost 50% of American energy consumption. While domestic reserves of natural gas seem adequate for the foreseeable future (209 trillion cubic feet were still available in 1990 according to the United States Geological Survey), the same cannot be said for oil. Domestic oil production peaked in 1970, while reliance on foreign, imported oil rose towards a figure approaching 50 percent of demand in the 1990s.

In light of our continued dependence on oil as an energy source, federal oil and gas becomes a potentially important domestic supply source. Oil and gas production from both onshore and offshore federal leases supplies approximately 10 percent of petroleum needed to satisfy total domestic consumption. Offshore leasing yields nearly three times the amount of oil and gas production supplied from onshore leases.

1. Royalties Management

One of the primary advantages of a leasing over a location system is that the federal government can obtain revenues from the extraction of its minerals in the form of royalties, annual rentals, and bonus payments. Mineral revenues collected are one of the largest sources of nontax income to the United States Treasury. Between 1982 and 1990, the Interior Department collected nearly $50 billion in royalties, rents, and bonuses from nearly 90,000 federal and Indian oil and gas leases.

Both the MLA and the Outer Continental Shelf Lands Act require that lessees pay the federal government a percentage royalty "in the amount or value of the [oil and gas] production." 30 U.S.C.A. § 223; 43 U.S.C.A. § 1337(a)(1)(A). For many years, however, excessive reliance on lessees' calculation of royalties was depriving the federal government of up to $500 million annually. To address this serious deficiency in the federal royalty management system, Congress in 1982 enacted the Federal Oil and Gas Royalty Management Act (FOGRMA), 30 U.S.C.A. §§ 1701–1757. FOGRMA created a new bureau within the Interior Department—the Minerals Management Service (MMS)—whose purpose is to ensure accurate and adequate royalty payments by federal oil and gas lessees. MMS regulations make up a comprehensive inspection, audit, accounting, and royalty collection system.

One of the primary tasks of the MMS has been to derive applicable standards for determining the "value of production" for royalty valuation purposes. These standards are then tested against a lessee's past royalty payments, and if this audit reveals a deficiency, the MMS may retroactively assess additional royalties (and interest on the unpaid royalties) against owing lessees. See, e.g., Mesa Operating Ltd. Partnership v. United States Dept. of Interior (1991) (lessee owed $1.5 million in unpaid royalties). Federal lessees have challenged the authority of the MMS to collect the increased royalties retroactively. Despite one early case suggesting the unfairness and invalidity of retroactive application of increased royalties, Continental Oil Co. v. United States (1950), the courts have generally sustained the practice for both onshore and offshore lessees. Amoco Production Co. v. Lujan (1989); Monsanto Co. v. Hodel (1987); Marathon Oil v. United States (1986). Retroactivity challenges have also been rejected when grounded on the Takings Clause, Norfolk Energy, Inc. v. Hodel (1990), and on estoppel against the government for agency acquiescence. Shoshone Indian Tribe v. Hodel (1990). The only notable lessee success in court against the MMS was in Diamond Shamrock Exploration Corp. v. Hodel (1988), where the Fifth Circuit held that payments by a pipeline purchaser to a lessee-producer did not trigger the lessee's duty to pay royalties to the federal government, since royalties were due only upon "production," i.e., when oil or gas was actually physically extracted from the earth. Also, the general six-year statute of limitations governing federal contract claims, 28 U.S.C.A. § 2415, may apply to audit reviews of royalty compliance. Philips Petroleum Co. v. Lujan (1989).

One of the statutory purposes of FOGRMA is "to fulfill the trust responsibility of the United States for the administration of Indian oil and gas resources." 30 U.S.C.A. § 1701(b)(4). This statutory charge has been interpreted to create in the United States a general fiduciary obligation toward Indian tribes with respect to the management of oil and gas leases on tribal lands. Jicarilla Apache Tribe v. Supron Energy Corp. (1986). The MMS has construed this fiduciary relationship to require private lessees on Indian lands to compute royalties (payable to the Indians) based on the market value determined by the highest price paid or offered for like quality oil or gas at the time of production. Pawnee v. United States (1987). Indian lessors may be barred by the federal six-year statute of limitations from bringing suit against the United States based on an alleged breach of the fiduciary duty to ensure that lessees properly calculate royalties. Sankey v. United States (1991).

2. Onshore Oil and Gas

a. *Predicates to the Leasing Decision*

(1) SECRETARIAL DISCRETION

The Supreme Court has interpreted the MLA as giving the Interior Secretary complete discretion to open or close federal lands to leasing. 30 U.S.C.A. § 226(a); Udall v. Tallman (1965). The Secretary's rationale for a refusal to lease may be based on conservation principles, United States ex rel. McLennan v. Wilbur (1931), or wildlife protection. Duesing v. Udall (1965) (lease tract closed when found to be breeding ground for moose). The possible sole exception to this otherwise unfettered discretion was advanced by a Wyoming District Court, which concluded that failure to lease in wilderness study areas was a de facto "withdrawal" which must comply with FLPMA withdrawal procedures. Mountain States Legal Foundation v. Hodel (1987).

(2) LANDS AVAILABLE TO LEASE

All BLM public lands and national forests are open to leasing unless specifically withdrawn. Oil and gas leasing is generally precluded in the national park system, in national wildlife refuges, in the Wild and Scenic Rivers System, and in wilderness areas. To lease in national forests requires explicit permission from the Forest Service.

(3) MINERALS ENCOMPASSED BY "OIL AND GAS"

While the MLA does not provide precise definition to the terms "oil and gas," the Interior Department has opted for an expansive construction. The word "oil" includes oil shale, native asphalt, solid and semisolid bitumen, and bituminous rock characterized by oil-impregnated rock or sands from which oil is recoverable by special treatment. See also Brennan v. Udall (1967). The Department of Interior has similarly defined "gas" broadly enough to include non-flammable gas, helium, carbon dioxide, coalbed gas, and other natural gases whose composition is not solely carbon and hydrogen. See Exxon Corp. v. Lujan (1990) ("gas" encompasses all naturally occurring gases which emerge at wellhead); Aulston v. United States (1990) ("gas" does not just mean fuel gas, but includes carbon dioxide).

b. The Leasing Decision

The 1920 MLA imposed a dual leasing system, which depended upon whether the lands open for lease were within known geological structures (KGSs). Those within a KGS must be leased by competitive bidding; those that were not (the vast majority of lands are non–KGS) were leased to the first qualified applicant. 30 U.S.C.A. § 226. This scheme had two inherent defects. First, the determination of whether an oil and gas structure was under a tract was more an art than a science, and subject to much challenge by lessees. See Bender v. Clark (1984); Arkla Exploration Co. v. Texas Oil & Gas Corp. (1984). Second, when the terms of non-competitive leases expired for failure to drill (many were held purely for speculative purposes, awaiting the price of oil or gas to rise), there was a mad scramble to be the first qualified applicant to refile. To address this situation, the Interior Department considered all lease applications as being "simultaneously" filed, so that the winning applicant would be by lottery. Many applicants used filing services to enhance their chances of being selected in the lottery. See Reppy v. Department of Interior (1989).

In 1987, Congress responded to these problems by enacting the Federal Onshore Oil and Gas Leasing Reform Act (Reform Act), Pub.L. No. 100–203. The Reform Act abolished the KGS/non–KGS distinction, and replaced it with a system that requires public lands first be offered by competitive bid, with a minimum acceptable bid of $2 per acre. If no minimum bid is received, the lands become available for noncompetitive leasing for a two-year period, after which they revert back to the competitive leasing process. 30 U.S.C.A. §§ 226(b)(1)(A), (c)(1).

The Reform Act gives federal land management agencies power to regulate the surface environmental consequences of oil and gas leasing operations on their lands, while continuing to vest in BLM ownership of the mineral estate. As a result, agencies other than BLM (e.g., the Forest Service, the Fish and Wildlife Service, the Park Service) have authority to control surface activities, and in the case of the Forest Service, it may actually veto BLM leasing decisions in national forests. 30 U.S.C.A. § 226(g), (h).

Under the MLA, the Forest Service had merely a consultative role with BLM. Forest Service regulations implementing the Reform Act identify four distinct roles that the Forest Service will play in the leasing decisions within national forest lands: (1) development of a land use plan for each national forest consistent with the National Forest Management Act of 1976 (see Chapter 7); (2) identification of lands within national forests administratively available for leasing; (3) making the decision to authorize BLM to offer site specific tracts for lease; and (4) approval of a lessee's "application" to the BLM for a "permit to drill" (APD), if the Forest Service is satisfied that drilling operations will not adversely affect surface lands or resources.

(1) LEASE TERMS AND EXTENSIONS

A lease is not for an indefinite time, but for a "primary" term (five years for competitive leases, ten for noncompetitive). If a lease has not achieved production of oil or gas in paying quantities by the end of the primary term, it expires. There are, however, three ways for the lessee to extend the term of the lease. First, if there is production at the end of the primary term, the lease may continue as long as there is paying production. 30 U.S.C.A. § 226(e). Second, if the lessee has initiated drilling operations within the primary term, then the lease is extended for an additional two years. Third, if the Interior Secretary decides, "in the interest of conservation," to suspend lease operations, then the primary term is lengthened by the duration of the suspension. 30 U.S.C.A. § 209. Compare Copper Valley Mach. Works, Inc. v. Andrus (1981) (stipulation in a lease denying lessee access to property for six months/year was a mandated lease suspension), with Getty Oil Co. v. Clark (1985) (suspensions requested by the lessee to extend the primary term may be denied or conditioned).

(2) LEASE STAGES

The lifecycle of a federal onshore oil and gas lease may go through several stages, where no given stage inevitably follows from the previous one. The would-be lessee first undertakes preliminary exploration work by reviewing aerial photos, geologic maps, or the exploration results of neighboring leases. If this effort suggests that certain lands hold promise, and if the applicable surface management agency has made these lands available for leasing, then a lease application may be submitted. An application does not obligate the Interior Department to issue the lease. If a lease is awarded by the BLM, the lessee then has the legal right to drill, Sierra Club v. Peterson (1983), but not the duty to do so.

After lease issuance, the lessee may conduct geological and geophysical prospecting, which does not entail drilling, but often does include such surface disturbing activities as recording seismic impulses from an explosive. If this prospecting is encouraging, the lessee may acquire surrounding leaseholds to prevent reservoir drainage from adjacent wells not under the control of the lessee. The next step may be to engage in exploratory "wildcat" drilling, which requires the lessee to submit and be granted an APD by the BLM. An APD will normally not be granted without approval of a surface use plan of operations, which will contain many environmentally-sensitive conditions.

If a wildcat well becomes a discovery well (a well that yields commercial quantities of oil or gas), additional development wells will likely be drilled to confirm the discovery and establish the extent of the field. The lessee must be granted APDs for such confirmation wells. If a well does not encounter oil or gas, it is plugged with cement and abandoned. If confirmation wells suggest the presence of a large reservoir (a "barn burner"), multiple wells will be drilled on the lease site and on surrounding leaseholds, consistent with well-spacing rules, to drain the reservoir efficiently. This is known as full field development. APDs for full field development typically include plans for additional storage facilities, pipeline networks, transportation corridors, as well as proposals for unitization and pooling. Norfolk Energy, Inc. v. Hodel (1990) (when federal lands are unitized with other lands, the federal agency may regulate operations on the nonfederal lands if not inconsistent with a preexisting lease); Cotton Petro. v. United States Dept. of Interior (1989) (Interior Secretary's rejection of a commutization (well pooling) agreement was arbitrary and capricious where Secretary failed to analyze relevant factors mandated by Departmental guidelines).

The lifespan of oil and gas fields varies. The average life of typical field is between 15–25 years. Abandonment of individual wells may start early in a field life, and reach a maximum when the field is eventually depleted. With abandonment comes well plugging and reclamation requirements, where the surface is usually restored to the specifications contained in the surface use plan of operations submitted with the initial APD.

Rarely does a prospective lessee encounter all these stages. As a practical matter, only one in ten leases is ever tested with an exploratory well. Of the ten percent tested, only a tiny percentage of these will yield a commercially productive well. Even if a well is commercially productive, the chances are no better than 50–50 that such a well will evidence a major reservoir, justifying the drilling of more wells for eventual full field development.

(3) Conditions to the Oil and Gas Lease

The Secretary of Interior is given broad powers "to do any and all things necessary to carry out and accomplish the purposes of [oil and gas leasing]." 30 U.S.C.A. § 189; Grindstone Butte Project v. Kleppe (1981). The authority to impose protective conditions and stipulations on leasing activities is consistent with this broad Secretarial authority. A lessee's failure to comply with lease conditions is grounds either for canceling a lease, Udall v. Tallman (1965), or for refusing to reinstate an expired lease. Ram Petroleums, Inc. v. Andrus (1981). Lease conditions should not be applied retroactively except where the purpose of the condition is to correct a lease based on an erroneous interpretation of a statute. Enfield v. Kleppe (1977).

Local governments have, with mixed success, sought to improve conditions on onshore federal oil and gas operations. See Western Oil and Gas Ass'n v. Sonoma County (1990) (lessee's constitutional challenge dismissed on ripeness grounds); Ventura County v. Gulf Oil Corp. (1979) (county regulation preempted by federal law).

(4) NEPA

Questions involving the timing, scope, and nature of an environmental impact analysis under NEPA have proven to be exceptionally difficult to answer in the case of federal onshore oil and gas leasing. This is because federal onshore leasing not only proceeds in stages, over time, but also over geographic space, at many lease sites. As noted above, the nature of federal onshore leasing is such that there is considerable uncertainty whether a leasing action at one stage, or at one site, will ever lead to the next stage, or to leasing at another site.

(a) Timing

Questions of EIS timing arise in considering whether an EIS should be prepared at the pre-lease planning stage, at the lease issuance stage, or at some post-lease stage, such as when an APD is filed. The Ninth Circuit has concluded that sale of a "no surface occupancy" (NSO) lease does not require preparation of an EIS. Conner v. Burford (1988). The District of Columbia Circuit has concluded that sale of *non*-NSO leases, which do not preclude surface disturbing activities, constitutes "the point of irreversible, irretrievable commitment of resources—the point at which NEPA mandates that an [EIS] be prepared." Sierra Club v. Peterson (1983). This is because, unless it is an NSO lease, the federal government may not totally preclude surface disturbing activities after lease issuance. Bob Marshall Alliance v. Hodel (1988). The Tenth Circuit disagreed with the Ninth and District of Columbia Circuits and concluded that a more realistic approach was to require only an EA at the lease sale stage, but to issue leases with sufficient stipulations aimed at protecting the environment. Park County Resource Council v. United States Dept. of Agriculture (1987). This permits deferral of full EIS review until the stage when drilling is more likely (the APD stage), provided that lease stipulations prevent proposed operations if their environmental consequences are unacceptable. The resulting apparent split in the circuits remains unresolved in light of the Supreme Court's refusal to review these cases. Sun Exploration & Production Co. v. Lujan (1989). In June, 1991, the Secretary of Interior reversed a decision by the Interior Board of Land Appeals holding that, as a general rule, an EIS is required for a "development well" (one drilled after an exploratory well shows that a site holds oil). The Secretary concluded that "the question of when to proceed with a full EIS [for onshore oil and gas operations] remains a fact-based determination." Michael Gold (1991).

(b) Scope

An important question involving NEPA "scope" is whether environmental review of onshore oil and gas leasing should be general, including broad expanses of federal land, or narrow and site specific. The answer to this question is critical to the nature of NEPA impact review, because the scope of an EIS is determined by the scope of the proposed action. In Kleppe v. Sierra Club (1976), the Supreme Court seemed to accept in dictum the proposition that site specific NEPA review could be deferred until site specific impacts were imminent. For onshore oil and gas leases, site-specific surface impacts are imminent and identifiable at the APD stage, not the lease issuance stage. Nonetheless, the leading case of Conner v. Burford, supra, mandates an EIS at the lease sale stage, even though it is extremely difficult then to ascertain whether, or where, drilling activity may occur. The *Conner* case is consistent with other non-oil and gas leasing cases calling for site-specific EISs where environmental impacts are still contingent on future actions. EDF v. Andrus (1980).

(c) Impact Analysis

If an EIS is done at lease sale, before post-lease APDs inform relevant surface management agencies of the location, number, or types of exploratory wells, should the lease sale EIS nonetheless make an educated guess about the environmental harms that might ensue? Cases like *Conner* hold that the government's inability at the lease sale stage to fully ascertain the future effects of its action "is not a justification for failing to estimate what those effects might be." In Robertson v. Methow Valley Citizens Council (1989), the Supreme Court concurred that agencies must describe environmental impacts "even in the face of substantial uncertainty." However, some onshore cases suggest that EISs are premature when environmental effects at lease sale cannot be readily identified, or if they are deemed only "remote and speculative possibilities." *Park County,* supra; Suffolk County v. Secretary of Interior (1977) (too much uncertainty involved in estimating the environmental effects of an onshore oil pipeline route at lease sale stage).

3. Offshore Oil and Gas

a. *Federal Jurisdiction*

As with federally-owned onshore oil and gas fields, offshore fields are leased to private developers pursuant to federal statute. As a result of the Submerged Lands Act of 1953, 43 U.S.C.A. § 1301, and the Outer Continental Shelf Lands Act of 1953, 43 U.S.C.A. § 1331, Congress controls outer continental shelf resources beyond the three-mile limit, while coastal states have ownership of submerged lands and "inland waters" within three miles of the coast. United States v. Louisiana (1985); United States v. California (1980); United States v. Maine (1975). State law governs disputes on the outer continental shelf only to the extent that it does not conflict with federal regulations. 43 U.S.C.A. § 1333(a)(2)(A);

Shell Offshore, Inc. v. Kirby Exploration Co. (1990). Within the three-mile limit, states may prohibit offshore drilling. Getty Oil v. State Dept. of Natural Resources (1982). The Alaska Native Indian Claims Act, 16 U.S.C.A. § 3101, which established a policy of preference for Alaskan Natives' use of certain Alaskan lands for subsistence, does not apply to the outer continental shelf. Amoco Production Co. v. Village of Gambell (1987).

b. The Outer Continental Shelf Lands Act (OCSLA)

(1) LEASING PROGRAMS

The OCSLA of 1953, as amended in 1978, requires the Interior Secretary to prepare an oil and gas leasing program for the outer continental shelf. 43 U.S.C.A. §§ 1331–1343. Offshore leasing is by competitive bid. Typically, bids are solicited on the basis of a cash bonus and a royalty agreement (averaging 12½%), with the highest bidder awarded the lease. When offshore leasing is permitted by the Secretary, it is not uncommon for the major oil companies to join together in a consortium and submit one bid on their collective behalf. If a single tract seems promising, it has not been uncommon for a consortium to bid nearly $100 million for that tract.

The Interior Secretary is granted broad discretion in choosing among systems for bidding on offshore leases. Watt v. Energy Action Educational Foundation (1981). Reviewing courts seem particularly inclined to defer to this discretion when the Secretary decides to exclude areas from a leasing program, or when existing leases are suspended for environmental reasons. See NRDC, Inc. v. Hodel (1988) (Secretary may exclude areas from an offshore leasing program for "political" reasons); Sun Oil Co. v. United States (1978) (Secretary has "power and authority to interfere with vested lease rights"). See also Secretary of the Interior v. California (1984). On the other hand, when the Secretary has proposed opening for leasing large portions of the outer continental shelf, courts have not been reluctant to either halt or scale down the leasing programs. Commonwealth of Mass. v. Watt (1983); California By and Through Brown v. Watt (1981).

(2) ENVIRONMENTAL CONCERNS

Because of the environmental hazards associated with off-shore drilling and production, both Congress and the Interior Department have imposed moratoria on leasing in certain areas. After the 1969 oil spill in the Santa Barbara Channel, the Secretary of Interior suspended operations there pending environmental review. In Union Oil Co. v. Morton (1975), the Ninth Circuit concluded that the Secretary's open-ended suspension of the lessees' property right was in effect a cancellation of the lease, constituting a taking.

After Interior Secretary Watt announced his decision in 1981 to lease nearly the entire outer continental shelf over a five-year period, several successful challenges to this unprecedented leasing plan were made under the 1978 OCSLA Amendments and other pertinent federal statutes. See California By and Through Brown v. Watt (1981) (program halted because Secretary had failed to consider environmental and coastal zone factors as required by section 18 of the 1978 Amendments, 43 U.S.C.A. § 1344(a)). In Commonwealth of Massachusetts v. Andrus (1979), the First Circuit temporarily halted a proposed lease sale on the Georges Bank off the New England coast (the Georges Bank is estimated to produce 15% of the world's annual fish catch). The court's decision was based on the 1978 OCSLA Amendments and the Marine Sanctuaries Act, both of which were found to impose a legal duty on the Interior Secretary to avoid unreasonable risk to fisheries in leasing offshore lands. The Georges Bank lease sale was later halted again on the ground that the leasing decision had not complied with NEPA. Massachusetts v. Watt, 716 F.2d 946 (1st Cir.1983).

c. The Coastal Zone Management Act (CZMA)

The CZMA requires Interior Department activities "directly affecting the coastal zone" to be conducted "in a manner * * * consistent with approved state management programs." 16 U.S.C.A. § 1456(c)(1). In Secretary of the Interior v. California (1984), the Supreme Court decided that a sale of offshore oil and gas leases was not an activity "directly affecting" a state's coastal zone. This conclusion was based on the nature of the four statutory stages of offshore leasing: (1) preparation of a leasing program; (2) lease sales; (3) exploration by the lessee; and (4) development and production. Unlike onshore oil and gas leasing, for offshore leases under the OCSLA, the lease sale is a relatively self-contained stage that does *not* entitle the lessee to go to the next stage— potentially environmentally damaging exploration work. Therefore, the lease sale itself cannot be said to "directly affect" a state's coastal zone.

d. NEPA

For offshore leasing, the Supreme Court in Secretary of the Interior v. California, supra, stated in dictum that NEPA requirements "must be met" at the lease sale stage, even while conceding that "the purchase of a lease entails no right to proceed with full exploration, development, or production." The Ninth, Second, and District of Columbia Circuits have focused on the "no right to proceed" reality of an offshore lease sale. Tribal Village of Akutan v. Hodel (1988); Village of False Pass v. Clark (1984); North Slope Borough v. Andrus (1980); Suffolk County v. Secretary of Interior (1977). For these circuits, the critical fact about an offshore lease is that, unlike an onshore lease, it does not provide lessees with any development rights. This is because, under the OCSLA, the lease sale is a purely paper transaction. As a result, these circuits have all held that an EIS for offshore leases at lease sale is premature. They have concluded that EISs are more appropriate when environmental impact analysis is not speculative, which is at the later exploration, production, and development stages.

When an EIS is prepared for an offshore leasing program, it is critical that it consider the cumulative impact on migratory marine species of offshore drilling and oil spills. For example, marine mammals, such as whales, are likely to migrate through an offshore oil and gas area and then be subjected to impacts outside the area (e.g., other offshore oil and gas operations, or municipal discharges to the ocean). NRDC, Inc. v. Hodel, 865 F.2d 288 (1988) concluded that NEPA was violated when the Interior Department failed to adequately assess such cumulative impacts of its late 1980s offshore leasing program.

B. COAL

The vast majority of coal extracted in the United States is consumed by electric utilities. Some coal is also used by the steel industry for its coke plants, and some is exported to foreign markets. Coal is in abundance in the United States. Just as the Persian Gulf region has been blessed with oil, the United States has a multi-century supply of coal. The federal government owns slightly over one-third of the nation's coal reserves. Fifty percent of total coal reserves is located in the western United States, and nearly two thirds of this coal is on federal lands (including Indian lands).

Federally owned coal in the West has several advantages over its chief competition—privately owned coal in the eastern and midwestern United States. Western coal has less sulfur, making it a preferred fuel source after the 1990 Clean Air Act Amendments. See Chapter Four. Coal in the western states is nearer the surface, which means it can be removed by surface mining techniques, which are less expensive than underground mining operations. Western surface mining also permits removal of more of the coal resource than underground mining. On the other hand, western coal has lower BTU heat content than eastern coal, it often has to be shipped longer distances to primary markets, and it is subject to strict reclamation requirements under the 1977 Surface Mining Control and Reclamation Act. In part because of these disadvantages, and in part because of a history of chaotic federal coal leasing practices, federal coal comprises a disproportionately small share of total domestic production (less than 20% of the country's coal production is from federal leases).

1. Pre–1976 Federal Coal Leasing

a. Coal Leasing Under the 1920 Mineral Leasing Act

After 1920, federal coal became a leasable mineral subject to the MLA. Between 1920 and the early 1970s, coal leases were basically issued on demand by the Interior Department. Most of these leases were noncompetitive, "preference right" leases. 30 U.S.C.A. § 201(b) (repealed 1976). Such a lease was acquired through a four-step process. First, a coal prospector applied for a prospecting permit. Second, if the permit was granted (which it inevitably was), then the prospector explored the lands set out in the permit area for a coal deposit. Third, if coal was discovered, then the prospector applied for a preference right lease. Fourth, if the Interior Department decided that the prospector had found coal in "commercial quantities," then it had a nondiscretionary duty to issue the lease.

This noncompetitive preference right leasing system became a speculative method of acquiring rights to coal without actually producing the coal. Lessees (or more accurately, lease "brokers") chose not to develop the coal while awaiting more favorable prices. Indeed, while the number of acres of federal land leased for coal development steadily increased through 1971, annual coal production from the lands decreased. By 1973, only 10% of federal leases were producing coal, accounting for less than 3% of total domestic production. The federal coal leasing system also had the disadvantage of bringing little revenue to the United States, and of ignoring environmental impacts in the rare case of coal development.

b. The 1971–1976 Moratorium

In response to the abuses under the MLA, the Interior Secretary imposed a moratorium on the issuance of new leases in 1971. Krueger v. Morton (1976) (moratorium not an abuse of discretion). Soon after the moratorium took effect, the Secretary ordered preparation of a national, programmatic EIS on the entire federal coal leasing program. See Kleppe v. Sierra Club (1976) (no additional "regional" EIS necessary without a coal program proposal on a regional scale). When the programmatic coal EIS was finally completed, it was found to be inadequate in NRDC v. Hughes (1977) (further coal leasing not warranted in light of low production from federal leases). The *Hughes* case injunction continued the Department's moratorium on coal lease sales into the late 1970s.

2. The Federal Coal Leasing Amendments Act (FCLAA)

a. Coal Leasing Under the FCLAA

During this chaotic time of Department moratoria and environmental litigation, Congress decided that the MLA was no longer working as it should, and therefore in 1975 it enacted the FCLAA, which became effective in 1976. 30 U.S.C.A. § 201. The FCLAA changed several key features of federal coal leasing. All leasing decisions must be preceded by comprehensive land use plans. In the plans, the Secretary must estimate the amount of coal deposits available, and the maximum economic recovery for each proposed lease tract. National Wildlife Federation v. Burford (1985) (plans for Powder River Basin coal lease sale acceptable). Noncompetitive leasing is replaced by competitive (sealed) bidding for all new leases. Prospecting permits are replaced by exploration licenses, which may be issued on tracts of up to 25,000 acres.

If a lease is issued, the lessee may control no more than 46,000 acres per state. The lease is for a term of 20 years (or longer if coal continues to be produced), and each lease must reflect a royalty rate that cannot be less than 12½ percent of the value of the coal. To avoid repeating the pre–1976 tendency of lessees to sit on non-producing leases, each FCLAA lease is subject to "diligent development." Before a lessee may "diligently" develop the claim, an exploration, operation, and reclamation plan must be filed with and approved by BLM. The Interior Secretary may also exchange lands leased under the FCLAA and MLA with unleased federal coal lands. The purpose of the exchange is usually either to consolidate a checkerboard pattern of coal lands, or to protect a pristine area from coal development. National Coal Ass'n v. Hodel (1987) (exchange permitted to prevent coal operations within Grand Teton National Park).

b. *Fair Market Value*

In the early 1980s, Secretary James Watt's Interior Department ended the moratorium and resumed federal coal leasing. The 1982 sale of leases in the Powder River Basin in Wyoming (Secretary Watt's home state) was particularly controversial. The sale disposed of a billion and a half tons of valuable federal coal, at a bid price that was widely thought to be considerably less than the "fair market value" of the leased coal. The FCLAA prohibits bid acceptance at less than fair market value, which is defined by Interior Department regulations as that "amount * * * for which the coal deposit would be sold or leased by a knowledgeable owner willing * * * to sell or lease to a knowledgeable purchaser." A special federal commission created to investigate this sale concluded that the federal government should have received between $60 million to $100 million more for the coal leases.

Another moratorium was quickly imposed. National Wildlife Federation v. Watt (1983). In 1987, a federal district court decided that it should defer to the Secretary's fair market value determination, in part because of the court's interpretation of fair market value as demanding only "fair return," not a maximization of revenues. Despite the loss of tens of millions of dollars of federal revenues, the Ninth Circuit sustained this determination and okayed the Powder River Basin sale in National Wildlife Federation v. Burford (1989).

c. *Retroactive Effect of the FCLAA*

The FCLAA created two issues for those with pre–1976 legal interests in federal coal that wished to be subject to the more generous terms of the MLA. First, since the FCLAA preserves "valid existing rights" (VER), when have applicants for a preference right lease under the MLA satisfied sufficient steps in the application process before 1976 to be considered a VER? Second, to what extent are VERs and valid pre–1976 leases subject to the more onerous requirements of the FCLAA?

(1) "Valid Existing Rights"

Courts did not consider pre–1976 applications for prospecting permits to be protectable property interests warranting VER status. Hunter v. Morton (1976); American Nuclear Corp. v. Andrus (1977); Peabody Coal v. Andrus (1979). If a prospecting permit had been granted, permittees requesting a time extension to apply for a preference right lease had a valid existing right to have the extension application considered on the merits. Peterson v. Department of Interior (1981). If a prospecting permit had been granted, and if the permittee had also discovered commercial quantities of coal, the permittee had a VER to the lease because the Interior Department then had a nondiscretionary duty to issue the preference right lease.

Since the test for what constituted "commercial quantities" of coal became more restrictive after 1976, a question arose about whether pre-1976 coal discoveries would be judged according the pre- or post-1976 test for commercial quantities. The rule that emerged was that if the Department had not previously determined that commercial quantities existed, the discovery could be tested against the post-1976 standard. NRDC, Inc. v. Berklund (1979) (whether a discovery was sufficiently "commercial" could hinge on application of a post-1976 standard requiring coal production to be profitable after incurring costs of environmental controls). See also Utah Intern., Inc. v. Andrus (1979). On the other hand, if the Department had previously determined that commercial quantities were present, then the Department could not later apply the stricter standard. Utah Intern., Inc. v. Andrus (1980).

(2) APPLICATION OF FCLAA TO PRE-1976 COAL LEASES

Neither VERs nor pre-1976 coal leases are immunized from the FCLAA. Under the terms of the FCLAA, any lease must meet all applicable environmental requirements, and be subject to the Clean Air Act, Clean Water Act, FLPMA, NEPA, and the Surface Mining Control and Reclamation Act. Pre-FCLAA leases are similarly subject to environmental requirements that flow from these statutes, unless these statutes specifically grandfather existing leases. NRDC, Inc. v. Berklund (1979); Utah Intern., Inc. v. Andrus (1980). The FCLAA also requires lessees to diligently develop and produce coal in commercial quantities; pre-FCLAA lessees had until the late 1980s to produce coal.

The FCLAA requires a minimum 12-½ percent royalty for all surface-mined coal. 30 U.S.C.A. § 207(a). Pre–1976 leases under the MLA were typically issued at a minimum royalty rate of 5¢ per ton, subject to the government's right to reasonably "readjust" the royalty at 20–year intervals. When 20 years passed, the question facing pre–1976 lessees was whether the FCLAA royalty rate could be considered a reasonable readjustment of the pre–1976 lease, even though the new royalty rate would be nearly a thousand times more than the MLA royalty of a few cents per ton.

The courts have consistently concluded that the lease reservation of readjustment power is subject to prevailing law at readjustment time. For example, the FCLAA's shorter readjustment interval of ten years automatically applies to pre–FCLAA leases after their 20–year readjustment period ends. Trapper Mining Inc. v. Lujan (1991). Since prevailing law applies at readjustment time, the much higher royalty rate under FCLAA is a reasonable readjustment condition. Western Energy Co. v. United States Dept. of Interior (1991); Western Fuels–Utah, Inc. v. Lujan (1990); FMC Wyoming Corp. v. Hodel (1987). The Interior Secretary also has authority to collect any resulting unpaid royalties by administrative action, without having to go to court. Arch Mineral Corp. v. Lujan (1990).

There are two exceptions to readjustment at FCLAA rates. First, a lower royalty rate is permissible when a lease covers underground coal. Coastal States Energy Co. v. Hodel (1987). Second, readjustment may not occur if the Department sends notice of readjustment long *after* the 20–year period has passed. Rosebud Coal Sales Co., Inc. v. Andrus (1982) (readjustment invalid when notice of readjustment was over two years after the 20–year anniversary date).

3. Coal Production and the Environment

a. NEPA

Environmental review under NEPA is an important component of every phase of federal coal leasing after passage of the FCLAA. Outstanding pre–1976 preference right leasing applications are considered by the BLM to be "proposals for major federal action," necessitating preparation of a full EIS. The Interior Department's overall Federal Coal Management Program calls for an EIS, whose adequacy has been challenged for failing to consider whether the Program's implementation might contribute to the greenhouse effect. Foundation on Economic Trends v. Watkins (1990). BLM regulations interpreting the FCLAA require preparation of an EA or EIS before issuing exploration licenses. If an EIS is prepared in conjunction with a lease sale, the sale may be suspended if the EIS is found to be inadequate. Northern Cheyenne Tribe v. Hodel (1988). Even land exchanges to consolidate coal tracts are subject to NEPA review. Northern Plains Resource Council v. Lujan (1989).

b. The Surface Mining Control and Reclamation Act (SMCRA)

After 1974, most domestic coal mining was done by surface mining techniques. By the 1980s, nearly two thirds of the nation's coal production was from strip mining operations. This surface mining is the most efficient and economical way of extracting coal; however, surface mining operations can have disastrous environmental and ecological consequences. In recognition of this fact, in 1977 the Congress enacted SMCRA, 30 U.S.C.A. §§ 1201–1328. SMCRA is primarily a reclamation statute, whose purpose is to prevent and repair damage caused by surface coal mining operations.

(1) SCOPE AND ADMINISTRATION

SMCRA applies to surface mining activities which "exist" as of August 3, 1977. Surface mining operations in place prior to the passage of SMCRA are regulated under state reclamation statues. Woytek v. Benjamin Coal Co. (1982). SMCRA defines "surface coal mining operations" broadly. The definition goes beyond just the site of a strip mine. 30 U.S.C.A. § 1291(28). For example, it reaches activities such as underground mines with surface impacts, and off-site processing facilities. National Wildlife Federation v. Lujan (1991). The dredging of a river for the purpose of producing coal is also "surface coal mining," Cumberland Reclamation Co. v. Secretary (1991), as is the recovery of anthracite silt. United States v. Devil's Hole, Inc. (1984).

The Act is administered through a cooperative effort by both federal and state officials. A new federal agency within the Interior Department, the Office of Surface Mining Reclamation and Enforcement, is charged with implementing a surface coal mining and reclamation program for public lands. 30 U.S.C.A. § 1273(a). States with approved programs may enter into cooperative agreements with the Interior Department to regulate surface coal operations on public lands. Non-federal private coal lands must be regulated by an approved state program, or, if the program is unsatisfactory, by the Interior Department. 30 U.S.C.A. §§ 1253, 1254. This federal intrusion into a field previously belonging to the states was deemed by the Supreme Court not to unconstitutionally infringe upon powers traditionally reserved to the states under the 10th Amendment. Hodel v. Virginia Surface Mining and Reclamation Ass'n (1981). State regulation of coal operations on private lands may be more stringent than SMCRA requirements. Budinsky v. Commonwealth of Pa. Dept. of Environmental Resources (1987).

(2) Statutory Scheme

SMCRA's regulatory scheme contains four key features. First, anyone intending to conduct a surface mining operation must submit a plan to reclaim the area of the mining operation, and apply for and obtain a permit to mine. 30 U.S.C.A. §§ 1257, 1258. The reclamation plan must demonstrate how the owner or operator will comply with various statutory performance standards.

Second, the Act spells out highly detailed performance standards governing how the operation must be conducted, and to what degree reclamation must take place. 30 U.S.C.A. § 1265. The Interior Secretary has implemented these standards in a series of regulations, most of which have been repeatedly attacked both by the National Wildlife Federation, and by the coal industry. The District of Columbia Circuit has sustained SMCRA regulations involving restoration of (1) prime farmland and pastureland, (2) subsided land overlying underground mines, and (3) alluvial valley floors. National Wildlife Federation v. Lujan (1991); National Wildlife Federation v. Hodel (1988). A facial challenge to SMCRA's "prime farmland" performance standard was found not to be a taking in Hodel v. Indiana (1981). However, application of the alluvial valley floor performance standard to a surface coal mine in Wyoming was found to be a taking in Whitney Benefits, Inc. v. United States (1991) (total diminution of value of coal resulted from a SMCRA prohibition of surface mining of coal located beneath alluvial valley floor). Because SMCRA worked an uncompensated taking, the *Whitney Benefits* court ordered the federal government to pay the coal owner $60 million plus interest for the lost value of the coal.

Third, no strip mining is allowed on lands determined to be "unsuitable" for surface coal mining operations. 30 U.S.C.A. § 1272. There are several ways for lands to be designated unsuitable. The Act itself prohibits surface mining within national parks, wildlife refuges, wilderness areas, or wild and scenic rivers. 30 U.S.C.A. § 1272(e)(1). National forests are unsuitable unless mining on a specific tract is otherwise consistent with federal land management statutes. The Interior Secretary is given discretion to determine unsuitability after a general "review of Federal lands." 30 U.S.C.A. § 1272(b). Also, any adversely affected person can petition the Secretary to make an unsuitability determination. Prager v. Hodel (1986).

Although an unsuitability designation effectively prohibits surface removal of valuable coal deposits, courts have been reluctant to characterize such a designation as a taking. Meridian Land and Mineral Co. v. Hodel (1988); Burlington Northern R. Co. v. United States (1985); Utah Intern., Inc. v. Department of Interior (1982). The rationale for these cases seems to be that an unsuitability determination only prevents coal extraction by inexpensive (and profitable) surface techniques; it is not an absolute ban on coal removal. Takings challenges are also minimized by a grandfather clause in the Act that exempts from an unsuitability designation "lands on which surface coal mining operations are being conducted * * * or under a permit * * * or where substantial legal and financial commitments were in existence [prior to the date of the Act's enactment]." 30 U.S.C.A. § 1272(a)(6).

Fourth, the Act requires mine operations to post a bond or indemnify the regulatory authority in the amount of the cost of reclaiming the operation. 30 U.S.C.A. § 1259; National Wildlife Federation v. Hodel (1988) (Department of Interior regulations on bonding consistent with the Act). Also, fees exacted from current strip mining operations are pooled into a reclamation trust, which the Interior Department distributes to any state or Indian tribe submitting an approved "abandoned mine reclamation program." 30 U.S.C.A. §§ 1231, 1232; Montana v. Clark (1984). The courts have adopted an expansive definition of "surface coal mining operations" subject to these reclamation fees. United States v.

Tri–No Enterprises, Inc. (1987) (company which purchased land upon which coal was stockpiled and then sold is liable for reclamation fees).

(3) VALID EXISTING RIGHTS

Section 522(e) of SMCRA prohibits the mining of coal within certain distances from buildings, roads, cemeteries and other surface land features, and also declares specific federal lands to be off-limits to surface coal mining. These restrictions are "subject to valid existing rights." 30 U.S.C.A. § 1272(e). Attempts to interpret this simple phrase have spawned a dozen or so years of Interior Department rulemaking and attendant litigation.

It would seem that, to constitute a "valid existing right" (VER), all three components of the VER phrase must be satisfied. If any is missing, the interest sought to be protected from the operation of SMCRA is without a necessary condition precedent to achieve VER status. The first question, then, is what is a "right"? A private interest in land or resources qualifies as a right if, under state or federal law, that interest is considered property. Cole v. Ralph (1920). A number of resource interests that are property interests have been given VER status in non-coal cases. See Ainsley v. United States (1985) (severed mineral estates); Sierra Club v. Hodel (1988) (right-of-way); Skaw v. United States (1984) (unpatented mining claims).

At one time the Interior Department interpreted SMCRA to permit use of "the VER definition contained in the appropriate state * * * regulatory program." When the VER definition includes rights arising under state law, the nature, characteristics, and range of state-created property rights should be determined by the states. Parratt v. Taylor (1981). One should not assume that rights recognized by state law should be denied VER status for lacking a state permit prior to the effective date of SMCRA. This is because the presence or absence of a permit does not define the existence of a right; a permit addresses only the extent of regulation of the right. Hodel v. Virginia Surface Mining & Reclamation Ass'n (1981) (requiring permits to be issued as a precondition to VER status under SMCRA not compelled by the statutory language).

A VER right "exists" if the right-holder has satisfied all the preconditions necessary under federal or state law prior to SMCRA's enactment. SMCRA's VER language has been liberally interpreted by the Interior Department to permit "continually created valid existing rights." Such rights would attach if, *after* enactment of SMCRA, a coal mining operation properly initiated on a particular parcel of land were later designated "unsuitable" for mining. Such a mine would be a VER which could continue to operate in the unsuitable area. See National Wildlife Federation v. Hodel (1988) (a continually-created VER is "a reasonable interpretation of SMCRA"); Belville Mining Co. v. United States (1991) (the Interior Department may not reverse a VER determination if the reconsideration was motivated by a change in regulatory policy rather than the discovery of an error).

For an existing interest in land or resources to be a VER under SMCRA it must also be "valid." An interest must be valid both under applicable pre–SMCRA law, and under post–SMCRA conditions. For example, an interest may be deemed invalid if, prior to SMCRA, it arose on land previously reserved or withdrawn. Wisenak, Inc. v. Andrus (1979). If an interest is invalid, SMCRA is not "subject to" it. Tetlin Native Corp. v. State (1988).

C. OIL SHALE

Oil shale was a locatable mineral until the MLA made it leasable in 1920. The MLA contains a savings clause which protects "valid claims existent on February 25, 1920, and thereafter maintained." 30 U.S.C.A. § 193. This savings clause raises two interpretative questions. First, even if there has been pre–1920 discovery of oil shale, can it be considered a discovery of a "valuable" mineral deposit in light of the failure of oil from oil shale ever to be competitive with the liquid petroleum industry? The Supreme Court answered this question in Andrus v. Shell Oil Co. (1980), decided at a time when the value of oil shale claims was sharply increasing due to oil shortages caused by an embargo of Iranian oil. The *Andrus* decision holds that the usual "present marketability" requirement of the discovery test should not be a prerequisite to oil shale being declared "valuable" under the 1872 Mining Law. The Court relied on an unjust enrichment-estoppel argument when it concluded that "if the Government were to succeed in invalidating [oil shale] claims * * * the Treasury would be substantially enriched * * *. The Government cannot achieve that end by imposing a present marketability requirement on oil shale claims."

The second question is whether failure to do assessment work on an otherwise valid oil shale claim inures to the benefit of the United States (which would then subject oil shale to leasing under the MLA), or to the benefit of other relocators (under the 1872 Mining Law). In Hickel v. Oil Shale Corp. (1970), the Supreme Court found for the United States, because the MLA seemed to favor giving the federal government the right to recapture lands which had not been "maintained" under the MLA savings clause. One unusual federal district court case has held that the federal government may by its acquiescence be estopped from raising a locator's failure to do annual assessment work. Tosco Corp. v. Hodel (1985). If an otherwise valid pre–1920 oil shale claim has been properly maintained, the Interior Department may not unreasonably delay in acting on an application for a patent. Marathon Oil Co. v. Lujan (1990).

D. GEOTHERMAL

1. Nature of the Resource

Unlike oil and gas, coal, or oil shale, the geothermal resource is not obviously a mineral. Physically, the resource is water, usually containing high salinity brines. Because it is high-temperature hot water or steam, when a geothermal reservoir occurs near the surface, its heat can be used to produce electricity. In light of its hybrid water-mineral nature, as well as its value as an energy fuel, questions arise regarding whether mineral reservations and conveyances include subsequently discovered geothermal reservoirs. Compare Pariani v. California (1980) ("mineral deposits" reserved to state include geothermal resources); United States v. Union Oil of Colo. (1977) (geothermal resources are included in reservation to United States of "coal and other minerals" in the 1916 Stock–Raising Homestead Act), with United States v. City and County of Denver (1982) (reservation of a hot spring did not reserve water for geothermal energy production).

2. The Geothermal Steam Act

Since 1970, the acquisition of property rights in geothermal resources on public lands has been pursuant to the Geothermal Steam Act of 1970, 30 U.S.C.A. §§ 1101–26. This 1970 Act treats the geothermal resource like a leasable mineral, subject to management by the Interior Department. A federal geothermal lease is immunized from an exercise of a state's condemnation powers. Grace Geothermal Corp. v. Northern Cal. Power Agency (1985). The Act allows holders of pre-existing mineral claims or leases to convert their federal property interest into a geothermal lease. See Crownite Corp. v. Watt (1985) (lease conversion denied when applicant had not initiated geothermal investigation). The 1970 Act was amended in 1988 to permit geothermal leaseholders to obtain lease extension of up to ten years, upon proof that the lessee had made a bona fide effort to develop the lease. Pub.L. No. 100–443.

The exploration phase of a federal geothermal leasing program does not constitute a "major federal action" triggering NEPA. Sierra Club v. Hathaway (1978). However, the Hawaii Geothermal Project, which contemplates private construction of a 500 megawatt electric power plant, was deemed to be a major federal action for purposes of NEPA when 80 percent of the project's funding was federal. Blue Ocean Preservation Soc. v. Watkins (1991).

III. THE LAW OF SALABLE, COMMON VARIETY MINERALS

As a general rule, ordinary and commonly occurring materials such as clay, sand, gravel, and stone were not considered locatable "hard rock" minerals under the 1872 Mining Law. An exception was made in the Building Stone Act of 1892, 30 U.S.C.A. § 161, which provided for the location of lands chiefly valuable for common building stone. This practice of treating common varieties as a separate category of minerals was codified in the Materials Act of 1947, 30 U.S.C.A. § 601. The Materials Act authorized disposal *by sale* of common variety "materials" such as sand, gravel, stone, clay, and vegetative resources. Later, the Common Varieties Act of 1955 (part of the Surface Resources Act), amended the Materials Act by removing from future location any "deposit of common varieties of sand, stone, gravel, pumice, pumicite, cinders [or] petrified wood." 30 U.S.C.A. § 611. Although neither Act defines the crucial term "common varieties," Interior Department regulations state that it includes "deposits which, although they may have value for use in trade or manufacture, do *not* possess distinct and special properties making them commercially valuable for such use over and above the normal uses of the general run of such deposits."

A. THE MATERIALS ACT AND COMMON VARIETIES ACT

The Materials Act was intended to create a method of minerals disposal distinct from the location or leasing systems. That method was sale, and it applied to common variety materials. The Common Varieties Act removed a large group of such common materials from the locatable minerals category. This was to prevent mining locations on public lands containing these materials, which under the 1872 Mining Law would have permitted the locator ultimately to obtain title to the lands. There was a perceived abuse of the mining laws, whereby prospectors would obtain title under the liberal terms of the 1872 Law, but put the land to non-mining purposes.

1. Lands Subject to Materials Sale

The Materials Act authorizes the disposal of common mineral materials from the "public lands of the United States." Disposals may be made from withdrawn lands, except lands withdrawn in aid of a function of the Departments of the Interior or Agriculture. 30 U.S.C.A. § 601. The Materials Act prohibits disposals from lands in national parks or monuments, and from Indian lands.

2. Sale of Materials Reserved as "Minerals" by Federal Land Disposal Statutes

In Watt v. Western Nuclear, Inc. (1983), the Supreme Court held that gravel had been reserved as a "mineral" under the Stock Raising Homestead Act (SRHA), and was therefore available for disposal by sale as a commonly occurring mineral under the Materials Act. It has also been held by a state court that a mineral reservation under the SRHA includes caliche (small rocks, dust, soil, and sand deposited in carbonates and carried into the crevices and pores of rocks). Champlin Petroleum Co. v. Lyman (1985).

Based on *Western Nuclear*, the BLM took the position that
caliche was similarly included in a Taylor Grazing Act reservation of "minerals." In Poverty Flats Land & Cattle Co. v.
United States (1986), the Tenth Circuit disagreed. The court
interpreted *Western Nuclear* as including common materials
within the term "minerals" only if they had been locatable
prior to 1955 (the date of the Common Varieties Act). Accord Andrus v. Charlestone Stone Products Co., Inc. (1978)
(for a substance to be "mineral," it must be the type of
valuable mineral that the 1872 Congress intended to make
the basis of a valid locatable claim). Unlike gravel, caliche
had not been considered a locatable mineral. The Tenth
Circuit Court reasoned that because caliche was of "common
occurrence generally and extensively," and because it had
never been considered locatable, it therefore was not a mineral reserved to the United States by the Taylor Grazing Act,
and it was not subject to the Materials Act.

B. THE LOCATION SYSTEM AND COMMON
VARIETY MATERIALS

1. Common Variety Materials Found in Association With Locatable Minerals

The ores of many hard rock minerals appear in combination with common varieties of rock, stone, and gravel. In
such a case, the Materials and Common Varieties Acts attempt to sort out conflicts that may emerge between the
location and sale systems. The 1955 Common Varieties Act
provides that nothing in the Act "shall affect the validity of
any mining location based upon discovery of some other
mineral occurring in or in association with such a deposit."
In effect, this provision is meant to ensure that mining
locations based on a discovery of gold in sand or gravel will
not be precluded by the presence of the common variety
material.

Conversely, the Materials Act allows the owner of an unpatented mining claim to use common variety materials for legitimate mining purposes, both on and off the claim, without having to obtain authorization under the Materials Act. 30 U.S.C.A. § 612(c). The unpatented claimant may thereby use materials like sand and gravel, but is not permitted to sell them to others. The owner of a *patented* claim can use or sell any mineral materials occurring on the claim.

2. Location of Pre–1955 Discoveries of Common Variety Materials

The 1955 Common Varieties Act does not apply retroactively. It contains a savings clause protecting any valid claim of a common variety located before the effective date of the Act. 30 U.S.C.A. § 615. To establish a valid pre–1955 location of a common variety, the most difficult requirement has been to show that there was a "discovery" of a valuable mineral before 1955.

For common varieties, the presence or absence of a discovery is determined according to conditions at the time of discovery; present conditions are not considered. Mendenhall v. United States (1984); Bell v. United States Forest Service (1974). The critical pre–1955 condition is whether, under the marketability test for discovery, the claimant can show that the claim could have been (or was) "extracted, removed and marketed at a profit." United States v. Coleman (1968). This marketability test requires, at the time of discovery, a market sufficiently profitable to attract the efforts of a person of ordinary prudence. Barrows v. Hickel (1971).

The federal courts, particularly the Ninth Circuit, have been strict in applying the marketability test to common varieties. See Dredge Corp. v. Conn (1984) (no discovery of sand and gravel when no evidence of pre–1955 sales, and when there was evidence that supply far exceeded local demand); Rawls v. United States (1978) (no discovery because costs of extracting, processing, and transporting sandstone would have made it unprofitable to market).

3. Location of Post–1955 Discoveries of Common Variety Materials

a. *"Distinct and Special Value"*

The 1955 Common Varieties Act provides that its terms do not apply to "deposits of such [common varieties] which are valuable because the deposit has some property giving it distinct and special value." 30 U.S.C.A. § 611. Thus, common varieties which otherwise must be purchased under the Materials Act may nevertheless be subject to location if they possess "distinct and special value." See United States v. Coleman, 390 U.S. 599 (1968) (while the 1955 Act removes from location common varieties of building stone, the location system remains "entirely effective" as to building stone with distinct and special value).

The distinct and special value test is really a comparison test which asks: Is this resource significantly different from other such resources? Federal courts and the Interior Department have posed this question in two ways. First, does the material have such a unique quality that it can be *used* in ways for which other materials may not be used? Alyeska Pipeline Service Co. v. Anderson (1981). Second, if uses are the same, does the material have some unique quality which gives it an *economic advantage* over competing materials? An economic advantage can be demonstrated either by showing a higher price for the material in question, or lower production costs and overhead. McClarty v. Secretary of Interior (1969).

So-called "uncommon varieties" meeting the distinct and special value test include: building stone with unique coloration; limestone suitable for use in the production of cement; clay used for the filtering of oils in the process of refining;

and "glass" sand. The economic advantage gained due to the proximity of a material deposit to the market does not make the deposit an uncommon variety.

b. Satisfying the Discovery Test

Even if a common variety material is found to have distinct and special value, to be locatable it must still satisfy the other requirements of location under the 1872 Mining Law. Again, the key requirement is that the mineral must not only be "distinct and special," but also sufficiently valuable to constitute a "discovery." Melluzzo v. Morton (1976) (marketability component of the discovery test may be satisfied if successful marketing *by others* has established that the claimant's comparable uncommon variety is itself marketable).

C. DISPOSAL OF SALABLE MATERIALS

The Materials Act establishes three means for disposal of common variety materials: competitive sales; noncompetitive sales; and free use permits. With certain exceptions, the Interior Secretary must sell the materials competitively "to the highest responsible qualified bidder after formal advertising." 30 U.S.C.A. § 602. The original term of a competitive materials sale contract may not exceed ten years. The Materials Act permits noncompetitive negotiation of sales contracts between the purchaser and the United States when it is impractical to obtain competition in the sale of the materials. For both types of sale, the United States must receive adequate compensation for the materials, which has been interpreted to mean not less than the appraised fair market value. The only time common varieties may be removed without charge is when some governmental or nonprofit entity obtains a "free use permit," which provides that the materials may not be resold or used for commercial or industrial purposes.

The United States may not dispose of common variety materials if an accompanying environmental report concludes that removal of the materials will cause unnecessary or undue degradation. The disposal of common variety materials does not limit the right of the United States to use the surface, or to issue permits that do not interfere with the production of the materials.

IV. FEDERAL RESERVED MINERAL RIGHTS

During most of the 19th Century, it was the intent of Congress to exclude known mineral lands from disposition to private parties. Thus, lands granted under the various homestead acts, and especially under railroad grants, generally excluded from patent those areas containing minerals. If such lands were subsequently found to be mineral in character, the courts held that the surface patentees owned the minerals. Union Pacific Land Resources Corp. v. Moench Inv. Co., Ltd. (1982); Burke v. Southern Pacific Railroad Co. (1914). However, it was impossible to know precisely which lands contained minerals and which did not. Lands classified as non-mineral were often mineral lands, and the minerals thereafter became subject to ownership by the surface patentee.

In order to correct this problem, most of the federal disposition statutes passed in the 20th century reserved the mineral estate (known and subsequently discovered) to the United States. The Coal Lands Acts of 1909 and 1910, 30 U.S.C.A. §§ 81, 85, provided that coal would be reserved in subsequent agricultural patents. The Agricultural Entry Act of 1914, 30 U.S.C.A. § 121, provided for a patent to the agricultural entryman while reserving to the United States specified minerals. Most important, the Stockraising Homestead Act of 1916, 43 U.S.C.A. § 291, reserved to the United States "all the coal and other minerals" in lands patented under the Act. This Act was the most widely used surface entry statute among those reserving minerals to the United States. The Taylor Grazing Act of 1934, 43 U.S.C.A. § 315g(c) (repealed 1976), also broadly reserved "all minerals to the United States" from federal lands exchanged for private lands to consolidate BLM grazing districts. The minerals thereby reserved under these settlement statutes become subject to location, lease, or sale. The method of mineral disposition depends upon the terms and language of the reservation, as well as the requirements of applicable federal mining statutes.

A. WHAT HAS BEEN RESERVED?

A recurrent interpretative problem has been ascertaining the nature of the mineral reservation in federal disposition statutes. Courts have devoted considerable energy in construing land grants and rights-of-way to railroads, particularly to the Union Pacific. Most cases have limited the extent of the interest granted the railroad, while expanding the nature of the reservation. In United States v. Union Pacific Railroad Co. (1957), the Supreme Court considered the grant of a right-of-way containing this exception: "That all mineral lands shall be excepted from the operation of this act." Although conceding the exception to be "inept," the Court nevertheless construed it to be a mineral reservation under the railroad right-of-way. The Union Pacific right-of-way was limited further in Energy Transportation Systems, Inc. v. Union Pacific R. Co. (1979), where the court held that the grant of the right-of-way did not convey title to the non-mineral subsurface estate. Another ambiguous Union Pacific grant reserving "all coal and other minerals" was held to cover oil and gas. Amoco Production Co. v. Guild Trust (1980).

The courts have sought to conform to Congressional intent when construing ambiguous mineral reservations in other federal land disposition statutes. For example, courts have decided that Congress wished the mineral reservation of "all the coal and other minerals" in the 1916 Stockraising Homestead Act to include: (1) geothermal resources, United States v. Union Oil of Cal. (1977); (2) caliche, Champlin Petroleum Co. v. Lyman (1985); and (3) gravel. Watt v. Western Nuclear, Inc. (1983). In *Western Nuclear,* the Supreme Court reasoned that Congress had intended for gravel to be reserved because in 1916 gravel was considered a mineral. Congressional intent was similarly determinative in Aulston v. United States (1990), where the Tenth Circuit reviewed historical and legislative materials before concluding that carbon dioxide deposits were meant to be included within the meaning of the "gas" reservation in the Agricultural Entry Act of 1914. Legislative intent is also important when the issue is whether Congress conveyed to private parties a particular mineral material as part of a patent grant of a subsurface estate. See Tyonek Native Corp. v. Cook Inlet Region, Inc. (1988) (sand and gravel part of subsurface estate when Congress created "dually owned [surface and subsurface] lands" under the Alaska Native Claims Settlement Act).

By contrast, when a federal disposition statute provides that the nature and extent of the mineral reservation is left to the complete discretion of the Interior Secretary, Congressional intent is then irrelevant. Such an unusual statutory provision for complete discretion is found in the equal value land exchange sections of the Taylor Grazing Act. 43 U.S.C.A. § 415g (repealed 1976). In construing reservations made under this provision, courts look to administrative practice and judicial interpretations, not legislative intent. Poverty Flats Land & Cattle Co. v. United States (1986) (caliche not a "mineral" reserved under Taylor Grazing Act).

B. RELATIONSHIP BETWEEN MINERAL AND SURFACE ESTATES

A mineral reservation severs the mineral from the surface estate. The former is typically held by a locator or federal lessee, while the latter is usually owned by a patentee receiving title under a settlement or agricultural entry statute. After a mineral reservation, the surface estate is servient to the dominant mineral estate, as long as the United States may realize a proper return from the extraction of the minerals. Kinney–Coastal Oil Co. v. Kieffer (1928). Although permissible surface uses are governed by the terms of the statute allowing surface entry, courts have favored the mineral estate, even when it damages the surface estate. *Kinney–Coastal,* supra (federal mineral lessees may halt use of surface for purposes inconsistent with mining operations); Transwestern Pipeline Co. v. Kerr–McGee Corp. (1974) (federal mineral lessee may subside the surface). The primary limitation on mineral owners is that the surface disruption may not be "negligent or excessive," and it must be necessary and incidental to the extraction of minerals. Gilbertz v. United States (1987); Holbrook v. Continental Oil Co. (1955).

FLPMA allows the surface estate owner to apply for a patent uniting surface and mineral estates. The mineral interest may be conveyed to the surface owner when there are no known minerals in the land, or when the mineral reservation interferes with non-mineral development of the land. 43 U.S.C.A. § 1719(b)(1). The surface owner must also pay fair market value for any remaining reserved mineral interest.

C. IMPLIED RESERVATIONS

When a surface owner obtains title from the United States, the instrument that transfers the legal interest is usually in the form of a patent, deed, or some other such document. If a statute or regulation establishes a reserved right associated with surface conveyances, but the patent or deed conveying the surface estate does not contain this reserved right, courts will nevertheless recognize and enforce the reserved right. Swendig v. Washington Water Power Co. (1924); Proctor v.

Painter (1926); Argo Oil Corp. v. Lathrop (1955). On the other hand, when neither a statute nor a patent reserves a right, courts will not imply a reservation. Leo Sheep v. United States (1979) (easement across private land to secure access to federal land must be *expressly* reserved when there is a federal conveyance to surface owner).

D. MINERAL RESERVATIONS WHEN LAND CONVEYED TO THE UNITED STATES

Under the Weeks Act of 1911, 16 U.S.C.A. § 521, the federal government purchased private land for inclusion in national forests. Many of the resulting surface land deeds that were conveyed to the United States reserved to the original private owners certain mineral rights. Two interpretative questions have arisen regarding these reservations in private conveyances. First, as with federal reserved rights, courts have had to determine whether a particular mineral resource has been reserved to the private owner. See Downstate Stone Co. v. United States (1983) (limestone not reserved because it comprised part of the surface). Second, questions have arisen about whether a mineral reservation carries with it the right to engage in serious surface-disturbing activities. See United States v. Stearns Coal and Lumber Co. (1987) (reservation of coal in non-broad form deed did not permit mineral owner to strip mine the surface).

CHAPTER SEVEN

TIMBER LAW

The physical characteristics of trees cause timber production to differ from the development of other natural resources. The same tree is both capital and output. The tree is productive capital while it is allowed to grow and produce wood. The tree becomes output when harvested. Timber thus raises a problem inherent in timber development—the decision when to harvest. For most resources, the amount available for development is fixed—there are just so many tons of coal or barrels of oil in the ground. However, the forester's decision as to when to harvest will affect the total amount of development possible. Harvesting a tree this year prevents the tree from producing more wood next year.

Further complications arise from the fact that a forest can physically depreciate in value. Old trees can die and decay. Entire forests can be lost through fire, disease, insect infestation, and ice storms. The long amount of time required for a seedling to grow into a merchantable product also creates planning difficulties for those in the timber business. In order to determine the types and numbers of trees to plant in any given year, the forester must predict the timber demand decades or more in the future. Other physical characteristics which affect timber development include the need for a large amount of land, the extensive processing needed to turn raw wood in the forest into a finished consumer good, and the unavoidability of on and off-site environmental impacts (including significant impacts on wildlife) associated with timber development.

Almost three-fourths of the nation's commercial forest land is in the eastern United States, with relatively little in the Rocky Mountain and Pacific Northwest regions. However, these acreage figures are somewhat misleading. Many eastern forests have supported commercial logging operations for over 100 years, and, consequently, consist of young-growth forests with relatively small timber inventories. On the other hand, because of the many large, mature trees in the old-growth and virgin forests of the Rocky Mountains and Pacific Northwest, these western regions account for approximately two-thirds of the nation's "sawtimber" inventory (live trees of commercial species which are large enough to yield at least one 12-foot log or two 8-foot logs).

Tree species also vary among regions. The western forests consist almost entirely of softwoods (conifers—such as firs, pines, spruces—and redwoods) which produce high quality lumber and plywood. Eastern forests produce mainly hardwoods such as oak, hickory, and maple. Southern pines are a source of pulp for the South's large paper products industry.

In the Northwest, the federal government owns more than half of the commercial timberland and can reclassify it at any time as wilderness or recreational areas. In the South, the government owns less than a tenth of the forested land. Much Southern timber comes from forests owned by farmers, who have the land cleared for planting. Because the land-owners are not in the timber business, they often do not replant.

Over 40 percent of the nation's timber harvest comes from private, non-industrial forests. These non-industrial owners may develop their lands themselves in the same way that a large timber company would. However, because many of these forests are small and the capital investments necessary to develop them are high, most small, non-industrial owners sell their timber to timber companies. This transaction can be accomplished in a number of ways, depending on how much control the landowner wishes to retain over timber development. The timber rights can be severed from the land, giving the timber company ownership of all the forest resources, with the landowner retaining ownership of the land and the right to use the land for all non-timber purposes. Another method is for the landowner to execute a timber sales contract under which the timber company buys the right to cut certain trees for a specified amount of time. The landowner who desires to retain the most control over timber development will cut the trees and then sell the felled trees to a timber company.

For those wishing to purchase timber from the United States, the most likely seller is the Forest Service, which retains full control over the management and development of the national forests. As mandated by the Resources Planning Act of 1974, 16 U.S.C.A. § 1601 (as amended by the National Forest Management Act of 1976), a great deal of planning is carried out at the national, regional, and local levels to assess the potential timber and nontimber uses of the national forests before a decision is made to sell timber from a particular forest. After a multiple-use survey is completed, the sale area's boundaries are marked and the timber's value is appraised. The sale is then advertised for bidding by timber companies. The Forest Service specifies most of the terms of the sale, such as the roads to be constructed, the area and individual trees to be cut, and the methods of logging, cleanup, and reforestation to be used.

The law governing timber development differs depending on whether development takes place on private lands or federal lands. Private timber law is a combination of tort, contract, and property law. State timber laws regulate the forestry industry by requiring reforestation or practices designed to minimize water pollution, soil erosion, and fire danger. Development on federal timber lands is controlled by government contract law, and by planning, environmental, management, and wildlife protection statutes.

I. PRIVATE TIMBER LAW

By far the greatest percentage of United States commercial timber land is owned by private parties. Of the 482 million acres of available commercial timber land, over 350 million acres (72%) is in private lands. Some 68 million acres is owned by the forest industry and 283 million acres is in non-industry private holdings. This enormous amount of non-forest industry private holdings represents nearly 60% of the total commercial United States timber holdings. The land is owned by an estimated four million non-industrial private forest landowners, many of whom are farmers. These owners harvest 38% of the nation's softwood and 76% of our hardwood. See City of Angoon v. Marsh (1984) (lands conveyed to Alaska Native Corporation valuable for timber harvesting became private lands under the Alaska National Interest Lands Conservation Act, even though lands were within National Forest).

A. OWNERSHIP

1. Timber

It is quite common for a timber owner to sell timber to a lumber company through a sales contract. Such companies have the resources and expertise to cut and remove the valuable timber, while the original timber owner desires the economic gain from selling the timber. Two difficulties involving timber ownership may occur with these contracts. First, the seller may not own the timber, in which case the contract is void. Thompson v. Flack–Haney Timber Co., Inc. (1990). Second, the timber owner may sell the same timber to more than one purchaser.

In the latter case, the common law rule is that once a grantor conveys all its interest, that grantor may not create further rights in the property in a third party absent any elements of estoppel. Recording statutes have now altered this rule so that it is now possible for a grantor to make a second conveyance divesting the first grantee, so long as the second grantee pays valuable consideration, records first, and acts in good faith. Recording a notice of lis pendens (warning that title to a certain property is in litigation) does not constitute a recording under these statutes. Crown Zellerbach Corp. v. Henderson (1986). State recording statutes often require the second purchaser to be without notice, actual or constructive, of the interest of the prior purchaser. Bohle v. Thompson (1989) (actual notice of prior timber sales contract excuses failure to record the contract). If a prior purchaser of timber fails to record, but pays taxes on the timber, posts "no trespassing" signs, and partially encloses the timber land with a fence, the second purchaser has constructive notice of the earlier sales contract. Wineberg v. Moore (1961) (subsequent purchaser has a duty of inquiry).

2. Land

Sometimes the absentee owner of timber land is not aware that someone has been cutting the trees on the land over a long period of time. Can tree cutting alone support an adverse possession claim? Courts are reluctant to establish adverse possession, when the only "hostile" act has been timber cutting. Bigham v. Wenschhof (1982); Thomas v. Davis (1982).

B. CONVEYANCES AND RESERVATIONS OF INTERESTS IN TIMBER

Private parties wishing to reap the economic benefits of timber on their land may execute timber deeds which either convey to others the right to enter the land to cut and remove timber, or reserve to themselves the right to the timber when the land is sold. Such conveyances and reservations create two separate property interests—one in the timber and one in the land. Although these interests are hopefully compatible, it is not uncommon for parties holding these interests to clash over (1) the nature of the timber right conveyed or reserved, (2) rights of access, and (3) damages to the land caused by the timber cutting operation.

1. Nature of the Interest

a. *Conveyances*

Failure of the parties to specify either the exact nature of the interest conveyed or the conditions of the conveyance causes numerous interpretative difficulties which often demand judicial resolution. Two commonly occurring issues involve (1) ascertaining what is conveyed, and (2) determining the consequence when some, but not all, of the timber is cut. The former question was addressed in the leading case of Arbogast v. Pilot Rock Lumber Co. (1959). At issue was a conveyance granting "all timber and logs." The grantees-logging companies urged that the phrase be interpreted to embrace all trees on the land at the time of the conveyance, without limitation as to size, type, or merchantability. The grantors argued that the phrase meant trees of a size and quality suitable for cutting into merchantable lumber at the time of the conveyance, not trees unsuitable then, but which had since attained that stature. The court decided that the *size* of the "timber" should be that which is suitable for manufacture into lumber for building purposes, and that the time for determining this size should be as of the date of execution of the contract. But see Baca Land & Cattle Co. v. Savage (1971) (all forms of forest growth are conveyed when deed grants "all the timber * * * and increment thereof").

When a contract conveys timber cutting rights for a specified removal period, and some trees remain uncut at the end of the period, the general rule is that unless otherwise set out in the contract, timber left standing belongs to the seller. Holmes v. Westvaco Corp. (1986). Similarly, if a timber owner conveys to a logging company "all timber," and gives the company a set time within which "to cut and remove the above-described timber," the company is contractually obligated to pay only for the timber actually cut, not for "all" the timber that had been on the land at the time of contract execution. Chavers v. Kent Diversified Products, Inc. (1989). The term of a timber conveyance may be extended by payment of an extension fee. Huey v. Tipton (1986) (forfeiture of contract for a 13–day delay in making extension payment would be unconscionable where delay was a result of an honest mistake).

Another interpretative problem occurs when a timber conveyance is signed but not executed before the death of one of the parties (usually the grantor). The question then is whether the conveyance becomes part of the deceased party's will or trust. Matter of Estate of Howard (1987) (sale of "land" including merchantable timber, is not a "sale of timber" within meaning of testamentary trust provision).

b. *Reservations*

A deed reserving "all timber" or "all of the timber" raises the same ambiguity as that raised by a conveyance using such indefinite phrases. Most courts follow a three-step analysis to construe such timber deeds: (1) look to the instrument itself to ascertain whether sufficiently modifying terms are employed in connection with the word "timber"; (2) if the intended meaning is still unclear, consider extrinsic evidence which may show a construction peculiar to the locality; and (3) apply the judicial definition of the word. McKillop v. Crown Zellerbach (1987); Walter v. Potlatch Forests, Inc. (1972). A reservation of "the right and privilege to remove any and all timber" does not reserve the title to the timber, but merely a profit a prendre. M & I Timber Co. v. Hope Silver–Lead Mines, Inc. (1967) (the owner of timber has the unlimited right to dispose of timber until the owner of the profit a prendre chooses to harvest it).

2. Access

Generally the right to cut and remove timber carries with it a right of access for that purpose only. Turlington v. McLeod (1988); Stephenson Lumber Co. v. Hurst (1935).

3. Relationship Between Landowner and Owner of Timber Rights

When the timber rights are severed from the land, those conducting logging operations owe the owner of the land a duty of reasonable care. Timber rights owners may be held liable only for such damage to the land caused by the negligent conduct of their operations, but not for damages incident to the employment of customary means of removing timber. Lawrence v. Saunders (1988); D.L. Fair Lumber Co. v. Weems (1944). The clearcutting method of harvesting trees may be an unreasonable infringement of the land-owner's rights if it produces a piling of slash to such an extent as to create a fire hazard. Baca Land & Cattle Co. v. Savage (1971).

C. CONTRACTS TO LOG AND MARKET TIMBER

Once a timber owner decides to cut and sell the timber, a series of contractual relationships are then established which tend to raise differing legal issues. First, the timber owner may enter into a contract with a logger, whose job is to cut and transport the timber to market, and to pay the owner for the timber. A contract for timber to be cut is a contract for the "sale of goods" under the UCC only if the trees to be cut are identified in advance. Conservancy Holdings, Ltd. v. Perma–Treat Corp. (1987). Such a contract may be breached if the logger unilaterally changes payment computations with no notice to the seller-timber owner. Georgia Kraft Co. v. Rhodes (1987). A logging contract may also be reformed if there is sufficient evidence of mutual mistake. Allen & Gibbons Logging, Inc. v. Ball (1988).

A second kind of contract is between the timber owner and a forester, whose job is to provide "forestry" services to timber owners (e.g., advice on marketing the timber), but not to purchase the timber. Timber owners must be explicit in stating whether a timber contract is to cut and sell, or to assist also in the marketing of the timber. Woodard v. Felts (1991).

A third kind of contract is between the logger and the saw mill. Such contracts should articulate the kinds of timber that the saw mill is willing to purchase. Toivo Pottala Logging, Inc. v. Boise Cascade Corp. (1987) (saw mill would pay only for "merchantable" timber). These contracts may be breached by the logger's failure to ship an agreed-upon quantity of timber by a specified date. Valley Timber Sales, Inc. v. Midway Forest Products, Inc. (1990). If a buyer of timber cancels a long term purchase contract, the seller-logger must mitigate damages by reselling the timber to other purchasers. Sprague v. Sumitomo Forestry Co., Ltd. (1985).

D. CUTTING TIMBER WITHOUT PERMISSION

1. Trespass

If someone enters another's land without permission of the owner and cuts down trees there, an action may be brought for trespass and destruction of trees. For there to be recovery, there usually must be a showing of trespass. This may be either by wrongful entry, or by entry with consent where: (1) the actions taken exceed the scope of the consent, McNamee v. Garner (1981), or (2) the consent is not by a proper agent of the owner. Smith v. Myrick (1982). No amount of private consent is adequate where the timber land is zoned for wildlife habitat protection, and the timber harvesting occurs without a government permit. Maine Land Use Regulation Com'n v. White (1987).

Often a state statute holds persons liable for wrongful timber cutting when they do not act in "good faith." Sparks v. Douglas County (1985) (lack of good faith when logger had sufficient notice of boundary dispute and still chose to cut trees). Before lack of good faith can be established, there must be some designation of a boundary line. Kirby Forest Industries, Inc. v. Dobbs (1987); Stevens v. Creek (1982).

2. Damages

In a trespass action for cutting trees without permission, the basic measure of damages varies from state to state, and is often dependent on a particular state's "wrongful timber cutting" statute. Usually, damages are the fair market value of the timber taken, at the time and place of the cutting, as well as cleanup and replanting expenses. Gibson v. Hardy (1985); Gewin v. Williamette Industries, Inc. (1981). Many states triple this basic award of damages to ensure "that timber buyers will exercise care in the cutting of timber." Wright v. Reuss (1982). Where the applicable statute does not provide for treble damages, courts may permit punitive damages. Leach v. Biscayne Oil and Gas Co., Inc. (1982).

II. STATE TIMBER LAW

Private timber law addresses neither the interests of persons outside the private party relationship nor the public policy implications of timber resource use and depletion. On state-owned lands, these issues are the topic of state timber law. A state may exercise most direct control over activities within state-owned forests, which comprise approximately 10 percent of the total national timber inventory. See North Fork Preservation Ass'n v. Department of State Lands (1989) (no EIS needed for state approval of oil and gas lessee's operating plan within state forest); Miller v. Commissioner of Dept. of Environmental Management (1987) (state agency may award exclusive use permit to private entity to operate cross-country skiing program in state forest). Timber harvesting practices in state forests are often governed by state forest practices statutes. West Norman Timber v. State (1950).

Outside of state-owned forests, state timber law is important because it regulates the actions of private timber owners.

A. REFORESTATION: STATE FOREST PRACTICE ACTS

Interest in some form of state regulation of private actions regarding forest land began as a reaction to the excessive harvesting that was occurring in the 19th century. In the absence of such regulations, logging companies undertook harvesting practices consistent with the prevailing myth of "inexhaustible resources." This assumption held, in effect, that resources such as timber were unlimited in supply in the United States, and that therefore clearcutting without reforestation was a proper harvesting technique. A logger having cleared one forest could simply move on to the next one. However, by the latter part of the 19th century, the fallacy of the inexhaustible resources assumption was becoming evident, especially with respect to the timber resource. The frontier had receded to the Pacific Ocean, and forests were found to be of finite, not infinite, supply. Fears of depleting the timber resource led to calls for government action to check the abuses of past harvesting techniques.

The initial federal-level response was the creation of the national forest system, discussed in Part III, below. The 1914 Weeks Act, 16 U.S.C.A. § 515–521, authorized federal purchase of privately-owned forested areas in the East for inclusion in national forests. Other federal statutes sought to encourage private timber owners to employ forest management techniques that conserved and replenished timber. Chief among those was the Clarke–McNary Act of 1924, 43

Stat. 653, which provided public subsidies for tree planting.

State regulatory statutes were passed throughout the first half of the 20th century to ensure future productivity of private timber lands. These laws were called "forest practice acts," and they usually had as their primary goal the reforestation of land harvested for timber. Most required that certain types of trees be spared cutting for forest regeneration purposes—thus these statutes were sometimes known as "seed tree laws." They prescribed minimum cutting diameters or a minimum number of seed trees to be left per acre. Some states authorized state inspection of forest areas being harvested, and performance bonds to guarantee restocking.

These forest practice acts are still in place. They impose varying negative restrictions and affirmative duties on private timber owners unaccustomed to (or unwilling to abide by) regulation. Often a permit has to be secured from the state forester before harvesting can take place. Also, logging operations on privately owned timberlands cannot begin without submission and state approval of a timber harvest plan. Sierra Club v. Board of Forestry (1991) (if the Department of Forestry determines that a timber harvesting plan may have a significant environmental impact, it may require the plan applicant to provide surveys of old growth-dependent wildlife species within the area to be harvested).

Uncomfortable with such state interference, many private owners challenged the constitutionality of the forest practice acts. The courts have by and large sustained the acts' constitutional validity. See State v. Dexter (1949) (no taking); Gallegos v. California State Bd. of Forestry (1978) (no taking); Laupheimer v. State (1988) (no due process or equal protection violation). A denial of a timber harvest permit under California's Forest Practice Act was found not to be a taking of property where the timber owner could still use the land for cattle ranching. MacLeod v. Santa Clara County (1984).

Most forest practice acts do not have as their primary purpose the protection of the environment. Their primary goal is to foster timber harvesting through maximum sustained production of timber, despite the industry's recognized potential for adverse environmental effects. Bayside Timber Co. v. Board of Supervisors (1971). Their scope is broad, regulating forest practice on public and private forest lands, including residential lots from which loggers remove timber at a profit. Department of Natural Resources v. Marr (1989). State forest practice acts preempt county authority to regulate commercial forest operations. 1000 Friends of Oregon v. LCDC (Tillamook Co.) (1987).

B. BEYOND REFORESTATION REGULATION

Another purpose of the forest practice laws is to preserve watershed lands for water supply, to prevent soil erosion, and to aid in flood control. These purposes have been found to be adequate justification for prohibiting widespread clearcutting of privately-owned timberland. Anderson v. Grays Harbor County (1956).

Several states have supplemented forest practices act regulation with special tax legislation whose purpose is to promote retention of land for forest. Over 20 states provide nonindustrial forest landowners and farmers with property relief by (1) assessing value on the basis of use (rather than market value), and (2) providing various means of deferring timber taxes. See Andrews v. Munro (1984). Other states encourage timber owners to undertake good forest practices by permitting them to pay a "yield tax" in lieu of an annual (and higher) property tax.

State law may seek to promote local timber processing by requiring that timber taken from state lands be processed within the state prior to export. The Supreme Court found such in-state protectionism to be violative of dormant Commerce Clause principles in South–Central Timber Development, Inc. v. Wunnicke (1984).

C. PROTECTION OF THE ENVIRONMENT

1. Federal Impetus

Two federal statutes passed in the 1970s help encourage state regulatory interest in the environmental impacts of private timber harvesting. Under the Cooperative Forestry Assistance Act of 1978, 16 U.S.C.A. § 2101, federal funds are made available for federal-state cooperative forestry activities that promote environmental quality. Under section 208 of the Clean Water Act, as well as section 319 of the Act's 1987 Amendments, states are to develop areawide and statewide water quality management plans that address the effects of water pollution from non-point sources, such as runoff from timber harvesting activities. 33 U.S.C.A. §§ 1288, 1329. On the other hand, the Clean Water Act also provides that commercial forestry operations in wetlands areas are generally exempt from section 404 "dredge and fill" permit requirements. 33 U.S.C.A. § 1344(f)(1)(A).

2. Environmental Protection

As noted in Chapter Four, many states have passed environmental protection statutes that are modeled after NEPA. These laws require environmental review of projects proposed or approved by the state which may affect the environment. Typically, a state forester's approval of a timber harvesting plan under a state's forest practice act triggers a need for an environmental impact review. Californians for Native Salmon and Steelhead Ass'n v. California Dept. of Forestry (1990) (cumulative environmental impact review must be included in each timber harvesting plan); Environmental Protection Information Center, Inc. v. Johnson (1985). Other state environmental protection laws allow private parties to bring an action against other private parties to protect "natural resources from impairment or destruction." Wrongful removal of trees from another's property constitutes "destruction of natural resources" under these statutes. Stevens v. Creek (1982).

3. Recreation and Preservation

Many states have set aside heavily forested lands as areas of critical state concern or nature preserves. The purpose of such reservations is to provide for recreational opportunities, and to preserve lands in their natural state. The cutting or clearing of wood in these reservations is forbidden. Harbor Course Club, Inc. v. Department of Community Affairs (1987) (clearing hardwood for golf driving range was improper when land was designated as area of critical state concern); Sierra Club v. Kenney (1981) (removal of trees in nature preserve burned by forest fire is a prohibited altering of natural conditions). Timberlands are also preserved by state or local open space laws. 1000 Friends of Oregon v. LCDC (Lane Co.) (1988).

4. Watershed Protection and Fire Prevention

Some states require anyone cutting timber near a watershed (especially one used by a city as a water supply) to remove waste debris in order to prevent spread of fire and consequent damage to the watershed. Perley v. North Carolina (1919). Other states have passed laws requiring timber owners to clear slash (inflammable debris created by logging) in order to reduce fire danger. Under these statutes, timberland owners are liable for firefighting costs if a forest fire results from an owner's failure to remove slash. State v. Anacortes Veneer, Inc. (1961).

III. FEDERAL TIMBER LAW

The United States owns and manages enormous tracts of forest land. The Forest Service, a Department of Agriculture agency, has jurisdiction over 191 million acres (an area larger than Texas) in 42 states. This land is organized into 156 national forests and 19 national grasslands. Of the 191 million acres, 90 million acres consist of potentially harvestable forest land, 33 million acres are managed as wilderness areas under the 1964 Wilderness Act, and the remaining acres include rangeland, high mountain country where timber is sparse, and "roadless areas" which have potential suitability for wilderness area designation. The national forests account for 18% of the country's commercial timber land. This land holds over half of the nation's inventory of softwood timber (used by the housing industry), and produces about 15% of the country's total commercial timber output.

Federal timber policy has primarily been guided by three key federal statutes. The 1897 Organic Act, 16 U.S.C.A. § 473, established general guidelines for managing national timber resources. The Multiple Use–Sustained Yield Act of 1960, 16 U.S.C.A. § 528, acknowledged that the national forests were to be administered not just for timber production, but also for "outdoor recreation, range, watershed, and wildlife and fish purposes." The National Forest Management Act of 1976 (NFMA), 16 U.S.C.A. § 1601, mandated extensive planning as a precondition to Forest Service action, and imposed substantive limitations on Forest Service discretion over timber harvesting decisions.

Pursuant to this legislation, Forest Service management policy has evolved from administering the national forests for timber harvesting purposes, to considering the multiple use potential of forest land, to making use decisions according to comprehensive forest plans, to protecting the environmental, recreational, wildlife, and wilderness values in forests. Although the Forest Service has traditionally enjoyed great discretion in managing national forests, the 1980s and 1990s have witnessed the emergence of an era where discretion has become limited in the clash between timber production and preservationist values.

A. USES OF NATIONAL FORESTLANDS

Forests and trees in national forests have many purposes. Trees harvested there become lumber for the construction and pulp and paper industries. National forest lands may also be commercially exploited for mining and grazing. Unharvested forest lands encourage stream flows, prevent floods, provide habitat for wildlife, and serve as a recreational playground for city dwellers. Despite the Forest Service's traditional reliance on a multiple use philosophy, the unfortunate reality is that timber harvesting (particularly by clearcutting), as well as mining and grazing, may not always be compatible with wildlife preservation or recreational use. This fundamental conflict between use and non-use has been the subject of heated debate within Congress, the courts, and the Forest Service.

1. Timber Harvesting

The United States Supreme Court has definitively ruled that the national forests were originally set aside for timber production and to conserve water flows, not for aesthetic, recreational, or wildlife preservation. United States v. New Mexico (1978). Consistent with this purpose, national forests have become an important source of timber for the lumber industry. Much of the national forest timber harvest comes from Washington, Oregon, and California, which enjoys a huge softwood inventory. The board feet of softwood per acre on national forest lands is greater than on private industry lands because national forests include many large "old growth" trees.

Apart from having such an attractive inventory, national forests are popular among timber companies because the Forest Service sells some of its timber to private interests at less than the cost of managing the forests. Forest Service studies suggest that sales of timber from all government-owned forests make money overall (for example, federal timber sales in fiscal 1987 exceeded costs by $540 million). However, most of this profit comes from the productive forests of the Pacific Northwest. In the remainder of the United States, below-cost prices often subsidize the timber industry and discourage timber companies from relying on private woodlands. This practice of below-cost sales is likely to continue, as many local communities depend on cheap federal timber for their employment base, and no federal statute or regulation directly requires that federal timber sales be on a "positive cash flow basis." Big Hole Ranchers Ass'n, Inc. v. United States Forest Service (1988).

Such federal largess may be coming to an end. Many national forests have experienced withdrawals and reservations for purposes inconsistent with timber harvesting. A national forest that becomes a national recreation area, or is designated wilderness, or wilderness study, or a segment of the wild and scenic river system, may be off limits to logging. See California v. Block (1982) (wilderness); Sierra Club v. Hodel (1988) (wilderness study); Wilderness Society v. Tyrrel (1988) (wild and scenic river). National forests that are habitat to endangered species, such as the northern spotted owl, may similarly be protected from timber sales. Northern Spotted Owl v. Lujan (1991). Land use plans required by NFMA may also designate some national forest lands as "not suited" for timber harvesting. 16 U.S.C.A. § 1604(k).

a. Timber Sales

(1) THE TIMBER SALE PROCESS

Federal timber sales are pursuant to the planning procedures set out by the Forest and Rangeland Renewable Resources Planning Act of 1974 (RPA), 16 U.S.C.A. § 1601, as amended by NFMA. Timber sales are also governed by the procedures of the 1897 Organic Act, 16 U.S.C.A. § 472a, as amended by NFMA. The forest planning process results in a forest plan for each national forest unit, and this plan determines what lands will be available for timber harvesting and the allowable timber supply. During the implementation stage of the forest plan, the Forest Service prepares and holds timber sales, and federal timber is harvested under timber contracts.

The timber sale process begins with an identification of the timber sale area. 16 U.S.C.A. § 472a(b). The Forest Service must consider the site-specific environmental impacts of timber harvesting in the sale area (in some NEPA document), and prepare an economic analysis of the sale. It next appraises the timber value, and this appraisal becomes the fair market value of the timber to be sold. 16 U.S.C.A. § 472a(a). All large timber sales are advertised for competitive bidding, where the sale price must not be less than appraised value. 16 U.S.C.A. § 472a(d). The Forest Service then opens bids, chooses the highest responsible bidder, and awards the timber contract.

(2) DEFEATING TIMBER SALES

The Forest Service's ability to hold timber sales may be seriously compromised by Congress and the federal courts. The Congress may circumscribe Forest Service discretion over particular timber sale programs. Even when Congress specifically allows timber sales by statute, these sales may be blocked by litigation or Forest Service decision. See Seattle

Audubon Society v. Robertson (1990) (statute permitting timber sales in old growth forests violated separation of powers by directing the outcome in pending litigation involving protection of the northern spotted owl); Gifford Pinchot Alliance v. Butruille (1990) (Forest Service may choose not to offer particular timber sales based on recommendation by Fish and Wildlife Service).

Forest Service regulations also give the Forest Service discretion to reject all bids. Earlier case law had suggested that the Service could reject bids without providing reasons for the rejection. Hi–Ridge Lumber Co. v. United States (1971); S & S Logging v. Barker (1966). However, in 1988, the Federal Circuit Court of Appeals found to be arbitrary and capricious the Forest Service's decision to change the bidding system after a company had won the bid. Prineville Sawmill Co., Inc. v. United States (1988). The *Prineville* holding is limited to its facts. Timber companies have no general statutory right to harvest timber from national forests; timber sales are left to the discretion of the Forest Service. Intermountain Forest Industry, Inc. v. Lyng (1988).

Litigation brought by environmental groups is yet another impediment to the Forest Service's ability to hold timber sales. Appeals from Forest Service decisions to hold timber sales rose from over 100 in 1985, to nearly 600 in 1990. The two most commonly used grounds for attacking timber sales have been NEPA and the Endangered Species Act (ESA). Successful NEPA challenges have been based on the following theories: (1) An EIS for a timber sale must adequately address environmental effects on biological corridors within the sale area. Marble Mountain Audubon Soc. v. Rice (1990). (2) An EIS for a timber sale must contain an adequate cumulative impact analysis. City of Tenakee Springs v. Clough (1990). (3) A group of timber sales requires an EIS. Sierra Club v. United States Forest Service (1988). (4) An EA must adequately assess the impacts of road construction associated with timber harvesting. Save the Yaak Committee v. Block (1988). But see Headwaters, Inc. v. BLM (1991) (designation of spotted owl as endangered species does not require a supplemental EIS under NEPA).

The ESA has been successfully invoked to defeat or delay timber sales in Sierra Club v. Yeutter (1991) (red-cockaded woodpecker), Northern Spotted Owl v. Lujan (1991) (northern spotted owl), and Thomas v. Peterson (1985) (grey wolf). The Clean Water Act has been a less useful tool in enjoining timber sales. Oregon Natural Resources Council v. Lyng (1989). One 1986 Ninth Circuit opinion suggests that failure of a timber sale EIS to discuss the water quality effects of timber harvesting may be grounds for halting the timber sale on NEPA grounds. Northwest Indian Cemetery Protective Ass'n v. Peterson (1986).

(3) TIMBER SALES CONTRACTS

(a) Timber Contract Terms

Most timber contracts are for less than ten years, and require Forest Service approval of a plan of operations. 16 U.S.C.A. § 472a(c). Timber contracts usually require a down payment, as well as advance payment for each area to be harvested. Virtually all federal timber contracts provide that the contract may be canceled or modified to prevent environmental harm. Stone Forest Industries, Inc. v. United States (1991) (denial of access to timber pending resolution of wilderness boundary issues). Cutting trees on Forest Service lands without a permit or timber sale contract is a federal offense. United States v. Lopez (1984).

A timber contract gives a logging company a property interest in the timber, which permits claims against the government under the Federal Tort Claims Act. Fort Vancouver Plywood Co. v. United States (1984). Timber sales contracts between the Forest Service and private companies are usually interpreted according to traditional rules of contract law. Summit Timber Co. v. United States (1982) (where contract represented that Forest Service will perform acts essential to contractual performance—e.g., accurately mark boundaries—the Forest Service may not avoid responsibility for its failure to perform such acts). The Forest Service is bound by its own timber contract regulations. Everett Plywood Corp. v. United States (1975).

(b) Modification and Cancellation of Existing Contracts

Through contract terms and federal regulation, the Forest Service retains the ability to change, and in some cases, to cancel ongoing timber contracts. Nearly all timber contracts may be revised to ensure conformity with NFMA plans, 16 U.S.C.A. § 1604, and rates of payment for timber may be adjusted throughout the contract term. Cedar Lumber, Inc. v. United States (1987). Timber contracts may also be canceled "to prevent serious environmental damage." Louisiana Pacific Corp. v. United States (1988).

If the federal government has not promulgated regulations or inserted provisions in the contract permitting modification or cancellation, it may not unilaterally impose post-contract changes. Everett Plywood Corp. v. United States (1981). However, where the modification is consensual and bilateral, private logging companies may not challenge the change on grounds of duress or unconscionability. Peters v. United States (1982); Louisiana–Pacific Corp. v. United States (1981).

(c) The Federal Timber Contract Payment Modification Act (FTCPMA)

Between 1977 and 1980, a combination of economic factors caused many timber companies to bid for timber at three to four times the Forest Service appraised value. In the early 1980s, the market for forest products declined substantially, leaving timber companies with contract obligation far above the market value for timber. The Forest Service responded by authorizing extraordinary interest-free extensions of time for contract performance, based on a finding of "substantial overriding public interest" pursuant to 16 U.S.C.A. § 472a(c)(B). This policy was known as the Multi–Sale Extension Program (MSEP). The 1984 FTCPMA ratified the MSEP, and authorized the Forest Service to permit purchasers to return a certain number of timber contracts upon payment of a "buy-out" charge. 16 U.S.C.A. § 618(a). Sierra Pacific Industries v. Lyng (1989). The amount of the buy-out charge varies with the financial structure of the timber contractor.

b. Harvesting Methods: The Clearcutting Controversy

One of the most important management decisions of the Forest Service is determining the appropriate method of timber harvesting. The two most commonly used methods are selective cutting and clearcutting (even-aged management). Under the former, only certain trees or areas of trees are removed at any given time; the remaining forest contains trees of many differing ages. Under the latter, all trees (regardless of age) are removed, and the trees of the next generation forest are all of the same age. Although clearcutting is preferred by timber companies because it entails less management costs, it can produce negative environmental impacts on wildlife, soil, and water resources. Clearcutting is also incredibly aesthetically ugly and offensive to environmental interests.

Around 1964 the Forest Service began to implement use of clearcutting in national forests. Conservation-minded plaintiffs eventually sued, claiming that Section 476 of the Organic Act permitted harvesting of only certain types of trees— namely, those that were "dead, matured, or [of] large growth." In West Virginia Division of Izaak Walton League of America v. Butz (1975), the Fourth Circuit agreed and ruled that the Organic Act was violated by timber sale contracts that did not provide for selective cutting of dead, matured, or large growth trees. A similar result was reached in Zieske v. Butz (1975). Congress responded to the Fourth Circuit case (known as the *Monongahela* decision, because the clearcutting was to occur in West Virginia's Monongahela National Forest) by passing NFMA. Under NFMA, Section 476 was repealed and replaced by 16 U.S.C.A. § 1604(g)(3)(F):

"[The Forest Service must] insure that clearcutting * * * and other cuts designed to regenerate an even-aged stand of timber will be used as a cutting method on National Forest System lands only where

(i) for clearcutting it is determined to be the optimum method * * *;

(ii) * * * interdisciplinary review * * * has been completed and the potential environmental * * * impacts assessed * * *;

2. Mining and Minerals Development

National forests may contain valuable hard rock minerals, oil and gas, or coal. Two legal issues arise with respect to development of these minerals within national forests: (1) As between federal and state law, whose law applies? (2) To the extent federal law applies, what does it require?

The first issue was addressed by the Supreme Court in California Coastal Com'n v. Granite Rock Co. (1987). The Granite Rock company had under the 1872 Mining Law located several valuable white limestone mining claims on national forest land in the scenic Big Sur area of California. Although the Forest Service had approved the company's mining plan proposal, the California Coastal Commission required Granite Rock to also obtain a state permit before beginning mining operations.

The Supreme Court (in a close 5–4 vote) found that there was no preemption. It reasoned that some of the federal laws alleged to preempt (e.g., the Coastal Zone Management Act, and regulations implementing the 1897 Organic Act) in fact affirmatively required compliance with applicable state law. More significantly, the majority characterized the state law as intending only to impose reasonable, environmentally sensitive conditions, not to prohibit mining on national forest lands. Because a state may regulate for environmental protection, and because California was not dictating federal "land use," there was no preemption. Accord, Gulf Oil Corp. v. Wyoming Oil and Gas Conservation Com'n (1985).

a. Hard Rock Mining

In 1974, the Forest Service promulgated regulations requiring all claimants to file a plan of operations for activities undertaken pursuant to the federal mining laws. The mere maintenance of buildings on a claim is an "operation" requiring a plan. United States v. Brunskill (1986). These regulations were found not to unreasonably interfere with a miner's rights under the 1872 Mining Law, and to be consistent with the Forest Service's authority to manage the national forests to prevent "destruction" and "depredation." United States v. Weiss (1981); United States v. Richardson (1979).

Under these regulations, if the proposed operation involves only minor sampling which is unlikely to do significant surface damage, and which does not involve cutting timber, then neither a plan of operations nor even a notice of intent to mine need be filed with the district ranger. Nor is a plan of operations necessary if access to the mine site is entirely by existing public or national forest road. If there is potential for significant surface damage, then mining activity may not begin without a detailed plan of operations and a bond to ensure compliance with the plan and with reclamation. United States v. Goldfield Deep Mines Co. (1981). The operator is entitled to access to the claims, subject to reasonable conditions. Montana Wilderness Ass'n v. United States Forest Service (1981).

The plan of operations is the standard of reasonableness for the mine's on-the-ground operations. A miner exceeding the terms of the plan may be subject to criminal penalties. United States v. Doremus (1989). After a mining plan is approved, a miner cannot avoid being judged by the reasonableness of the plan by withdrawing it. United States v. Nordwick (1987).

Forest Service approval of mineral development activities within national forests triggers NEPA. Cabinet Mountains Wilderness/Scotchman's Peak Grizzly Bears v. Peterson (1982); Foundation for North American Wild Sheep v. United States, Dept. of Agriculture (1982). An EIS for a plan of operations for a mine located on national forest land need not discuss remote and conjectural environmental consequences, only reasonable alternatives. Havasupai Tribe v. United States (1990).

b. Oil and Gas

Throughout the 1980s, a difficult task facing the Forest Service was how to manage its oil and gas leasing program in light of three federal statutes—NEPA, NFMA, and the Federal Onshore Oil and Gas Leasing Reform Act of 1987 (Reform Act), 30 U.S.C.A. §§ 188, 195, 226. NEPA requires environmental review at the "go/no go point of commitment." NFMA mandates preparation of Forest Service management plans for every national forest, where such plans are to be consistent with NEPA. The Reform Act gives the Forest Service an enforceable veto over BLM oil and gas leasing decisions in national forests, and permits the Forest Service to regulate all surface-disturbing, environmentally damaging activities conducted pursuant to any oil and gas lease.

While the demands of these three statutes is clear, what was not clear was how to apply them to federal onshore oil and gas leasing. Problems arise because it is impossible to predict at a preleasing stage whether a lessee will proceed through any of the stages theoretically possible after lease issuance—e.g., no action, geophysical prospecting, acquisition of surrounding leaseholds, exploratory drilling, discovery of oil and gas, or full field development. As a practical matter, only one in ten leases is ever tested with an exploratory well. Of the ten percent tested, only one in ten yields a commercially productive well, and less than half of these will evidence a major reservoir justifying full field development.

This uncertainty caused the Forest Service initially to adopt a "tiered" or staged environmental review process. Tiering entails a more general NEPA review for a leasing program over a wide area, coupled with an EA at lease issuance, and front-loading leases with standard stipulations and conditions. Site-specific NEPA review and an EIS is delayed until the lessee actually decides to undertake exploratory operations in a localized area or, upon discovery, seeks permission to conduct full field production. This sequence, which parallels the judicially approved cause of conduct for offshore oil and gas leasing (Village of False Pass v. Clark (1984)), was found to be acceptable by the Tenth Circuit in Park County Resource Council, Inc. v. United States (1987).

The eventual 1990 Forest Service regulations under the Reform Act reject this earlier (and more sensible) approach. These oil and gas leasing regulations reflect instead the rationale of the District of Columbia and Ninth Circuit Courts of Appeal, which have concluded that lease issuance is the critical point of commitment triggering NEPA and an EIS, unless it is a no-surface occupancy lease. Bob Marshall Alliance v. Hodel (1988); Conner v. Burford (1988); Sierra Club v. Peterson (1983). Because of the resulting significance of the leasing stage, the 1990 regulations provide that the Forest Service must make three key decisions prior to lease issuance, and *each must comply with NEPA.* These three decisions are: (1) the adoption of a forest management plan under NFMA; (2) the decision to make certain lands administratively available for leasing; and (3) the decision to issue a lease for specified lands. The "lands administratively available" decision may be included in the Forest Plan.

c. Coal

The Surface Mining Control and Reclamation Act of 1977 prohibits the mining of coal on Forest Service lands without a permit. 30 U.S.C.A. § 1256. The only exception to this requirement is when the coal operator can demonstrate a pre–1977 "valid existing right" to engage in coal mining. Ramex Mining Corp. v. Watt (1985).

3. Multiple Use

The 1897 Organic Act established that national forests were to be administered primarily for timber harvesting and watershed protection. The Multiple–Use Sustained–Yield Act of 1960 (MUSYA), 16 U.S.C.A. §§ 528–531, substantially broadened the purposes of the national forests to include "recreation, range, timber, watershed and wildlife and fish purposes." 16 U.S.C.A. § 528. These purposes are, however, "supplemental to, but not in derogation of, the purposes for which the national forests were established [i.e., for timber harvesting and watershed protection]." 16 U.S.C.A. § 528; United States v. New Mexico (1978).

a. Non-timber Uses of National Forests

MUSYA reflects the reality of national forest use. The national forests are, and have been, subject to uses which sometimes compete or conflict with timber harvesting. See United States v. Weiss (1981) (mining may be regulated within national forests); Hunt v. United States (1928) (deer herds may be reduced); Light v. United States (1911) (Forest Service has power to license grazing); Otteson v. United States (1980) (Forest Service does not have obligation to maintain logging roads for recreational purposes); Headwaters, Inc. v. BLM (1988) (wilderness, fish, and wildlife preservation sought). In addition, the bark of a sparsely distributed tree in the Pacific Northwest, the Pacific yew, has been found to be the source of a new cancer drug that can melt away tumors that resist all other treatments. Since forests have value for purposes other than timber harvesting, the language of MUSYA raises a question for courts and the Forest Service as to whether commercial timber production can remain the dominant use in national forests.

b. *Judicial Views on Multiple Use in National Forests*

One wishing to allege that multiple use principles are enforceable limitations on unfettered Forest Service discretion to sell timber would argue that consistency with MUS-YA is reviewable in court, and that MUSYA sets out applicable standards that must be followed by the Forest Service. These standards derive from the language of MUSYA, which states that timber harvesting is only one of five listed *coequal* uses, and that each of these uses is entitled to due consideration by the Forest Service. 16 U.S.C.A. § 528. Several courts have already either adopted this view, or tested Forest Service decisions against MUSYA requirements. See Intermountain Forest Industry Ass'n v. Lyng (1988) (MUSYA "gives range, recreation, and wildlife an equal footing with timber production"); United States v. Means (1988) (Forest Service properly denied permit for religious and cultural community, when residential use would not comport with MUSYA requirements).

However, the bulk of case law suggests that MUSYA provides few, if any, discoverable standards to limit the Forest Service's land management discretion. Most cases have found the Forest Service's multiple use decisions to be reviewable, but only for "irrationality" in agency determination of fact. NRDC, Inc. v. Hodel (1985) (agency plans acceptable if not "irrational"); Perkins v. Bergland (1979) (MUSYA "breathes discretion at every pore"); Strickland v. Morton (1975). The general sentiment among federal courts seems to be that MUSYA's requirement that the Forest Service give "due" consideration to various uses be interpreted as "some" consideration, not "equal" consideration. Sierra Club v. Hardin (1971); National Wildlife Federation v. United States Forest Service (1984). Other courts have been more blunt in their assessment of non-timber uses: "The primary use [of forests] * * * is for timber production to be managed in conformity with * * * recreation * * * as a secondary use." O'Neal v. United States (1987).

c. *Future Multiple Use Management*

Although the courts have rejected the notion that MUS-YA's multiple use principles are enforceable limitations, multiple use may become a standard in the future through two different routes. First, RPA and NFMA plans expressly tie timber sales to the multiple use concept. 16 U.S.C.A. §§ 1604(g); 472a. See also Intermountain Forest Industry Ass'n v. Lyng (1988). Second, several non-timber statutes (e.g., NEPA, the Endangered Species Act, the Wilderness Act) have been and will continue to be raised to defeat claims that timber harvesting is the dominant use for national forests.

B. FOREST MANAGEMENT BY PLANNING

The 1970s ushered in a new era of forest management practices where planning became the indispensable precondition to agency action. Although primitive planning for specific forest areas took place under the 1987 Organic Act, and multiple use planning was undertaken pursuant to MUSYA of 1960, it was not until passage of three significant statutes in the 1970s that systematized, comprehensive planning became the foundation of national forest management. These three statutes are (1) the Forest and Rangeland Renewable Resources Planning Act of 1974 (RPA), 16 U.S.C.A. § 1601–1613; (2) the National Forest Management Act of 1976 (NFMA), 16 U.S.C.A. § 1600–1614; and (3) for forested BLM lands, FLPMA of 1976, 43 U.S.C.A. § 1701 et seq.

1. The Resources Planning Act of 1974

The RPA established a national planning system for the national forests in 1974. It directs the Secretary of Agriculture (i.e., the Forest Service) to prepare a long-range assessment of the nation's renewable forest and rangeland resources. This assessment is to project future supply and demand for those resources, and result in a program to guide Forest Service activities. The intent of the RPA is to set timber and other resource output levels *nationally*, not regionally or locally, and to rationalize the budget process. The RPA recognizes that national forests are a limited renewable resource, and that future use of this resource requires planning regarding the activities that deplete it, and the federal funds needed to reforest and maintain it.

The RPA formally requires (1) an Assessment every ten years describing the renewable resources in all the national forests, (2) a Program every five years setting long-range objectives for Forest Service activities, (3) a Statement of Policy from the President every five years to set budget requests based on the Program, and (4) an annual Report which tests actual forest activities against the Program objectives. 16 U.S.C.A. §§ 1601[a], 1602, 1606[a], 1606[c]. Each region and each forest within a region is to accomplish the objectives set out in the Program and Statement of Policy. Neither the Program nor Statement of Policy are binding on the Forest Service or the President's actual budget requests. National Wildlife Federation v. United States (1980).

Although most Forest Service timber management plans are now prepared pursuant to NFMA, some were earlier adopted under the RPA. The timber cutting that occurs under these plans must comply with NEPA requirements, American Timber Co. v. Berglund (1979), but need not be consistent with the harvest level specified in the plan. Intermountain Forest Industry Ass'n v. Lyng (1988). In 1987 and 1988, Congress amended the RPA to bar judicial challenges to such plans "on the sole basis that the plan in its entirety is outdated." This same amendment then permitted challenges to "any and all particular activities to be carried out under existing plans." This confusing statutory language has been interpreted to preclude challenges to Forest Service timber sales which raise NEPA concerns in the context of individual sales based on RPA plans. Oregon Natural Resources Council v. Mohla (1990); Portland Audubon Soc. v. Lujan (1989). The rationale for these cases seems to be that if a NEPA claim succeeds, the result will likely be a modified land use decision, which in effect will be a successful challenge to the forest plan, which the RPA amendment was intended to prevent.

2. The National Forest Management Act of 1976

a. *The Planning Process*

NFMA requires the Forest Service to promulgate regulations implementing the statute's provisions, and then to prepare forest plans for each national forest that are consistent with (1) the regulations, and (2) the President's Statement of Policy issued under the RPA. The regulations were adopted in 1979, and by 1990 most of the forest plans were completed.

Unlike the RPA's national focus, NFMA contemplates planning at a regional and local level. The plans are prepared by interdisciplinary teams with considerable public involvement. These plans must comply with multiple use objectives and NEPA; they must "provide for outdoor recreation (including wilderness), range, timber, watershed, wildlife, and fish." 16 U.S.C.A. §§ 1604(e), (g)(1), (3)(A). NFMA directs that all of these uses be considered, not necessarily those producing the greatest dollar return or the greatest unit output. 16 U.S.C.A. § 1604(g)(3)(E)(iv). After review of public comments and the draft plan's EIS, the regional forester adopts the final forest plan that maximizes long-term net public benefits in an environmentally sound manner.

NFMA plans must accomplish several tasks. They must inventory all renewable resources. 16 U.S.C.A. § 1604(g)(2)(B). They must classify each national forest for land use suitability. The plans must determine in particular which lands are "not suited" for timber harvesting, 16 U.S.C.A. § 1604(k), and which are suitable for timber management. 16 U.S.C.A. § 1604(g)(2)(A). For lands suitable for timber harvesting, the plans must calculate the amount of timber that will be harvested from the inventory. This "allowable cut" is to be calculated on the basis of the applicable volume of timber, and the time that must pass before a second harvesting can begin. 16 U.S.C.A. §§ 1604(m); 1611(a). Finally, the plans must identify conditions "involving hazards to the various resources." 16 U.S.C.A. § 1604(g)(2)(B).

Once a forest plan has been adopted, all subsequent Forest Service actions and timber sales determinations must be consistent with the plan. 16 U.S.C.A. § 1604(i). As a result, once plans designate certain areas within national forests as primarily valuable for nontimber uses, timber cutting will likely be forbidden there. Even if timber harvesting is permitted by the plan, NFMA provides that timber sales must still be consistent with other protective conditions (e.g., restocking within five years; protection of watershed, wetlands, and water quality), as well as with other relevant statutes, such as NEPA and the Clean Water Act. 16 U.S.C.A. § 1604(g)(3)(E)(i–iii); Northwest Indian Cemetery

Protective Ass'n v. Peterson (1985); National Wildlife Federation v. United States Forest Service (1984).

Now that NFMA regulations are promulgated, and NFMA plans are completed for virtually all national forests, the next legal step will surely be judicial challenge to and review of these plans. See, e.g., Sierra Club v. Cargill (1990); Citizens for Environmental Quality v. United States (1989).

b. *Substantive Requirements*

(1) ENVIRONMENTAL CONSTRAINTS

NFMA and its implementing regulations require that a draft and final EIS be prepared on each forest plan. The EIS must present a broad range of alternative plans emphasizing different multiple use values. The Forest Service's inability (or unwillingness) to comply with NEPA in preparing its forest plans has resulted in several successful challenges to proposed timber sales and accompanying road building. Marble Mountain Audubon Soc. v. Rice (1990) (EIS did not adequately address effect of timber sale on biological corridor); City of Tenakee Springs v. Clough (1990) (supplemental EIS failed to consider alternatives to timber harvest contract requirements); Save the Yaak Committee v. Block (1988) (EIS needed for entire road to be constructed, not just a road segment), Sierra Club v. United States Forest Service (1988) (forest-wide EIS needed for nine timber sales in a California national forest).

NFMA also requires forest service plans to "provide for diversity of plant and animal communities." 16 U.S.C.A. § 1604(g)(3). In the early 1980s, the Forest Service issued a regulation known as the "well-distributed" rule which imposes a wildlife management and protection mandate on forest plans. This rule seeks to ensure that viable populations of wildlife will be maintained, and that "habitat must be provided to support a minimum number of reproductive individuals and that habitat must be well distributed so that those individuals can interact with others in the planning area." The well-distributed rule has the potential to completely prevent timber harvesting in habitat conservation areas created pursuant to the rule.

(2) METHOD OF HARVEST

NFMA was enacted in large part because Congress wished to impose environmental and aesthetic constraints on the even-aged clearcutting method of timber harvesting. NFMA sets out three general standards when contemplating the clearcutting method. First, NFMA regulations ban timber harvesting of even-aged stands until they "generally have reached the culmination of mean annual increment of growth." This fulfills the NFMA directive that harvesting be postponed until optimal tree growth has occurred. 16 U.S.C.A. § 1604(m)(1). Second, clearcutting may not be chosen simply because it is the cheapest way of harvesting the maximum number of trees. 16 U.S.C.A. § 1604(g)(3)(E)(iv). Third, clearcutting must satisfy five statutory conditions: (1) it is the "optimum" method; (2) all impacts have been assessed; (3) the clearcuts blend with the terrain; (4) they are limited in size; and (5) they are carried out "consistent with the protection of soil, watershed, fish, wildlife, recreation, and aesthetic resources, and the regeneration of the timber resource." 16 U.S.C.A. § 1604(g)(3)(F)(i)–(v). Even if the clearcutting plan complies with all these NFMA conditions, this harvesting method may still be barred for violating some other applicable statute. Sierra Club v. Yeutter (1991) (even-aged management practices violate the Endangered Species Act). See also RACE v. United States Dept. of Agriculture (1990) (Forest Service may reject clearcutting for not meeting visual quality objectives).

(3) Timing and Amount of Harvest

NFMA requires forest plans to determine timber harvesting levels, and to set "the planned timber sale program * * * necessary to fulfill the plan." 16 U.S.C.A. §§ 1604(e)(2), (f)(2). Forest Service regulations carry out this statutory charge by requiring forest plans to (1) establish the "allowable sale quantity" (ASQ), and (2) set out the "quantity of timber planned for sale by time period." ASQ is typically expressed as the average number of board-feet that may be harvested each year.

The ASQ and the sale schedule must conform to three NFMA standards. First, cutting is prohibited unless "stands of trees * * * generally have reached the culmination of mean annual increment of growth." 16 U.S.C.A. § 1604(m). This provision appears to be statutory ratification of the *Monongahela* rule that harvesting occur at biological maturity, not economic maturity. Second, timber may be harvested only where "there is assurance that such lands can be adequately restocked within five years after harvest." 16 U.S.C.A. § 1604(g)(3)(E)(ii); Sierra Club v. Cargill (1990) (seven year restocking plan invalid). Third, timber sales must be limited "to a quantity equal to or less than a quantity which can be removed from [each] forest annually in perpetuity on a sustained-yield basis." 16 U.S.C.A. § 1611(a). This language seems to reflect the philosophy of "nondeclining even flow," which limits the harvesting schedule to an annual cut that is exactly equal to annual growth. See also Citizens for Environmental Quality v. United States (1989) (Forest Service reliance on computer program to develop timber harvest schedule improper for using inaccurate price assumptions, and for not setting timber production goals in light of environmental considerations).

(4) LOCATION OF HARVEST

Both Congress and the Forest Service have been particularly sensitive to the kinds of lands on which timber may be harvested. NFMA requires forest plans to identify lands that are "not suited for timber production," where "economic" factors (e.g., below-cost sales) may be considered in determining unsuitability. 16 U.S.C.A. § 1604(k). Plans may not permit harvesting either on lands too "marginal" to ensure reforestation, or on lands where logging would adversely affect "diversity of plant and animal communities." 16 U.S.C.A. §§ 16094(k), (e), (g)(3)(B). NFMA permits harvesting only where (1) watershed is not damaged, (2) water quality is protected, and (3) the decision to harvest is not based primarily on economic grounds. 16 U.S.C.A. § 1604(g)(3)(E).

Forest Service regulations implement this statutory mandate through a three-stage timber land suitability process. The first stage removes land from timber harvesting for environmental reasons (e.g., if harvesting will damage soil productivity). See Citizens for Environmental Quality v. United States (1989) (final decision on soil damage may be deferred until site-specific soil survey done prior to timber sale). During the second stage, the Forest Service identifies lands which would be most feasible and economic for timber harvesting. In the third stage, lands may be eliminated to protect wildlife or roadless-area wilderness values.

(5) COST OF HARVEST

Some individual timber sales lose money for the United States when certain costs (e.g., road construction) exceed revenues generated by the sale. NFMA provides little guidance on the validity of such below-cost sales, other than stating that economics should be "considered," and that any harvesting system should not be "selected primarily because it will give the greatest dollar return." 16 U.S.C.A.

§ 1604(g)(3)(E)(iv). Limited case law stands for the proposition that the Forest Service need not "proceed with a timber sale on a positive cash flow basis." Big Hole Ranchers Ass'n, Inc. v. United States Forest Serv. (1988); Thomas v. Peterson (1985). Forest Service administrative precedent requires justification of below-cost sales as either (1) the most efficient way of providing nontimber benefits (e.g., wildlife enhancement), or (2) necessary to satisfy concerns regarding timber-reliant community stability.

3. Timber Harvesting on BLM Lands

While the BLM is not subject to NFMA, its timber sales are governed by three other federal statutes. Procedurally, the BLM must comply with NEPA requirements. See Headwaters, Inc. v. BLM, Medford Dist. (1987). Substantively, BLM timber sales must comport with FLPMA's planning and land management standards. 43 U.S.C.A. §§ 1712, 1732(a). Although BLM timber actions must also reflect FLPMA's multiple use philosophy, it appears that all that is required is for BLM simply to prepare a multiple use analysis, after which it may favor timber harvest objectives. Headwaters, Inc. v. BLM (1988). Third, for heavily forested Oregon and California (O & C) lands that were originally granted to, and later relinquished by railroads, the BLM must satisfy the Oregon and California Act of 1937, 43 U.S.C.A. §§ 1181a–1181j. The courts have interpreted this statute as making timber production the primary use of O & C lands. O'Neal v. United States (1987).

C. ENVIRONMENTAL AND PRESERVATIONIST VALUES

Federal statutes other than NFMA reflect environmental and preservationist values. Such values have become central to Forest Service planning and forest management. If federal forest managers are not sufficiently sensitive to these values, their decisions will likely be challenged in court, often successfully.

1. NEPA

As described more fully in Chapter Five, agencies seeking to comply with NEPA first decide whether their contemplated action requires preparation of a full environmental impact statement (EIS). This task usually is accomplished by performing an environmental assessment (EA), which is an abbreviated version of the EIS. If the EA determines that the likely impacts will be marginal, the agency then files a "finding of no significant impact" (FONSI) instead of an EIS. If the EA suggests significant impacts will occur, the agency prepares an EIS. If new or changed circumstances occur after the EIS is prepared, the agency may file a supplemental EIS (SEIS). NEPA challenges to Forest Service actions typically allege either that a full EIS, not just an EA and a FONSI, should have been prepared, or that an existing EIS was inadequate, or needing supplementation.

a. Failure to Prepare EIS

The Forest Service's decision not to prepare an EIS is reviewed under the "arbitrary and capricious" standard of the federal Administrative Procedure Act. 5 U.S.C.A. § 706(2)(A); Marsh v. Oregon Natural Resources Council (1989). Under this deferential standard of review, a Forest Service FONSI (and resulting lack of an EIS) is rarely overturned in federal court. See Lockhart v. Kenops (1991) (no EIS needed for land exchange). The rationale used most often by the Forest Service for stopping at the EA stage is that the proposed action is itself relatively minor, and unconnected to other similar actions. Texas v. United States Forest Service (1986) (EA sufficient when proposal was to clear only one and one-half percent of forest's total acreage);

Big Hole Ranchers Ass'n, Inc. v. United States Forest Service (1988) (EA sufficient when a timber sale in a roadless area was not connected to the other timber sales).

Not even an EA is called for if NEPA does not apply. NEPA has no applicability to Forest Service actions which are not substantive proposals, but which are characterized as budgeting or scheduling programs. National Wildlife Federation v. Coston (1985). See also Klickitat Cty. v. Columbia River Gorge Com'n (1991) (NEPA does not apply to plans prepared under Columbia River Gorge National Scenic Area Act).

b. Adequacy of EIS

The Forest Service has not fared well in defending completed EISs in court. Forest Service EISs have encountered two difficulties. First, the agency has been inclined to divide projects (e.g., road building to harvest areas), so that each has an insignificant environmental impact, while collectively they have a substantial impact. In such cases, courts have demanded an EIS addressing cumulative impacts for the collective, connected actions. Sierra Club v. United States Forest Service (1988); Save the Yaak Committee v. Block (1988); Thomas v. Peterson (1985).

Second, EISs have been found to be inadequate for various fact-specific reasons: (1) Failure to consider reasonable alternatives that would have resulted in less timber being made available. City of Tenakee Springs v. Clough (1990). (2) Failure to address effect of timber sale on a "biological corridor." Marble Mountain Audubon Soc. v. Rice (1990). (3) Failure to disclose water quality effects of road building and timber harvesting. Northwest Indian Cemetery Protective Ass'n v. Peterson (1986). (4) Failure to sufficiently address site specific impacts of logging company's road construction. City of Tenakee Springs v. Block (1985).

c. Failure to Prepare Supplemental EIS

The subject of post-decision, post-EIS supplemental EISs is not expressly addressed in NEPA. However, judicial interpretation of NEPA and pertinent regulations provide the Forest Service guidance. The Supreme Court has opined that EIS supplements are required when there "are significant new circumstances or information relevant to environmental concerns and bearing on the proposed action or its impacts." Marsh v. Oregon Natural Resources Council (1989). In determining whether to prepare a supplemental EIS, the Forest Service should apply a "rule of reason," which requires it to take a "hard look" at any new information which comes to light, but does *not* require a supplemental EIS every time new information surfaces. The standard which controls the decision of whether a supplemental EIS is required is similar to the decision to prepare an EIS in the first place. Headwaters, Inc. v. BLM (1991) (no SEIS needed as a result of spotted owl being designated as an endangered species); Cronin v. United States Dept. of Agriculture (1990) (no SEIS needed for timber sale); Churchwell v. Robertson (1990) (no SEIS needed for timber sale).

2. Wildlife Protection

The Endangered Species Act (ESA) has had a procedural and substantive constraining impact on the Forest Service's timber sale program. Procedurally, the Forest Service must engage in a lengthy and complex interagency consultation process with the Fish and Wildlife Service before it may proceed with any timber sale. This consultation will eventually yield a jeopardy or nonjeopardy opinion on wildlife impacts in the sale area. Substantively, the Forest Service must ensure that its actions will not "take" a listed species, or threaten its habitat. 16 U.S.C.A. §§ 1536, 1538.

Several species have had considerable impact on timber sales. The Pacific Northwest's northern spotted owl has been listed as a threatened species under the ESA, and its habitat (old growth forests) has been designated as "critical." Northern Spotted Owl v. Lujan (1991). Clearcutting in parts of Texas has been halted because of the presence of the listed red-cockaded woodpecker. Sierra Club v. Yeutter (1991). Road construction into national forests has been enjoined because of failure to adequately protect endangered grey wolves. Thomas v. Peterson (1985).

Apart from the ESA, the Migratory Bird Treaty Act (MBTA), 16 U.S.C.A. § 703 et seq. may also deter Forest Service timber harvesting. The MBTA bans the taking of any bird identified by the Secretary of Interior as migratory. If ESA regulations prohibiting modification of "essential habitat" of threatened or endangered species also apply to birds on the migratory bird list, many national forests used by migratory birds may become off limits to timber cutting.

3. Wilderness

The saga of the Forest Service's experience with the 1964 Wilderness Act is recounted in Chapter Three. To recap briefly here, the Act initially directed the Secretary of Agriculture to review Forest Service primitive areas for possible wilderness designation. Parker v. United States (1971) (no action may be taken to develop lands predominantly of wilderness value contiguous to primitive areas). The Forest Service then inventoried other roadless areas within its jurisdiction to ensure that suitable national forest areas were not overlooked as potential wilderness areas. This review, known as roadless area review and evaluation (RARE I), generated controversy and litigation over its scope. Wyoming Outdoor Coordinating Committee v. Butz (1973). RARE II was initiated to remedy the inadequacies of RARE I, but it was rejected in court on NEPA grounds for failure to perform site-specific analyses of all nonwilderness designations. California v. Block (1982).

Following California v. Block, the Forest Service revised its regulations for roadless areas. These "RARE III" regulations permit the Forest Service to manage roadless areas for preservation of their roadless *de facto* wilderness characteristics, even if they have been designated as nonwilderness. But see Wilson v. Block (1983) (Forest Service not required to manage nonwilderness lands as wilderness). The revised regulations also require all roadless areas reviewed in RARE II, or identified in NFMA forest plans, to be considered for later wilderness designation.

Two issues will likely arise during the RARE III process. First, the Forest Service must continue to be sensitive about whether and when to prepare EISs for roadbuilding/timber harvesting programs in roadless wilderness study areas (WSAs). Thomas v. Peterson (1985). Second, the Forest Service must grapple with the problem of the extent of access allowed in roadless WSAs to valid, pre-existing mining or timber claims. Montana Wilderness Ass'n v. United States Forest Service (1981) (access permitted across a WSA for harvesting); Utah v. Andrus (1979) (access to mine in WSA may be regulated to prevent unnecessary and undue degradation of land).

4. Clean Water Act

a. *Water Quality*

As noted more fully in Chapter Four, the federal Clean Water Act requires states to establish water quality standards for waterbodies, which may not be exceeded by activities (e.g., timber harvesting) that contribute pollutants to water. 33 U.S.C.A. § 1313. The relationship between state water quality standards and timber production (i.e., road building and timber cutting) becomes relevant in two contexts. First, timber sales may be challenged directly for threatening a violation of state water quality standards. Compare Marble Mountain Audubon Soc. v. Rice (1990) (timber sale may violate water quality standards), with Oregon Natural Resources Council v. Lyng (1989) (timber sale would not violate water quality standards). Second, a federal timber sale may run afoul of NEPA, either because no EIS was prepared discussing the sale's impacts on water quality, Sierra Club v. United States Forest Service (1988), or because an EIS inadequately discussed harvesting effects on water quality. Northwest Indian Cemetery Protective Ass'n v. Peterson (1986).

b. The Silvicultural Exemption to the Dredge and Fill Permit Requirement

Section 404 of the Clean Water Act, the primary federal mechanism for the regulation of activities affecting wetlands, requires permits for the discharge of dredged or fill material into "navigable waters." 33 U.S.C.A. § 1344. The term navigable waters includes wetlands. United States v. Riverside Bayview Homes, Inc. (1985). Because many wetlands are forested, and capable of commercial timber production, Congress provided an exemption to the permitting requirements of section 404 for "normal * * * silvicultural * * * activities." 33 U.S.C.A. § 1344(f)(1)(A). This exemption, however, is conditioned by a "recapture provision" of the Act, under which a silvicultural activity may still be subject to section 404 permitting if it has "as its purpose bringing an area * * * into a use to which it was not previously subject, where the flow or circulation of navigable waters may be impaired or the reach of such waters reduced." 33 U.S.C.A. § 1344(f)(2).

The EPA has interpreted both the silviculture exemption and its recapture provision in a general counsel memorandum. According to the EPA, the exemption applies to "normal" activities, defined as "ongoing" or "established." An activity need not be ongoing itself, but it must be part of a larger ongoing operation. For the recapture clause to be triggered, the activity must constitute a "new use," and it must cause an impairment of flow or circulation of wetlands waters. A new use is not present because of the nature of the activity, but because the activity adversely affects the wetland character of an area.

5. Chemical Spraying

For many years, the Forest Service relied on heavy use of insecticides and herbicides to protect its trees. Then, as a result of litigation and a growing awareness of the negative secondary effects of chemical spraying, the EPA and the Forest Service began to restrict the use of chemicals in national forests. Outright prohibitions on the use of some chemicals in national forests were upheld in United States v. Vertac Chemical Corp. (1980). By the end of the 1980s, the Forest Service's use of herbicides had been sharply curtailed. This was in large part due to a number of lawsuits brought against the agency which successfully alleged that EISs for spraying programs were inadequate for failing to perform an acceptable "worst case analysis." Save our Ecosystems v. Clark (1984); SOCATS v. Clark (1983). The worst case analysis requirement has subsequently been watered down by Council on Environmental Quality regulation. Robertson v. Methow Valley Citizens Council (1989).

CHAPTER EIGHT

WATER LAW

Water, like timber and minerals, is a natural resource that has important economic value to the United States. Unlike these other economic resources, water is absolutely essential to the existence of the human race. Its use, ownership, and distribution are thus of critical importance.

Water is a renewable natural resource because a new supply is furnished each year in the form of precipitation. This precipitation flows from watersheds into the streams, lakes, and groundwater basins that constitute the nation's primary sources of fresh water. Moreover, water is capable of being used a number of times in sequence, such that the same water molecules can be used and discharged by one user, and then become the source of supply for the next user. Despite the fact that water is naturally replenishable and reusable, there is not enough water everywhere in the United States to allow every user sufficient usable water whenever and wherever the water is demanded. A condition of scarcity occurs when natural events (e.g., droughts) reduce the precipitation that renews the resource, when human demands on the resource grow to the point where they exceed average available supply, or when water becomes polluted, either by discharges or by hydrologic modifications (e.g., dams and diversions) that concentrate pollutants.

Water law does not operate by providing for the ownership of water, in the way that real property law allows for ownership of land. Rather, water law generally grants rights to the use of water. These rights are important in resolving conflicts between private persons, where the rights of one party are measured against the rights of another. A user's water right may be like a right under property law where the user "owns" a right to do certain things; a water right may also be like a right under tort law where one water user may not unreasonably interfere with another user's right. Western states tend to follow the former "property" system of water rights, while states in the East use a "tort-like" system. Many states do not initially rely on courts or common law analogies in the water law field; they instead use administrative schemes where permits are issued to water users. These administrative systems also regulate private water rights with reference to broader public interests (e.g., environmental protection).

Despite the fact that state law can be preempted by federal action, federal acquiescence and ratification has allowed state water law to dominate. In the East, lands and resources were either never owned by the federal government (e.g., in the original 13 states), or were quickly passed out of federal ownership by numerous disposition statutes. Free of federal control, these states adopted the English common law doctrine of "riparianism," which was further modified to meet the needs of an American society that had greater demands for the water. Western lands, on the other hand, were in large part owned by the United States, which had the power to dispose of these lands and the water, together or separately. A series of federal statutes and court decisions not only severed the estate in water from these western public lands, but also established that state water law and local custom would apply on public lands. See California–Oregon Power Co. v. Beaver Portland Cement Co. (1935). Many of these western states have adopted the "prior appropriation" doctrine, which has arisen as a preferred alternative to riparianism in the water-scarce West.

I. STATE WATER LAW

The water law that is practiced at a state level varies by state. Some use a riparian system, some the prior appropriation doctrine, and some are "dual doctrine" states which use both. Every state also recognizes some public rights in water. The nature of state water law also depends on the type and location of the water. Most surface water not governed by federal law is subject to one of the above four state water law systems. State water law also regulates (1) surface water to maintain instream flows, lake levels, and dilution flows for water quality; (2) diffused surface waters; and (3) groundwater.

A. SYSTEMS OF WATER LAW

1. Riparian Rights

a. Nature and Characteristics of Riparian Right

The riparian system applies in twenty-nine states, virtually all of which are east of the Missouri River. The essence of the system is that only the owner of a parcel of land touching a watercourse has riparian rights; such rights attach only to an owner's land within the watershed of the watercourse. A riparian landowner may in some jurisdictions be unable to use the water outside the watershed. Stratton v. Mt. Hermon Boys' School (1913). In other jurisdictions, use outside the watershed of origin is subject to a reasonable use restriction. Little Blue Natural Resources Dist. v. Lower Platte North Natural Resources Dist. (1980).

Waters subject to use by adjacent lands include most surface waters with definable, natural borders. Thus, the waters of rivers, streams, and even above-ground springs flowing from underground sources in well-defined channels may become a source of riparian water rights. Owners of land abutting natural lakes or ponds have riparian ("littoral") rights to the water there. Stewart v. Bridges (1982). The riparian owner on a lake takes title under common law to any unsurveyed islands which fall within an area bounded by lines drawn from the edges of the riparian tract to the center of the lake. Wheeler v. United States (1991).

Riparian rights do not attach to diffuse surface waters, groundwater (if no connection to surface water), non-naturally occurring water, or water in non-natural waterways. Alburger v. Philadelphia Elec. Co. (1988). Although ownership of land bordering on an artificial watercourse (e.g., a dam, ditch or lake) does not give the landowner riparian rights to the water, over time one may acquire a prescriptive right which may be used to estop other riparians from interfering with it. Kray v. Muggli (1901).

Riparians have a right to make reasonable use of a watercourse so long as such use does not interfere with reasonable uses of the water by other riparians. This "reasonable use" rule requires harm to other riparians before a use can be alleged to be unreasonable. Pursuant to the theory of reasonableness, each riparian has a right equal to the rights of other riparians along the watercourse. The twin notions of equal, correlative rights and the no-harm-to-other riparians rule produce two kinds of disputes. First, one riparian may not interfere with the quality of water to the injury of other riparians. Swanson v. Bishop Farm, Inc. (1982) (a riparian has the right to unpolluted water in its "natural" condition). Second, one riparian may not interfere with the supply of water available to other riparians. Cooley v. Clifton Power Corp. (1984) (dam operator which obstructed the natural flow of a river could be enjoined).

The reasonable use doctrine reflects a preference for natural over artificial uses of water. Prather v. Hoberg (1944). In the 1990s, a natural use is usually defined as a use which is reasonable in light of the reciprocal rights of other riparians. A riparian use will therefore support domestic, irrigation, industrial, mining, and hydropower uses on riparian lands. Storage of water is acceptable so long as the reasonable uses of others are not impaired. Heise v. Schulz (1949). If a city owns riparian land, then it may make reasonable municipal uses of the water. Botton v. State (1966). In order to avoid owning sufficient riparian land to justify the large supply of water needed to supply municipal residents, many cities have either condemned private riparian water rights, or have been given special statutory powers. Dimmock v. New London (1968). A riparian may also make recreational uses of an adjoining waterway. Collens v. New Canaan Water Co. (1967).

While a riparian landowner does not own the water in the watercourse, the landowner does have a property right in the waterbody that provides several legal rights. These include the right of access, the right to build a wharf, the right to maintenance of the flow within the stream, the right of reasonable use, and the right to a certain degree of water quality. The right to discharge waste depends upon whether the discharge constitutes a changed use, and whether other riparians are injured. Borough of Westville v. Whitney Home Builders, Inc. (1956).

b. *Conveyances*

If a riparian landowner transfers riparian land to another party, the general rule is that the conveyance presumably includes riparian water rights appurtenant to the land. However, the riparian right to the use of the water may be separately reserved or granted, either when a riparian divides a riparian tract, or when riparian rights are transferred to non-riparians. A riparian grantor may divide a riparian parcel, convey a divided portion to the grantee, and either reserve the water rights for the retained portion, or convey the water rights to the grantee. Copeland v. Fairview Land & Water Co. (1913). Similarly, a riparian grantor may divide a riparian tract so that a portion of the original riparian land is no longer contiguous to the watercourse, convey the now non-riparian land to the grantee, and either reserve the water rights for the retained riparian portion, or convey the water rights to the non-riparian portion. Strong v. Baldwin (1908).

If a riparian proprietor conveys only that part of the land that does not front the watercourse, the riparian water rights are severed from the conveyed land. In a "source of title" jurisdiction, land severed from the water can never regain riparian rights. Yearsley v. Cater (1928). In "unity of title" jurisdictions, any person owning riparian land is entitled to riparian rights, regardless of whether some of that land did not front a watercourse when it was originally conveyed to the riparian owner. Clark v. Allaman (1905).

c. Limits on Riparian Rights

The most important traditional, common law limitations on riparians are: (1) the reasonable use rule, which allows riparians to use adjacent waters only if the use does not interfere with the reasonable use of other riparians; (2) the reciprocal right of other riparians to make reasonable use of waters, including the surface of waterways; (3) the prohibition against any use of water on land outside the watershed (although the Restatement (Second) of Torts § 855 tests non-riparian uses according to a reasonableness standard relative to riparian uses); and (4) public rights, discussed below in Part I A 4.

In addition, many eastern riparian states have adopted statutory permit systems to regulate water use. These permit systems typically are triggered either when drought or unanticipated diminution of water quality call for regulation, or when one seeks to divert or impound surface water. Permits must be obtained from a state administrative agency which decides (1) whether one may divert water, (2) the quantity that may be diverted (and how much must remain in the stream), (3) the method of diversion, and (4) when the water may be diverted. In its decision the agency considers the effect on other riparians, on fish and wildlife, on water quality, and on the public's interest in water. As between competing riparians, priority of use is irrelevant, and domestic and municipal uses are generally favored.

d. Loss of the Riparian Right

Riparian rights can be lost by the presence of conditions leading to either common law or statutory bases for termination. Although non-use alone will not destroy riparian rights, an abandonment may occur if the owner does not use the right *and* indicates an intent to abandon. Since few riparian owners will likely ever manifest an intent to abandon, its loss is more commonly brought about when another party (typically an upstream user) obtains a prescriptive right (against a downstream user) under adverse possession rules. An upper riparian's use is not adverse unless it unreasonably interferes with the rights of downstream users. Pabst v. Finmand (1922). Downstream users, either riparian or non-riparian, cannot acquire prescriptive rights against upstream riparians.

If "avulsion" occurs (where a river suddenly abandons its channel and occupies a new channel because of natural or human-induced conditions), the river may move away from a riparian landowner's property. In such a case, the property boundary does not change and riparian land becomes non-riparian, depriving the landowner of riparian rights. Baxter v. Utah Dept. of Transp. (1989). When a waterbody gradually changes course, "accretion" and "reliction" may occur. Accretion is the slow and imperceptible deposit of silt on one riverbank, and erosion of the other bank, that gradually changes the location of the river. City of Lawrence v. McGrew (1973). Reliction is the process by which land is bared by gradual recession of water. Matter of Ownership of Bed of Devils Lake (1988). With either accretion or reliction, the property boundary changes with the waterline and with the borders of the watercourse, and riparian rights are not lost. 101 Ranch v. United States (1990) (under doctrine of reliction, landowner takes title to lands uncovered by gradual recession of water); California ex rel. State Lands Com'n v. United States (1986).

Some states require permits for existing uses. If permits are not obtained, the riparian right may be forfeited. Many permit states require forfeiture if water use under a permit is discontinued for a set period of time. Matter of Deadman Creek Drainage Basin (1985).

2. Prior Appropriation

The prior appropriation doctrine is the established rule for recognizing and administering water rights in 19 states. All of the eight most arid states in the central Rocky Mountain region, and Alaska, have adopted a "pure" version of the prior appropriation doctrine. The nine states bordering these mountainous states, as well as Mississippi, employ a mix of riparian and prior appropriation doctrine in their water laws.

Although in both riparian and appropriation systems the legal property interest is the right to the use of the water, not the water itself, there are significant differences in the doctrines. Ownership of riparian land is not the basis for the appropriation water right; the water right exists when water is appropriated (diverted and used) for a beneficial purpose. Appropriated waters need not be used on riparian lands and there is no watershed limitation. Appropriated waters may be used any place, regardless of the distance from the stream. There is no reasonable use limitation; the extent of the water right is the amount that historically was put to a beneficial purpose. In an appropriation system the water right has a "priority" date, which is the date of the original appropriation. The holder of the oldest water right (with the most senior priority date) is entitled to full delivery of water. In times of shortage there is no prorationing of available water among riparians. The senior appropriation right is entitled to full delivery of water, which must be accomplished before the next junior appropriator is entitled to take water. Appropriative rights are acquired by use and may be lost by non-use.

a. *Acquisition of Water Right*

(1) WATERS SUBJECT TO APPROPRIATION

(a) Waters From Natural Watercourses

In most states the prior appropriation doctrine does not apply to diffused surface water, and to the extent it applies to groundwater, it is usually modified to reflect the unique nature of groundwater's physical occurrence. The appropriation doctrine has primary applicability to surface waters, and particularly to waters from "natural" watercourses. As a general rule, water that is not in a watercourse as a result of naturally occurring precipitation or runoff, but instead is there because of human labor, is not subject to appropriation and use except by those responsible for its presence. But see Arizona Public Service Co. v. Long (1989) (sewage effluent is subject to appropriation by downstream users).

A watercourse includes rivers, streams, lakes, ponds, and all the tributaries that feed into them. Spring waters may be subject to appropriation if they form a definite stream. Oklahoma Water Resources Bd. v. Lawton (1977). To be a watercourse a waterbody usually must have a definite bed, bank, and channel; some jurisdictions require that the water be in the channel throughout the year, not just during seasonal runoff or during a rainstorm. State v. Hiber (1935). Other jurisdictions demand that there be sufficient water in the stream to be used for irrigation. Hoefs v. Short (1925).

(b) Foreign or Developed Water

When water is not naturally a part of a watershed, when it is introduced into a watercourse as a result of human effort, that water is referred to as "foreign" or "developed" water. The most common example of foreign water in the West is the water that is brought to a river by some transbasin (different watershed) diversion. Such a diversion often entails tunneling and pumping water many miles through mountains to the eventual watercourse. A developer (or importer) of foreign water has the right to use, reuse, successively use, sell, or entirely consume such water. City and County of Denver By and Through Board of Water Com'rs v. Fulton Irrigating Ditch Co. (1972); Water Supply and Storage Co. v. Curtis (1987).

Unlike other appropriators, the foreign water developer need not be concerned about providing an adequate return flow for downstream appropriators. The normal "no harm" to junior downstream appropriators does not apply to foreign water because by definition the water was never naturally in the watercourse. Thus, as to foreign water, junior appropriators' rights are subject to change in time, place, or nature of use by the developer of the water, even when the change eliminates the water otherwise available. City of Florence v. Board of Waterworks of Pueblo (1990). This right of a developer of foreign water to use the water regardless of other appropriators may be modified by contract. Denver v. Consolidated Ditches Co. (1991). When the importer of foreign waste loses physical possession of the water, it may be used (but not appropriated) by others. Dodge v. Ellensburg Water Co. (1986).

(c) Waste or Salvaged Water

When water has escaped from a ditch or diversion channel by drainage or seepage, it is known as "waste" water. When it is recaptured before it rejoins a natural watercourse, it is sometimes known as "salvaged" water. The rule is that such waters may be recaptured and reused by the original appropriator. There are three limitations on this right of recapture and reuse. First, the total quantity of water used may not exceed the quantity in the appropriator's water right. Cleaver v. Judd (1964). As long as total use does not exceed the water right, the original appropriator may increase consumption by recycling the water, even if this injures downstream users that have come to rely on historical return flows. Second, waste water must be used for the original purpose of the right. Water salvaged by more efficient irrigation systems for a new purpose is considered a change of use that violates the "no harm" to downstream junior rule. Comstock v. Ramsey (1913). Third, the reuse must occur on the land from which the original appropriation was made. Salt River Valley Water Users' Ass'n v. Kovacovich (1966) (water salvaged by lining irrigation ditches may not be reused on adjoining parcel).

In Colorado, an appropriator may not enlarge an original decreed right by removing phreatophytes (plants along streams that consume water), by draining an adjacent peat bog, or by cutting trees that take water from streams. Southeastern Colorado Water Conservancy Dist. v. Shelton Farms, Inc. (1974); RJA, Inc. v. Water Users Ass'n (1984); Giffen v. State (1984). Although these decisions deter activities which "create" new water, the rationale has been that the saved water was originally in the stream and therefore was part of the appropriation by downstream juniors.

In Nevada and Arizona, sewage effluent is waste water that is subject to appropriation by others. United States v. Orr Water Ditch Co. (1990); Arizona Public Service Co. v. Long (1989). Those responsible for the sewage may discontinue its discharge without violating the rights of downstream users that had appropriated it.

(2) Perfecting the Appropriative Right

The requirements of an appropriation vary by jurisdiction, and most states have supplanted the traditional common law elements of appropriation with specific statutory requirements which must be met before a permit may be granted. Nevertheless, even the permit system jurisdictions generally impose three traditional preconditions on a valid appropriation: (1) intent to appropriate and notice of the appropriation; (2) diversion; and (3) application of the water to a beneficial use within a reasonable time. Non-permit jurisdictions, primarily Colorado, apply these three elements somewhat differently, and their system of perfecting an appropriation will be addressed separately below.

(a) Intent and Notice

Since most appropriation states require a permit for a valid appropriation, application for the permit supplies the requirements of intent and notice. However, one may not apply for a permit and then seek a place to use it. Lemmon v. Hardy (1974). Manifestations of intent and notice are also important for purposes of establishing a priority date. Colville Confederated Tribes v. Walton (1985). If an appropriator proves that intent and notice were manifested before physical diversion of water (e.g., by undertaking a survey), the doctrine of "relation back" allows the priority date to be set at the earlier intent-and-notice date. Olsen v. McQueary (1984) (a warranty deed conveying a decreed water right not an overt physical act giving notice to others).

(b) Diversion

The diversion requirement serves several important purposes. It determines the extent of the water appropriated, a fact useful to downstream appropriators. Such downstream users also rely on the location of the upstream diversion; the "no harm" to junior appropriators rule often prevents upstream appropriators from changing the initial point of diversion. The diversion requirement also provides notice, and the date of diversion may be used to establish an appropriator's priority date.

In some jurisdictions, it may not be necessary for there to be an actual physical diversion of water by some device that takes water from a waterbody. Many states permit state agencies to make instream appropriations of water so that a minimum amount of water will continue to flow in order to protect fish, wildlife, or recreation. Diack v. City of Portland (1988). Other jurisdictions do not require a physical diversion if intent and application to a beneficial use is already established. Thomas v. Guiraud (1883) (overflow from a dam onto a meadow is an adequate diversion). Some states permit the diversion requirement to be satisfied if livestock drink from a stream. Waters of Horse Springs v. State Engineer (1983). One federal court concluded that the mist from a natural waterfall was a diversion. Empire Water & Power Co. v. Cascade Town Co. (1913).

In permit jurisdictions which allow the priority date to relate back to the date of the application, the appropriator must begin and complete construction of the diversion project with "due diligence," and put the water to a beneficial use with a fixed time period. Application of Plains Elec. Generation and Transmission Co-op., Inc. (1988). There are two exceptions to the due diligence requirement. First, many states allow municipalities to appropriate water for future water supply requirements. Second, extensions of the time period for demonstrations of due diligence may be granted upon a showing of "good cause." In re Hood River (1924) (financial difficulties are a good cause exception to due diligence).

(c) Beneficial Use

The definition of beneficial use is similar among appropriation jurisdictions, and generally includes the following uses: domestic, municipal, industrial, commercial, agricultural, hydropower production, stockwatering, and mining. Neubert v. Yakima–Tieton Irr. Dist. (1991) (frost protection is a beneficial use); Benz v. Water Resources Com'n (1988) (use of water to leach boron in soil is a beneficial use). By the 1990s, recreation, fish and wildlife maintenance, and preservation of environmental and aesthetic values had been declared beneficial uses. Despite the broad sweep of the beneficial use definition, some uses are still suspect. See Danielson v. Milne (1988) (drilling and testing wells with temporary pumps, without more, is not a beneficial use).

If an appropriator puts water to a use deemed beneficial by state law, it may not be defeated by a junior use thought to be more socially or economically important. However, one who has perfected an appropriative right by applying it to a beneficial use may lose it if the means of diversion or ultimate use is found to be wasteful. Denver v. Consolidated Ditches Co. (1991); Imperial Irr. Dist. v. State Water Resources Control Bd. (1990).

(d) The Prior Appropriation Right in Non–Permit Jurisdictions: The Colorado Experience

In non-permit jurisdictions like Colorado, priority is established when the applicant (1) decides to use water, and (2) makes an "open, overt physical demonstration of the intent." These physical acts must be sufficient to constitute notice to third parties. Lionelle v. Southeastern Colorado Water Conservancy Dist. (1984). Evidence of future needs, without firm contractual commitments, is insufficient to show intent. Colorado River Water Conservation Dist. v. Vidler Tunnel Water Co. (1979).

Colorado allows for "conditional decrees," which give the rightholder a particular quantity of water for a specific future use. An applicant seeking a conditional decree must prove that the appropriation will be completed with diligence. Evidence of diligence on one part of a large integrated project may properly be attributed to the entire project. In re Application For Water Rights (1987). Failure to exercise diligence may be supported by the following evidence: the applicant failed to (1) acquire financing commitments, Trans-County Water, Inc. v. Central Colorado Water Conservancy Dist. (1986); (2) obtain legal ownership of the land on which a proposed storage project was to be located, FWS Land and Cattle Co. v. State, Div. of Wildlife (1990); (3) finalize firm contracts for the use of the water. Rocky Mountain Power Co. v. Colorado River Water Conservation Dist. (1982); or file timely application of diligence. Fort Lyon Canal v. Purgatoire River (1991). Failure to proceed with diligence cancels the conditional right. Broyles v. Fort Lyon Canal Co. (1985).

In Colorado, an appropriator's priority date is the date the "first step" is taken toward appropriating water, which often is the first overt physical act taken to construct diversion facilities. Four Counties Water Users Ass'n v. Colorado River Water Conservation Dist. (1966); City and County of Denver v. Sheriff (1939). If a water right is then perfected with reasonable diligence, the priority date will relate back to the date on which the appropriator took this first step. Closed Basin Landowners Ass'n v. Rio Grande Water Conservation Dist. (1987).

(3) STATUTORY AND ADMINISTRATIVE REGULATION AND PERMITTING OF APPROPRIATIVE RIGHTS

In all appropriation jurisdictions except Colorado a prospective water user must apply to a state agency or official (e.g., the state engineer) for a permit to appropriate water. Colorado still adheres to a court-supervised administrative system.   The permit-granting body serves three important functions.   First, it issues permits for feasible projects that meet statutory criteria for a valid appropriation (e.g., permit issuance may not impair existing rights).   While a finding that unappropriated water is available is usually a standard criteria, such a finding may in reality mean that water will be available only in years of heavy flow or low senior usage.

Most states may reject applications not in the "public interest."   See Steamboaters v. Winchester Water Control Dist. (1984) (proposed hydro project may affect public interest in fishing); Shokal v. Dunn (1985) (application must be considered in light of public's interest in water quality).   Some states have gone so far as to impose a "public trust" duty on permitting agencies.   United States v. State Water Resources Control Bd. (1986) (state agency must grant permits in light of water quality goals); United Plainsmen Ass'n v. North Dakota State Water Conservation Com'n (1976).   Administrative agencies also impose permit conditions that restrict how the water right may be exercised.   East Bay Municipal Utility Dist. v. Department of Public Works (1934).

Second, permitting agencies distribute water to users, so that as western streams diminish in flow during the summer, the diversion works of appropriators are shut off in inverse order of priority.   This policing of distribution rights is ministerial, and therefore requires no prior notice before a head is open or shut.   Hamp v. State (1911).   The agency's distribution function also includes making decisions on requests for changes in the point of diversion or place of use.   Compare Bonham v. Morgan (1989) (Utah state engineer must consider public welfare when contemplating applications for changes in point of diversion, place, or nature of use), with Application of Sleeper (1988) (New Mexico state engineer need not consider public interest in ruling on applications for transfer or change of water rights).

Third, rights are "adjudicated" in order to place on record relative dates of priority, amount of water appropriated along a watercourse, and purpose and place of water use. Once there has been a final tabulation of competing rights within each state's watershed, a court decree is entered for all rights thus adjudicated. South Adams Cty. v. Broe Land Co. (1991); McDonald v. State (1986).

b. Nature and Characteristics of the Appropriative Right

(1) PRIORITY

An appropriator's right is judged in relation to the rights of other appropriators; one is either senior or junior to all others along a waterbody. If one is senior to a junior appropriator, the senior may take water needed by downstream juniors, while upstream juniors must permit the water to flow past their diversion points if the senior needs the water. The senior is entitled to the full senior allotment before the junior may use any water. R.T. Nahas Co. v. Hulet (1988) (downstream seniors entitled to damages for upstream junior's impoundment of water which resulted in crop losses). This senior right is protected even if there are dramatic physical losses in flow between upstream juniors and a downstream senior. State ex rel. Cary v. Cochran (1940) (seniors may shut off upstream juniors, despite the fact that 77% of the water was lost in transit through seepage and evaporation). But see Glenn Dale Ranches, Inc. v. Shaub (1972) (appropriators may not divert more than is needed to irrigate crops to compensate for losses while water is flowing to the crops).

There are still several recourses available to juniors. First, some states allow juniors to take water that would otherwise go to senior appropriators so long as the junior substitutes or exchanges it for "new" water that can be used by the senior. Reno v. Richards (1918) (stored water may be released to satisfy senior); Board of Directors of Wilder Irr. Dist. v. Jorgensen (1943) (foreign water may be delivered to senior). Second, each appropriator may agree to a rotation system, whereby an appropriator takes the total share for all for only a short time period (to afford each a practical "head" for irrigation). Albion—Idaho Land Co. v. Naf Irr. Co. (1938). Third, a junior can prevent enforcement of a senior right if the senior's use is not for a beneficial purpose, or if a "futile call" will result (when no junior water will reach the senior due to poor flow, natural seepage, or evaporation). Finally, a senior may not transfer the senior right to another, or change the point of diversion, place or purpose of use, if the junior's right is thereby harmed. Matter of May (1988).

(2) QUANTITY

The amount of water that may be used by an appropriator is measured by the quantity of water that historically could be applied to a beneficial use. Neubert v. Yakima–Tieton Irr. Dist. (1991); United States v. Alpine Land & Reservoir Co. (1983). Because early appropriators often grossly over-claimed the amount that could be used beneficially, many current statutory systems condition water rights on proof by new and existing appropriators that all the water may be beneficially used and not wasted. State ex rel. Erickson v. McLean (1957).

There are important limitations on the right to a specific quantity of water. An agency or court may deny an application to change the place or purpose of use, or point of diversion, or transfer of a water right, if the change or transfer will result in an increase in the amount of water that has historically been put to a beneficial use. As a result, the change or transfer may not be permitted unless the quantity of the right is reduced to historic use, which is typically less than the amount of the original appropriation. Orr v. Arapahoe Water & Sanitation Dist. (1988). This rule is subject to modification by private agreements among appropriators. Matter of Water Rights of Fort Lyon Canal Co. (1988).

The extent of an appropriator's right may depend on the efficiency or wastefulness of the appropriator's method of diversion and manner of use. As a general rule, an appropriator must employ a reasonably efficient means of diversion. In re Water Rights in Silvies River (1925) (efficiency is to be judged not by standards prevailing at the time diversion works are constructed, but by current state-of-the-art technology). The rationale behind this rule is to ensure that upstream junior appropriators will not have to supply water to downstream seniors who require amounts in excess of their use to compensate for losses caused by inefficient diversion facilities. Schodde v. Twin Falls Land & Water Co. (1912). Another limitation occurs in states which by statute allow appropriators a fixed amount of water per acre irrigated. In determining an appropriator's "duty of water," the appropriate state official may use a formula based on the average needs of the group of users along a stream, rather than the needs of a particular user. State ex rel. Reynolds v. Niccum (1985).

(3) TRANSFERS AND INTER-BASIN DIVERSIONS

Since water rights are generally appurtenant to the land upon which the water is used, a conveyance of land will pass the water right title to the grantee unless the grantor reserves the water right. A water right may also be granted separately from the land in the absence of legislation restricting such transfers. Where state law permits a severance of the water right from the land, the holder of the right does not have priority. Aside from statutes forbidding transfers away from the land, the transferor is limited to transferring either the amount of the decreed right or actual historic use, whichever is less. Basin Electric Power Co-op. v. State Bd. of Control (1978).

Unlike the riparian doctrine, the appropriation doctrine permits transfers of water across watersheds. Coffin v. Left

Hand Ditch Co. (1882). A number of principles limit transbasin diversions. First, if the diverter purchases rights from appropriators in the area of origin, the "no harm to other appropriators" rule becomes applicable to resulting changes in use. Second, several states have enacted "area of origin" protective legislation designed to mitigate the harm to an area about to be de-watered by a transbasin diversion. California permits such diversions only if the area of origin is still able to appropriate the water when it is needed. Colorado requires diverters to demonstrate that future water supplies for the area of origin "will not be impaired." Third, the Commerce Clause prohibits one state from preventing water within that state from being used in adjoining states. Sporhase v. Nebraska ex rel. Douglas (1982).

(4) Changes that Cause Harm to Other Appropriators

Approximately 50% of water diverted for irrigation is consumed, while the other 50% returns to the hydrologic cycle to join a surface stream or to recharge a groundwater aquifer. This sizeable return flow is used by other downstream appropriators. If an appropriator transfers the water right, or changes the point of diversion, or changes the location, nature, or time of use, such an alteration may adversely affect the return flow. This change may in turn harm downstream appropriators that have come to rely on it for their water supply. Downstream seniors are legally protected from such changes by their prior rights to the water. But so too are downstream appropriators protected by a rule that recognizes a right of juniors "in the continuation of stream conditions as they existed at the time of their respective appropriations." Farmers Highline Canal & Reservoir Co. v. City of Golden (1954).

This rule means that upstream senior appropriators may not make changes in the diversion point, or the place, nature, or time of use, when the change results in injury to downstream appropriators. See Matter of Steffens (1988) (change in *point of diversion* would injure junior by enabling senior to overuse his water rights); Heine v. Reynolds (1962) (change in *location* prohibited if it adversely alters quality of waters available to juniors); Westminster v. Church (1968) (change in *nature* of use resulting in a more consumptive use harms juniors); Matter of Water Rights No. 101960–41S (1991) (change of use from flood irrigation to sprinkler irrigation resulting in lesser return flows is a violation of the "no harm" rule); Cate v. Hargrave (1984) (change in *season* of use may harm juniors who have relied on off-season use of the senior's water).

The burden of proving no harm to others is on the one seeking the transfer or change. Matter of May (1988). An application to change will be denied if conditions cannot be imposed to protect other appropriators from resulting harm. Brighton Ditch Co. v. City of Englewood (1951). The "no harm" rule is not applicable to the recapture and reuse of waste water on the same land for the original purpose, nor does it apply to foreign water. Twin Lakes Reservoir & Canal Co. v. Aspen (1977).

Upstream appropriators may not transfer their water right to others where the transfer results in a change that causes harm to other appropriators. Green River Dev. Co. v. FMC Corp. (1983). Only the amount that has been historically consumed by the transferor may be transferred, because the amount consumed has not been part of the return flow, and hence has not been relied on by others. Green v. Chaffee Ditch Co. (1962).

(5) STORAGE

A right to divert water from a waterbody (a direct flow right) does not necessarily entitle the right holder to store the water. Some jurisdictions assume that capture of water in a reservoir is a sufficiently beneficial use under a direct flow right. Pueblo West Metropolitan Dist. v. Southeastern Colorado Water Conservancy Dist. (1984). Others require a separate permit or decree for storage rights (e.g., Arizona, Nebraska, Wyoming). Once obtained, a storage right is integrated into the priority system, with neither storage nor direct flow rights given preference. Donich v. Johnson (1926).

A storage right may be applied for future use (carryover storage). Federal Land Bank v. Morris (1941). It may also be leased to another user, or exchanged for direct flow diversions upstream. There are two primary limitations on storage rights. First, the total water impounded during a year is limited to the capacity of the reservoir (an empty reservoir filled once, not emptied and successively filled). Wheatland Irr. Dist. v. Pioneer Canal Co. (1970). Second, the "no harm" rule prohibits storing water if the storage is a change which harms other appropriators.

c. *Loss of Appropriative Rights*

There are three ways by which an appropriator may lose part or all of a water right by non-use. *Abandonment* follows when non-use is coupled with intent to abandon. Legal difficulties preventing water use may excuse non-use, Hallenbeck v. Granby Ditch & Reservoir Co. (1966), but economic infeasibility will not. Southeastern Colorado Water Conservancy Dist. v. Twin Lakes Associates, Inc. (1989). Some states have provided that an unreasonable period of non-use creates a rebuttable presumption of intent to abandon. Denver v. Snake River Water Dist. (1990). This presumption may be rebutted by the holder of the water right. People ex rel. Danielson v. City of Thornton (1989) (water right owner's testimony of desire to place water right on market for sale does not rebut presumption of abandonment). If water is abandoned, it is subject to appropriation by others.

Many states provide for *forfeiture* of water rights when there is non-use for a period of time set by statute. Nephi

City v. Hansen (1989). For there to be forfeiture, there must be no use at all within the statutory period; application to a beneficial use within the period prevents forfeiture. McAtee v. Faulkner Land & Livestock, Inc. (1987). A water right may also be forfeited if a would-be appropriator does not proceed with due diligence in constructing diversion works. Montana Dept. of Natural Resources and Conservation v. Intake Water Co. (1976). Some state statutes provide that municipalities and water conservancy districts shall not forfeit water rights as a result of non-use when the water is appropriated for future needs. City of Raton v. Vermejo Conservancy Dist. (1984).

Rights to the use of either appropriated or unappropriated water usually cannot be acquired by *adverse possession.* Lewis v. State Bd. of Control (1985). Prescriptive rights to water are also not good against the state. People v. Shirokow (1980). Nor may use of water by an upstream junior appropriator which is adverse to a downstream senior result in a reversal of priorities. Coryell v. Robinson (1948). Even in jurisdictions which permit adverse possession of a water right, there is a strong bias against ownership by adverse use. Joe Johnson Co. v. Landen (1987); College Irr. Co. v. Logan River & Blacksmith Fork Irr. Co. (1989) (there is a presumption against acquisition of a water right by adverse use). But see Matter of Water Rights of V–Heart Ranch, Inc. (1984).

3. Dual Systems

The three Pacific Coast states, the six states divided by the 100th meridian (Texas, Oklahoma, Kansas, Nebraska, South and North Dakota), and Mississippi, are "dual system" states. In these states the law of prior appropriation has been superimposed on a pre-existing system of riparian rights, and each state has had to reconcile the two somewhat inconsistent doctrines, and administer the competing water rights of riparians and appropriators.

In most dual system states the solution to the contradictions in the two water law doctrines has been to restrict existing riparian rights and do away with unused riparian rights. These restrictions have taken four forms. First, riparians are often limited in quantity to the amount that can be reasonably used for a beneficial purpose, and subsequent appropriations are permitted which do not harm the riparian's reasonable use. Brown v. Chase (1923). Second, the critical problem of extinguishing unused riparian rights so that they may become subject to appropriation has been solved by legislation and case law recognizing only riparian rights vested through use; all other "unused and unusable rights predicated upon [riparian] theory" have largely been eliminated. State ex rel. Emery v. Knapp (1949). Third, in order to resolve disputes among riparians and appropriators, states employing a permit system that quantify riparian rights integrate these rights with appropriative rights. The priority date of riparian rights is usually senior to appropriators. Fourth, acquisition of a water right through prescription, otherwise allowed in riparian jurisdictions and disallowed in appropriation states, is permitted in dual systems. Pabst v. Finmand (1922) (non-riparian may acquire rights by prescription against lower riparians who did not suffer actual harm, but riparians may gain a prescriptive right only if their use caused harm to lower riparians).

Two dual system states, Nebraska and California, continue to recognize unused riparian rights. Wasserburger v. Coffee (1966) (riparian may require appropriator to release water if riparian lands were severed from public domain); San Joaquin & Kings River Canal & Irr. Co. v. Worswick (1922) (unused riparian rights may be successfully exercised against appropriations made on private land). In 1979, the California Supreme Court limited riparian owners' future right to use water by affording such rights lower priority than rights administratively recognized in the interim by the State Water Resources Control Board. In re Waters of Long Valley Creek Stream System (1979).

4. Public Rights

An important limitation on the rights of riparians and appropriators is the right of the "public" (via state or federal governments) to (1) the *land* underlying waters, (2) the *surface* use of waters, or (3) the general *use* of waters. Public rights have been recognized through several legal theories.

a. Federal Regulatory Power

Private ownership rights to water arising under state law are subservient to federal laws regulating water resources. First Iowa Hydro–Elec. Co-op. v. FPC (1946) (state water law doctrine remains applicable only to the extent it is not superseded by federal law). Constitutional power justifying federal regulation of waters is based on the right of Congress to regulate "navigable" waters as an element of commerce. The legal definition of navigability is a liberal one which asks whether the waterbody was navigable in fact when the state came into the Union. A waterbody is navigable for purposes of federal regulation if it could be made navigable by artificial improvements; it may also be used strictly in intrastate commerce. United States v. Appalachian Elec. Power Co. (1940). The navigation power extends to non-navigable tributaries of navigable streams. Oklahoma v. Guy F. Atkinson Co. (1941).

b. Title to Beds Underlying Navigable Waters

Navigability at the time of statehood also determines ownership of the underlying bed. If a waterbody is navigable, then title to the bed passed to the state upon admission to the Union. Pollard v. Hagan (1845). However, navigability for bed title purposes uses a different test than that relevant to navigability for federal regulation. Bed title navigability is decided under federal law, which requires that the water in its "natural" and "ordinary" (i.e., without artificial improvement) condition be usable by customary modes of travel. Utah v. United States (1971) (Utah may claim bed ownership of Great Salt Lake because it was navigable when Utah achieved statehood). Bed title extends beneath a navigable waterway to the "mean high water line," a line determined by averaging a waterway's high water marks.

Several consequences may follow if a waterbody was navigable under the federal test at the time of statehood. First, since title to the bed passed to the state, riparians are deprived of their right to the bed. See United States v. Keenan (1985) (title to beds of waters deemed *non*-navigable pass to riparians). When the bed under the water is state-owned, riparians may not build wharves, piers, docks, or bridges which interfere with public rights to navigation. Second, some states view public rights to the surface of water as a function of state ownership of the bed, thereby limiting private uses which conflict with public surface uses. Third, some courts have concluded that riparian property bordering watercourses whose beds are state-owned should be burdened with an easement of public access.

c. *"Navigability" Under State Law*

Certain jurisdictions have chosen to adopt a more liberal "state" test of navigability. In these states a waterway is navigable if the river can float logs or recreational boats (rafts or canoes). Edwards v. Severin (1990). When a river is navigable under the state test, two legal consequences may occur. First, title to the beds of waters not navigable under the federal test may be owned by the state. Shortell v. Des Moines Elec. Co. (1919). Second, public rights to water may attach even when the beds are in private ownership. Muench v. Public Service Com'n (1952). In either case, riparian rights and appropriator's uses are qualified to the extent necessary to allow public uses. Wilbour v. Gallagher (1969) (landfill must be removed as an obstruction to recreational navigation).

d. The Public Trust Doctrine

States that took title to lands under navigable waters defined by the federal test hold these lands in trust for the people of the state. The public trust doctrine allows the public to "enjoy the navigation of the waters, carry on commerce over them, and have liberty of fishing therein freed from interference of private parties." Illinois Central Railroad Co. v. Illinois (1892). Some states have acknowledged a public trust duty that emerges for state laws declaring public rights or ownership to state waters. In these states, the public trust applies to waters not considered navigable under the federal test. Galt v. State by and through Dept. of Fish, Wildlife and Parks (1987); Orion Corp. v. State (1987) (public trust extends to tidelands and shorelands).

Where the public trust is applicable, state conveyances of submerged lands will be examined to determine if they are inconsistent with the trust doctrine. Caminiti v. Boyle (1987); Kootenai Environmental Alliance, Inc. v. Panhandle Yacht Club, Inc. (1983). In addition to limiting conveyances, the public trust doctrine has been used to protect public environmental rights and recreational uses. Marks v. Whitney (1971); Borough of Neptune City v. Borough of Avon–By–The–Sea (1972).

e. Non-navigable Waters

Normally, the public has no right to the use of purely non-navigable waters. State ex rel. Meek v. Hays (1990). Nonetheless, some states have recognized public rights to waters that meet neither the federal nor state tests of navigability, and where the public trust doctrine does not apply. Nonnavigable waters have been made public (1) by state statute, (2) by judicial interpretation of state constitutional law, and (3) by the common law doctrine of dedication (e.g., when a riparian manifests an intent to dedicate and the public accepts). Montana Coalition for Stream Access, Inc. v. Hildreth (1984); Day v. Armstrong (1961). Colorado courts have rejected theories of public rights to the surfaces of nonnavigable waters. People v. Emmert (1979) (the public has no right to the use of waters overlying private lands for recreational purposes).

B. SOURCES OF WATER

1. Surface Water

a. *Regulation of Instream Flows and Lake Levels*

State governments and the federal government may want to ensure that certain waterbodies maintain a minimum flow or surface level so as to protect fish and aquatic life, to provide sufficient dilution flows for ambient pollutants, and to preserve recreational and aesthetic values. At a state level, instream flows may be maintained in three ways. First, to overcome the legal difficulties associated with the lack of a diversion, a state legislature may specifically recognize the right of a state agency to make an instream appropriation. Colorado River Water Conservation Dist. v. Colorado Water Conservation Bd. (1979). Second, certain waters may be statutorily removed from appropriation, and thereby protected from damage by private diversions and public projects. Third, some states rely on the public trust doctrine to dedicate water to instream uses. Ritter v. Standal (1977).

Federal protection of instream flows occurs under the Wild and Scenic Rivers Act. 16 U.S.C.A. § 1271–87. Federal reserved water rights may also preserve instream flows.

Park Center Water Dist. v. United States (1989). However, the federal reserved rights doctrine is a source of authority only if maintenance of instream flows is among the original purposes of the federal reservation. United States v. New Mexico (1978). For example, courts are still wrestling with whether Congress intended to reserve instream flows in national forests when it added to the 1897 Organic Act the following language: "No national forest shall be established, except * * * for the purpose of securing favorable conditions of water flows." 16 U.S.C.A. § 475, United States v. Jesse (1987). Nor is it clear whether Congress intends to reserve rights for instream flows when it designates wilderness areas. Sierra Club v. Lyng (1987).

When government agencies alter lake levels for flood control, to improve navigation, or to maintain water supplies, the rights of the government and the littoral owner clash. If the government action is for a legitimate public purpose, the littoral owner usually has no legally protected interest in the maintenance of a lake at any particular level. Wood v. South River Drainage Dist. (1967).

b. Diffused Surface Waters

There are important definitional and legal differences between waters in a natural watercourse and diffused surface waters. The former includes waters flowing in a defined channel with bed and banks, while the latter encompasses waters from rain, melting snow, or seepage that do not yet form a part of a watercourse or lake. See Island County v. Mackie (1984) (waters in a natural drain flowing from higher to lower lands not diffused waters). If waters are in a natural watercourse, they may be used or drained only in relation to the rights of other riparians and appropriators along the watercourse. Diffused surface waters may be captured, or their flow otherwise directed, without as much regard for the rights of lower landowners.

The general rule is that a landowner who captures diffused surface water is entitled to use and control it. This control ends when the water enters a definite watercourse. Oklahoma Water Resources Bd. v. Central Okl. Master Conservancy Dist. (1968). In three ways states have modified the "capture" doctrine: (1) Redefine "watercourse" to include diffuse waters. Hoefs v. Short (1925). (2) Make all "natural streams" subject to state water law, and include within the phrase all waters, from whatever source, that naturally flow into such streams. Nevius v. Smith (1929). (3) Subject diffuse surface waters to the reasonable use rule. State by and Through Dept. of Highways v. Feenan (1988).

Apart from capturing diffused water, a landowner may wish to redirect the flow of such waters, or otherwise change natural drainage patterns. For non-diffused waters, or waters that have been artificially brought upon the land, the rule is that drainage through the property of a lower landowner may occur only if that owner gives permission or is not injured. City of Benton City v. Adrian (1988). Also, if one impounds water in a reservoir, release of that water onto another's land may give rise to strict liability, even if the water originally was diffused water. Gossner v. Utah Power and Light (1980). But see Murphy v. Kentucky Utilities Co. (1991) (no liability where utility released water from a dam after heavy rains, when downstream landowner would have sustained flood damage even without the release).

If diffused surface water is not impounded, the extent to which a landowner may drain or divert it depends on which of three "rules" has been adopted in the landowner's state. In states that have adopted the common enemy rule, landowners may take action to avoid diffused surface waters without liability to others. Pickett v. Brown (1991). Many common enemy rule states have tempered the rule with a reasonable use standard. Jacobs v. Pine Manor College (1987). In states using the civil law rule, each landowner has a reciprocal duty to not alter diffused waters in ways that affect others. Dougan v. Rossville Drainage Dist. (1988). In states applying the reasonable use rule, interference with diffused surface waters is tested by balancing the gravity of harm against the utility of the conduct. Braham v. Fuller (1986).

Drainage of protected wetland areas is subject to special state and federal regulation. Many states require a state-issued permit before designated wetlands may be drained or altered. Mario v. Town of Fairfield (1991). The federal Clean Water Act requires a "dredge and fill" permit from the Army Corps of Engineers before constructing projects that affect wetlands. 33 U.S.C.A. § 1344; Avoyelles Sportmen's League, Inc. v. Marsh (1983). A "wetland" is defined as any area where the soil is saturated to the surface for several days, or has standing water for approximately two weeks each year.

2. Groundwater

a. *Resolving Conflicts Among Competing Users*

States may choose from among five doctrines for determining liability when groundwater users interfere with each other. The first four rules discussed below are primarily applicable to "percolating" groundwater—waters which slowly seep beneath the earth's surface in no known identifiable natural channels. The fifth rule—prior appropriation—is most often applied to groundwater sources connected to, and following, surface watercourses.

Under the rule of absolute ownership, the owner of the surface land owned all of the water within or under it, because it was thought that the water was part of the soil. As a consequence, landowners had no liability for any use of groundwater, even though the use may have injured others. Because the rule leads to depletion of groundwater, and incurs no obligation for harm to others, most states have rejected or modified it. State v. Michels Pipeline Const., Inc. (1974).

The reasonable use rule permitted landowners to withdraw any amount of groundwater for reasonable uses, regardless of the consequent harm to neighboring landowners, so long as it was taken in connection with beneficial enjoyment of the land from which it was taken. This rule was applied to produce unreasonable results. See Finley v. Teeter Stone, Inc. (1968) (although defendant's well caused subsidence, no liability because defendant's use of groundwater on land was reasonable).

The California Supreme Court repudiated both the absolute ownership and reasonable use rules in favor of the correlative rights doctrine. This doctrine is based on a theory of proportionate showing of withdrawals among landowners overlying a common aquifer; each landowner was held to have rights in the common groundwater pool in proportion to the land overlying the pool. Katz v. Walkinshaw (1903). The correlative rights doctrine was a direct result of growing scientific evidence about groundwater hydrology; scientists and then courts realized that when a number of persons owned land overlying an aquifer, withdrawal of water by one would affect all.

Section 858 of the Restatement (2d) of Torts (the fourth rule) states that well owners are liable if a groundwater withdrawal (1) causes harm to a proprietor of neighboring land through lowering the water table, (2) exceeds the proprietor's reasonable share of the groundwater, or (3) affects a surface waterbody in a way that unreasonably causes harm to a person entitled to use its water. The first restriction holds liable parties who lower the water table. Maerz v. United States Steel Corp. (1982). The second is similar to the correlative rights doctrine in that it seeks to apportion rights in the common groundwater pool (though without reference to amount of land ownership). The third is reflected in states that integrate management of interconnected ground and surface waters.

The fifth rule, prior appropriation, is premised on the notion that senior appropriators should not have their expectations defeated by subsequent junior wells that damage existing rights. Current Creek Irr. Co. v. Andrews (1959). Because the resulting "junior liable" rule theoretically permits seniors to exhaust an aquifer's water, and because the senior's well or pumping system may be outmoded, many states have modified the prior appropriation doctrine with respect to groundwater rights. A more limited form of protection of seniors is provided for only "unreasonable interference." Mathers v. Texaco, Inc. (1966) (lowering of water table of aquifer not a *per se* unreasonable impairment of senior rights). Other states have imposed a statutory permit system that protects senior rights only to the extent allowed by permit. Fundingsland v. Colorado Ground Water Com'n (1970) (a junior permit may be denied only if the rate of pumping results in a 40% depletion of groundwater under a circle with a three mile radius around the proposed well within 25 years). Senior groundwater rights are also limited by cases requiring the senior's well to be reasonably adequate. City of Colorado Springs v. Bender (1961) (senior rights limited by well which reaches to such a shallow depth that virtually any nearby junior well would adversely affect it). But see Baker v. Ore–Ida Foods, Inc. (1973) (seniors not expected to improve their means of pumping "beyond their economic reach").

b. Public Administration of Groundwater Use

A state may declare ownership of groundwaters beneath the state to be public, and thereby subject private ownership rights to certain public obligations. See Matter of Permit No. 47–7680 (1988) (not in public interest to use water from geothermal aquifer to irrigate crops). Public rights may be granted to public agencies, which may acquire appropriative and storage rights to groundwater. For example, in California, special water districts may obtain imported water from water-rich northern California, which they may then store it in natural underground reservoirs. City of Los Angeles v. City of San Fernando (1975). In some jurisdictions like New Mexico, waters imported and stored in underground aquifers become public waters subject to capture by other appropriators. State ex rel. Reynolds v. Luna Irr. Co. (1969).

Public administration of groundwater use usually involves permitting for groundwater withdrawals. One important goal of groundwater permits is to ensure that a proposed or existing well will not adversely interfere with existing groundwater rights. Stokes v. Morgan (1984) (permit may authorize change in place of use of groundwater rights when change would have minimal effect on quality of groundwater). Where withdrawals from an aquifer threaten to exceed the recharge rate, many state statutes allow state officials to designate such aquifers as "critical areas," so that pumping is restricted to those with pre-existing permits. Doherty v. Oregon Water Resources Director (1989). Rather than halt overdrafts through critical area designation, some states (e.g., Colorado, Oklahoma) allow gradual depletion of certain aquifers over a fixed period of time. In states that provide for what is, in effect, groundwater mining, new permits are granted if the lowering of the water table is not so rapid as to injure other permitted wells overlying the mined aquifer.

c. Regulation of Groundwater Pumping to Protect Surface Users and Groundwater Quality

Groundwater pumping may have two negative consequences on others: (1) it may affect surface water flows if the groundwater and a surface watercourse are interconnected; (2) it may either cause pollutants to migrate from a contaminated aquifer into a relatively clean one, or concentrate existing pollutants. Both consequences have been regulated by state law.

In cases where surface and groundwater sources are interconnected, many prior appropriation states (e.g., Colorado, California, Utah, New Mexico) have chosen to regulate them together. Conjunctive management is particularly appropriate where surface sources are over-appropriated, and juniors seeking water turn to groundwater sources which may be interconnected to a senior's surface source. In these states, a primary goal is to protect the rights of senior surface appropriators from junior well owners whose pumping reduces surface supplies. Wyoming State Engineer v. Willadsen (1990). In New Mexico, a senior surface appropriator unable to divert surface water because of groundwater pumping may drill a well to tap the groundwater under the stream. Langenegger v. Carlsbad Irr. Dist. (1971). In Colorado, juniors may tap underground sources if they supply ("augment") affected surface users with supplemental water to compensate for the surface effects of groundwater removal. Danielson v. Castle Meadows, Inc. (1990).

In order to prevent groundwater contamination, states may impose permit conditions on wells. Permitting agencies seek to prevent introduction of pollutants into groundwater by examining whether a well will draw a contaminant into an aquifer. These agencies seek to prevent concentration of pollutants by restricting the amounts that may be pumped from an aquifer. But see Stokes v. Morgan (1984) (a certain amount of groundwater pollution may be justified in the interest of full development of water resources).

II.   FEDERAL AND INTERSTATE WATER LAW

A.   FEDERAL WATER PROJECTS

1.   The Navigation Servitude

Unlike the navigation power (discussed above in Section I A 4), which is the source of authority for Congress to legislate on issues involving navigation, the navigation servitude permits federal interference with private rights in waterways without the need for just compensation. Unless otherwise modified by Congress, the navigation servitude applies to the surface of navigable waters, to the water power value attributable to the flow of a moving stream, to the bed and banks of navigable waters up to the average high water mark, and even to lands valuable because of their proximity to navigable waters. Because of the servitude, federal water projects (such as dams) which damage private property subject to the servitude (such as bridges, oyster beds, or lands up to the high water mark), need not pay just compensation for the damage. United States v. Cherokee Nation of Okl. (1987) (no need to balance the public interest served by the navigation servitude in light of the intended use of streambed interests of private owners).

Despite the reach of the servitude, there are limits. It generally does not apply to non-navigable tributaries of navigable waters. United States v. Kansas City Life Ins. Co. (1950). It does not apply where federal improvements to navigation result in erosion to land located above or outside the bed of a stream. Owen v. United States (1988). Nor does it apply to non-navigable water subsequently made navigable by private effort. Kaiser Aetna v. United States (1979); Boone v. United States (1990).

2. Reclamation

The Reclamation Act of 1902, 43 U.S.C.A. § 371, was passed to develop the West's water resources for irrigation and agricultural production. The Act authorized construction of dams, canals, and diversion projects to bring federally "developed" water to privately owned land. These projects could be managed by irrigation districts under contract to the Interior Department. ETSI Pipeline Project v. Missouri (1988) (Lake Oahe in South Dakota not a reclamation project, primarily because the Army Corps of Engineers built it and controls its operation). The Act requires federal compliance with state water law. California v. United States (1978) (the Interior Secretary must decide whether state law allows appropriation of water rights for reclamation projects); United States v. Alpine Land and Reservoir Co. (1989). Other federal reclamation acts provide that state law shall govern in disputes between federal reclamation water and water rights arising under state law. Application of City and County of Denver By and Through Bd. of Water Com'rs (1991) (Denver's right to divert Blue River water is subject to the federal government's senior right to fill Green Mountain Reservoir, where reservoir is part of Colorado Big Thompson Project).

B. FEDERAL RESERVED WATER RIGHTS

1. Nature and Effect of the Reserved Right

The federal reserved water rights doctrine holds that when federal lands are withdrawn or reserved for specific purposes, unappropriated water will impliedly be reserved in an amount sufficient to satisfy the purposes of the withdrawal or reservation. The doctrine applies to Indian lands, Winters v. United States (1908), and to public lands. Arizona v. California (1963). Thus, if Congress reserves land for a national park, national forest, national monument, military base, wilderness area, or other purpose that may require water, the reservation carries with it an implied reservation of water. Cappaert v. United States (1976) (legislation creating Devil's Hole National Monument reserved sufficient water to preserve the pupfish there).

The doctrine may be asserted regardless of whether the withdrawal or reservation mentions water, and it acknowledges the prerogative of the federal government to establish and exercise reserved rights in disregard of state law. Private rights arising under state law are protected only if they vested prior to the date of the reservation or withdrawal;

after that date private parties may use the water pursuant to
state law, but risk divestment if the federal government later
asserts its prior superior rights. Navajo Development Co. v.
Sanderson (1982) (when conveying a water right, private
grantor does not warrant that the federal government will
not assert dormant reserved rights). The federal government
need not use the reserved water after the reservation in
order to protect its right to the water. In appropriation
states, the federal government's water has a priority as of the
date of the reservation. United States v. Denver (1982)
(reclassification of national forest land to national park status does not change the priority date of reserved water
rights).

2. Purpose and Quantity of Water Reserved

Reserved water rights cases establish two principles that
turn on the "purpose" of the reservation. First, water is
reserved, and may be used, only for the purpose of the federal
reservation. In United States v. Denver (1982), the Colorado
Supreme Court rejected the argument that the 1960 Multiple
Use Sustained Yield Act had subsequently reserved water in
addition to that already reserved for national forest purposes
by the Forest Service Organic Act. The *Denver* case also
rejected the argument that reserved rights existed for recreational purposes (river rafting) within Dinosaur National Monument. See also In re General Adjudication of All Rights to
Use Water in the Big Horn River System (1988) (intent at
time of creation of Indian reservation was to create a reservation with a sole agricultural purpose, not a homestead purpose). However, in Sierra Club v. Lyng (1987), a Colorado
federal district court held that reserved water rights are
created for instream flows when Congress creates a wilderness area. See also United States v. Jesse (1987) (federal
reserved right to preserve instream flows over national forest
lands should be acknowledged if the purpose of the Organic
Act would otherwise be defeated). The original allotment of

a reserved water right may be used for a use not encompassed by the original purpose after the right has been specifically quantified. Arizona v. California (1979).

The second principle is that the quantity of water subject to the reserved right is limited to the amount necessary to fulfill the reservation's purpose. United States v. New Mexico (1978) (there must be a "careful examination" of the purposes of reservation land to determine the quantity of water reserved). Uncertainty over the exact quantity of water reserved adversely affects both those with a right to the reserved water (who do not know how much water they may use), and upstream and downstream appropriators impacted by some future use of the reserved water. The need to make certain the quantity of water reserved has resulted in adjudications, initiated both by private parties and the federal government, which ask a court to quantify the reserved rights granted a reservation. Because a private party may sue neither the United States nor Indian tribes without congressional consent, Congress waived sovereign immunity in water rights adjudications with the passage of the McCarran Amendment, 43 U.S.C.A. § 666. Dugan v. Rank (1963) (McCarran Amendment extends to general stream adjudications, not to actions against the United States by individual appropriators). Once the federal government is joined, it must comply with state procedural requirements. United States v. Bell (1986).

3. Effect of State Water Law

When a reserved right is claimed in a prior appropriation jurisdiction, the rightholder need not comply with state water law requirements. A reserved right may not be attacked for not constituting a reasonable or beneficial use; the test is whether the use meets the reservation's purpose. Federal reserved rights are superior to all state water rights vesting after creation of the reservation, regardless of whether the holder of the state right had notice of the existence or quantity of the federal right. The holder of the reserved right need not acquire a state permit to exercise the right. Federal reserved rights may not be lost for non-use. State ex rel. Greely v. Confederated Salish and Kootenai Tribes (1985).

In riparian jurisdictions, conditions normally required by the reasonable use doctrine (e.g., no interference with the rights of fellow riparians; equal sharing by riparians in times of shortage) may not be imposed on a federal reserved right if the state rule would interfere with the accomplishment of the reservation's purpose. The United States may also acquire normal riparian water rights as a proprietor with respect to its own lands. In re Water of Hallett Creek Stream System (1988).

4. Location of Water Reserved

As a general proposition, the reserved rights doctrine is limited to waters flowing across, or bordering, reservation lands. It also applies to groundwater beneath the reservation. *Cappaert,* supra; Park Center Water Dist. v. United States (1989). In Arizona v. California (1963), the Supreme Court went so far as to assume that if Congress creates a reservation that has no water, then it has impliedly reserved sufficient non-contiguous nearby water to satisfy the reservation's purposes.

C. INTERSTATE ALLOCATION OF WATER

1. Interstate Compacts

One way for states to resolve their differences over the waters of an interstate waterway is by compact. Art. I, § 10, cl. 3. Pursuant to the compact power given states by the Constitution, over 20 interstate compacts relating to water resources have been negotiated and approved by Congress. Most interstate stream compacts allocate water among the signatory states. Oklahoma v. New Mexico (1991). Such a compact allows states to allocate unapportioned water for future use, which courts are usually unable to do because of the ripeness barrier. Besides allocating water, compacts are formed for purposes relating to water storage, flood control, and pollution control. West Virginia ex rel. Dyer v. Sims (1951) (interstate river pollution).

Compacts are binding upon citizens of the compacting states, regardless of whether individual citizens were parties to the compact. Hinderlider v. La Plata River & Cherry Creek Ditch Co. (1938). State law conflicting with the terms of a compact is preempted by the compact.

2. Adjudication

Judicial resolution of water disputes between states most commonly occurs in the absence of a compact, when a state either restricts out-of-state access to state water supplies, or asks the United States Supreme Court to assert original jurisdiction in order to make an "equitable apportionment" of contested interstate waters. In the former case, the state law may be an unconstitutional burden on interstate commerce. New England Power Co. v. New Hampshire (1982) (state may not prohibit utility from selling hydroelectric power generated within the state to out-of-state users). In Sporhase v. Nebraska ex rel. Douglas (1982), the Supreme Court held that groundwater was an article of commerce, and that a Nebraska statute which imposed a reciprocity requirement on other states was an unconstitutional form of discrimination against interstate commerce.

Resolution of interstate water disputes in the Supreme Court is usually pursuant to the equitable apportionment doctrine, a form of federal interstate common law first used in Kansas v. Colorado (1907). Because the two contesting states in Kansas v. Colorado used differing water law systems (riparian and prior appropriation), the Court turned to a neutral "equitable" principle to apportion the waters of the Arkansas River. Equitable apportionment has been used by the Court in cases involving interstate water pollution affecting two riparian states, New Jersey v. New York (1931), and in a case involving anadromous fish living in interstate waters. Idaho ex rel. Evans v. Oregon (1983). In controversies between two states using the appropriation system, the Court has applied the prior appropriation doctrine. Wyoming v. Colorado (1922). However, the Court has refused to apply strict priorities between two appropriation states when the effect would be to protect wasteful and inefficient downstream uses. Colorado v. New Mexico (1984).

*

PART IV

ENERGY RESOURCE DISTRIBUTION AND USE

Law As a Means of Facilitating the Conversion of Natural Resources to Energy Needed by End–Users

The first stage of the energy fuel cycle is the exploration and exploitation of natural resources, followed by their transportation and processing. After natural resources are processed, they are converted into usable energy and then the energy is distributed for consumption. Part IV considers the government's regulatory response to the energy fuel cycle. Chapter Nine explains the domestic pattern of energy regulation that has dominated domestic policy-making for over a century. In the next two chapters, individual natural resources are examined as they move through the energy fuel cycle. Chapter Ten discusses oil, coal, nuclear power, hydroelectricity, and alternative resources, from exploration through transportation. Chapter Eleven addresses energy conversion and consumption in the context of traditional public utility regulation of electricity and natural gas.

CHAPTER NINE

FEDERAL ENERGY POLICY

Although Congress requires the President to submit to it a biannual national energy plan, it is fair to say that the United States has no coherent and comprehensive plan. Still, as a general proposition, since the late 19th Century the United States has developed an identifiable pattern of energy decisionmaking. This pattern forms what can be properly termed the dominant model of United States energy policy. The dominant model is not richly detailed nor does it coordinate the nation's several energy markets and industries. Nevertheless, the dominant model contains recognizable variables and themes to be explored in this chapter.

Over the last 100 years, the United States government has fairly consistently implemented energy policies that support private ordering by markets, and correct market defects through industry-specific government regulation. Furthermore, the dominant model relies on fossil fuels (oil, natural gas, and coal) for over three-fourths of the nation's energy production and consumption. Occasionally, particularly during the Carter Administration, the federal government has promoted alternative energy resources. However, alternative sources, with the possible exception of conservation, have neither displaced nor superseded traditional fossil fuels and nuclear power.

The first part of this Chapter explains the dominant model of U.S. energy policy and its heavy reliance on conventional, predominantly fossil, fuels. The second part discusses emerging alternative policies and fuels in the context of contemporary world economics and environmental sensitivity.

I. ENERGY FACTS

Energy industries involve hundreds of billions of dollars of our domestic and global economies, even though relatively few natural resources are used in the production of energy. The domestic energy economy is roughly divided between oil and electricity, which do not compete with one another. Oil is primarily used in the transportation sector. Natural gas, coal, and nuclear power are used to generate electricity, which in turn is primarily used for commercial and residential heating, air conditioning, lighting, and for industrial manufacturing. A more detailed discussion of facts about the natural resources used to produce energy, and the uses to which that energy is put, will help illuminate our nation's energy laws and policies.

The Department of Energy, through its Energy Information Administration, gathers data on various aspects of energy industries. The following diagram, taken from the Energy Information Administration's Annual Energy Review–1990, shows the total amount and composition of the energy produced and consumed in the United States in 1990.

Diagram

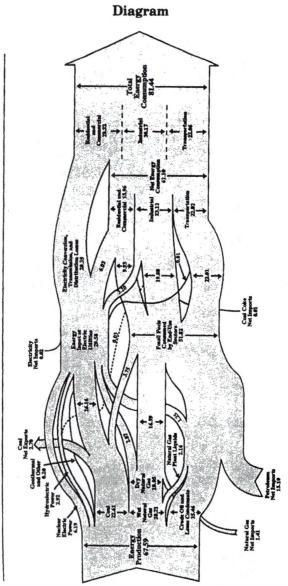

Total Energy Flow, 1990
(Quadrillion Btu)

At the start of the 1990s, the United States was consuming 81.44 quads of energy while producing only 67.59 quads. (One quad equals one quadrillion BTUs of energy.) The shortfall between consumption and production, most notably in oil, is covered by imports.

Of the 81.44 quads of energy consumed, petroleum accounted for 33.64 quads (41%), followed by natural gas at 19.41 quads (24%), coal at 19.05 quads (23%), nuclear power at 6.2 quads (7.6%), and hydropower at 2.94 quads (3.6%). According to the Energy Information Administration Annual Report, less than one percent of electricity consumed (.21 quads) is derived from geothermal, wood, solar, wind, biomass and other alternative energy forms.

Total energy use in this country may be broken down by sector: residential and commercial energy users consumed 36% of all energy; industrial users consumed 37%; electric utilities consumed 36%; and, transportation consumed 27%. These figures exceed 100% because electricity is also counted in the figures for the residential, commercial, and industrial sectors.

There is a limited cross-substitutability of natural resources. All of the natural resources listed above can be used to generate electricity for the residential, commercial, and industrial sectors of the economy. However, electricity is rarely used in the transportation sector and, as a result, petroleum is almost the exclusive natural resource for transportation.

The nation consumes 33.64 quads of oil and produces only 15.46 quads, signifying the importance of the country's dependence on imported oil to make up the shortfall between domestic oil production and demand. As the world price of oil drops, the country becomes more dependent on foreign oil and more susceptible to a foreign oil embargo similar to that of the middle and late 1970s and to the supply disruption caused by Iraq's invasion of Kuwait in 1990. Although a net importer, the United States regularly exports some of its natural resources. In 1990, it exported coal (2.77 quads), crude oil and petroleum products (1.84 quads), and hydroelectricity and natural gas (.30 quads). During that year, the United States also imported crude oil and petroleum products (16.93 quads), and natural gas (1.51 quads).

The preceding data provide current information. However, in order to make policy, it is also necessary to have useful projections about the future availability of and need for resources, although such projections are not highly reliable. The Department of Energy gathers and sorts data for the purpose of making such predictions. Table 9–1 was developed by the Energy Information Agency of the Department of Energy, in its Annual Energy Outlook—1990.

Table 9-1

Supply and Deposition	1988	1989	1990	1995	2000	2005	2010	Annual Percent Growth 1988-2010

Energy Summary (Quadrillion Btu)

Primary Production

	1988	1989	1990	1995	2000	2005	2010	1988-2010
Petroleum	19.5	18.5	17.9	16.0	15.1	14.0	12.7	-1.9%
Natural Gas	17.5	17.4	17.8	19.4	21.2	20.9	20.4	0.7%
Coal	20.7	21.3	21.6	23.5	25.5	29.9	35.2	2.4%
Nuclear Power	5.7	5.6	5.9	6.1	6.2	6.5	6.5	0.6%
Renewable Energy	6.0	6.5	6.8	7.7	8.3	9.2	10.1	2.4%
Total Production	**69.4**	**69.3**	**69.9**	**72.7**	**76.4**	**80.4**	**84.9**	**0.9%**

Net Imports

Petroleum (including SPR)	13.9	15.2	16.1	19.3	21.0	23.4	26.0	2.9%
Natural Gas	1.2	1.3	1.4	2.1	2.7	2.9	2.9	4.1%
Coal/Other (- indicates export)	-2.1	-2.2	-2.1	-2.1	-2.6	-3.5	-4.9	4.0%
Total Net Imports	**13.1**	**14.3**	**15.4**	**19.2**	**21.1**	**22.8**	**24.1**	**2.8%**

Consumption

Petroleum Products	34.2	34.1	34.4	36.0	37.2	38.3	39.9	0.7%
Natural Gas	18.6	18.9	19.2	21.3	23.6	23.4	22.8	0.9%
Coal	18.8	19.0	19.0	20.7	22.0	25.2	28.9	2.0%
Nuclear Power	5.7	5.6	5.9	6.1	6.2	6.5	6.5	0.6%
Renewable Energy/Other	6.1	6.6	6.9	7.7	8.5	9.4	10.3	2.4%
Total Consumption	**83.4**	**84.2**	**85.4**	**91.9**	**97.4**	**102.8**	**108.4**	**1.2%**
Discrepancy	*-0.9*	*-0.6*	*-0.1*	*0.0*	*0.0*	*0.5*	*0.5*	

End-Use Prices (1989 dollars per million Btu)

Residential

Heating Oil	6.05	6.20	6.11	6.99	8.20	9.10	10.02	2.3%
Natural Gas	5.53	5.49	5.41	6.01	6.96	8.05	9.27	2.4%
Electricity	22.86	22.41	22.19	22.38	22.94	23.74	24.14	0.2%

Industrial

Residual Fuel Oil	2.22	2.46	2.49	3.19	4.47	5.31	5.98	4.6%
Natural Gas	2.97	2.89	3.00	3.37	4.35	5.44	6.63	3.7%

Transportation

Motor Gasoline	8.03	8.51	8.38	8.95	10.47	11.37	12.04	1.9%
Diesel Oil	6.84	6.95	6.69	7.55	8.76	9.76	10.56	2.0%

Electric Utilities

Coal	1.54	1.46	1.47	1.59	1.66	1.76	1.86	0.9%
Heavy Oil	2.52	2.78	2.75	3.48	4.70	5.54	6.21	4.2%
Natural Gas	2.36	2.36	2.39	2.90	3.83	4.92	6.00	4.3%

Table 9-1 presents DOE's "base case" for predicting the production, consumption, and price of energy from 1988 to 2010. The base case is DOE's central forecast and depends on assumptions about world oil prices, economic growth, supply and demand for energy, and technologies for producing and using energy. The base case shows that from 1988–2010, oil production will decline annually by 1.9% with modest annual growth in natural gas (.7%) and nuclear power (.6%), and greater annual growth in coal production (2.4%) and renewable resources (2.4%). Total imports will experience an annual growth of 2.8%. Prices are expected to rise annually, from a modest .2% for residential electricity to over 4% annually for industrial and utility oil and natural gas.

The base case assumes relatively low oil prices, due to instability in the Organization of Petroleum Exporting Countries (OPEC), which will increase supplies. The base case also assumes a concentration of oil supply by Middle East producers and concentrated demand by market economies, excluding Eastern Europe, the Soviet Union, and China. Finally, the base case assumes annual economic growth between 2.1% and 2.8%.

Such assumptions do not necessarily hold up well. For example, the DOE report did not anticipate Iraq's invasion of Kuwait. When the assumptions change so do the forecasts. Alternative DOE forecasts are presented in Table 9–2, also taken from DOE's Annual Energy Outlook—1990. Table 9–2 shows energy production, consumption, and price projections to the year 2010 under alternative assumptions. Because oil plays such a crucial role in energy policy, the price of oil, whether higher or lower than the norm, dramatically affects production and consumption patterns.

Table 9–2

	1988	Base Case	Low Oil Price Case	High Oil Price Case	Low Growth Case	High Growth Case
Primary Production (Quadrillion Btu)						
Petroleum	19.5	12.7	11.3	14.5	12.7	12.8
Natural Gas	17.5	20.4	20.0	20.6	19.7	20.9
Coal	20.7	35.2	35.2	34.7	31.4	38.0
Nuclear Power	5.7	6.5	6.5	6.5	6.5	6.5
Renewable Energy	6.0	10.1	10.1	10.1	10.1	10.1
Total Primary Production	**69.4**	**84.9**	**83.0**	**86.4**	**80.4**	**88.3**
Net Imports (Quadrillion Btu)						
Petroleum	13.9	26.0	31.8	22.3	24.6	28.1
Natural Gas	1.2	2.9	2.9	2.9	2.7	3.2
Coal/Other (− indicates export)	−2.1	−4.9	−4.8	−4.9	−3.0	−6.5
Total Net Imports	**13.1**	**24.1**	**29.9**	**20.3**	**24.2**	**24.8**
Consumption (Quadrillion Btu)						
Petroleum Products	34.2	39.9	44.1	37.6	38.4	42.0
Natural Gas	18.6	22.8	22.5	23.0	21.8	23.7
Coal	18.8	28.9	29.1	28.4	27.0	30.1
Nuclear Power	5.7	6.5	6.5	6.5	6.5	6.5
Renewable Energy/Other	6.1	10.3	10.3	10.3	10.3	10.3
Total Consumption	**83.4**	**108.4**	**112.5**	**105.8**	**104.0**	**112.6**
Prices (1989 dollars)						
World Oil Price (dollars per barrel)	15.27	36.90	25.90	47.40	36.90	47.40
Domestic Natural Gas Wellhead (dollars per thousand cubic ft.)	1.76	5.63	4.59	5.51	4.57	6.09
Domestic Coal Minemouth (dollars per short ton)	23.02	28.55	28.66	28.33	26.58	29.76
Average Electricity Price (cents per kilowatt hour)	6.62	7.01	6.81	7.03	6.61	7.34

II. CONVENTIONAL POLICIES AND CONVENTIONAL FUELS

Energy law as a specific field of study and as an area of law practice is a relatively recent development. The flurry of legislative activity that resulted as a reaction to the Arab Oil Embargo in 1973 and the Iranian Revolution in 1979 is generally considered to constitute the primary body of what is now referred to as energy law. This corpus of law generally involves the federal regulation of the energy fuel cycle. It affects the industrial structures used to extract, transmit, convert, and distribute energy products, and the sectors of the economy that consume the energy.

A. HISTORICAL ANTECEDENTS

Although energy law has emerged only in recent years, it has identifiable antecedents. These antecedents help us to recognize the dominant model of federal energy policy, to appreciate recent events, and to understand the implications of both on future energy planning.

Since the Industrial Revolution, government regulation has been used to control the production and distribution of the social necessity called energy. Government regulation has paralleled—and supported—the growth and development of energy industries and markets. Perhaps the single most trenchant observation about the history of energy regulation is to note the symbiotic relationship between private energy industries and public energy regulation.

1. 1887–1900

Modern energy regulation began near the end of the nineteenth century with the Supreme Court's opinion in Munn v. Illinois (1876). Although *Munn* involved grain elevators, its holding helped to create a major precedent for regulated industries generally, which later had bearing for energy law. The Court recognized the existence of "natural monopolies" and ruled that states could regulate such industries in the public interest. The Court's message was that government would not tolerate the private exercise of market power and that such an exercise could be restrained by the heavy hand of government price-setting. *Munn* was the first in a series of opinions allocating ratemaking power and establishing government authority for energy decision-making and policy-making. See also Federal Power Com'n v. Hope Natural Gas Co. (1944); Missouri ex rel. Southwestern Bell Tel. Co. v. Public Serv. Com'n (1923); Smyth v. Ames (1898); Jersey Central Power & Light Co. v. Federal Energy Reg. Com'n (1987). In 1887, ratemaking became an active part of our political economy through the creation of the Interstate Commerce Commission (ICC), the first modern administration agency. Although the ICC regulates the rail industry, its ratemaking authority established the pattern for price setting for natural monopolies such as public utilities.

At the end of the nineteenth century, energy was produced on local or regional bases. Consequently, decisions were made and policies developed first at the local and then at the state levels, tracking the structure of the energy industries themselves. At the turn of the 19th Century, there was no overarching energy policy coordinating the development and use of natural resources. Instead, specific energy resources like oil, coal, and natural gas were regulated independently of one another.

Modern energy industries and markets began to take shape during the last quarter of the nineteenth century. During this period, the country found itself in two significant energy transitions: the transition from wood to coal was completed, and the transition from coal to oil and natural gas was beginning. The second transition was from local and state, to regional and national markets, again mirroring industry development. Even in this initial phase of energy regulation, the dominant policy model can be discerned in its embryonic form. The model defined energy law and policy as a series of rules and regulations promoting the development of individual natural resources industries. Energy regulation emanated from a fundamental tension between an energy delivery system based on private ownership and the need for public regulation. The consequence of this tension was a series of government policies promoting energy business.

As the production and distribution of energy moved from local to state, and then to regional, national, and international markets, individual natural resources industries grew accordingly. Firms became larger and more integrated to capture economies of scale. Government regulation followed the pattern of these changes.

2. 1900–1920

During the first two decades of the twentieth century, modern energy industries, energy markets, and federal energy regulation assumed the shape they have today. The country was no longer a low energy society, but was becoming a high energy one dependent on large-scale, capital-intensive, centralized, interstate energy production and distribution. This transition occurred first in oil, then in electricity. The general intent of federal energy regulation was to promote production and industrial stability and, occasionally, to smooth out gross social and economic distortions caused by the exercise of market power by some energy firms.

Coal reigned king during the Industrial Revolution and well into the 20th Century. Throughout this period, however, oil and natural gas markets also expanded, signaling a transition from coal to the other fossil fuels. The oil and natural gas markets were expanding as new end uses, such as refined petroleum products and automobiles, increased demand. Because of coal's reputation as a dirty burning fuel, the cleaner alternatives of oil and natural gas were preferable. By 1925, oil constituted almost one-fifth of the energy market. Despite the transition from the solid to the liquid and gaseous fossil fuels, the federal government never abandoned coal. Instead of allowing an unimpeded transition to occur in the market, the federal government intentionally supported the use of coal to buoy the industry.

Structurally, the coal, oil, and natural gas industries had similarities and differences which affected government regulation. The basic difference concerns the degree of competition within each industry and the demand for each resource. Coal production was, and continues to be, the most competitive of the three industries. The basic similarity is that each industry has a transportation bottleneck. In the oil and natural gas industries, pipelines are the bottleneck, and in the coal industry railroads are the bottleneck.

During the first two decades of the twentieth century, oil became the paradigm of big industry. In 1911, Standard Oil and related entities controlled 65% of the market, down from 90% in 1900 due to the federal government's successful antitrust litigation. See, Standard Oil Co. of N.J. v. United States (1911). Still, in 1919, thirty-two firms controlled 60% of production, and, in 1920, the thirty largest oil firms controlled 72% of the country's refining capacity.

The natural gas industry was less concentrated during these early years because natural gas was seen as a nuisance by-product of oil exploration and was wasted rather than exploited. Before the turn of the century, small, local natural gas companies were the rule. Municipal gas companies controlled local gas primarily for street lights. By the end of the first third of the century, however, natural gas was seen as a valuable commodity and the transportation network became dominated by a few interstate pipeline companies. This development, paralleling the market power of the oil companies, ultimately led to the passage of the Natural Gas Act in 1938, and federal regulation of the gas industry.

During this formative period, energy markets moved from local and state, to regional and national levels. Federal intervention into private energy industries was episodic, allowing interindustry and interfuel competition to develop and later flourish. Whenever there were serious blips in energy markets, primarily when production was not flowing smoothly or when distribution was congested, the government would intervene in an attempt to smooth out the blip. In general, pre-World War I intervention was motivated by a sense of progressivism colored by antitrust sentiment. Government would protect consumers from the exercise of monopoly power by large energy firms. The Hepburn Act, 34 Stat. 584 (1906), (which curtailed big oil's control of interstate pipelines), the Interstate Commerce Commission (which regulated the coal-hauling rail industry), the Federal Trade Commission (which protected against economic abuses by monopolies like the domestic oil industry), and the rise of state public utility commissions (which controlled utility rates for gas and electricity) were all aimed at curtailing market power.

World War I only slightly shook the country out of its Golden Age complacency. Professor John Clark has argued in his book, Energy and the Federal Government Fossil Fuel Policies, 1900–1946 (1987), that the war solidified the position of private energy industries. He states, "For business, the war in Europe opened great opportunities for profit through an expanding foreign trade. As many businessmen viewed it, America's entrance into the conflict provided no compelling reasons for a swollen federal economic role." Although the federal government did establish the United States Fuel Administration (USFA), the first energy agency with the power to regulate prices, transportation, and distribution, the USFA did not exercise these powers. The agency was administered locally, and its principal goal was to mobilize natural resources for the war, not to coordinate energy industries.

The USFA relied on decentralized administration and on the rhetoric of volunteerism, patriotism, and industry-government cooperation, rather than on the heavy hand of federal intervention. As a consequence, coal production did not appreciably increase during the war, pricing policies were a failure, rail carriers moved coal to the highest bidders first, and coal allocation regulations were conducted on an uncoordinated regional zone basis. The coal industry paid a price for exercising its grip on the nation's energy markets. At the height of World War I, coal was being replaced by oil and natural gas. Nevertheless, the federal government continued to support the coal industry.

Not surprisingly, federal oil and natural gas policies followed a pattern similar to coal regulation, also garnering federal favor. During World War I, several restrictions on oil and natural gas were implemented, including fuel-switching, licensing, price and production controls, and rationing. However, these controls were not integrated into an overall energy policy and they ended with the Armistice.

The regulatory experience from 1900–1920 firmly established cooperative industry-government relations. In the initial two decades of the twentieth century, energy markets were structured by:

(1) seemingly inexhaustible supplies of oil, natural gas, and coal;

(2) a shift from local to regional and interstate resource production and distribution;

(3) continuous growth in markets and in energy efficiency;

(4) increasing industrial concentration, integration, and large-scale production; and,

(5) transportation bottlenecks in each industry.

These aspects and trends generated a pattern of federal energy regulation that persists to this day. Federal energy regulations reacted to market conditions and mirrored the specific industries being regulated. Regulators did not treat energy industries either in a coordinated fashion or comprehensively. Instead, the coal, oil, natural gas (and electricity) industries have been regulated separately, by tracking each resource through its fuel cycle. Regulation occurs at each of the production, processing, distribution, and marketing stages. Federal regulation has focused on separate markets and industries, rather than on energy production and distribution as a whole system.

3. 1920–1933

During the Roaring Twenties, coal reached the end of its prominence as the nation's energy supplier, yielding this position to oil. This shift did not come without stark socioeconomic difficulties, most notably those suffered by coal miners. Mine operators, naturally, were interested in maintaining their market shares. However, since the coal market was shrinking, the most logical and simple way for the industry to maintain profitability was to reduce wages. With the industry in decline due to excess capacity and reduced demand, what resulted was cutthroat competition, pressure for wage reduction, and miner's strikes. Coal's shrinking market and consumers' growing preference for oil and natural gas underscored the significance of fuel substitution, that is, the ability of individuals or firms to switch from one energy resource, such as coal, to another, such as oil.

Promoting fuel substitution is consistent with the country's political economy because it fosters competition. Active fuel substitution also stimulates efficiency as consumers alter their energy demands based on price. Consequently, one theme of government energy regulation has been to encourage several private markets, rather than only a favored few or a single large government energy market.

To encourage the development of oil, the common law developed the rule of capture: oil belongs to the person who captures it. The rule of capture promotes production, but it also results in waste, as producers will capture as much as they can before their neighbors do. In order to reduce such waste, the states enacted gas and oil conservation statutes.

At the federal level, the Federal Oil Conservation Board (FOCB) was created to look into the perceived weaknesses of the oil industry. The primary weaknesses were waste, declining reserve estimates, and price instability due in part to the occasional flush field. Instead of curbing production, the FOCB promoted the oil depletion allowance and opened up the public domain under the Mineral Lands Leasing Act of 1920, 30 U.S.C.A. §§ 49, 50, 181, 351 et seq. Both responses favored industry. In short, the FOCB pressed for government controls in order to stop waste and stabilize prices as a form of oil industry protectionism. The FOCB also allowed large firms to control production and reduce the amount of oil on the market, which permitted these firms to capture economic rents. In these ways the FOCB regulatory efforts worked to the great benefit of the major oil companies.

By the end of the 1920s, the fossil fuel industries (oil, natural gas, and coal) were well entrenched. Energy markets, with the exception of coal, were expanding. In addition, interfuel competition and industry concentration were increasing.

The 1930s brought with them a peculiar test of the nation's energy policies. Not only did the country experience a national economic depression that put a downward pressure on prices, but rich oil fields were discovered in the oil producing states, most notably in eastern Texas. These discoveries flooded the market with remarkably cheap oil, with prices dropping below ten cents per barrel. As a result, the majors pushed for firm production controls to insure higher prices. In addition, global oil markets were developing, giving the east coast refineries the option to buy cheap foreign oil. Here again, the majors sought government intervention in the form of import tariffs to protect their markets.

On the eve of the New Deal, the nation's energy industries, markets, and regulations had developed a pattern which continues to dominate energy planning. Oil replaced coal as the dominant fuel, and large, integrated domestic firms continued to prosper. The New Deal did little to alter this pattern, with the notable exception of federalizing the regulatory structure. Federalization came predominantly in the form of regulation of interstate energy sales. It was not, however, an alternative form of energy planning. Rather, it was an adaptation to the nationalization of energy markets.

4. The New Deal Era to World War II

The New Deal experiment introduced federal regulation into nearly every sector of the national economy. Roosevelt's economic philosophy was industrial revitalization through market stabilization and business support. Although energy industries were looked upon with some skepticism, their prior development ensured their survival and growth.

Big oil was the big winner of New Deal regulation. In 1937, twenty companies controlled 70% of the proven reserves and 76% of the refining capacity. In 1941, the Temporary National Economic Committee reported the findings of its investigation into the oil industry and concluded that the "major integrated oil companies markedly increased their pre-depression control of reserves and crude production and maintained a great supremacy in refining capacity, refining output, pipeline ownership, and marketing."

Coal's troubles continued during the New Deal. The bituminous industry was plagued by productive overcapacity, underemployment of miners, poor working conditions, and chaotic pricing. Instead of recognizing and accepting the declining fortunes of the coal industry, New Deal coal policies attempted to increase wages and promote job security. The result was a labor-sensitive coal policy that did not address either the real capital problems facing the industry or the need to reduce production to reflect market demand. The coal codes of the National Recovery Administration, like the oil codes before them, were administered by the industry in the coal fields. They were not centralized. In a declining industry, government could not keep mines open and increase miners' wages, even though these were the goals of the New Deal. Nevertheless, the government attempted to pull off the impossible by trying to coordinate prices to the satisfaction of mine operators, mine workers, and consumers. To this end, two National Bituminous Coal Commissions were created to promulgate minimum prices and enforce codes of unfair trade practices.

Coal slightly improved its position during World War II. Production increased, and, more importantly, coal found the market that would serve as its largest customer—public electric utilities. Although the utilities' consumption of coal did not completely offset coal losses in the railroad, commercial, and residential sectors, electric utilities maintained a long-term, reliable market for coal.

The two most significant and lasting pieces of New Deal energy legislation are Part II of the Federal Power Act, 16 U.S.C.A. §§ 824a–825r, passed in 1933, and the Natural Gas Act, 15 U.S.C.A. § 717 et seq., passed in 1938. These two statutes focus on regulating the interstate sales of electricity and natural gas, respectively, due to market power in the transportation sectors of those industries. The intent of the two laws was to regulate the electricity and natural gas industries separately, in part because interstate electricity and natural gas markets developed in dramatically different ways (described in Chapter 11).

If the New Deal was not up to the challenge of coordinating energy policy in the 1930s, would World War II stimulate such a movement? Not really. The basic regulatory agencies, the Petroleum Administration for War, and the Solid Fuels Administration for War, were divided between oil and coal and continued the old pattern of being guided by the industries themselves. Obviously, energy resources, particularly oil, needed to be mobilized, and, as during the World War I, energy policies were greatly influenced by the industries themselves. Worse, industrial concentration continued and war policies favored large firms as major oil companies received the bulk of federal largess being dispensed to build $1 billion of new refineries.

The New Deal response to economic problems was to encourage and support industry by stimulating the national market. Regulatory objectives consisted of encouraging production, promoting growth, and providing economic stability for energy industries as a means of supporting the economy as a whole. By limiting objectives to energy production and industrial stability—both in the name of efficiency—there was little room for either energy planning or redistribution of wealth from producers to consumers.

5. Post–World War II to 1973

There were four notable energy developments between World War II and the energy cataclysm of the 1970s. First, although the coal industry had long lost its prominence, it found a new stable market in the electricity industry. Second, the natural gas industry was destabilized and, beginning in 1954, entered a period of confusion from which it has yet to emerge. Third, the oil industry went from surplus to shortage as the government attempted to rationalize domestic production and foreign imports. Fourth, the entire country jumped headlong into the commercial nuclear market, a market that in the 1990s is stagnant.

Despite fits and starts in these several industries, the country's energy program emerged relatively unharmed during this period. The energy market generally was transformed from a market of cheap abundant resources to one of more costly energy and conservation efforts. However, brownouts, gas lines, and curtailments were short-lived. The ability of the country to recover from significant market changes attests to the stability of the dominant model of energy policy.

a. Coal

While the volume of coal production remained relatively even, production shifted from eastern coal, which was mined from deep pits, to western coal, which was surface mined.

Although coal prices were not directly set by government, government health and safety regulations made the coal business more expensive. Regulations protecting miner health and safety, and the environment, raised the cost of doing business. These increased costs raised industry concerns about the ability to maintain market share when nuclear generated electricity was being touted as "too cheap to meter."

b. Natural Gas

The natural gas story is a favorite of pro-market advocates because government intervention has been judged to be a gross failure. There is fairly straightforward language in the Natural Gas Act exempting gas producers from federal regulation, while regulating the interstate pipelines that transported the gas to markets. The congressional intent of the Natural Gas Act was to protect consumers from the market power of interstate pipelines. The structure of the industry is such that pipelines constitute a transportation bottleneck. Pipelines purchase gas from producers in the field and transport it to distributors or end users. Consequently, without producer price regulation, any price charged by the producer to the pipeline is fully passed through to consumers. Because of this automatic pass through, consumer pressure was brought to regulate producer prices. Federal regulation of natural gas producers first occurred in Interstate Natural Gas Co. v. FPC (1947). In *Interstate,* natural gas prices of producers affiliated with pipelines were subjected to federal regulation because of the direct pass through. In 1954, the Supreme Court justified federal price setting for non-affiliated interstate producer prices in Phillips Petroleum Co. v. Wisconsin (1954).

The direct effect of the *Phillips* ruling was to subject thousands of individual producers to trial-type ratemaking hearings before the regulatory agency set up to handle such matters under the Natural Gas Act—the Federal Power Commission (FPC). However, the FPC was unable to administer the increase in its docket. Natural gas ratemaking evolved from individual adjudications, to area ratemaking, and finally to national ratemaking through rulemaking. Instead of individual hearings for each natural gas producer, the FPC set rates prospectively for large areas of the country, then it set national rates.

Area and national ratemaking were based on the concept of "vintaging," or two-tier pricing in which "old" gas prices (before regulation under the Natural Gas Act) were based on historic or embedded costs, and "new" gas prices (post-regulation) were allowed to float to market levels. The direct effect of two-tier pricing and cost-based ratemaking was to create a double dual natural gas market. Federally regulated natural gas prices in interstate markets were kept down because the price of "old gas" was based on embedded or historic costs rather than being based on current market prices, which occurred with "new" gas. The other dual market arose between the intrastate and interstate markets. The prices in the unregulated intrastate market were set at the current market level and were allowed to rise, while federally regulated interstate prices were depressed.

The problems associated with these dual markets were further aggravated by strict abandonment rules that prevented federally regulated producers of gas dedicated to the interstate market from switching to the more lucrative unregulated intrastate market. See 15 U.S.C.A. § 717f(b); California v. Lo–Vaca Gathering Co. (1965). Federal regulatory policies kept gas prices artificially low, which reduced domestic production and caused natural gas shortages. This regulatory structure hamstrung the industry and had to be dismantled.

The first governmental response was not complete deregulation, however, but rather regulatory reform and partial deregulation through the Natural Gas Policy Act of 1978

(NGPA) 15 U.S.C.A. § 3301 et seq. The intent of the NGPA was to unify the dual markets and to begin to deregulate prices. Today, although most gas is now deregulated, pipelines continue to present regulatory problems that are discussed more fully below.

c. Oil

World War II marked the emergence of oil as the dominant energy resource, largely as a result of oil's dominance in fueling the country's transportation sector. Shortly after the war, imports exceeded exports, causing concern among domestic producers. The recurring problem with foreign imports is that cheaper foreign oil shrinks the market for domestic producers. A further problem with foreign imports is the political instability that makes oil supplies unreliable.

In order to shore up the domestic oil industry, government placed quotas on imports. With quotas, domestic producers were assured a share of the market. Consistent with past practices, government first relied on the market to limit imports, and then government asked industry to limit imports voluntarily. Not surprisingly, volunteerism did not prove to be an effective way to cut imports because imported oil was cheaper than domestically produced oil and was attractive to refiners. During the 1950s, various political and rhetorical arguments were made to reduce imports for national security reasons, but the economic reality tilted in favor of cheap oil. At the end of the 1950s, oil import quotas were made mandatory, and they continued until the early 1970s when domestic production peaked, making them superfluous.

The 1970s caught oil in an unfamiliar setting—price regulation. Oil prices initially were set as part of President Nixon's wage and price controls. These regulations took on a life of their own after the Nixon economic stabilization program ended, and oil prices became regulated as a result of soaring gasoline prices caused by the OPEC oil embargo of 1973–74. Oil price regulations required an elaborate bureaucratic machine for their administration. Oil price controls, like natural gas price regulations, were thought to have distorted the market rather than stimulated it, and they were ultimately dismantled by President Reagan in January, 1981.

d. Nuclear Energy

The single most notable energy event in the post-World War II period was the major commitment of capital to commercial nuclear power. The several hundred billion dollar industry began at the end of World War II as a way to channel the destructive force of nuclear power into more benign and beneficial uses. In 1946, the Atomic Energy Act, 42 U.S.C.A. § 2011, was passed for the purpose of moving nuclear power away from the military and into civilian hands. The Act, however, still allowed the government a monopoly on controlling uranium. That monopoly existed until the Act was significantly amended in 1954 to permit private ownership of uranium. This control was crucial for private sector investment. Such investment became substantial in 1957 with the passage of the Price–Anderson Act, 42 U.S.C.A. § 2210, which limited the liability of nuclear facilities in the case of an accident.

After the passage of the Price–Anderson Act, thousands of megawatts of nuclear generating capacity were ordered by private firms. The expansion of commercial nuclear energy continued throughout the 1960s and into the early 1970s, spurred by a pro-nuclear consensus. The prevailing wisdom was that private producers had a new, modern, "safe and clean" technology, that consumers were pleased to receive a cheap product, and that the government was happy to find beneficial civilian uses for this technology of the future.

Toward the end of the 1960s and into the 1970s, however, the promises that had built the pro-nuclear consensus showed signs of fatigue. Instead of being safe, clean, cheap, and abundant, the nuclear enterprise was discovered to have large social costs, involving enormous environmental, health, safety, and financial risks. By the 1990s the industry was moribund. No new nuclear plants have been ordered since 1978, and all plants ordered since 1974 have been canceled. Although there were 111 plants in operation in 1990 and 8 more with construction permits, nuclear power, particularly large-scale plants of 1000 megawatts and more, is stalled.

B.　PRESIDENTS CARTER AND REAGAN TEST THE DOMINANT MODEL, 1973–1988

The history of energy law and policy until 1973 demonstrates the development of a dominant model of energy policy. The decade following 1973 tested that model as world energy markets experienced dramatic changes. In response to those changes, President Carter attempted to centralize energy policymaking and decisionmaking and tried to develop a comprehensive and coordinated national energy plan. That plan never coalesced. President Reagan tried to deregulate energy on a broad scale and dismantle the Department of Energy. He failed as well. In short, neither the Carter hyper-regulatory approach nor the Reagan deregulation approach was effective in radically altering energy regulation, which continued to hew closely to the dominant model policy that had developed over the previous century. The inability of the two presidential administrations to control energy policy demonstrates the tenacity of the model.

1.　President Carter and Centralized Energy Policy

There were four significant energy events during the Carter Administration which generated a cascade of energy regulations. First, Carter sought to centralize energy administration in the cabinet level Department of Energy (DOE). The DOE was unable, however, to design a comprehensive national energy plan because energy decisionmaking and policymaking responsibilities were scattered over several branches of the federal government, and even within the DOE itself authority was fragmented.

Second, Carter's "moral equivalent of war" speech on April 18, 1977, outlined the substantive principles of a national energy policy which led to the passage of the National Energy Act in October of the following year. The National Energy Act consists of five pieces of major legislation: the National Energy Conservation Policy Act, Pub.L. No. 95–619, 92 Stat. 3206 (codified as amended in scattered sections of Titles 12, 15, 25, 31 and 42 U.S.C.A.); the Powerplant and Industrial Fuel Use Act of 1978, Pub.L. No. 95–620, 92 Stat. 3289 (codified as amended in scattered sections of Titles 15 and 42 U.S.C.A.); the Natural Gas Policy Act of 1978, Pub.L. No. 95–621, 92 Stat. 3350 (codified at 15 U.S.C.A. §§ 3301– 3432 & 42 U.S.C.A. § 7255); the Public Utilities Regulatory Policies Act of 1978, Pub.L. No. 95–617, 92 Stat. 3117 (codi- fied as amended in scattered sections of Titles 15, 16, 26, 42, and 43 U.S.C.A.); and the Energy Tax Act of 1978, Pub.L. No. 95–618, 92 Stat. 3174 (codified as amended in scattered sec- tions of Titles 26 and 42 U.S.C.A.).

The component parts of the National Energy Act addressed conventional fuels in several ways. Their purpose was to move the country away from a dependence on foreign oil, promote the use of coal, increase energy efficiency, modernize utility ratemaking, stimulate conservation, encourage the creation of a new market for alternative energy sources in electricity, and restructure a distorted market in natural gas.

The third major event was President Carter's energy ad- dress on April 5, 1979, which stressed the need to decontrol oil prices as a means of increasing domestic oil production. The address led to the passage of the Crude Oil Windfall Profit Tax Act of 1980, Pub.L. No. 96–223, 94 Stat. 229

(codified as amended in scattered sections of Titles 7, 19, 26 and 42 U.S.C.A.), designed to capture the economic rents realized by domestic oil producers as a result of the rise in world oil prices.

Fourth, on July 15, 1979, the President delivered another major energy address, returning to his moral equivalent of war rhetoric. Again, Congress responded, this time with the passage of the Energy Security Act of 1980. The Energy Security Act, Pub.L. No. 96–294, 94 Stat. 611, (codified as amended in scattered sections of Titles 7, 10, 12, 15, 16, 30 and 42 U.S.C.A.), also consists of several pieces of legislation, including: the Defense Production Act Amendments of 1980, Pub.L. No. 96–294, 94 Stat. 617 (codified in 50 U.S.C.A. §§ 2061–2166); the United States Synthetic Fuels Corporation Act of 1980, Pub.L. No. 96–294, 94 Stat. 633 (codified as amended in scattered sections of 42 U.S.C.A.); the Biomass Energy and Alcohol Fuels Act of 1980, Pub.L. No. 96–294, 94 Stat. 683 (codified as amended in scattered sections of Titles 7, 15, 16 and 42 U.S.C.A.); the Renewable Energy Resources Act of 1980, Pub.L. No. 96–294, 94 Stat. 715 (codified as amended in scattered sections of Titles 16 and 42 U.S.C.A.); the Solar Energy and Energy Conservation Act of 1980, Pub.L. No. 96–294, 94 Stat. 719 (codified as amended in scattered sections of Titles 12 and 42 U.S.C.A.); and the Geothermal Energy Act of 1980, Pub.L. No. 96–294, 94 Stat. 763 (codified in scattered sections of 16 U.S.C.A.).

The Energy Security Act was a dramatically conceived package of legislation that turned energy policy away from conventional resources and toward the development and promotion of synthetic oil and gas derived from coal, oil shale, and tar sands. The Act also attempted to stimulate a third energy transition, from fossil fuels to renewable resources such as solar, biomass, alcohol, wind, and geothermal steam. The Act also sought to make conservation a larger part of the country's energy planning.

The legislation that emerged during the Carter Administration did not achieve the intended result of coordinating national energy policy. Regulatory authority throughout the federal government was fragmented, and competition among and within the several energy industries resisted comprehensive planning. Nor did it stimulate the so-called third energy transition, from fossil fuels to renewable resources and conservation. Instead, Carter's energy program went contrary to the country's entrenched model of energy policy. The attempted coordination failed because of the model's resistance to centralization; the transition also failed because of the model's traditional reliance on the market to signal a move into other resources. Simply put, centralization and planning conflicted with competition and private markets.

2. President Reagan and Deregulation

If President Carter's highly centralized, pro-government energy policy failed, it would seem to follow that President Reagan's private sector, supply-side, anti-government deregulation efforts surely would succeed and that the DOE would be dismantled. Indeed, President Reagan made his energy intentions clear in one of his first acts in office by decontrolling oil prices on January 28, 1981. The oil price decontrol was largely symbolic, however, because they were scheduled to terminate on October 1st of that year.

The Reagan deregulation program did not spring from whole cloth. Natural gas deregulation, like oil deregulation, was scheduled to occur consistent with phased deregulation contemplated by President Carter's Natural Gas Policy Act of 1978. Similarly, although President Reagan campaigned to dismantle the United States Synthetic Fuels Corporation, the synfuels program failed because the market was unable to support it. Synfuels producers were not able to process coal into natural gas or extract oil from tar sands or oil shale at costs competitive with traditionally extracted oil and natural gas.

In President Reagan's campaign against big government, the Department of Energy and the Solar Energy Research Institute (SERI), a federal laboratory devoted to renewable energy research, were to be abolished as part of the new president's program of supply-side economic deregulation. The continued existence of DOE and SERI (renamed in 1991 the National Renewable Energy Laboratory), and President Reagan's failure to deregulate energy in substantial ways, may be explained by the intransigence of bureaucracies. That explanation is, however, too superficial. A more refined explanation, like the explanation for President Carter's failure to centralize national energy planning, can be found in the dominant model. This model demonstrates that government regulation of energy is embedded in the country's political economy. By acting inconsistent with that model through overreliance on the market and underreliance on government support of conventional fuels and producers, President Reagan's initiatives at deregulation were destined to fail.

C. THE DOMINANT MODEL OF ENERGY POLICY

The energy policies of the Carter and Reagan administrations did not last much beyond their immediate causes. The Carter and Reagan policies were similar in that both were inconsistent with the dominant energy policy model and with the prevailing market. The dominant model requires support of conventional resources, and recognition that some segments of the energy industries possess market power requiring regulation. Stable energy production, distribution, and consumption occur as a consequence of the interplay of government and industry within the boundaries of our mixed-market political economy.

The key to understanding the political economy of energy is recognizing the symbiotic relationship between government and industry, which is manifested by four characteristics. First, in some instances energy resources are complementary, so that regulation of one does not necessarily adversely affect the other. Oil (for transportation) and electricity divide the energy pie into two more or less equal but noncompeting shares. Electricity does not occupy much of the transportation sector, and oil is an uneconomic means of producing electricity. Therefore, federal energy policy can support both oil and electricity production. Second, energy resources are susceptible to inter-fuel competition. A federal policy that promotes the use of coal to generate electricity simultaneously discourages the use of nuclear power for the same purpose, thus promoting competition. Third, industry and government depend on each other for the distribution and allocation of benefits and burdens. The federal government, for example, controls most of the new oil reserves but depends on private industry for their development. Finally, both business and government are stimulated to act by market disequilibria. Oil price controls were responses to Middle East embargoes, and increased exploration for natural gas was a reaction to a loosening of federally established prices. This interplay between government and industry has created the dominant model.

Domestic energy policy, from the late nineteenth century to the early 1990's, was based on the fundamental assumption that a link exists between the level of energy production and the gross national product (GNP). Consistent with this assumption is the hope that economies of scale in energy production can still be realized. As more energy is produced, prices will remain stable, or relatively low, and the GNP will grow. Implicit in this simple formula is the supposition that the general welfare increases in direct proportion to the GNP. Energy policy continues to rely on this fundamental market-based assumption.

As a consequence, domestic energy policy favors large-scale, high-technology, capital-intensive, integrated, and centralized energy producers which rely on fossil fuels. These archetype energy firms are favored over alternatives, such as small solar or wind firms, because energy policy-makers believe that larger firms can continue to realize economies of scale. Policy-makers gamble that greater energy efficiencies can be achieved by traditional, fossil fuel-reliant firms, rather than by alternative firms. Such traditional firms seemingly have an advantage through technological innovation, discovery of new reserves, and discovery of new energy sources. This belief may or may not be true. Nevertheless, it persists, and the favoritism it engenders will continue as alternative firms carry the burden of persuading policy-makers otherwise. Put another way, as long as energy production, consumption, and prices remain stable, the embedded assumptions of the dominant energy policy model will continue.

This dominant model of energy policy thus has the following general goals:

(1) to assure abundant energy supplies, even if these supplies have to be imported;

(2) to maintain reasonable prices;

(3) to limit the market power of archetype firms;

(4) to promote inter- and intrafuel competition;

(5) to support conventional fuels (oil, natural gas, coal, hydropower, and nuclear power); and

(6) to allow energy decisionmaking and policymaking to develop within an active federal-state regulatory system.

This policy, developed over the last 100 years, has served the country well by providing long periods of reliable energy at relatively low prices and with respectable degrees of economic stability. In light of this historical intransigence, one can assume that the dominant policy will continue in the future, and that alternatives to conventional systems will be an insignificant component of domestic energy policy.

III. ALTERNATIVE FUELS AND POLICIES

Discussion of alternative energy sources can trace its recent history to the environmental movement of the late 1960s. Indeed, alternative energy policy can be discerned as having three periods. In the late 1960s and early 1970s, the environmental movement provided the impetus for energy policies sensitive to clean air and water, particularly for cleaner burning coal and for the promotion of renewable resources. The energy "crisis" of the mid–1970s moved alternative policies in two directions. First, the crisis demonstrated that conservation could play an important role in energy planning. Second, renewable alternatives to fixed supplies of oil and natural gas were sought. The final period is just beginning. The late 1980s, especially with the publicity surrounding global warming, reinvigorated the earlier discussion about renewable resources and conservation.

A. ALTERNATIVE FUELS

The phrase "alternative fuels" encompasses two distinct ideas. In more common parlance, alternative fuels are frequently equated with renewable resources such as solar, wind, biomass, waste, and geothermal. Alternative resources also include such fuels as oil shale, tar sands, and gas from coal, that serve as direct substitutes for oil and natural gas. These latter alternative resources are other forms of fossil fuels and easily fit the dominant model, unlike renewable resources which supplant that model.

Alternative energy resources should be analyzed from four perspectives regarding feasibility. Before an alternative energy resource supplants a conventional fuel it must be feasible scientifically, technologically, legally, and financially.

Scientific feasibility means that the basic science regarding a particular alternative is known. Technological feasibility means that the basic science can be applied. The basic science and technology is known for most alternative resources. Nuclear fusion (the combination of atomic nuclei) is an example of one technology that is not yet on line. Legal feasibility refers to the creation of a legal regime, usually in the form of a property interest, so that the alternative resource can be owned, transferred, and used. Occasionally, legal feasibility requires innovation, such as the development of property rules for sunlight and geothermal power.

However, the single largest obstacle to marketing alternative energy resources is their financial feasibility. Put most simply, the question is whether the alternative source is cost competitive with conventional sources. Unless and until solar generated electricity is less expensive than utility generated electricity, there will be little or no market for solar power. Likewise, synthetic fuels will replace conventional fossil fuels only when synfuels are less costly and economically competitive with natural gas and oil. Sometimes government regulation can narrow the cost differential by subsidizing the development and distribution of an alternative resource. Examples of such regulation include the oil depletion allowance, and tax credits for conservation measures. Eventually, the alternative resource must develop a market to survive, and the costs and benefits of law (i.e. government regulation) must fit into the picture.

B. ALTERNATIVE ENERGY POLICIES

The dominant model of United States energy policy relies on the hard path of large-scale, capital intensive high-technologies. The Energy Security Act of 1980 evinced a government commitment to experiment with and fund research and development of alternative fuels, and a willingness to try alternative policies. As things turned out, this commitment and willingness dissipated with the Reagan Administration.

President Reagan's anti-DOE, pro-market program was antithetical to government support for alternative fuels and policies. As if presidential disapproval were not enough, the economy of the 1980s also turned against alternatives. Energy prices dipped, supplies of conventional fuels increased, and the market for alternatives evaporated. This condition of a weak, virtually non-existent, market for alternatives lasted throughout the decade of the 1980s. Although there is no immediate, dramatic reason, like the 1973 Arab Oil Embargo, to expect a radical change of policy in the 1990s, there are signs of potential change.

The first sign comes from the Reagan legacy—energy policy-makers are placing more reliance on market mechanisms rather than on heavy-handed government price-setting and resource allocation. This change may or may not help alternative fuels and policies, depending on the relative prices of alternative fuels compared with the prices of conventional fuels.

The second sign is environmental sensitivity. Energy and the environment will continue to be an important energy topic for as long as we can peer into the future. Until recently, the terms "energy" and "environment" were used in an uncomfortable alliance. Indeed, "energy," and the "environment" were seen as distinct systems of policy and planning. By the 1990s, however, one can no longer afford to juxtapose these words to represent distinct ways of thinking about the future of the natural world; the realization is that there is an interconnection between the energy produced from natural resources and the environmental effects of that production.

1. Energy Futures

Although several energy futures are possible, two extremes are frequently discussed. The first is simply a continuation of the dominant fossil fuel model with a large dose of nuclear power. The other extreme is a near apocalyptic world as described in D. Meadows, The Limits to Growth (1972) and B.

McKibben, The End of Nature (1989). These authors argue that human activity has already irreversibly and negatively altered nature. They further argue that drastic steps regarding energy must be taken or else the future is uncertain. In particular, greater conservation, use of renewable resources, and increased energy efficiencies are necessary if the planet is to survive.

It is wrong to limit the nation's energy future to these two visions—a continuation of the past century or an explicitly counter-cultural one. It is also wrong to assume that these two visions of our energy future, a future made complicated by an ambiguous environmental forecast, are equal alternatives or that policy-makers can choose one over the other as if both were situated on a level playing field. Rather, the dominant model of energy policy has a decided edge.

The dominant model is an integral part of our culture because of massive investment, public subsidies, a century of experience, and because of the existence of perplexing questions about future environmental uncertainties. Any alternative vision, including an *End of Nature* hypothesis, carries the heavy burden of overcoming this history. In no small part, choosing an alternative requires policy-makers to make, in Kenneth Boulding's terminology, heroic, financially risky policy choices and strategic decisions.

The economic downturn of the late 1970s, early 1980s, and early 1990s, and the future threats posed by global climatic shifts and changes in world markets, challenge both energy and environmental policy-makers. Neither can proceed with business as usual. Energy policy-makers must anticipate the long-term social costs associated with large-scale projects, even as they set policy for short- and medium-term energy needs. Likewise, environmental policy-makers must factor into their more ambitious programs the short- and medium-term energy needs of active and productive national economies.

2. An Alternative Energy Policy: The Sustainable Development Model

One emerging alternative energy policy is called the sustainable development model. "Sustainable development" is defined as a policy or program that "meets the needs of the present without compromising the ability of future generations to meet their own needs." World Commission on Environment and Development, Our Common Future (1987). Sustainable development makes two promises. First, it is to serve as a bridge between economic reality and social aspirations. Second, energy production and environmental protection may work together through the common language that sustainable development provides.

The sustainable development model is more politically sensitive and asks more technically difficult questions of economists. Under this model, the common language spoken by energy and environmental policy-makers will look to safety, intergenerational effects, democratic political participation, and environmental care, as much to efficiency, productivity, and wealth creation. The common language will be one of political economy, rather than a narrow language of either the short-term satisfaction of individual needs (economics) or the long-term creation of utopias (politics). It is estimated that a sustainable energy plan can move from fossil fuels to solar power, increased efficiency, renewable resources, and conservation by 2030. See L. Brown, State of the World—1990 (1990).

Does the choice of a new energy/environmental vision necessitate a change in life style? This is the important cultural question. It is the cultural question that makes decisionmakers hesitate before they adopt alternatives to the dominant model. The dominant vision promises wealth creation, economic efficiency, and energy production for a healthy society. The alternative vision promises an equitable distribution of goods, environmental protection, and ecological sensitivity. The sustainable development vision promises a melding of all of these.

Although the dominant fossil fuel driven model has demonstrated its tenacity, there are signs of new thinking about United States energy policy. In 1991, the Bush Administration published a *National Energy Strategy* which begins: "The National Energy Strategy lays the foundation for a more efficient, less vulnerable, and environmentally sustainable energy future." President Bush also proposed extensive legislation, entitled the National Energy Security Act of 1991, to implement the National Energy Strategy.

This comprehensive legislation addresses the new and the traditional. Espousing faith in the market, the proposal seeks to bring about energy efficiency in consumption and use, as well as in the oil and electricity markets. The proposal also explores coal technology and electricity, oil exploration on the outer continental shelf and in the Arctic, and natural gas and nuclear power. On the "alternative" energy side, the Bush proposal contains initiatives for renewable energy, as well as research and development, and demonstration projects, for new energy technologies.

Although the Bush legislation is fundamentally consistent with the traditional model, the National Energy Strategy, like the Clean Air Act Amendments of 1990, begin to link energy concerns with environmental resources. Further, the Bush proposal subjects energy and environmental initiatives to a market test and to cost-benefit analyses.

IV. CONTINUED RELIANCE ON THE DOMINANT MODEL

Speculation about the energy future must comport with the real world. Not only did 1990 bring attention to the global climatic consequences of traditional fossil fuel policies, the year also demonstrated the country's and the world's preoccupation with and dependence on the dominant model.

The Iraqi invasion of Kuwait on August 2, 1990 and the 1991 War in the Gulf were dramatic events that temporarily changed the world energy picture. Combined, Iraq and Kuwait produce 4.6 million barrels of oil per day, constituting 16% of world oil production. The United States imports 8 million barrels per day and approximately 13.3%, or 600,000 barrels per day, of its daily requirement from Iraq and Kuwait. The shortfall in world oil production as a result of removing Iraqi and Kuwaiti oil from the global market was ultimately made up by increased output from other Middle Eastern countries, non-OPEC countries, and by the release of oil from United States strategic petroleum reserves. Regardless of this coverage, the consequences to domestic and world economies were severe.

After the invasion, oil prices climbed higher than at any time since the 1973 Arab embargo. Although they eventually receded to near normal levels, these steep price increases exerted forceful downward pressure on the economy as a whole and increased inflation. Oil stock and bond prices were volatile, reflecting general uncertainty in the markets. In September, 1990, Congress approved and President Bush signed into law legislation that extended the United States Strategic Petroleum Reserve through September 30, 1994. The goal is to store one billion barrels of oil. The 1990 extension also authorized the President to draw down for sale up to five million barrels on a test basis. In January 1991, the President authorized the release of one million barrels of oil a day to stabilize the oil market.

Once again, reminiscent of the mid–1970s, energy policymakers called for energy policy planning, a strategy for reducing dependence on foreign oil, possibly greater use of nuclear power, increased conservation, and increased domestic oil exploration. Although the oil shortfall caused by the Iraqi invasion of Kuwait was made up, the hypersensitive geopolitics of the Middle East oil supply, and the ease with which disruptions can occur, tend to destabilize energy planning. In a period of such destabilization, the likely course is to follow familiar paths. In other words, future energy policies are more likely to resemble traditional fossil fuel policies than alternative policies such as the sustainable development model. The last decade of the 20th century will be an important one for energy law and policy planning as the dominant model confronts global challenges.

CHAPTER TEN

DEVELOPING ENERGY RESOURCES

Energy is simply defined as the capacity to do work. Before natural resources can be harnessed to do that work, they must be transformed from their natural state into a useful form. This transformation occurs throughout a period called the fuel cycle. Generally speaking, the fuel cycle entails five stages: exploration and recovery; processing; transportation; conversion to usable energy; and distribution to end users. Individual resources, and the industries surrounding those resources, have peculiarities deserving special attention.

Chapter Nine argued that the United States has no comprehensive, coordinated national energy plan which links all energy resources to national goals in a detailed fashion. Rather, the government regulates individual natural resources industries and markets. Government regulates those industries and markets along individual fuel cycles. Chapter One noted how government intervenes in private enterprise when a market failure or imperfection is identified, and when a regulatory justification for that intervention can be made. Consequently, energy regulation attempts to correct market failures usually in an attempt to prevent a concentration of market power or to enhance economic efficiency. In the sections that follow, a specific resource industry is described and then followed by a discussion of the government regulations surrounding that industry.

This chapter focuses on: oil, coal, nuclear power, hydropower and alternative resources, in the first three stages of the fuel cycle—exploration and recovery, processing, and transportation. The last two stages of the fuel cycle—conversion and distribution—are discussed in Chapter Eleven. It should be noted that each of the resources presented in this chapter can be converted into electricity. Once converted, the electricity is then distributed to end users. The conversion and distribution of electricity almost exclusively occurs through a public utility. Natural gas is distributed also by public utilities. Therefore, Chapter Eleven discusses both the conversion of natural resources into electricity, and the distribution of electricity and natural gas in the context of public utility regulation.

I. OIL

Oil has occupied center stage in domestic and international energy policy and planning for over a century. See D. Yergin, The Prize: The Epic Quest for Oil, Money, and Power (1991). As the 1990 Iraqi invasion of Kuwait attested, the disruption of the oil supply can affect domestic and world economies. Since the early 1970s, with President Nixon's Project Independence, freedom from foreign oil, especially oil from the Middle East, has been an aspiration of United States energy policy. Unfortunately, that independence has not been forthcoming. In 1970, domestic oil production peaked, and has been in decline ever since. Domestic reserves remain elusive and increasingly expensive to extract. Globally, particularly in the Middle East, large oil reserves can be produced more cheaply than in the United States, thus making foreign oil attractive to domestic refiners and consumers.

It is a curiosity of United States energy policy that, even though oil is the central actor as a resource, oil is subject to few government regulations. The primary reason offered for the light regulatory hand is that the oil industry is competitive and does not exercise monopoly power, therefore extensive federal government oversight is unnecessary. The exercise of monopoly power was a major concern at the turn of the 19th Century. That concern dissipated with the break-up of the Standard Oil Trust in 1911. Standard Oil Co. v. United States (1911). Since then there has been only intermittent government regulation of oil.

A. OVERVIEW OF THE OIL INDUSTRY

The oil fuel cycle can be divided into four parts: exploration and production, refining, transportation, and marketing. Large oil companies such as Amoco and Exxon are involved with each stage and are known as integrated companies. Nonintegrated companies, of which there are about 40,000, are those that are engaged in one of these phases. Semiintegrated or partially integrated companies have two or more but not all phases.

The fuel cycles for oil and natural gas are structurally similar in the beginning because oil and natural gas are often found together. After a given reservoir produces a certain amount of oil, enhanced (more expensive) recovery techniques are required. Where oil is depleted from older wells, new and deeper wells in harder to drill places such as the outer continental shelf are needed. Oil is then transported by tanker, truck, or pipeline to one of about 300 oil refineries in the United States. Refineries separate the petroleum into more than 3000 products, ranging from jet fuel to petrochemicals used to make plastics. Gasoline is the largest component of all petroleum products and accounts for about 50% of refined product consumption. The transportation sector accounts for about 54% of all oil consumed, followed by residential and commercial users (24%), industrial users (17%), utilities (4%) and miscellaneous (1%).

B. REGULATORY OVERVIEW

With the exception of antitrust enforcement and regulation of interstate transportation of oil pipelines in the early 20th century, the federal government has not regulated the oil industry heavily. Rather, the federal government, primarily through favorable tax treatment such as a resource depletion allowance and foreign tax credits, has supported the industry.

In the first third of the 20th Century, government regulation was accomplished through state oil and gas conservation laws. Through such devices as pooling, unitization, well spacing, and prorationing, states attempted to affect how much oil was produced and put on the market at a given time. Producing states such as Texas, Louisiana, and Oklahoma, which were interested in keeping the petroleum industry viable, passed legislation to insure that oil did not glut the market and lower oil prices to the point of incurring waste.

In the 1930s, several rich oil fields were discovered in East Texas and Oklahoma, and existing state conservation laws were unsuccessful in stemming production. Oil prices plummeted. The federal government then sought to play a supporting role to state conservation regulation by trying to restrict the amount of oil traded in interstate commerce in excess of amounts allowable under state statutes. Known as "hot oil," the federal government first banned its trade in interstate commerce by Executive Order, through the Department of the Interior under Harold Ickes. Next, as part of Franklin Roosevelt's National Industrial Recovery Act, an oil code setting production quotas was adopted to reduce production and stabilize prices. That code was invalidated in the celebrated anti-delegation case, Panama Refining Co. v. Ryan (1935). Immediately following the Court's rejection of the oil code, Congress passed the Connally Hot Oil Act of 1935, 15 U.S.C.A. § 715 et seq., that specifically prohibited interstate or foreign commerce in amounts of oil greater than the amounts allowed by state law. Soon thereafter, the demand for oil increased as the nation mobilized for war.

The oil market changed after World War II. First, oil replaced coal as the nation's dominant fuel, a transition that had begun during World War I. Second, oil production expanded throughout the world. And third, in 1948 U.S. oil imports exceeded exports for the first time. Consequently, global production by the major integrated oil firms has kept the world economy in a delicate state.

When foreign oil is cheaper than domestic oil, it is desired by domestic refiners. Domestic producers prefer to limit foreign imports and they intermittently seek import quotas for the sole purpose of protecting their industry. Early in the Eisenhower Administration, voluntary quotas were tried and failed. Then in 1957, the President instituted the Mandatory Oil Import Programs (MOIP). This program limited the amount of foreign oil that could be imported into the country in an effort to aid domestic producers. The MOIP remained active and in effect until the Arab oil embargo of 1973. In 1970, domestic production peaked at 9.6 million barrels per day, thus relieving the need for mandatory quotas on imported oil. In 1973, oil prices rose to such an extent that domestic price regulation rather than quotas occupied federal attention.

Oil prices became regulated as part of President Nixon's Economic Stabilization Program. Under Phase IV price controls of the Economic Stabilization Act of 1970, 12 U.S.C.A. § 1904, oil prices were regulated at each stage of the industry, including production, refining, reselling, and retailing. These controls were first administered through the President's Cost of Living Council, the now defunct Federal Energy Administration, and finally through the Department of Energy (DOE). Oil prices were deregulated in January, 1981.

One statutory response to the oil embargo of 1973 was the Emergency Petroleum Allocation Act, 15 U.S.C.A. § 751 et seq., that enabled the President to provide equitable allocations of petroleum products because of an oil shortage which threatened the normal flow of commerce and constituted a

national energy crisis.   Powerine Oil Co. v. FEA (1976);
Bonnaffons v. DOE (1980).   See also the Energy Policy and
Conservation Act, 42 U.S.C.A. § 6201 et seq. (also regulating
oil prices).

Although oil price regulations were decontrolled in 1981,
and generally judged overly complex and counter-productive,
a brief discussion of them should be instructive.   Price controls are a regulatory tool often used by government, and the
oil price regulations have a counterpart in natural gas regulation.

C. THE ERA OF PRICE AND ALLOCATION CONTROLS, 1970–1980

1. Pricing

The complex set of oil regulations in the 1970s spawned
equally complex court cases and an intricate price-resource
allocation structure.   This section addresses two-tier pricing,
entitlements, exception relief, small refiner bias, and the
stripper well exemption, to name a few of the arcane terms
that have become associated with the regulation of petroleum
at the federal level during the 1970s.

Oil price controls were motivated by two goals: to spur
new domestic production through higher prices, and to prevent oil firms from capturing economic rents from existing
production.   Hence, a two-tier pricing system was created—
"old" oil and "new" oil.   Emergency Petroleum Allocation
Act, 15 U.S.C.A. §§ 751, 753 (1973).   Old oil prices were
determined by reference to historical and then to current
levels of production from a given property.   Even the term
"property" produced litigation.   Texaco, Inc. v. DOE (1980).
The quantity of oil produced from a property in the designated base year was known as the "base production control
level."   Production at or below that level was "old" oil, while

quantities of oil produced in excess of that level was "new" oil. Pennzoil Co. v. DOE (1979).

Under the regulations, if producers were willing to invest capital in new production, the cost of producing this "new" oil was passed through to refiners and then to consumers, and the price of new oil rose to the market level. Consumers Union of U.S., Inc. v. Sawhill (1975); Cities Service Co. v. FEA (1975); Delta Refining Co. v. FEA (1977).

The two-tier system did not go far enough. The disparity between the price of controlled and uncontrolled oil had an unequal impact on different groups of refiners. With a dual pricing system, the major integrated oil companies, which as a class had greater access to old oil, had significantly lower refining costs than did small independent refiners. The government's response was the Entitlements Program under the Energy Policy and Conservation Act, 42 U.S.C.A. § 6201 et seq. A refiner was required to have an "entitlement" for each barrel of old oil it refined. All refiners were issued monthly entitlements equal to their proportionate share of old oil refined during a base period on a nationwide basis. This meant that refiners that used more old oil than the national average were required to buy additional entitlements from refiners that went below the national average. This equalized the costs between controlled and uncontrolled oil used by refiners.

Another disparity existed within the class of small producers known as stripper wells that produced only 10 barrels of oil per day or less. Stripper well volume was so low that the incentives for new oil production were not sufficient to encourage them to increase production through more costly techniques. These producers were exempted from price controls. Southern Union Production Co. v. FEA (1978). Another refinement of this pricing system was needed for small refiners in order to keep them competitive. The entitlements program had built into it a small refiner bias under which small refiners were allocated additional entitlements. Pasco,

Inc. v. FEA (1975). The practical effect was that even "new" oil became controlled for small refiners. These new controls thus set up a three-tier pricing system. Mapco Inc. v. Carter (1978). With the stripper well exemption and the incentives for enhanced recovery, oil price controls became multi-tiered.

Market distortions had been created between integrated and nonintegrated companies, and among large and small refiners and various producers. Price disparities also developed between domestic and imported oil. Some refiners argued that the two-tier system caused refiners to purchase more imported oil instead of reducing imports. In addition, price disparities appeared in different geographical markets within the United States. To deal with these peculiarities, the DOE was empowered to grant exception relief to the pricing regulations. Rock Island Refining Corp. v. DOE (1979); New England Petroleum Corp. v. FEA (1978). Exceptions to the entitlements program protected the competitive position of oil firms that were adversely affected in the market because of government regulations.

Price controls also contained an enforcement component. If sales of controlled products were made in violation of the pricing regulations, then the DOE had enforcement authority and violators could be ordered to refund overcharges. Quincy Oil, Inc. v. FEA (1979); Plaquemines Oil Sales Corp. v. FEA (1978); Naph–Sol Refining Co. v. Cities Service Oil Co. (1980). These overcharges could be large. In United States v. Exxon Corp. (1979), the government sought to have Exxon refund over $183,000,000.00. Oil companies were ordered to refund large overcharges in Phillips Petroleum Co. v. DOE (1978); Standard Oil Co. v. FEA (1978); Standard Oil Co. v. DOE (1978); United States v. Metropolitan Petroleum Co., Inc. (1990).

2. Allocation

One way to affect the distribution of a good is to alter its price. Another regulatory tool is resource allocation. The

DOE was empowered to allocate oil supplies for the purpose of maintaining an oil company's competitive position in the industry.

On November 12, 1979, in response to the taking of hostages by Iran, President Carter issued a proclamation banning the importation into the United States of oil produced in Iran. The Iranian government then placed an embargo on the export of its oil to the United States. In an effort to alleviate the hardships caused by this supply disruption, the DOE implemented a mandatory allocation program. Under this program, a domestic refiner injured by the embargo could receive cheaper oil from other domestic refiners. Marathon Oil Co. v. DOE (1979); New England Petroleum Corp. v. FEA (1978). The DOE also limited or set the amount of an oil product that suppliers could sell to their customers. Shell Oil Co. v. Nelson Oil Co., Inc. (1980).

The power of the DOE to allocate supplies also became important to consumers affected by shortages throughout the market. The regulations under the mandatory allocation program distributed supplies to help keep firms competitive in the industry. When oil supplies were reduced as a result of the Iranian embargo, the fear was that some end-of-the-fuel-cycle customers would also be indiscriminately disadvantaged. Rules for rationing gas at the pump were a kind of allocation that affected consumers most directly. Reeves v. Simon (1974). In an effort to allocate gasoline in a "fair and equitable" manner, Congress also passed the Emergency Energy Conservation Act of 1979, which required the President to develop a "standby" rationing plan for gasoline and diesel fuel.

D. OFFSHORE EXPLORATION AND OIL SPILLS

The discomfort caused by dependence on foreign oil puts pressure on domestic producers. Domestic producers, in turn, look to federal lands, both onshore and offshore, as areas for new exploration. Federal lands, however, carry with them a high degree of environmental sensitivity that have a direct impact on oil production and price. Oil producers are looking for oil in more exotic and protected locales, such as Alaska's North Slope, federal forests, and on the outer continental shelf (OCS).

The United States, rather than any individual state, is entitled to exercise sovereign rights over the seabed and subsoil of the ocean lying more than three miles seaward from the coastline. United States v. Maine (1975); the Outer Continental Shelf Lands Act, 43 U.S.C.A. § 1331. This property regime has spawned a significant federal-private market which relies on exploration and development of the OCS for oil and gas. As noted in Chapter Six, the federal government, primarily through the Department of the Interior, leases areas of the OCS to oil companies through a competitive bidding process. The leases allow for exploration and development. Bids are solicited on the basis of a cash bonus with a fixed royalty, a royalty bid with a fixed cash bonus, or various combinations of the two. The bidding system is designed and intended to balance the economic, social, and environmental concerns of developing these offshore lands, as well as to assure a fair market price to the government. Watt v. Energy Action Educ. Foundation (1981).

The DOE has authority to develop the OCS so that the nation might increase its supply of oil and gas. In a real sense, the OSC and federal onshore lands are the last domestic frontiers, certainly in the foreseeable future. However, development of the OCS raises concerns that the ecological dangers inherent in tapping offshore resources will require a great deal of caution. The major challenge is whether the Department of Interior's environmental impact statement (EIS) for offshore leasing satisfies the requirements of the Natural Environmental Policy Act. Suffolk County v. Secretary of Interior (1977); Natural Resources Defense Council, Inc. v. Hodel (1988). If the EIS is inadequate, then the leasing can be enjoined. Commonwealth of Massachusetts v. Andrus (1979).

Oil spills present the greatest environmental risk and they can occur as a result of a blow out, pipeline leak, or tanker spill, as the Exxon Valdez accident in Alaska's Prince William Sound demonstrated. In Commonwealth of Massachusetts v. Andrus (1979), the First Circuit Court of Appeals considered a preliminary injunction, issued by the district court, which enjoined the Secretary of the Interior from proceeding with the proposed sale of oil leaseholds in the OCS off the coast of New England. The injunction had been granted on the basis that safeguards against oil spills were lacking. In response to the dangers inherent in oil spills, Congress amended the Outer Continental Shelf Lands Act to create an oil spill fund. Conservation Law Foundation of New England, Inc. v. Andrus (1979).

Oil spills are indeed vexatious on many fronts. In Sun Oil Co. v. United States (1978) and Pauley Petroleum Inc. v. United States (1979), numerous lessees of federal offshore lands brought lawsuits against the United States contending that their leasehold rights were impaired due to new restrictions on exploration following the Santa Barbara blow-out. The oil companies' claims for damages were denied. The costs of purchasing the now largely useless leaseholds, which ran into the hundreds of millions of dollars, had to be absorbed by the oil companies and passed through to consumers and shareholders.

Oil spills may endanger shorelines, aquatic life, wildlife, and the stability of entire ecosystems. In Commonwealth of Puerto Rico v. SS Zoe Colocotroni (1980), the federal Court of Appeals upheld in part a district court's award of damages for the clean up costs of an oil spill against a tanker. Costs can also be recovered by the government pursuant to the Clean Water Act. United States v. Dixie Carriers, Inc. (1980). In North Slope Borough v. Andrus (1980), environmentalists obtained an injunction against the Department of the Interior from issuing leases for the exploration of Alaska's North Slope until the EIS was supplemented. In *North Slope,* suit was brought under NEPA, the Outer Continental Shelf Lands Act, the Endangered Species Act, the Marine Mammal Protection Act, the Migratory Bird Treaty Act, and the Agreement on Conservation of Polar Bears.

Congress, in response to the Exxon Valdez disaster, has further addressed the problem of oil spills in the Oil Pollution Act of 1990, Pub.L. No. 101–380, 104 Stat. 484. This extensive legislation establishes a system of compensation and liability, including the creation of an Oil Spill Liability Trust Fund and a system of fines and penalties.

II. COAL

Coal is our nation's most abundant source of energy. Eighty-six percent of the coal consumed in the United States is used as fuel for plants generating electricity. The remainder is used as primary fuel for certain enterprises. Because coal is a useful substitute for other fuels such as oil, nuclear power, and natural gas, occasionally there is a movement toward having energy users convert from other resources to coal. The relative resource abundance of this energy fuel is significantly offset by its health, environmental, and economic problems.

A. OVERVIEW OF THE COAL INDUSTRY

The coal industry is large, varied, and complex. The coal fuel cycle is similar to that of oil and gas in that it encompasses mining, transportation, refining, and then combustion. There are four types of coal that differ in heat content and in sulphur content: bituminous, anthracite, sub-bituminous, and lignite. The types of coal are listed from highest heat content (bituminous) to lowest (lignite). Sub-bituminous and lignite, found mostly in the western states, have less sulphur, which is better for the environment, but they also have less heat. Coal with the highest heat content, but which is dirtier to burn, is found in the East. The coal with acceptable heat properties and a lower sulphur content is mined in the West. Moreover, western coal is easily surface mined, while eastern coal is generally recovered through deep-pit mining techniques.

There are an estimated 3.9 trillion tons of coal in the United States, and 1.7 trillion tons are classified as "identified resources." Identified resources are defined as deposits of coal occurring in beds of a minimum thickness and depth. Only a portion of these reserves are capable of being mined. Approximately 438 billion tons are included in the "demonstrated reserve base." This category is important because it attempts to measure the amount of coal that is able to be mined technically and economically. The greater part of the reserve occurs in the western United States.

The federal government is estimated to own approximately one half of the nation's coal reserves. Coal on federal lands is managed by the Department of the Interior, where different aspects of coal production are handled by different agencies. The Bureau of Land Management issues leases and licenses for coal mining, pursuant to an extensive statutory and regulatory overlay. The key federal statutes are the Mineral Lands Leasing Act of 1920, 30 U.S.C.A. § 181; the Federal Coal Leasing Amendments Act of 1975, 30 U.S.C.A. § 201(a); and the Mineral Leasing Act for Acquired Lands, 30 U.S.C.A. § 351 et seq. The United States Geological Survey has authority over mines; the Office of Surface Mining Reclamation and Enforcement implements the Surface Mining Control and Reclamation Act of 1977, 30 U.S.C.A. § 1201; the Department of Labor exercises jurisdiction over the Federal Mine Safety and Health Act of 1977, 30 U.S.C.A. § 801; and the Department of Energy has acquired some jurisdiction formerly held by the Department of the Interior.

B. COAL REGULATION

The federal government does not directly regulate either the price or the allocation of coal. However, coal prices and allocation are affected by the government's health, safety, and environmental regulations.

1. Coal Conversion

Given coal's abundance, and the realization that coal use can reduce dependence on foreign oil, conversion from oil to coal once struck the federal government as a good idea. That legislation was a failure, but the lessons learned from that failure are useful.

It was hoped that legislation designed to increase coal consumption would have reduced reliance on foreign oil and gas. Thus, in 1974, the Congress passed the Energy Supply and Environmental Coordination Act of 1974, 15 U.S.C.A. § 791 et seq. This Act authorized the then Federal Energy Administration to order powerplants and "major fuel burning installations" to substitute coal for oil or gas as their boiler fuel. In addition, the Act contained measures to ameliorate environmental problems caused by expanded coal production. Then in December, 1975 as part of the Energy Policy and Conservation Act, Congress amended ESECA to extend FEA's authority to issue prohibitions and construction orders. Coal conversion legislation was further amended by the Powerplant and Industrial Fuel Use Act of 1978, 42 U.S.C.A. §§ 8301–8484 (1982).

This coal conversion legislation was largely unsuccessful. Utilities and industrial users that found coal conversion too expensive avoided costly government orders by obtaining exemptions. For example, according to one DOE report, between January 1, 1983 and December 31, 1985 *all* requested exemptions to the coal conversion legislation were granted. The ineffective and underenforced coal conversion legislation was eventually repealed. The Powerplant and Industrial Fuel Use Act of 1978 Amendment, Pub.L. No. 100–42, 101 Stat. 310 (May 7, 1989).

2. Health and Safety Concerns for Mine Workers

Some have described underground mining as the most hazardous occupation in the United States. Explosions, cave-ins, flooding, and suffocation threaten lives and are responsible for the deaths of tens of thousands of miners. Coal dust threatens the long-term health of miners and can be fatal, as can working the massive machinery now employed in modern mining operations. Historically, the states were responsible for the health and safety of miners. State enforcement was inadequate because inspections were not rigorous and little attention was paid to the long-term health effects on mine workers. These inadequacies led to federal government involvement.

Federal legislation addressing health and safety aspects of coal mining includes: the Federal Coal Mine Safety Act 30 U.S.C.A. § 451 et seq.; the Federal Coal Mine Health and Safety Act of 1969, (codified in various provisions of U.S.C.A. titles 15 and 30); significant amendments to the 1969 act in the Federal Mine Safety and Health Amendments Act of 1977, 30 U.S.C.A. § 801 et seq.; and the Black Lung Benefits Act of 1972, 30 U.S.C.A. § 901 et seq.

Federal intrusion into coal miner health and safety is broad based. State laws, unless they are more stringent than the federal standards, are preempted and federal inspectors have the authority to conduct warrantless searches and the power to close mines which are in violation of federal standards. Donovan v. Dewey (1981). Federal health and safety laws subject violators to civil and criminal penalties. The state must set health and safety standards at a level necessary "for the protection of life and the prevention of injuries," and it must set standards for toxic materials which occur during the mining process at levels "which most adequately assure on the basis of the best available evidence that no miner will suffer material impairment of health or functional capacity even if such miner has regular exposure to the hazards dealt with by such standard for the period of his working life." This latter test is intended to reach the "attainment of the highest degree of health and safety protection for the miner." 30 U.S.C.A. § 811(a)(6)(A) (1982).

In Usery v. Turner Elkhorn Mining Co. (1976), the United States Supreme Court upheld the constitutionality and retroactive effect of the Federal Coal Mine Health and Safety Act of 1969 as amended by the Black Lung Benefits Act of 1972. This legislation established a compensation system for coal miners affected by pneumoconiosis (black lung disease), which is caused by long-term inhalation of coal dust.

C. LAND RECLAMATION

Costs and risks borne by workers are imposed, at least partially, on mine operators, and are to be reflected in the cost of coal. Similarly, environmental legislation involves the redistribution of the benefits and burdens of coal mining. The costs of reclaiming land after coal mining, as well as the costs of cleaning the coal before or during burning, must be imposed on someone. These costs will be reflected in the cost of a ton of coal, and they will be imposed on the coal's purchaser.

Sixty percent of the coal mined in the United States is surface or open-pit mined. In the eastern United States, about 50% of coal is surface mined and 50% is extracted from underground mines. In the western United States, a greater percentage of coal is surface mined, and in the Great Plains nearly 100% of the coal is surface mined. Surface mining is cheaper and is less hazardous to the health and safety of mine workers than deep pit mining. However, surface mining injures the environment through soil erosion, water contamination, vegetation destruction, wildlife disruption, and aesthetic degradation.

Surface mining requires the removal of topsoil and then the removal of the layer of soil underneath the topsoil. This second layer is called the "overburden" and it is often acidic. The topsoil and the overburden must be separated. If the overburden is placed above the topsoil, then rain can cause leaching which ruins the topsoil, and the accompanying run-off is acidic, which can cause damage to surrounding water systems. After the coal is extracted, the abandoned mine, with its exposed layers of acidic soil, can continue to pollute the area with acid run-off. The way to avoid these adverse environmental problems is through land reclamation.

Like miner health and safety regulations, environmental regulations to promote land reclamation were once the province of the states. Land reclamation was not rigorously enforced in part because states were protective of their coal industries. In order to combat these harmful environmental effects, Congress enacted two statutes: the Resource Conservation and Recovery Act of 1976 (RCRA), 42 U.S.C.A. §§ 6901–6987 (1982), providing for standards for disposal sites and waste treatment; and the Surface Mining Control and Reclamation Act of 1977 (SMCRA), 30 U.S.C.A. §§ 1201–1328, requiring that mined land be restored to its original condition.

RCRA is discussed in Chapter Four. The SMCRA, administered by the Office of Surface Mining Reclamation and Enforcement of the Interior Department, is enforced through a system of permits, inspections, and fines. Not surprisingly, the Act met with considerable resistance. Not only did private mine owners wish to avoid the costs that the Act imposed, states did not welcome federal intervention in an area that was traditionally left to local regulation. The SMCRA was challenged in the United States Supreme Court, which upheld the Act against several constitutional challenges in Hodel v. Virginia Surface Mining & Reclamation

Ass'n (1981), and Hodel v. Indiana (1981). Application of SMCRA to a particular coal property has in one case been found to be a taking by the United States Federal Circuit. Whitney Benefits v. United States (1991).

The structure of the SMCRA includes a large role for state regulation. Once the state develops a reclamation plan approved by the Interior Department, then state agencies administer the plan and state courts have exclusive jurisdiction. Haydo v. Amerikohl Mining, Inc. (1987).

It has not been an easy task to have states and the Interior Department develop and enforce reclamation plans. In September 1981, two environmental groups filed a lawsuit against the Secretary of the Interior and the Director of the Office of Surface Mining seeking to compel these enforcement duties under the SMCRA. The plaintiffs claimed that Interior Department officials had failed (1) to assess and collect mandatory civil penalties, and (2) to take proper enforcement action against mine operators found in violation of the SMCRA. In Save Our Cumberland Mountains, Inc. v. Watt (1982), the district court held that the Secretary of the Interior had a mandatory duty to enforce the SMCRA, and he was ordered to do so. That case was overturned on appeal due to improper venue in Save Our Cumberland Mountains, Inc. v. Clark (1984). Following these developments, the parties pursued negotiations which led to a settlement of the lawsuit and to attorney's fees for the plaintiffs for their successful settlement. Save Our Cumberland Mountains, Inc. v. Hodel (1985).

D. CLEAN AIR AND WATER

Once coal reaches its destination, it is burned for its stored energy. The burning of coal presents perhaps the most sensitive and complex environmental issues of the coal fuel cycle. Coal combustion generates four main sources of pollution: sulfur oxide, nitrogen oxide, carbon dioxide, and particular matter, all of which spoil land, water, and air. Sulfur oxide, which increases with the sulfur content of the coal, causes human health problems, crop damage, and acid rain. Nitrogen oxide contributes to these problems and causes smog. Tons of particulate matter are emitted from coal burning facilities daily and cause property damage and health hazards. Finally, carbon dioxide causes what is known as the greenhouse effect, which is an increase in the temperature of the earth's surface. The principal form of water pollution caused by burning coal is thermal pollution.

The Clean Air Act, 42 U.S.C.A. § 7401 et seq., as amended in 1990, is the basic federal law governing pollution controls for coal burning electric power plants. The law is complex and detailed. See Chapter Four. The object of the Clean Air Act is to establish standards for the emission of pollutants. The Act is administered by the states and the federal government and includes provisions that force power plants to develop and use new technologies to improve environmental quality. The Clean Air Act authorizes the EPA to set performance standards for sources of air pollution. Because electric utilities burn approximately 80% of the coal produced in this country, they are a major source of air pollution. In 1979, the EPA set restrictions on the amount of sulfur dioxide and particulate matter that can be emitted from coal-fired electric power pants. The EPA regulations were challenged by environmental groups for being too lax and by utilities for being too stringent. The District of Columbia Circuit sustained the regulations in Sierra Club v. Costel (1981). The Clean Air Act was significantly amended in 1990 and these amendments are briefly explained in Chapter Eleven.

Coal burning facilities also contribute to the problem of acid rain. Acid rain is defined broadly as the long range transport and deposit of pollutants. Acid rain begins with combustion. As coal is burned in electric powerplants, large quantities of sulphur dioxide (SO_2) and nitrogen oxides (NO) are released into the air. The sulfates and nitrates then combine with cloud vapor to form sulfuric and nitric acids that may be carried long distances before falling to earth. Acid rain damage is predominant in the northeastern United States and eastern Canada.

E. COAL TRANSPORTATION

Railcars, barges, and trucks transport the mined coal to points of distribution or consumption after it has been refined and sorted. There has been interest in the coal industry over the development of coal slurry pipelines. Slurry pipelines come into direct competition with rail transportation, and these two transportation modes are the most significant for the coal industry.

1. Rail Transportation

Railroads account for approximately two-thirds of all coal carriage. Coal, the largest single commodity carried by rail, is transported by unit trains often reaching 100 units in length. In the eastern United States, there is a measure of competition for carriage contracts among railroads, barges, and trucks. Railroads also compete among themselves for the carriage of various commodities and passenger service. However, in the western United States, because of the great distances involved and the absence of a network of navigable waterways, the rail industry has a dominant competitive position for coal carriage.

Because rail carriage is the indispensable link between coal production at the mine and end-use by consumers such as electric utilities, railroads have what is called a "bottleneck" monopoly position, analogous to the bottlenecks created by natural gas and crude oil pipelines. Electric utilities which must depend on this monopolistic type of rail transportation are called captive shippers or captive customers. Thus, without rail transport there effectively can be no viable coal industry. Primarily for that reason, the federal government has intervened in the coal industry by requiring that rates for coal carriage be regulated.

Rail rates for coal haulage are set by the Interstate Commerce Commission (ICC). Rate setting jurisdiction rests with the ICC rather than the courts. Burlington Northern Inc. v. United States (1982). The ICC attempts to set rates that are just and reasonable, and nonconfiscatory. Historically, rail rates were based on a cost-of-service plus reasonable rate of return formula. Northern Pacific Railway Co. v. North Dakota (1915). The electric utility, under this formula, pays the railroad a rate which covers the railroad's transportation costs plus a percentage profit. Any higher rate would be confiscatory.

Because of the weakened financial condition of the railroad industry in the 1970s, Congress passed the Railroad Revitalization and Regulatory Reform Act of 1976 (4-R Act), Pub.L. No. 94-210, 90 Stat. 31. The 4-R Act was expressly intended to bolster the rail industry financially. To this end, the Act allowed the ICC to set rates so that rail carriers in competitive markets earn "adequate revenues," 49 U.S.C.A. § 10701a(b)(3), which, in turn, was defined "to cover total operating expenses, including depreciation and obsolescence, plus a reasonable economic profit or return (or both) on capital employed in the business." 49 U.S.C.A. § 1074(a)(2). The 4-R Act also authorized the ICC to inquire into the reasonableness of rates charged carriers which may dominate their market. In other words, the ICC has authority to assess whether the rates charged by railroads are the result of their possible monopoly position.

In addition to the 4-R Act, Congress attempted to assist the rail industry by freeing them from rate hearings for every rate increase they sought. In the Staggers Rail Act of 1980, 49 U.S.C.A. § 10101 et seq., Congress broadened the authority of the ICC to set "rate flexibility zones." These zones allowed railroads to set their own rates within a pre-established geographical zone without formal ICC rate hearings. With the 4–R and Staggers Rail Act, the ICC has moved away from a simple cost-of-service formula. In order to help railroads stay competitive with other transporters, the ICC has given railroads the power to set a rate "zone" to avoid numerous rate hearings, and their rates may be based on comparative industry costs.

Through a rate design known as Ramsey rates (also known as differential rates), a railroad can establish two sets of rates. One may be based on cost of service to noncaptive customers, and the other may be based on value of service to captive customers. For example, a utility (a captive customer) with no other source of coal supply is assumed to be willing to pay more than the actual cost of service for coal transportation. Thus, a utility accepting such an arrangement effectively subsidizes other cost-of-service users of rail transportation.

2. Coal Slurry Pipelines

Coal slurry pipelines operate much like oil pipelines. Coal is mined, impurities are removed, and the coal is then crushed and mixed with water. A slurry mixture of about equal weights of water and coal is transported in the pipeline from the mouth of the mine to the point of consumption or distribution. At the end of the system, the mixture is removed from the pipeline and the coal is dewatered. Coal slurry transportation may be cheaper than rail transportation once the pipelines are built. Because coal slurry pipelines represent direct competition with rail transportation, the development of such pipelines are opposed by railroads.

Pipeline proponents face numerous hurdles. First, rail transporters resist the construction of slurry pipelines and lobby against them because they fear that slurry transportation will reduce their market in coal transportation. Second, before a pipeline can be constructed, the project developer must acquire land or easements for the pipeline which cross several parcels of land. This situation presents a classic holdout problem, in that even one landowner unwilling to sell the necessary fee estate or easement can "hold-out" by asking exorbitant prices for the land necessary for the construction of the pipeline. Energy Transportation Systems, Inc. v. Union Pacific Railroad Co. (1979) (railroad which owned only a surface right-of-way had to provide a right-of-way to a slurry pipeline). Because of the holdout problem, pipeline developers wishing to acquire the land at fair market value need the power of eminent domain. However, the necessary state legislation allocating that power generally has not been forthcoming.

In addition to land rights, slurry pipelines must acquire water rights. Water is a scarce, sacred, and extremely valuable resource in the western United States. So much so, that some states have passed legislation attempting to restrict the use of water, and such restrictions may preclude coal slurry pipeline production. Montana, for example, has enacted a statute which states that the "legislature finds that the use of water for the slurry transportation of coal is detrimental to the conservation and protection of the waters of the state," thus preventing slurry pipelines from acquiring necessary water rights. Mont.Code Annot. §§ 85–2–104; 41–3–115. These state restrictions on water use are of questionable constitutionality because the states are favoring their own citizens and impeding interstate commerce. In Sporhase v. Nebraska (1982), the Supreme Court held that Nebraska's right to restrict the transportation of water out of the state was subject to Commerce Clause analysis. Although not directly apposite to slurry pipeline development, the *Sporhase* decision has a signficant impact. If a state law restricting the out-of-state transportation of water impedes interstate commerce in coal, then the law may be unconstitutional.

In Missouri v. Andrews (1986), the Secretary of the Department of Interior executed a contract with Energy Transportation Systems, Inc. giving a slurry pipeline company the right to withdraw 20,000 acre feet of water per year from a federal reservoir in South Dakota for forty years. (An acre foot of water is the amount of water that covers an acre to the height of one foot). Missouri, Iowa, and South Dakota contested the authority of the Secretary of the Department of the Interior to award such a contract. The states argued that the federal reservoir was governed by a series of regulations, including the Flood Control Act of 1944, and that the Secretary could not unilaterally execute a water service contract for industrial purposes to the detriment of the states. Both the United States District Court and the United States Court of Appeals for the Eighth Circuit ruled that the Secretary did not have unilateral authority to award the contract. The United States Supreme Court affirmed this holding. Energy Transportation Systems, Inc. Pipeline Project v. Missouri (1988).

III.　NUCLEAR POWER

Nuclear power once promised to be the safe, clean, cheap and abundant energy source for the future. Today none of those claims are accurate. Health and safety issues have arisen regarding plant operation and waste disposal. Increased construction and back-end costs have made nuclear power more expensive than anticipated, and uranium has also become very costly to process. However, the cost of the electricity generated by coal-fired and nuclear powered plants is roughly equivalent.

A.　OVERVIEW OF THE NUCLEAR POWER INDUSTRY

There are approximately 110 nuclear power plants operating in the United States, and these produce about 20% of the Nation's electricity. Sixty-six of these commercial reactors are due for permanent shutdown by the year 2010. All are fission reactors. Fission is a chain reaction which splits the uranium nucleus and results in the release of energy (heat). Nuclear fusion also produces energy, but it uses an opposite process where a reaction and consequent heat are obtained by combining nuclei. Although fusion produces a great deal more energy than fission, fusion is both technologically and financially prohibitive.

Plutonium is a fuel that can be used in fast "breeder" reactors. The fast breeder reactor creates more fuel than it burns. Plutonium does not occur in nature and must be converted from the excess uranium that is created after a chain reaction. Plutonium has a higher toxicity and longer life than any element now known, therefore safety concerns over its development and use run high. In Westinghouse Elec. Corp. v. United States Nuclear Regulatory Com'n (1979), the Third Circuit upheld a Nuclear Regulatory Commission (NRC) order suspending its decisionmaking processes dealing with the recycling of spent nuclear fuel. This recycling process produces plutonium.

The nuclear power fuel cycle, as originally conceived, was to be a closed system. The ore would be mined, processed, used by reactors, and then reused by reactors. This has not come to pass. The first step in the fuel cycle involves locating and mining uranium ore. Once the ore has been mined, it is milled into uranium oxide (UO_2), a substance which is commonly referred to as "yellow cake." The "yellow cake" is then converted into gaseous uranium hexaflouride. This gas is then subjected to an enrichment process which raises the concentration of uranium 235 contained within the uranium hexaflouride from 1% to almost 3%, which is enough to cause a chain reaction. After the enrichment process has been completed, the enriched gas is returned to a solid state. The enriched product is fashioned into pellets and then made into fuel rods, which are used in reactors to create heat through fission, which, in turn is used to generate electricity. These steps constitute the front end of the fuel cycle, and each phase, and attendant costs, are fairly well known. This is not so of the back-end of the fuel cycle, where many problems are associated with plant decommissioning, emergency planning, waste storage, transportation, and disposal.

B. LEGISLATIVE OVERVIEW

The federal government has been pivotal in the development, regulation, and promotion of nuclear technology since its inception. After World War II, the shift from the military to the commercial use of nuclear power did not remove the federal government from the regulatory process. In fact, the federal government steered the course of this technology through its infancy. The Atomic Energy Act of 1946, Pub.L. No. 79–585, 60 Stat. 755 (1946), formally shifted control over nuclear development from the military to the civilian government. Very little development of commercial nuclear power occurred during the 1946–54 period because the 1946 Act maintained a government monopoly over the control, use, and ownership of reactors and fuels. The Eisenhower Administration revised the nation's atomic energy policy and encouraged private commercial development through passage of the Atomic Energy Act of 1954, Pub.L. No. 83–703, 68 Stat. 919 (1954).

The 1954 Act ended the federal government's monopoly over nonmilitary uses of atomic energy and allowed private ownership of reactors under Atomic Energy Commission (AEC) licensing procedures. The 1954 Act, the bulk of which remains applicable, set the tone and the goals for commercial nuclear energy. Private sector public utilities were designated to take the lead, by owning and running the reactors. Lewis Strauss, Chairman of the AEC, interpreted the 1954 Act as a mandate to rely principally on private industry to develop civilian reactor technology. The Power Reactor

Demonstration Program of 1955 was an attempt to involve private industry in a competitive program to test several separate reactor technologies. Government and private industry were to develop reactors jointly. Once the reactors were completed, government was to step out of the project, and privately owned utilities were to assume fiscal responsibility.

Private industry was not receptive to bearing the financial burden and was unenthusiastic. The critical impediment was the possibility of a nuclear accident. Officials of General Electric, one of the major reactor builders, threatened withdrawal from nuclear development activity, stating that GE would not proceed "with a cloud of bankruptcy hanging over its head." In response, Congress passed the Price–Anderson Act of 1957, that limited the liability of the industry and assured compensation for the public. Pub.L. No. 85–256, 71 Stat. 576 (codified as amended at 42 U.S.C.A. § 2210). The Act removed the last obstacle to private participation. Congressional hearings on the Price–Anderson Act revealed that there would be no commercial nuclear power plants built by the private sector without a financial safety net provided by the government.

After several amendments, the Act continues to limit a public utility's financial exposure in the event of a nuclear incident. Duke Power Co. v. Carolina Environmental Study Group, Inc. (1978) (Price–Anderson Act held constitutional). The ceiling for liability was set at $560 million in the original Act. This amount consists of all the private insurance that the utilities could raise, which from 1957 to 1967 amounted to $60 million, with the government standing good for the remainder. Every ten years the Act comes up for renewal. Under the 1988 amendments of the Act, there are two layers of financial protection. The first consists of prepaid insurance from commercial insurance companies. In 1990, this insurance amounted to about $200 million per facility. The second layer consists of deferred premiums paid by each facility to be used after the first layer is exhausted. Each facility must pay premiums up to $63 million, not to exceed $10 million per year. In 1990, the second layer amounted to $6.9 billion, in addition to the $200 million first layer.

Until Congress passed the National Environmental Policy Act of 1969 (NEPA), 42 U.S.C.A. §§ 4321–70, requiring environmental impact statements for all major federal activities, the AEC had no formal environmental assessment mechanism. In Calvert Cliffs' Coordinating Committee, Inc. v. U.S. AEC (1971), the federal appeals court held that NEPA's provisions applied to the AEC, which subsequently drafted its own environmental provisions. NEPA continues to limit NRC actions. Limerick Ecology Action, Inc. v. United States NRC (1989) (NRC policy statement addressing severe accident mitigation did not satisfy NEPA).

In the 1970s, the temper of nuclear regulation changed. People were no longer complacent about nuclear power safety, or convinced by environmental claims made by industry and government. Throughout the 1960's and into the early 1970's, the demand for electricity was growing at an attractive rate; coal burning facilities were an environmentally unattractive alternative. With the staggering oil price hikes of the mid–1970's, nuclear power not only remained economically desirable, it was also given a prominent position in national energy plans. Still, a rift in the government-industry partnership started to develop which would first manifest itself in a bureaucratic realignment.

The AEC had conflicting functions: promoting the use of nuclear technology and, at the same time, insuring that the technology was applied safely. In 1974, realizing the cross purposes of both promotion and safety oversight, Congress split the AEC. It created the Nuclear Regulatory Commission (NRC), an independent agency responsible for safety and licensing, and formed the Energy Research and Development Administration (ERDA), later absorbed by the Department of Energy, responsible for promotion and development of nuclear power. Energy Reorganization Act of 1974, P.L. 93–438, 88 Stat. 1233 (1974) (codified as amended at 42 U.S.C.A. §§ 5801–79). This alignment did not completely remove a fundamental regulatory conflict for the NRC. The NRC had the responsibility both for licensing plants and for safety oversight. If the NRC too vigorously exercises its safety role, then the attendant compliance costs act as a disincentive to invest in nuclear plants, which cuts across the NRC's licensing grain.

The NRC, successor to the AEC, is an independent regulatory agency which regulates nuclear power reactors. 42 U.S.C.A. §§ 5801–91. The primary form of regulation is a two-step licensing process. One license is required for construction and another for operation. Vermont Yankee Nuclear Power Corp. v. Natural Resources Defense Council, Inc. (1978); San Luis Obispo Mothers for Peace v. U.S. NRC (1986); Power Reactor Development Co. v. International Union of Elec., Radio and Machine Workers (1961). The NRC also issues licenses for the use of nuclear materials, and for transportation, the export and import of nuclear materials, facilities, and components.

Nuclear power regulation is highly centralized by the federal government, which enjoys a large degree of preemptive authority over nuclear safety and radiological hazards. Northern States Power Co. v. Minnesota (1971). Nonradiological issues are not preempted if they involve either the financial capability to dispose of waste or state tort liability. Pacific Gas & Elec. Co. v. State Energy Resources Conservation & Development Com'n (1983); Silkwood v. Kerr–McGee Corp. (1984).

After the 1979 Three Mile Island (TMI) accident, the NRC increased safety inspections, stepped up enforcement, and developed backfitting and emergency preparedness rules. See Union of Concerned Scientists v. United States NRC (1987). Off-site emergency preparedness did not become an issue until after TMI, and these regulations have been the primary reason for continued delays in opening nuclear power plants. Suffolk County v. Long Island Lighting Co. (1984). The Department of Energy formally began planning for the disposal of nuclear wastes, imposing most of the associated costs on industry. Nuclear Waste Policy Act of 1982, 42 U.S.C.A. §§ 10101–226. With the back end costs so escalated, regulators have tried to reduce front end costs.

C. NUCLEAR WASTE

The nuclear fuel cycle, from mining through reprocessing, produces four major types of waste: high level, low level, mill tailings, and gaseous effluents. Mill tailings are the residues from uranium mining and milling operations. High level wastes, a classification based primarily on heat and radiation emission rates, derive from spent nuclear fuel rods generated in the processing of the fuel and the fabrication of plutonium. These wastes are highly toxic and remain so for hundreds of thousands of years. Low level wastes are generated by almost all activities involving radioactive materials. Currently, low-level nuclear waste may be disposed of in several ways: transfer to a facility licensed by the NRC; burial pursuant to a license granted by the NRC; disposal at sea; incineration; or discharge into a sanitary sewer.

The effects of low level radiation on humans are still largely unknown. Moreover, methods used to extrapolate effects are in dispute. The consequences of high level radiation are known to have a series of adverse effects, but it is not known if the effects of low level radiation are proportional or whether long term exposure to low level wastes is linear (with each higher dosage the negative reaction is proportionately greater). Exposure to high level doses may be lethal or may induce a variety of somatic effects, including leukemia, other forms of cancer, and genetic mutations. Thus, wherever radioactive materials accumulate there are sensitive health problems. Nuclear waste disposal also carries with it large economic costs. Pacific Gas & Elec. Co. v. State Energy Res. Conserv. & Develop. Com'n (1983). Waste storage may well be the final stumbling block to a complete nuclear policy.

Radioactive waste is stored on reactor sites. When spent fuel rods and other waste products fill the storage capacity at utility plants, then plants have to expand their storage capacity, or permanent off-site storage areas must be established. Expansion of on-site capacity is a delicate temporary solution in light of the uncertainties surrounding the development and implementation of safe methods for the ultimate disposal or even long-term storage of wastes. Ultimately, what will be required is the shipment of nuclear wastes off-site. This solution will entail extensive transportation of wastes to some central repository.

Transportation of nuclear materials poses problems similar to those of waste disposal. Transportation occurs at both the front and back ends of the fuel cycle, but it is the back end transport that will cause most problems in the future. If radioactive material escapes, health risks are extreme. States will want to forbid movement of nuclear wastes through the state. Both the Department of Transportation and the NRC have jurisdiction over nuclear materials transportation, and state laws prohibiting such transport are likely preempted. Illinois v. General Elec. (1982).

The federal government had no comprehensive program governing the disposal of nuclear wastes until passage of the Nuclear Waste Policy Act of 1982 (NWPA). Under the original 1982 Act, the Secretary of the Department of Energy was to nominate several potential sites for nuclear waste disposal. On May 28, 1986, the Secretary nominated five sites: Richton Dome, Mississippi; Yucca Mountain, Nevada; Deaf Smith, Texas; David Canyon, Utah; and Hanford, Washington. Of these five sites, the Secretary recommended and the President approved for site characterization studies the three sites in Nevada, Texas, and Washington.

There was so much opposition to the multiple site selection process that Congress amended the Act in December, 1987, Pub.L. No. 100–203. Now only one site, Yucca Mountain in Nevada, is earmarked for site studies. If this site satisfies DOE, NRC, and EPA standards, it will begin receiving nuclear waste by the early part of the Twenty First Century. County of Esmeralda, Nevada v. United States DOE (1991) (prior to designation of this Nevada site, DOE must consider the potential for groundwater contamination, and the risks associated with various transportation routes). If Nevada is selected as the host state of a high level nuclear waste repository, it may receive up to $50 million per year in benefit payments pursuant to the amended Nuclear Waste Policy Act.

The NWPA sets out the government's responsibility for the disposal of spent nuclear fuel and high-level nuclear waste. However, requirements imposed by the NWPA on the storage of spent nuclear fuel do not apply to all federal storage of spent nuclear fuel. State of Idaho v. United States Dept. of Energy (1991).

Low-level waste is regulated by the states and the federal government under the Low–Level Radioactive Waste Policy Act, 42 U.S.C.A. §§ 2021b–2021j. Radioactive mill tailings are regulated under the Uranium Mill Tailings Radiation Control Act of 1978, 42 U.S.C.A. §§ 7901–12. See American Mining Congress v. U.S. NRC (1990); Environmental Defense Fund v. U.S. NRC (1990).

The cost of dismantling spent nuclear plants will likely be enormous. By the year 2025, over 100 nuclear reactor licenses are scheduled to expire. The decommissioning of the plants will entail removing most radioactive elements within the plant's nuclear reactor, and then razing the entire plant. The cost, per plant, will be over one billion dollars, to be paid by the utility customers in their rates.

IV. HYDROELECTRIC POWER

A. THE HYDROPOWER INDUSTRY

Hydropower, the energy derived from falling water, has long been an energy resource in the United States. It was first used to provide mechanical energy to grind grain and run industrial machinery. In the twentieth century, hydropower has been used almost exclusively to generate electricity.

The first hydroelectric facility was built at Appleton, Wisconsin in 1882. However, most of the hydropower development in the United States began in the early part of the twentieth century with the installations of the Hoover Dam on the Colorado River and large plants on the Tennessee and Columbia Rivers. There are over 1,500 licensed hydroelectric sites in the United States. Forty-two percent are owned by utilities; 22.5% by municipalities; 10% by industrial firms; and the remainder by cooperatives and independent developers.

Hydroelectricity is produced by the passage of water through a turbine. The water is captured by a dam built to cause trapped water to flow downward by gravity through the turbine to a lower elevation downstream. The amount of hydroelectricity that can be derived from a plant is proportional to the energy delivered to the turbine, which in turn depends on the speed and amount of water flowing through it. Generally speaking, the larger and higher the dam, the more energy that can be generated. This energy is then transferred to a generator which converts the energy to electricity.

Hydroelectricity is an attractive energy resource for a number of reasons. First, the cost to produce electricity by hydropower is less expensive than the cost to produce electricity from either fossil fuel or nuclear power plants because the "fuel"—water—is relatively costless. Second, the price charged for hydroelectric power is generally stable and does not fluctuate with changes in the price or availability of fuel. This is because the large capital costs of dam construction are sunk and operating costs are low. The availability of hydropower does, however, depend on the amount of water in the stream or river. Third, hydroelectric facilities do not present the environmental concerns that fossil fuel and nuclear power plants create, such as acid rain or hazardous waste disposal. Yet hydropower does have environmental consequences, primarily associated with the construction of dams and the consequent changes in the surrounding area. Also, changing the flow of streams and constructing hydroelectric facilities may adversely affect wildlife and fish in the area. Federal agencies, such as the Environmental Protection Agency and the Army Corps of Engineers, will deny a permit or license if there is thought to be too much environmental damage to the surrounding area. Such was the case in 1990 when the EPA vetoed a license to build the huge Two Forks hydroelectric plant in Colorado because of environmental concerns.

Hydroelectricity is limited by the small number of sites on which a facility may be located, and by the limits that streams and rivers themselves impose on facility size and output. Drought can be a problem, as in 1988, when the amount of hydroelectricity produced reached the lowest point in twenty-two years due to a two-year drought in the United States.

While the total amount of hydroelectric energy generated in the United States has increased in recent years, its share of the total energy used by consumers in this country has declined. In the 1940s and 1950s, hydropower provided 40% of the nation's electric energy. By the 1990s, that amount has dropped to 10%.

Finally, hydroelectric use varies throughout regions of the country. Hydroelectricity provides a major source of electricity in the Pacific Northwest, where appropriate water sources are especially abundant, and the Southeast, where the Tennessee Valley Authority operates in the Tennessee and Mississippi River Basins.

B. FEDERAL REGULATION

Electricity derived from water power was initially considered to be under the jurisdiction of state and local governments because the electricity produced by hydropower was confined to local use. With the rise of interstate commerce, the need arose for uniform controls. The federal government has jurisdiction over the use of the country's navigable waterways because they are essential for national defense, and are a major transportation system for interstate and foreign commerce, as well as a source of energy. Early federal legislation authorized the Secretary of the Interior, under the Yosemite National Parks Act of 1901 (codified as amended at 16 U.S.C.A. § 79 and 43 U.S.C.A. § 959) and under the General Dam Act of 1906 (codified as amended at 33 U.S.C.A. § 491), to grant rights-of-way and leases for energy production at hydroelectric facilities. The General Dam Act also provided for a municipal preference for hydropower and, as significantly amended in 1910, incorporated provisions for monetary charges, a fifty-year permit limitation, and recovery of privileges by the federal government. Even with substantial amendments, the General Dam Act did not successfully coordinate hydroelectric planning.

It was not until 1920 that Congress passed the Federal Water Power Act of 1920 (FWPA), 16 U.S.C.A. § 791 et seq. The purpose of the FWPA was to assert widespread jurisdiction over waterpower sources, to begin comprehensive planning for national water power, and to create the Federal Power Commission (FPC), now the Federal Energy Regulatory Commission (FERC). Passage of the FWPA was partly the result of efforts by conservationists who fought to ensure a comprehensive nationwide water power plan. One objective was to reconcile conflicting uses such as navigation, recreation, hydropower, and wildlife presentation within one framework.

Federal jurisdiction is most frequently based on the fact that hydroelectric plants use water from navigable waterways that fall under federal domain. Federal jurisdiction is also based on the Commerce Clause of the U.S. Constitution, Art. I, sec. 8, cl. 3. Under the FWPA, the FPC had authority to issue licenses for 50 years, and the federal government had the authority to recapture the power at the end of the license. These powers now reside in the FERC.

In 1935, Congress passed Title II of the Federal Power Act (FPA), 16 U.S.C.A. § 824 et seq., which extended the Federal Power Commission's authority to include ratemaking and licensing power over hydroelectric facilities. The FPC had (and the FERC has) authority to issue licenses to citizens, corporations, or state and municipal governments to construct and operate hydroelectric plants. In addition, the FERC has jurisdiction over the transmission of electric energy in interstate commerce, and over the sale of such energy at wholesale in interstate commerce.

C. FEDERAL JURISDICTION

The FERC's jurisdiction for licensing is limited. The 1935 FPA delegated to the Commission the authority to license nonfederal hydroelectric projects consistent with certain guidelines. The guidelines state that the project must (1) be within the United States; (2) be located on navigable waters; (3) use water or waterpower from a government dam; and (4) affect interstate commerce. Whether a potential site meets these FERC licensing criteria has been the subject of much litigation.

Although federal hydropower authority under the above enabling legislation is intended to result in comprehensive water power planning, it is nevertheless limited. In First

Iowa Hydro–Electric Cooperative v. FPC (1946), a hydropower cooperative had been granted a license by the FPC to build a dam on a tributary of the Iowa River, although the dam would significantly impede the flow of the river and compliance with Iowa law was virtually impossible to obtain. The Supreme Court allowed the dam to be built, holding that section 9(b) of the Federal Power Act, which required a showing of compliance with state law, was merely informational and that the Commission's decision must be binding in order to allow the FPC to provide for comprehensive nationwide planning.

Most often, federal authority will preempt state authority. For example, states explicitly retain their proprietary rights in water resources under § 27 of the Federal Power Act, 16 U.S.C.A. § 821, but they cannot require dam permits for federal projects. See also State of California, ex rel. State Water Resources Bd. v. FERC (1989) (FPA vests sole authority to set flow rates of hydropower projects in FERC).

In determining the extent of federal authority, the critical issue is the navigability of waters for a proposed hydroelectric plant site. In United States v. Appalachian Electric Power Co. (1940), contrary to the findings of the lower district and circuit courts, the United States Supreme Court held that part of the New River in West Virginia was "navigable" and subject to FPC jurisdiction. The Court admitted that there was no definitive test for navigability, but found that the waterway was suited for "use of the public for purposes of transportation and commerce," and as such was considered "navigable" for purposes of the Federal Power Act. Federal preemption of hydroprojects also extends to the waters on United States reservations. FPC v. Oregon (1955).

The Supreme Court has also held that the FERC has jurisdiction over a pumped storage facility located on a nonnavigable tributary of a navigable waterway because the hydropower derived on the tributary would be used in interstate commerce. Federal Power Commission v. Union Electric Power (1964). The Supreme Court found that the facility could affect navigability downstream because the proposed "pumped storage" facility—where water would be pumped to a high reservoir, stored, and then released to generate power during periods of peak demand—could affect navigability downstream.

Another problem arises when a hydroelectric plant is erected on a waterway contained completely within the borders of one state and whose electricity is used only within that state. In City of Centralia v. FERC (1981), a court held that the FERC did not have jurisdiction in the circumstances of that case because any effect on interstate commerce was insubstantial. Subsequently, that same court upheld FERC jurisdiction for the same project on a finding of navigability, rather than effects on interstate commerce. City of Centralia v. FERC (1988).

The FERC does not, however, have exclusive authority over hydropower facilities. Local, state, and federal agencies also have statutory powers to regulate hydroelectric projects, as long as state or local regulations do not impede the exercise of federal authority. Under the Clean Water Act § 401, 33 U.S.C.A. § 1341(d), for example, states may set water quality standards for hydropower projects. Also, the federal government may not preempt state tort law. South Carolina Public Service Authority v. FERC (1988). Further, under the FPA, states may not set minimum water flow requirements for fish preservation if the requirements conflict with a FERC license. California v. FERC (1990). States may establish a water use plan when the Federal Bureau of Reclamation is the regulating authority. California v. United States (1978).

D. LICENSING

1. Federal Power Act

Once the question of jurisdiction is settled, the next step is licensing a hydroproject. The FERC can authorize preliminary permits, licenses, new licenses, annual licenses, and exemptions. In choosing among permit applicants, the groundwork is set out in the Federal Water Power Act of 1920. Section 10(a) of this Act requires the FERC to choose the project "best adapted" to improve or develop a waterway for interstate or foreign commerce or hydropower development. If no applicant can demonstrate a specific project's superiority using this criteria, then section 7(a) of the Act states that preference be given to state or municipal applicants over private developers. This so-called "municipal" preference is valuable because of the low cost of hydroelectricity relative to electricity generated from coal-fired, oil-fueled, or nuclear powered plants. Because there often is a strong public interest in granting licenses to public applicants, if a private developer's application is more comprehensive than that of the public entity, the FERC must allow time for the public developer to revise the application to equal that of the private applicant. Finally, the FERC may deny an application from nonfederal developers if the Commission decides that, for the benefit of the public, the facility should be constructed and maintained by the United States itself.

Federal licensing of hydroelectric projects is done pursuant to the 1920 Federal Water Power Act and the 1935 Amendments to that statute. Because both acts grant licenses for up to 50 years before relicensing is necessary, the date of the project is important. The FERC may grant licenses to voluntary applicants of projects built on nonnavigable streams before 1935 under the jurisdiction of § 4(e) of the 1920 Act. 16 U.S.C.A. § 797(e); Cooley v. FERC (1988). In Farmington River Power Co. v. FPC (1972), the court held that § 23(b) of the 1935 Amendments required a license of any project constructed on a navigable waterway built between 1920 and 1935. Puget Sound Power & Light Co. v. FPC (1977). FERC authorization is also required for substantial reconstruction of projects built before 1920. Minnesota Power & Light Co. v. FPC (1965); Northwest Paper Co. v. FPC (1965). Compare

Aquenergy Systems, Inc. v. FERC (1988) (permit required for major post–1935 reconstruction by new owner on nonnavigable stream), with Washington Water Power Co. v. FERC (1985) (no license needed for project completed in 1911); Puget Sound Power & Light Co. v. FPC (1977) (no permit required to repair damaged pre–1935 project).

Conflicts over licenses became a major problem in the mid–1960s when licenses, which had been granted for a fifty year period, began to expire. Private license holders sought renewal of their licenses in opposition to municipal or state bodies that wished to take over the facilities, and the private developers objected to the preference given to public entities in licensing.

This tension between private projects and municipal preferences in a relicensing context was discussed in an important FERC opinion, In re City of Bountiful, Utah, FERC Opinion No. 88 (June 27, 1980), Util. Law Rep. (CCH) 12,331. There, private developers argued that the preference clause for municipalities pertained only to applications for original licenses, not relicensing. The FERC held that "new licensee" referred to any license, and therefore public bodies were meant to receive preference in relicensing of hydro facilities as well as for original licenses. The controversy regarding the continuation of preferences on relicensing was addressed by Congress in the Electric Consumers Protection Act of 1986, 16 U.S.C.A. § 800(a), which eliminated the preference. Kamargo Corp. v. FERC (1988). Courts have held that the preference applies only to original licenses, not to relicensing. Alabama Power Co. v. FERC (1982); Clark–Cowlitz Joint Operating Agency v. FERC (1987). Still, new licenses are to be granted to applicants whose plans are best adapted to serve the public interest, and license transfers will not be made for "insignificant differences." 16 U.S.C.A. § 808(a)(2). Thus, incumbents are still favored, even though the preference has been eliminated.

2. Environmental Laws

Environmental concerns began to play a part in the licensing procedures of hydroelectric projects beginning in the 1960s. As a precursor to NEPA requirements, in 1965, environmental groups won a ruling that the FPA required that Consolidated Edison's request to build a pumped storage facility on the Hudson River should include an examination of the environmental value of preserving that area of the river in its present condition. Scenic Hudson Preservation Conference v. FPC (1965). See also Udall v. FPC (1967); Platte River Whooping Crane Critical Habitat Maintenance Trust v. FERC (1989).

Hydropower licenses are subject to federal environmental regulations, most notably the environmental impact statement requirement of NEPA. Federal hydropower projects are subject to NEPA for licenses, La Flamme v. FERC (1991), and for relicensures, Confederated Tribes and Bands of Yakima Indian Nation v. FERC (1984). In addition to NEPA, applicants may be subject to other environmental legislation, such as the Clean Water Act, 33 U.S.C.A. § 1251 et seq., and the Wild and Scenic Rivers Act, 16 U.S.C.A. §§ 1271–87. In National Wildlife Federation v. FERC (1986), the Ninth Circuit remanded to the FERC its decision to grant seven preliminary permits for hydroelectric power projects along the Salmon River in central Idaho. The court reasoned that the FERC had failed to demonstrate why a comprehensive plan was unnecessary for such extensive hydropower development along a navigable river. The court further held that the FERC was required to address the project's impacts on fish and wildlife under the Pacific Northwest Electric Power Planning and Conservation Act, 16 U.S.C.A. § 839(6).

Environmental considerations have also been highlighted by the Electric Consumers Protection Act of 1986 (EPCA), 16 U.S.C.A. § 808. The EPCA amends FPA § 4(e) by requiring the FERC to make licensing decisions which give "equal consideration" to environmental matters as well as power production.

3. Small Hydropower Projects and the Public Utility Regulatory Policies Act

The 1970s were a volatile time for energy markets as prices rose, supplies contracted, and the commercial nuclear power industry collapsed. These energy disruptions of the 1970s motivated the United States to reduce dependence on foreign oil. In the electricity market, alternative sources of electricity promised to reduce electricity prices by increasing supplies and stimulating competition. In 1978, Congress passed the Public Utilities Regulatory Policies Act of 1978 (PURPA) to aid small hydroelectric plant operators. PURPA section 401, 16 U.S.C.A. § 2701, required the Secretary of Energy to establish a program to encourage the development of small (less than 80 megawatts) hydroelectric sites, by authorizing federal loans for feasibility studies and for project costs. PURPA also requires the FERC to establish a regulatory program to facilitate licensing procedures for small hydropower projects in connection with existing dams.

PURPA promotes cogeneration and small power production, including small hydropower facilities. To make investment in small power production attractive, PURPA includes statutory provisions that obligate local utilities to connect with small power producers, to furnish back-up power when necessary, and to purchase the small producer's excess electricity at the utility's "avoided cost." Thus, if the small power producer generates electricity at a rate lower than that of the local public utility, the small power producer saves money on electricity and has a market for the excess product. PURPA has proved highly successful in stimulating this market. When the cost of electricity from traditional large-scale electric power producers rises, then alternative electricity sources such as small hydropower plants are attractive.

PURPA provides for exemptions from the FPA licensing requirement for "small conduit" (15MW) projects. The Energy Security Act, 16 U.S.C.A. § 2705(d), also provides for a 5MW exemption. The purpose of the exemption is to promote power production by reducing administrative costs for small electricity-producing projects, like small hydro facilities. Exemptions have been preferred to preliminary permits. City of Centralia v. FERC (1986). Exemptions have been upheld without a showing of a need for hydropower. Idaho Power Co. v. FERC (1985). However, exemptions have been restricted in order to protect the environment. Tulalip Tribes of Washington v. FERC (1984).

4. The Electric Consumer Protection Act

In 1986, Congress passed the Electric Consumers Protection Act (ECPA), 16 U.S.C.A. § 791 et seq. ECPA amended the FPA to resolve the question of whether the preference given to municipalities and states in licensing hydroelectric facilities applied to relicensing as well as to the development of new sites. Section 7 of the act makes it clear that the preference is to be given to states and municipalities only for an "original" license and not where an expired license is up for renewal. While this section does not call for preference to an incumbent, it does state that "insignificant differences" between applicants will not result in the transfer of a license from a previous licensee to a new holder. Applications to run a preexisting facility are now to be evaluated according to whose application the FERC determines is best adapted to serve the public interest without preference for municipalities. There is still a disposition toward granting the previous license holder's renewal if that holder has a "record of compliance with the terms and conditions of the existing license." 16 U.S.C.A. § 808(a)(3)(A).

Open competition for hydroelectric facility licenses would be thwarted, however, if previous licensees were allowed to use their existing control over established electric distribution systems in gaining an unfair advantage over new applicants. The ECPA contains two provisions aimed at preventing this practice.

First, under section 15(d)(1) of ECPA, the FERC may not consider an incumbent's advantage with respect to transmission facilities in determining license proposals. Second, the ECPA attempts to ensure that any new applicant who is awarded a license will have access to needed transmission facilities, if the FERC determines that it is "not feasible" for the new licensee to operate the facility without obtaining transmission services from the original licensee. The Commission must attempt to have the original and new licensees work out an agreement for use of the transmission facilities. If negotiations fail, however, the FERC will order the original licensee to file a tariff, subject to a refund, to ensure that the new licensee will be able to begin operations on the date that the license is transferred. The FERC will then issue a final order, setting the tariff at a "reasonable rate," but the Commission may not order the original licensee to make substantial improvements to its transmission system, or interfere with the previous licensee's ability to service its customers.

Another new licensing criteria that the ECPA established involves energy conservation. Under section 4(e), the Commission is to give "equal weight" to energy conservation in making licensing decisions, in order that those who receive licenses will consider energy conservation as an energy supply alternative. Section 3(b) of the ECPA also requires the FERC to consider "the electrical consumption efficiency improvement program of the applicant * * * for encouraging or assisting its customers to conserve electricity."

Public bodies such as states and municipalities do receive preference over private entities in the purchase of power from a hydroelectric facility. Construction of a federal dam allows the government to sell electric power, as authorized by a number of federal statutes. Reclamation Project Act of 1939, 43 U.S.C.A. § 485(c); the Flood Control Act of 1944, 16 U.S.C.A. § 825s. Because the cost of federal hydropower is usually well below the cost of other fuels, competition for this energy is often intense.

This practice, mandated under the federal statutes through which the federal marketing agencies sell electricity, has been attacked in court most often by public bodies who do not receive preference as purchasers of hydroelectric power, either because it was sold to a private utility or to another preference entity. Such was the case in Metropolitan Transportation Authority v. FERC (1986), where two state agencies, the Metropolitan Transit Authority of New York and the Vermont Department of Public Service, claimed preference status under the Niagara Redevelopment Act. The FERC's orders, which rejected preference status for both entities, was upheld by the Court of Appeals for the Second Circuit. The court stated that "for purposes of 16 U.S.C.A. § 836(b), 'public bodies' are 'publicly-owned entities capable of selling and distributing power directly to consumers of electricity at retail,' not consumers or brokers."

The ECPA also has provisions which affect PURPA. In the late 1970s and early 1980s, there was a rush in the United States to develop small hydroelectric facilities. This was because of PURPA's extensive incentives for renewable sources, and because of favorable tax legislation. Opposition arose when the FERC decided to extend PURPA benefits to new dam or diversion projects by interpreting the "renewable sources" language in PURPA to include such new projects.

The ECPA responded to these concerns by limiting the availability of PURPA benefits involving new dams or diversions, establishing a moratorium on PURPA benefits for such future projects. However, to aid developers who had relied on the promise of PURPA benefits and had begun planning and developing new facilities, the ECPA established a grandfather clause, exempting most of these projects from the moratorium on PURPA benefits. Projects which fall under the grandfather clause are those which had already been approved by the Commission, as well as those for which proposals had been received by the Commission before enactment of the ECPA. Additionally, ECPA does not affect any project located on a federal dam at which nonfederal hydroelectric development is permitted.

The ECPA contains a pertinent provision relating to the enforcement of its regulations. Concerns were raised prior to its enactment that a number of hydroelectric facilities, which came under federal jurisdiction, were operating without a license from the FERC, making it extremely difficult to monitor the safety conditions and environmental effects of these projects. Additionally, the FERC was accused of failing to diligently monitor compliance with the terms of the licenses it granted. In response, the ECPA states that the FERC "shall" monitor compliance with licensing and exemption requirements. The ECPA gives the FERC more authority to enforce these requirements by granting the Commission power to revoke licenses and exemptions for noncompliance with their terms, and to impose civil penalties of up to $10,000 per day of such noncompliance.

V. ALTERNATIVE ENERGY RESOURCES

As noted in Chapter Nine, the phrase "alternative energy sources" has two distinct meanings. Sometimes the phrase encompasses an alternative energy culture, and the reference is to renewable resources such as solar, wind, or biomass. Other times the reference is to substitutes for conventional fossil fuels, such as oil shale or coal gas. In either case, alternative energy resources must be scientifically and technologically feasible. More significantly, the alternative must satisfy a market test and be financially feasible. Although law, through government regulation, cannot directly affect science and technology, it can further both through government support of research and development, and demonstration projects. Law can also affect the financial feasibility of alternative sources by creating and sustaining markets, either through property rules or price supports.

A. SOLAR POWER

Solar energy is principally used for water and space heating, with a growing application in the production of electricity with photovoltaic cells and large solar collectors. The largest solar collector generates 55 megawatts of electricity. A large nuclear plant, by contrast, generates over 1000 megawatts.

An early estimate anticipated that solar power would account for up to 23% of the country's energy needs by the year 2000. R. Stobaugh & D. Yergin, Energy Future (1979). By the early 1990s, solar power accounted for substantially less of the country's energy production. Nonetheless, solar energy is considered the premier renewable energy source. It is safe, inexhaustible, and not subject to cartelization, attributes which do not belong to oil, coal, gas, or uranium.

Solar energy is both "passive" and "active." Passive solar energy is a system designed with no moving parts, such as a house facing south with large double-paned windows. Passive solar energy, together with improved insulation, also incorporates the principle of conservation. Active solar energy involves mechanical moving parts, such as solar collectors that heat air or water which then move through pipes. The air or water is fanned or pumped through a heat exchanger in a water-filled storage tank. This hot water can be used to heat a house directly, or indirectly by pumping it through a radiator.

Sunlight can also be converted into electricity through photovoltaic conversion. Photovoltaic cells, like transistors and integrated circuits before them, are semiconductors. Sunlight generates electricity when it falls on specially treated silicon chips. These cells are used in the aerospace industry, but costs have not been reduced sufficiently to make them marketable for mass consumption. Solar Photovoltaic Energy Research, Development, and Demonstration Act of 1978, 42 U.S.C.A. § 5581; Solar Energy and Energy Conservation Act of 1980, 12 U.S.C.A. § 1451 et seq., and 42 U.S.C.A. § 6347 et seq.

Sunlight is not susceptible to ownership and centralization like real property. In order to receive the beneficial use of this energy source, the user must have access to sunlight. Generally, access is secured through local or state laws, such as zoning, easements, conversion law, nuisance, or prior appropriation. See Prah v. Maretti (1982) (construction of a house created a private nuisance because it would obstruct an adjoining property owner's access to sunlight, and significantly impair the use of a solar energy system).

The federal regulation of solar energy concentrates on stimulating the market through such devices as the promotion of small power production using solar energy, favorable tax depreciations, and research and development. Solar Energy Research Development and Demonstration Act of 1974, 42 U.S.C.A. § 5551–66.

B. BIOMASS AND ALCOHOL FUELS

These two sources are discussed together because they are the subject of Title II of the Energy Security Act of 1980, which is known as the Biomass Energy and Alcohol Fuels Act of 1980, 42 U.S.C.A. § 8801 et seq. "Biomass" has been broadly defined as "any organic matter which is available on a renewable basis, including agricultural crops and agricultural wastes and residues, wood and wood wastes and residues, animal wastes, municipal wastes, and aquatic plants." 42 U.S.C.A. § 8802. Biomass is converted to methane gas through the decomposition of organic matter. The energy derived from biomass is actually solar energy stored in organic matter through the process of photosynthesis. This energy can be reclaimed from the harvesting of live plants or from wastes. "Alcohol" simply means alcohol which is produced from biomass, which can then be used either alone or in combination with other substances. The most widely used form of alcohol is gasohol, made from ethanol, which is marketed for mass consumption. Ethanol may play a role under the 1990 Clean Air Act Amendments.

The Solar Energy Research, Development and Demonstration Act of 1974, 42 U.S.C.A. § 5551, authorizes and funds research into the field of biomass conversion. The Resource Conservation and Recovery Act of 1976 creates a federal-state program to study the energy potential of solid wastes. 42 U.S.C.A. § 6901 et seq. The Biomass Energy and Alcohol Fuels Act furthers the federal effort in this area by encouraging biomass development. The Act is designed to provide financial assistance for biomass and alcohol energy projects in the form of loans, loan guarantees, purchase agreements, and price guarantees.

C. GEOTHERMAL

Geothermal energy is generated by the heat from the earth's interior. This heat can be used to turn turbines to generate electricity. It is a relatively safe and clean fuel. The environmental repercussions in developing this resource include noise, odors, thermal pollution, the discharge of dissolved materials into surface or ground waters, and subsidence. The relative environmental safety and cleanliness of this resource stems from the fact that these hazards occur principally at the site rather than throughout the fuel cycle, as is the case with coal or oil.

Most geothermal heat resides in the earth's molten core and mantle below the earth's crust at depths incapable of being tapped by drilling. However, there are locations around the globe, called "hot spots," where the earth's protective crust is sufficiently shallow to permit human access to geothermal heat. In certain places, there are hot springs or geysers (like Old Faithful in Yellowstone National Park) where geothermal energy has broken the earth's surface. In the United States, as much as 1.3 million acres of land, including Alaska and Hawaii, have potential for power production from geothermal energy. Most of the potential domestic geothermal sites are located in the western United States, the most productive of which is the Geysers region of California.

In 1960, the Pacific Gas and Electric Company became the first American utility to generate electricity from geothermal steam in the Geysers region. In 1986, the Geysers region generated 10.3 billion kilowatt hours of electricity, and at a lower cost than fossil fuel generation in the same area. Electricity generated from geothermal sources peaked in 1987 at 11 billion kilowatt hours. Geothermal steam has high economic value. In Grace Geothermal v. Northern Cal. Power Agency (1985), one prospective purchaser offered $145 million for an interest in a federal geothermal leasehold.

The Energy Security Act addressed the field of geothermal development with the enactment of the Geothermal Energy Act of 1980, 30 U.S.C.A. § 1501. The Act is designed to promote this resource by overcoming economic and institutional barriers. Loans will be made in connection with the Geothermal Energy Research, Development, and Demonstration Act of 1974, 30 U.S.C.A. § 1101, to assist the exploration of geothermal reservoirs. The Act also provides for a study of the feasibility of establishing a reservoir insurance program, and for a study of financial incentives for the development of geothermal resources for nonelectric applications.

One state and federal law problem with geothermal resources has been to determine whether they belong to the owner of the underlying "mineral" estate or to the surface estate owner. Geothermal resources have been held to be the property of the mineral estate rather than the property of the surface owner. Geothermal Kinetics, Inc. v. Union Oil Co. (1977). The geothermal owner may enter the surface estate and build an electrical generating plant, even when the surface owner objects. Occidental Geothermal, Inc. v. Simmons (1982).

The United States owns a significant amount of land where geothermal resources are located. Congress early adopted a policy of leasing geothermal resources on federal lands pursuant to the Geothermal Steam Act of 1970, 30 U.S.C.A. § 1001. Crownite Corp. v. Watt (1985); Getty Oil Co. v. Andrus (1979). The Ninth Circuit has held that the federal government reserved the rights to the geothermal resources in the Stock–Raising Homestead Act of 1916. United States v. Union Oil Co. (1977).

D. SYNTHETIC FUELS

The Energy Security Act of 1980 established the United States Synfuels Corporation to stimulate the commercialization of synthetic oil and gas. According to the Act, a "synthetic fuel" is generally defined as "any solid, liquid, or gas which can be used as a substitute for petroleum or natural gas and which is produced by chemical or physical transformation of domestic sources of coal, shale, tar sands, and water." 42 U.S.C.A. § 8702. Synthetic fuels development was to be accomplished through a federal subsidy of private efforts to extract liquids and gas from coal, oil shale, and tar sands. Federal subsidies were in the form of loans, loan guarantees, price guarantees, purchase agreements, joint ventures, and, as a last resort, ownership by the federal government. The original goals of the Synfuels Corporation were to subsidize production of 500,000 barrels a day of synfuels by 1987, and 2,000,000 barrels a day by 1992. These goals were never met.

Basically, synfuels are oil replacements which result from processing oil shale and tar sands into liquid, and gas from the gasification of coal. Because of the great abundance of oil shale, tar sands, and coal, and because technologies exist for their transformation, synfuels are scientifically and technologically promising energy sources. However, synfuels are not commercially feasible. They are more expensive than conventional fuels. Environmental problems also surround synfuels processes, not the least of which is the possibility of climatic change due to the release of massive amounts of carbon dioxide into the atmosphere as a result of the burning of carbon-based fuels.

The most advanced synthetic fuels technology is coal gasification. In this process, coal is heated together with steam in a "gasifier." The gasifier causes some of the hydrogen in the steam to join with the carbon in the coal to form methane, the primary ingredient of natural gas. Coal gasification has certain environmental and distributional advantages. Gasification of coal removes harmful sulphur, other particulates, and heavy metals to produce a clean burning gas. In addition, there already exists a network of natural gas pipelines to transport the gas to end-users.

Coal can also be converted to oil through a process of liquefaction. Liquefaction was used extensively by Germany during World War II. Millions of barrels of oil a year were produced directly from coal in Germany during the war years by using inexpensive, disposable catalysts. Other liquefaction methods first convert coal to gas and then convert the gas to oil. The DOE has experimented with several coal-to-oil technologies.

Oil shale is sedimentary rock containing an organic rock-like material called kerogen. The kerogen may be processed by heating it into shale oil, a form of crude oil. The United States has an abundance of oil shale. Known reserves are about 600 billion barrels of oil and possible reserves may exceed two trillion barrels of oil. The most extensive and highest grade of oil shale deposits in the United States are located in the Rocky Mountain States of Colorado, Utah, and Wyoming. In this region, oil shale is contained in 3 basins, the Piceance Basin, the Green River Basin, and Uinta Basin. The Piceance Basin in northwestern Colorado has the largest deposits of high-grade oil shale, estimated at 1.3 trillion barrels of oil (more than the amount of oil under Saudi Arabia).

Oil may be extracted from oil shale either by conventional mining and surface processing (surface retorting), or by the use of water to extract the oil from the shale while it is still in the ground (in situ processing). The major problems associated with recovery of oil from shale are water availability and pollution. Shale oil development on a scale of 1 million barrels of oil a day is estimated to require between 121,000 to 189,000 acre-feet of water per year. Oil shale also produces waste water which is high in salt content. In addition, spent shale must be disposed of, and the retorting process produces emissions which deteriorates air quality.

Tar sands are deposits that bear hydrocarbons which are not capable of production through ordinary oil wells because of the high viscosity of the tar hydrocarbons. Tar sands include oil sands, bitumen sands, and rocks that bear oil or bitumen. In North America, the richest known tar sands deposits are in Utah (up to 30 billion barrels or more) and Alberta, Canada (up to 250 billion barrels). Most tar sands are not near the surface and thus may not be strip mined. However, once recovered, extraction of the hydrocarbon from tar sands is much more efficient and consumes less energy than the extraction of kerogen from oil shale. There are no commercial tar sands operations in the United States. Even if developed, the impact of tar sands on the total domestic energy supply is thought to be limited.

While synfuels are scientifically and technically feasible, synfuel projects are not economically competitive with conventional oil and natural gas resources. Ever since 1984, the

United States has enjoyed a glut of oil and a "bubble" of natural gas. With so much supply, the price of oil and gas has been low, and there is little pressure to develop synfuels. Not surprisingly, the federal government has removed itself almost completely from synfuels development. The Synfuels Corporation was funded initially at $24 billion dollars. In the early 1980s, the Corporation's budget was slashed to $8 billion, of which $5.7 billion was required to meet the substantive commitments already undertaken by the Corporation. On December 12, 1985, the Synfuels Corporation was abolished.

E. CONSERVATION

Another "alternative fuel source" is conservation. Energy conservation has two meanings. First, energy is conserved simply by consuming less. Second, energy is conserved as energy production and use become more efficient. Conservation through greater efficiency can take place on a number of fronts. Retrofitting of buildings and appliances or producing more fuel efficient cars can conserve energy. Tax credits and deductions can be used to encourage installation of conservation measures. Taxes can also be used to raise the price of energy, thus reducing demand and use. The decontrol of fuel prices in a time of shortage will also bring about conservation by causing prices to rise and demand to fall. The government can directly curtail supplies, and thus force conservation (a crude example of this is lower speed limits).

Three federal statutes enacted during the energy "crisis" days of the 1970s promote conservation. The Energy Policy and Conservation Act, 42 U.S.C.A. § 6201, includes such measures as appliance and car efficiency standards, industrial conservation targets, federal conservation efforts, and grants for state conservation programs. The Energy Conservation and Production Act, 42 U.S.C.A. § 6801, establishes an office for energy information and analysis, and proposes energy conservation standards for new buildings. The National Energy Conservation Policy Act (NECPA), 42 U.S.C.A. § 8201, part of the National Energy Act of 1978, requires utilities to adopt a comprehensive conservation program. Each utility must inform its residential customers who own or occupy a residential building of suggested conservation measures, the savings in energy costs that are likely to result, a list of suppliers and lenders for energy savings installations, and suggestions regarding energy conservation techniques.

The statutes described in this chapter do not exhaust the list of conservation measures. They are the major legislative efforts, however, together with Title V of the Energy Security Act, which establishes a Solar Energy and Energy Conservation Bank. 12 U.S.C.A. § 3601.

F. CONCLUSION

Alternative energy sources must compete with conventional fossil fuels and with the dominant model of U.S. energy policy. The competition will be won in the market place and frequently that market place will be shaped by government rules and regulations. If the United States is to move from the traditional path of heavy reliance on fossil fuels and nuclear power to an alternative path of renewable resources and conservation, then government support may well be necessary. Support has come from the Congress through legislation such as the Renewable Energy and Energy Efficiency Technology Competitiveness Act of 1989, 42 U.S.C.A. § 12001. The purpose of the act is to "pursue an aggressive national program of research, development, and demonstration of renewable energy and energy efficiency technologies in order to ensure a stable and secure future energy supply." 42 U.S.C.A. § 12001(b). One suspects, however, that alternative energy sources will remain an insignificant part of the energy picture until some catacylsmic event, such as another embargo of imported oil, convinces Americans that our fossil fuel supplies are not inexhaustible.

CHAPTER ELEVEN

ENERGY CONVERSION AND DISTRIBUTION

Chapter Ten discussed the exploration, production, and transportation of most of our nation's energy resources. Each of those resources can be used to produce electricity, although electricity production is dominated by coal and nuclear power. This final chapter focuses on the back-end of the fuel cycle. Specifically, it examines the conversion of natural resources into electricity, and then the distribution and pricing of electricity and natural gas to consumers. The discussion of natural gas production and transportation was deferred to this chapter for two complementary reasons. First, gas exploration and production are very similar to those stages of the oil fuel cycle already discussed. Second, the distribution and regulation of natural gas is very similar to the same stages of the electricity industry discussed in this chapter. Consequently, discussing electricity and natural gas together better focuses on the conversion and distribution stages of the fuel cycle.

Examination of the natural gas and electricity markets demonstrates how natural resources are converted into usable energy. The ultimate beneficial use of many of the natural resources addressed in this book is for energy—the ability to do work. This work occurs when one turns on the ignition to start a car, flip a switch to light an office, or move a thermostat to heat or cool a home. Energy is also used to fly airplanes, manufacture steel and glass, and run appliances from computers to escalators. Once converted to a usable form, energy must be distributed to consumers. Further, because both natural gas and electricity have monopoly characteristics and are deemed to be goods "in the public interest," they are regulated by the government. Basically, government regulation aims at providing reliable service at reasonable prices. This chapter examines public utility regulation in the context of ratemaking, which best exemplifies the regulatory compact between government and industry once energy crosses interstate boundaries and is at the point of distribution to end users. Historically, state utility commissions regulate the setting of retail prices for such energy sources as natural gas and electricity.

I. NATURAL GAS

Natural gas is a relatively abundant resource, although as recently as the late 1970s that has not been the case. The story of natural gas regulation demonstrates the impact that government regulation has on markets. In particular, from the 1960s to 1990, federal regulations created a dual natural gas market. The final chapter on a large portion of federal natural gas regulation seems to have been written with the decontrol of producer prices in 1989. See The Natural Gas Wellhead Decontrol Act of 1989, 15 U.S.C.A. § 3301. At the federal level, natural gas is regulated through the Federal Energy Regulatory Commission. The Natural Gas Act of 1938, 15 U.S.C.A. § 717, together with the Natural Gas Policy Act of 1978, 15 U.S.C.A. § 3301 (a portion of the National Energy Act), are the primary organic laws governing natural gas regulation. State public utility commissions (PUCs) regulate the retail pricing and distribution of the commodity to end users.

A. OVERVIEW OF THE NATURAL GAS INDUSTRY

The natural gas industry, like the oil industry, consists of integrated and nonintegrated firms. Integrated gas companies explore for and produce natural gas, and then the gas is transported through pipelines (some intrastate and some interstate). After transport, the gas is refined and distributed. Nonintegrated companies perform one or more but not all of these functions.

The industry can be divided into four primary parts: producers, pipelines, local distribution companies (LDCs), and end users. Pipelines play a key role in the distribution system. They offer two services—selling natural gas and transporting it. There are approximately 933 municipally owned natural gas distribution companies in the United States as opposed to over 1000 investor-owned utilities. Investor-owned utilities, however, enjoy a 90% to 95% share of the market. Generally, municipal gas distributors, like municipal electric companies, are much smaller.

In 1990, natural gas accounted for approximately one quarter of the United States energy consumption. The United States produces about 92% of the natural gas it consumes and imports the remaining 7%. Both Canada and Mexico have large supplies of natural gas and provide 6% of the U.S. supply. Other sources of gas include synthetic gas (SNG) which is manufactured from coal. At present, synthetic gas cannot be manufactured at a price lower than that of natural gas. Another source of natural gas is liquified natural gas (LNG), which is imported from Algeria and constitutes one percent of U.S. consumption. LNG consists of natural gas that is liquified at low temperatures then shipped on specially designed tankers. Once delivered into the United States, the LNG is processed into its gaseous form and placed into pipelines. LNG is highly explosive, and thus it presents the threat of a catastrophic accident should a tanker be damaged, particularly while loading or unloading in port. In addition, the cost of LNG development is expensive, and current use of LNG rather than natural gas is not economically viable. Natural gas is consumed by various sectors of the economy: industries (42%); residential sources (25%); commercial sources (15%); electric utilities (15%); and transportation (3%).

B. REGULATORY OVERVIEW

The federal regulation of natural gas is grounded in the Commerce Clause of the Constitution, Art. I, sec. 8, cl. 3. Because of the federal system, there is a division of authority between the state and federal governments. West v. Kansas Natural Gas Co. (1911) (states cannot prohibit interstate shipment); Public Utilities Com'n v. Attleboro Steam & Elec. Co. (1927) (same). This dual jurisdictional authority has caused market distortions, the effects of which are being felt in the 1990s.

1. The Natural Gas Act

The federal government's first major involvement with the regulation of natural gas came in 1938 with the passage of the Natural Gas Act (NGA), 15 U.S.C.A. § 717. The Act was prompted by a 1935 Federal Trade Commission report stating that interstate pipelines exercised abusive monopoly power. In response to these market abuses, the NGA conferred on the Federal Power Commission (now FERC) authority to regulate interstate sales of natural gas. The Act allowed the FPC to approve rates that were "just and reasonable" and that did not grant any "undue preference" or "maintain any unreasonable difference" among purchasers. 15 U.S.C.A. § 717c. This power was held to be constitutional in FPC v. Hope Natural Gas Co. (1944). The *Hope* case sets the constitutional standard for administrative ratemaking authority in the face of a company's claim that rates are too low, confiscatory, and violative of the taking clause of the Fifth Amendment. Under the Act, the FERC may assert jurisdiction over sales of intrastate natural gas that are commingled with interstate gas. California v. Lo–Vaca Gathering Co. (1965); Louisiana Power & Light Co. v. FPC (1973).

The NGA divided regulatory authority between the federal government and the states. Under the NGA, federal regulators had jurisdiction over: (1) wholesale sales by interstate pipelines; (2) transportation by interstate pipelines; and, (3) imports and exports. The states had regulation of retail sales and intrastate transactions.

From 1938 until 1954, the FPC asserted its jurisdiction over interstate pipelines but did not assert jurisdiction over producers. Interstate sales were defined to exclude the price that producers charged in the field (the wellhead price) to the pipeline. Naturally, the prices charged by producers to distributors were passed through to customers, hence any protection afforded customers could easily be vitiated by excessive prices at the wellhead. In 1947, the Supreme Court ruled that the FPC had jurisdiction over the prices that producers charged affiliated pipelines. Interstate Natural Gas Co. v. FPC (1947). Then, in 1954, the Supreme Court expanded FPC jurisdiction to cover producer prices. Phillips Petroleum Co. v. Wisconsin (1954).

One immediate consequence of the *Phillips* decision was the imposition of a massive administrative burden on the FPC. It was estimated that the FPC could not finish its 1960 caseload until the year 2043. At that time, rate schedule hearings proceeded as adjudicatory hearings under the Administrative Procedure Act. These kinds of hearings allow companies to air their individual case before FPC hearing examiners. To relieve this burden, the FPC moved away from individual hearings and began relying on rate-setting by gas producing regions. First, the FPC set area rates. In re Permian Basin Area Rate Cases (1968); Southern Louisiana Area Rate Cases v. FPC (1970). The consequence was a change from ratemaking by adjudication under the APA to ratemaking by rulemaking. Instead of individual producers and distributors having hearings, all the producers and distributors within a region were parties to a single ratemaking procedure.

This regional ratemaking functioned neither smoothly nor quickly. The FPC then set national natural gas rates. This procedure was upheld in Shell Oil Co. v. FPC (1975), and American Public Gas Ass'n v. FPC (1977).

The exercise of jurisdiction by the FPC over interstate sales had another serious repercussion. Two natural gas markets were created—one interstate and the other intrastate. Eventually, the prices charged in these markets became uneven. The prices in the largely unregulated intrastate market rose faster than those in the federally regulated interstate market because the federal rates were based on cost-of-service rather than being allowed to float upwards toward the market level. The result of this price differential was that the intrastate market producers had more funds which they could use to develop new sources of natural gas. Because of strict abandonment rules in the federal legislation, producers with gas dedicated to interstate commerce could not move into the intrastate market without federal approval. 15 U.S.C.A. § 717f(b); United Gas Pipe Line Co. v. McCombs (1979); California v. Southland Royalty Co. (1978). Ironically, due to the natural gas "shortage" caused by less interstate gas production, the FPC, and later the FERC, were not liberal in granting abandonments because of fears that these would be an adverse effect on the interstate market.

The dual market created by federal and state natural gas regulation had produced artificial shortages. The regulatory response to those shortages was that the FPC had to apportion supplies. The FPC adopted a policy of end-use curtailment for interstate pipelines. These pipelines were required to sell gas according to certain priorities. Schools, hospitals, and small residential users had top priority, while large industrial customers capable of switching to other fuels would have their supplies curtailed first. American Smelting & Refining Co. v. FPC (1974); City of Willcox and Arizona Elec. Power Co-op., Inc. v. FPC (1977).

Soon a cry arose to deregulate the market prices of natural gas. The deregulation advocates argued that the industry was competitive, that the so-called natural gas shortage was artificially created by excessive and counterproductive federal regulation, and that suppressed prices prevented the development of new sources of natural gas which would relieve the "shortage." Antideregulation proponents argued that regulation was needed because the industry was not competitive, that consumers would suffer in disproportionate amounts, and that other means of exploration and development could be equally effective. These arguments failed. The reality is that two markets did exist, and they had created market distortions so that prices and allocation of gas were uneven, and new sources were needed. The result was the passage of the Natural Gas Policy Act of 1978 (NGPA).

2. The Natural Gas Policy Act of 1978 (NGPA)

The NGPA was the intended centerpiece of President Carter's National Energy Act. The NGPA initiated four significant changes in the law. First, federal price controls were imposed on the intrastate market, 15 U.S.C.A. § 3301. Second, the NGPA created a formula for monthly increases in the wellhead price of "new" post–1978 natural gas. Third, the ceiling price on delivered "new" natural gas was pegged to the price of refined oil. Finally, the NGPA provided for the elimination of price controls starting January 1, 1985, subject to reimposition on certain natural gas sales (e.g., "new" natural gas, new onshore production wells, and certain intrastate contracts). 15 U.S.C.A. § 3331. The overall thrust of the NGPA was to begin price decontrols, stimulate production, and unify the natural gas market.

Title I began to ease the downward pressure on wellhead prices and started price decontrol. Wellhead price decontrol was set for January 1, 1993. 15 U.S.C.A. § 3301. The NGPA also created categories and vintages of natural gas with the intent of stimulating the production of some markets. Each category had a maximum lawful price tied to inflation. The incentive categories included "high-cost" gas, "deep gas," new natural gas from the outer continental shelf, and new on-shore gas.

Title II of the NGPA provides for "incremental pricing." Essentially, incremental pricing is a type of marginal cost pricing, which means that the prices at which natural gas is sold reflect the additional costs of production. See Chapter One of this book. Instead of "rolling-in" or averaging the costs of natural gas, higher costs are charged to users as they are incurred. Title II passthrough regulations allow the passing through of certain "incremental costs" of natural gas to industrial facilities. 15 U.S.C.A. § 3341. This means that wellhead price increases permitted under Title I of the NGPA in an effort to deregulate the price of natural gas will not be borne wholly by high priority customers. Rather, the prices are absorbed by "industrial boiler fuel facilities" as defined in the Act. The Act also provides for exemptions so that passthrough costs are not suffered by such users as existing small industrial boiler fuel facilities, agricultural users, schools, hospitals, and similar institutions. 15 U.S.C.A. § 3346. Thus, the NGPA protects certain classes of users by channeling the increased costs to certain industrial customers.

In general, the following costs are subject to the pass-through: new natural gas; natural gas under intrastate rollover contracts, which is an expansion of federal jurisdiction in an effort to counter the effects of the dual market; gas from new onshore production wells; certain natural gas imports; stripper well (small producer) gas; "high-cost" gas, also defined in the Act; Alaskan natural gas; and some other identified costs, such as state severance taxes. 15 U.S.C.A. § 3343. The theory behind passthrough costs is a classical economic one: as prices increase for certain products, the supply of these products should increase. By allowing certain identified costs to be passed through, the production of those types of natural gas should be encouraged.

A fair question is raised as to whether it is unfair and perhaps even confiscatory to have industrial users absorb all of these costs. There should be a ceiling price above which the passthrough costs cannot go. The logical ceiling is the alternative price of replacement fuel. If the costs of natural gas rise too high, then the users subject to the passthrough will find it cheaper to buy some other fuel. Thus, the Act gives the user the option of purchasing other fuel, or limiting the amount it must pay under the incremental pricing provisions of the NGPA. This ceiling does not include the cost of coal because of a fairly uniform national policy of encouraging coal use. Thus, the incrementally priced natural gas cannot go higher than the price of alternative fuels except coal. 15 U.S.C.A. § 3344(e). Because of concerns involving the fairness of passthrough regulations, and the difficulty in identifying an appropriate ceiling, the incremental pricing provisions were repealed in May, 1987. Pub.L. No. 100–42.

3. Public Utility Regulatory Policies Act

Title III of the Public Utility Regulatory Policies Act of 1978 (PURPA), also part of the National Energy Act, applies to natural gas rate design issues. In order to conserve energy, increase the efficient use of facilities and resources, and promote equitable rates to consumers, state regulatory agencies and nonregulated gas utilities, as defined in PURPA, are required to hold hearings to consider rate design standards proposed by the Act. At the conclusion of the hearings the standards shall be adopted "if and to the extent * * * that such adoption is appropriate and is consistent with otherwise applicable state law." 15 U.S.C.A. § 3203(a)(2).

Under PURPA, the Secretary of the DOE together with the FERC was required to conduct a gas rate design study which examines the effects of incremental pricing, marginal cost pricing, end use gas consumption taxes, wellhead natural gas pricing policies, demand rate design, declining block rates, interruptable service, seasonal rate differentials, and end user rate schedules. 15 U.S.C.A. § 3206(a). The study of these various designs must make reference to the effect of the design on pipeline and distribution company load factors, rates to each class of user, consumption of natural gas, change in total costs, end use of gas, and competition for alternative fuels. Rate design can be used simply for the accumulation of enough revenue to keep a responsible utility operating with a fair rate of return without gouging customers, or it can be utilized to accomplish other social policy objectives, such as conservation of resources, redistribution of wealth among classes of users, and the reallocation of various resources. After all, if a particular rate design raises the cost of natural gas to industrial consumers, for example, higher than the cost of coal, then the industrial consumer will switch to coal. A pervasive issue with rate design then becomes the purposes for which a specific design is being proposed.

C. POST NGPA REGULATION

As complex as it was, the NGPA had positive effects. Most simply, it increased domestic natural gas production. Market unification and price deregulation stimulated that production. Nevertheless, the natural gas market did not function entirely as desired. During the natural gas shortage and curtailment period of the 1970s, pipelines entered into long-term contracts with producers to assure the pipelines' supplies. Unfortunately, these contracts were entered into during a period when supplies were low and they contained a harsh "take or pay" clause that adversely affected pipelines.

1. Take-or-Pay Contracts

In order to have reliable supplies, pipelines entered into long-term supply contracts with producers which contained take-or-pay clauses. Such clauses required the pipeline to either take the amount of gas they contracted for, or pay up to 100% of the price of that gas. Prenalta Corp. v. Colorado Interstate Gas Co. (1991) (remedy for breach of take-or-pay contract is the value of the quantity of gas not taken). In a shortage period, this clause is desirable. The pipeline has a reliable supply and the producer has cash flow. When there is a surplus of gas, however, the clause hurts pipelines and their customers. In a period of surplus, natural gas prices will decline. The long-term contracts, however, prevent the lower priced gas from getting to consumers because the pipelines must take or pay for contracted supplies. In the early 1980s, take-or-pay liability was estimated to cost $8 billion. Because of the tie-up in the flow of cheap natural gas from producers to customers, the FERC was asked to provide relief.

2. FERC Natural Gas Initiatives

A significant market dislocation in natural gas occurred in the mid–1970s. It was caused by dual natural gas markets, price deregulation, take-or-pay contracts, and increased supplies. The FERC responded with natural gas regulation during the 1980s which has been considered nothing short of revolutionary. Through a series of rulemaking orders, as interpreted by the D.C. Circuit Court of Appeals, the natural gas industry is facing its most significant restructuring since the 1978 Natural Gas Policy Act.

In response to the distortion in the natural gas market caused by regulation and long-term contracts, pipelines, producers, and consumers petitioned the FERC for relief. Pipelines tried to ensure their cash flow to pay their fixed and variable costs through minimum billings. In Order No. 380, the FERC ordered the elimination of the variable cost from all minimum commodity bills. Wisconsin Gas Co. v. FERC (1985) (fixed cost provisions of minimum billings are to be addressed in individual proceedings); Transwestern Pipeline Co. v. FERC (1987). If a company can rebut the presumption that minimum bills are anti-competitive, then they can be used. Transcontinental Gas Pipe Line Corp. v. FERC (1990).

In a brief period, 1983 to 1985, the FERC attempted to increase pipeline competition through "special marketing programs" (SMPs). Under a SMP, the producer and pipeline would amend their contract to enable the producer to sell the contract gas on its own and credit the sale to its contract with the pipeline. The FERC would grant the necessary abandonment.

The SMP satisfied pipelines and producers but not customers. Pipelines tried to get access to the surplus market, and producers simply wanted to get their gas to market. Small residential consumers, however, protested the new marketing programs that excluded them from participation. In effect, the SMP moved low cost gas to large industrial consumers but not to small residential consumers. The D.C. Circuit remanded the SMP to the FERC for this reason, and then the programs expired. Maryland People's Counsel v. FERC (1985); Maryland People's Counsel v. FERC (1985).

Other concerns of producers, pipelines, and consumers did not fall on deaf ears. The FERC reacted to requests for relief and to changing market conditions by attempting to loosen pricing and entry and exit controls for the purpose of letting gas flow more smoothly through the distribution system from producer to end-user (in industry jargon, from wellhead to burnertip). Because pipelines were the bottleneck in the natural gas fuel cycle, they were the targets of FERC regulatory efforts.

In Order No. 436 (1985), the FERC proposed to separate the merchant and transportation roles of pipeline companies as a means of opening access for captive customers and others who found it difficult to switch fuels or supplies. The purpose of Order No. 436 was to pressure producers and pipelines to move gas to end users through easier regulation. The elements of Order No. 436 included:

(1) open-access transportation by pipelines, meaning that the pipeline would not discriminate between customers;

(2) if demand is greater than capacity, then the open-access pipeline will transport natural gas on a first-come, first-served basis;

(3) rate regulation will be done within a zone;

(4) local distribution companies may switch their "contract demand" to transportation service, and have the option to reduce contract demand; and

(5) the FERC may expedite licensing for new pipeline facilities and services who choose to avail themselves of the open access provisions.

Although the D.C. Circuit generally agreed with the purposes of Order No. 436, the order was remanded to the FERC in Associated Gas Distributors v. FERC (1987), because of the FERC's failure to address the problem of take-or-pay burdens. The court upheld the FERC's jurisdiction to promulgate open access provisions as long as the provisions were nondiscriminatory, and it also sustained the order's flexible rate treatment. This approach to ratemaking allowed pipelines to set rates within a zone of reasonableness and to give discounts rather than have the pipelines tied to a single cost-based rate. More innovatively, the court upheld regulations that allowed pipeline customers to modify their contracts with pipelines unilaterally. Under certain circumstances, the customers could convert a percentage of their contract demand from a gas purchase obligation. As a result, *Associated Gas*

Distributors is an important decision for natural gas regulation.

Take-or-pay liability continued to congest the natural gas market and regulatory relief was not forthcoming. The D.C. Circuit told the FERC to look more closely at the take-or-pay issue. Maryland People's Counsel v. FERC (1985); Associated Gas Distributors v. FERC (1987); Consolidated Edison Co. of New York, Inc. v. FERC (1987). The FERC responded with Order No. 500 (1987). According to FERC Chair Martha Hesse, the underlying philosophy of Order No. 500 is "spreading the pain," with the goal of making open access "a fact of life in the gas industry." Order No. 500 in large part was a readoption of Order No. 436, with some attention paid to take-or-pay liability. Under the new order, producers had to credit the pipelines' take-or-pay liability with the volumes of gas transported under the open access provisions. Provision was also made for sharing accrued take-or-pay obligations and for avoiding future take-or-pay liability. See American Gas Ass'n v. FERC (1990). Order No. 500 was dealt a temporary setback by the Fifth Circuit, but it was sustained by the Supreme Court in Mobil Oil Exploration & Producing Southeast Inc. v. United Distribution Companies (1991).

Order Nos. 436 and 500 form the heart of the regulatory revolution in the natural gas industry. Both attempt to pry open access to markets through pipelines, and both seek to resolve the multi-billion dollar take-or-pay liability problem. The FERC has been moving toward the objective of promoting a more competitive natural gas market by focusing on pipelines. By easing entry and exit controls and by expanding price decontrols, these natural gas regulations constitute a new form of regulation. The thrust of the FERC gas initiatives is to increase competition by lightening the regulatory touch. This same philosophy is behind FERC's proposed electricity regulations.

II. ELECTRICITY

Electricity is not a natural resource; it is the product of electric generators. Energy resources such as oil, natural gas, coal, uranium, hydropower, and alternative resources, are used to create steam which turns a turbine shaft which rotates coils of wire within stationary magnets which then generates electricity. The fuel cycle consists of an energy resource being converted into electricity, where the electricity is then transmitted from the source of production directly to end users or to local public utilities for distribution.

Like the natural gas industry, the electricity industry is regulated at the federal and state levels. Unlike the natural gas industry, electricity regulation has not suffered the problem of dual markets. Instead, the electricity industry has market problems of its own. From the end of World War II until the mid 1960s, the demand for electricity grew at a steady rate of 7% per year. After 1965, the growth in demand became erratic, even to the point of negative growth in one year. After the 1990s, the rate of growth in demand hovered between 2% and 3% per year.

The great problem with the shift from steady, predictable 7% growth to erratic then lower growth is that traditional public utilities are large-scale, capital intensive, and dependent on high technology. These power producers committed large amounts of capital to expansion that did not materialize, leaving the industry with excess capacity and weak cash flow.

A. INDUSTRY OVERVIEW

The following diagram shows the resources used in electricity production.

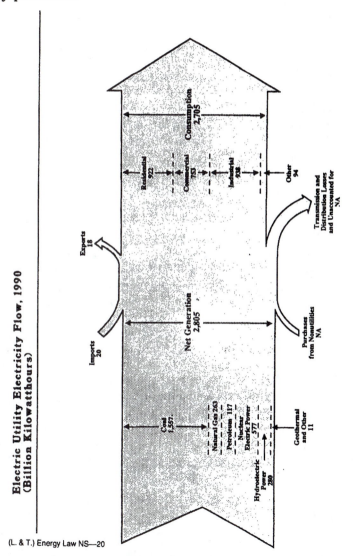

Electric Utility Electricity Flow, 1990
(Billion Kilowatthours)

According to the DOE, Annual Energy Review 1990 (May, 1990), coal generates 62% of United States electricity, followed by nuclear power (20%) natural gas (9.47%), hydropower (10%); and oil (4%). Historically, the electricity industry has enjoyed tremendous growth. Utility companies continuously expanded the size of their plants, and power generation became more cost and energy efficient. That is, the per unit costs of electricity decreased, and the ratio of the amount of the energy used to the amount generated increased. Thus, utilities were able to provide more electricity to more people for more uses at lower costs. Declining unit costs for electricity continued until the late 1960s and the early 1970s. After that time, costs rose due to slowing technical advances, inflation, rising capital costs, and high fuel costs.

There are three segments in the electricity industry— generation, transmission, and distribution. Structurally, the dominant actor in the industry is the investor-owned utility. Out of the approximately 3100 utility systems, only 400 are owned by private investors, yet they generate about 77% of total production. Forty systems are federally owned, 2000 are owned by state or local government, and the remainder are electric cooperatives. Investor-owned utilities are, for the most part, vertically integrated and dominate the industry.

Once generated, electricity is transmitted through high-voltage lines ranging from 69 kilovolts (kv) to 745kv. Transmission lines perform two functions—the movement of electricity from generator to distribution center, and the formation of a grid. Today, most of the country is covered by an electricity grid which allows different generators to connect with different transmission systems to enable the industry to realize economies of scale.

One of the problematic aspects surrounding the use of electricity is that it cannot be stored. Batteries are in the primitive stages of technological development for this task. Thus, the generation of electricity is in a constant and delicate balance. "Base-load" generators are operated continuously to meet customer demand. These have high capital costs but the lowest operating costs. Base-load plants are most often nuclear powered or coal-fired. Intermediate load plants, such as oil fired plants, are used as demand peaks. When demand is highest, "peak-load" generators are brought into operation. The difficult part of the balance is to have enough base-load generation for the constant and assured demand, and enough peak load for demand increases without having too much excess capacity, i.e., unused electricity. To promote economy, electric utilities interconnect with each other and transfer their excess as demands vary. The interconnections of these many utilities form power pools which attempt to maintain the highest degree of efficiency available through an increase in economies of scale.

B. REGULATORY OVERVIEW

The regulation of the electricity industry is divided between the states and the federal government. State public utility commissions establish the utility's franchise and set its retail rates. The federal government, through the FERC, sets wholesale and interstate rates. Mississippi Power & Light Co. v. Mississippi (1988); Nantahala Power and Light Co. v. Thornburg (1986).

Most of the federal regulation of the electricity industry is governed by three federal statutes. The primary legislation is the Federal Power Act of 1935 and the Public Utilities Regulatory Policy Act of 1978 (PURPA). The Public Utility Holding Company Act, 15 U.S.C.A. §§ 79 to 79z-6, is administered by the Securities Exchange Commission and governs holding company abuses and utility finance. Arcadia v. Ohio Power Co. (1990). The electricity industry is also subject to federal anti-trust law. Otter Tail Power Co. v. United States (1973).

Title II of the Federal Power Act, 16 U.S.C.A. § 824, confers ratemaking and licensing authority on the FERC.

Federal rate regulation mandates that rates be "just and reasonable" and nondiscriminatory, otherwise the rates are unlawful. 16 U.S.C.A. § 824(d)(a). The FERC has jurisdiction over the transmission of electric energy in interstate commerce and the sale of such energy at wholesale in interstate commerce. 16 U.S.C.A. § 824(a). The FERC also functions as a coordinator for interconnections which are made pursuant to the Act and by voluntary agreement. 16 U.S.C.A. § 824(a)(A).

As part of the National Energy Act, Congress passed the Public Utility Regulatory Policy Act of 1978 (PURPA), 16 U.S.C.A. § 2601. PURPA affects electric utilities in two significant ways. First, it amends the Federal Power Act in order to expand FERC jurisdiction over wheeling, interconnection, and assorted industry structural items. Secondly, FERC authority and involvement over electric utility ratemaking is expanded.

Title II of PURPA grants to the FERC the power, in limited circumstances, to issue an order requiring the utility to interconnect. The theory behind this power is that such an order would be designed to serve the public interest by encouraging conservation of energy and capital, as well as improving the reliability and efficiency of the electric system. 16 U.S.C.A. § 824(i). The Federal Power Act is also amended by PURPA to allow the Commission to order the "wheeling" of electricity, i.e., the transmission of electricity over another utility's transmission lines. Wheeling should encourage conservation and efficiency. 16 U.S.C.A. § 824(i). In an effort to promote pooling for similar purposes, 16 U.S.C.A. § 824a–1 grants the FERC the authority to exempt certain utilities from state laws which prohibit or prevent the voluntary coordination of electric utilities.

Occasional brownouts and blackouts are due to electric power shortages. In an effort to stem these shortages, 16 U.S.C.A. § 824a–1(a) requires public utilities to provide plans for shortages. PURPA also requires the Commission to undertake a study of proposed wholesale rate increases, and a study of the level of reliability needed to adequately serve the public. U.S.C.A. §§ 824a–1(b); 824a–2. These provisions of Title II encourage conservation and efficiency in the electricity industry by attempting to tighten energy use in the existing production and distribution networks.

PURPA gave a significant boost to alternative forms of energy production. Among other things, the act creates a market for the sale and purchase of electric power produced by certain facilities that meet the statute's requirements for cogeneration or small power production. Firms that satisfy these regulations are known as qualifying facilities (QFs). See Empire Lumber Co. v. Washington Water Power Co. (1987) (conventional utility need not purchase electricity from a facility which is not a QF). To promote cogeneration and small power production, PURPA also exempts QFs from certain regulation under the Federal Power Act, the Public Utility Holding Company Act, and some state and financial regulations.

Section 201 of PURPA defines "small power production" facilities to mean those facilities that have a capacity of 80 megawatts (Mw) or less. By comparison, a large central station power plant may have a capacity of 500 Mw or more. Small power production facilities, to qualify, must not have over one-half ownership by an electric utility. More than 75 percent of its total energy production must be from waste, biomass, geothermal, or renewable resources. 16 U.S.C.A. § 796(17).

"Cogeneration" is the use of a single fuel source like coal, oil, or gas to make sequentially two usable forms of energy, usually electricity and heat. For example, oil or gas is used first in a boiler to fuel an electric turbine which produces electricity. The boiler also gives off excess heat in the form of steam, and the steam is then used to provide heating. The steam may also be used to generate electricity. Cogenerated electricity accounts for 20,000 Mw out of total United States capacity of more than 600,000 Mw. Companies build cogeneration facilities to cut energy costs, or to turn a profit by selling power to the local utility.

PURPA requires the FERC to promulgate rules requiring electric utilities to buy and sell electricity from and to qualifying cogenerators and small power producers. Utilities are also obligated to interconnect with qualifying facilities in order to buy and sell electricity. This insures a market for the electricity from cogeneration and small power production facilities, and places them in competition with electric utilities. Section 210(b) of PURPA also requires the FERC to ensure that the rates for the purchase and sale of electricity from and to cogenerators and small power producers are (1) just and reasonable to the consumers of the electric utility, (2) in the public interest, and (3) nondiscriminatory to cogenerators and small power producers. In addition, the FERC is to ensure that any rate does not exceed the incremental cost to the electric utility of alternative electric energy (i.e., electricity obtained from other than the qualifying facility). 16 U.S.C.A. § 824a–3. The assumption behind section 210 is that if a market for electricity produced from cogeneration and small power production facilities is to be viable, there must be purchases of that electricity, there must be a physical interconnection to the electric facilities, and there must exist the right of cogenerators and small power producers to have their electricity transmitted to purchasers by electric facilities.

Section 210 of PURPA was held constitutional by the Supreme Court in FERC v. Mississippi (1982). In American Paper Institute, Inc. v. American Electric Power Service Corporation (1983), the Court upheld the FERC rule that requires utilities to buy electric energy from a qualifying facility at a rate equal to the utility's "full avoided cost." This is the cost which the utility would incur in generating or buying the electricity from a source other than the qualifying facility. See also Snow Mountain Pine Co. v. Maudlin (1987).

American Paper also sustained the FERC rule issued under PURPA that requires utilities to make the necessary physical interconnections with cogeneration and small power producers to effect purchases and sales under PURPA.

PURPA added sections 211 and 212 to the Federal Power Act, 16 U.S.C.A. § 824j and k. Those sections provide that if a cogenerator or small power producer requests a third party utility to provide electric transmission service (wheeling) to a willing buyer, and the generator is refused, the FERC may order the third party to wheel in certain limited circumstances. In addition, a wheeling order must not result in an uncompensated economic loss or undue burden for any affected party. Nor can the order impair the ability of any electric utility to render adequate service to its customers. Section 211(c)(1) also requires that no wheeling order "may be issued unless the Commission determines that such an order would reasonably preserve existing competitive relationships." 16 U.S.C.A. § 824j(e)(1).

C. TRANSMISSION AND POWER POOLS

Under section 202(a) of the Federal Power Act, the FERC is authorized to divide the country into regional districts to promote voluntary interconnections and coordination of electricity transmission. These interconnections form power pools that try to achieve economies of scale in transmission and use of electricity. The FERC has the authority to approve power pools. Central Iowa Power Co-op. v. FERC (1979).

It was earlier noted that in an effort to increase efficiency, electric utilities are linked through interconnections. These interconnections form power pools. These power pools are agreements among electric generation, transmission, and distribution companies to sell power to each other at certain times and rates. The idea is to have a pool in which members with excess capacity can transfer that load to other members experiencing shortages. Ideally, waste is reduced, less expensive electricity is being generated, and the most efficient generating units are operating at all times. PURPA indeed encourages this by giving the FERC authority to order interconnections.

Pooling and interconnections are not without problems, however. Pooling puts traditionally competitive utilities into the position of reducing competition. This is particularly true in the battle between small utilities and larger ones. The larger utilities can achieve greater economies of scale and can sell their products and services more cheaply than can smaller utilities. Hence a disincentive exists for allowing smaller utilities to become members of a power pool. Small utilities cannot be ignored though, given that there are close to 3,000 small utilities out of a total of 3,100 utility systems. One technological hurdle which remains is that electricity transmission is not perfectly efficient, and electricity cannot be transmitted over very long distances. More specifically, it is not economic to transfer electricity from the western United States (where there is much low sulfur coal and excess capacity) to the East (where there are most end-users).

D. FERC ELECTRICITY INITIATIVES

There is a consensus interpretation of why there were changes in growth in the electricity market after World War II. An unprecedented climate of competition arose due to excess capacity, slowed growth in demand, greater price elasticity of demand, new entrants in the generation end of the fuel cycle, and merger, acquisition, and spin-off activities. Yet, as in the natural gas market, there is a paradox accompanying increased competition. Although there are more options available for the generation of electricity on the supply side and more options for consumers to choose from on the demand side, these options are not available to all consumers. Specifically, purchasing flexibility exists for large industrial consumers, but typically does not filter down to smaller customers.

In a controversial series of proposed rulemakings, the FERC is gravitating away from prices artificially set by regulation, and toward greater reliance on market-like competition to align more closely supply, demand, and price. The FERC's free market favoritism is theoretically sound. However, there are structural impediments in the electricity industry—just as there are in the natural gas industry—that make undesirable a complete transition from regulation to market. Like the natural gas industry, the electricity industry may be able to promote more competition in the generation segment of its fuel cycle, but the transmission segment exhibits monopoly characteristics, and, hence, it should be regulated. Regulation of transmission is also necessary to prevent captive customers (small commercial and residential users) from being forced to absorb excess utility costs.

The FERC's rulemaking activities aspire to achieve two goals. First, the FERC wants to discontinue setting wholesale rates administratively and to have them set in something like a competitive market. Second, following the successful lead of PURPA, which opened up markets in cogeneration and small power production, the FERC proposes to even further expand generation options to encourage competition.

PURPA began developing generation alternatives by creating a new electricity market. Under PURPA, a co-generation facility, or small power producer, can become a "qualifying facility" (QF) entitled to sell its excess product to a utility, up to the utility's avoided cost. Therefore, any QF that can produce more electricity than it can use at a cost lower than the purchasing utility's cost of electricity can make a profit on those sales. This PURPA scheme successfully brought new entrants into the market and increased the energy efficiency of electricity production.

Building on that success, the FERC issued three notices of proposed rulemaking (NOPR) that have the potential to revolutionize federal regulation of electricity to the same degree as FERC's initiatives regarding natural gas. Two NOPRs concern avoided cost determinations. In one, the FERC proposes the establishment of bidding procedures to be implemented by both state regulatory authorities and nonregulated electric utilities as a means of establishing rates for QF power purchases. This proposed rule would create an artificial market for price setting and would avoid a fixed reliance on a utility's full avoided cost. If successful, such bidding would encourage cogeneration and small power production, energy conservation, efficient use of facilities, and equitable rates. In the second FERC rulemaking, guidelines are provided for states that choose to set rates administratively rather than through an auction-like market.

In its third NOPR, the FERC proposes the creation of a new entity in the electricity market, independent power producers (IPPs). An IPP is defined as a power producer that does not have a franchise area and does not own transmission facilities. In other words, an IPP is not structured like a classic public utility. Like QFs, IPPs compete with traditional public utilities, and among themselves, for a share of an emerging market. Traditional public utilities may have reached their technological capacity, as evidenced by the fact that they are producing electricity at a cost higher than other producers. Through IPPs, the FERC intends to exploit this gap.

The IPP notice proposes that rates will be set according to a bidding process similar to that for QF power. In other words, IPP ratemaking will be determined in a constrained market rather than on a historic cost basis. This rate regulation is an attempt to reform traditional ratemaking by setting rates more competitively. It is also an attempt to rationalize electricity pricing by treating the new class of suppliers uniformly. IPPs and QFs fit the economic theory behind competitive markets. As new entrants, they must offer electricity below the buyer's (incumbent's) incremental cost in order to profit and stay in the market. Most frequently, buyers of IPP power will be traditional franchised utilities, often vertically integrated, that will buy when electricity is cheaper in the market than it is to produce.

The FERC natural gas and electricity rulemakings are revolutionary in two ways. First, they rest on the FERC's existing authority and not on some new legislative mandate. Second, they break away from traditional utility-type regulation. Still, these proposals are consistent with the dominant model of energy regulation described in Chapter Nine. The model aspires to mimic the market when it can, and it resorts to regulation only when a market imperfection can be pointed out as a justification for government intervention. One cautionary note is that the regulatory transitions, like any such transition, will have associated costs, and complaints will be heard from the losers. For example, traditional public utilities, faced with new competition, will face a potential loss of market power. Captive consumers of natural gas and electricity may also complain. The realignment of these two industries should improve allocative efficiency as natural gas and electricity are sold at accurate prices without an accompanying loss of social welfare. Yet captive consumers of natural gas and electricity may bear an unreasonable amount of the transition costs, and a general move to the market will not, on its own, protect these consumers. There will therefore likely be associated regulation, possibly from the states, to reduce these imperfections.

Federal natural gas and electricity initiatives are motivated by one overriding goal—to move energy regulations closer to the market. This movement is premised on the recognition that natural gas is abundant, as is the coal and nuclear power that produces electricity. Also, old electricity technologies seem to have peaked, while new technologies in production and distribution appear available. Adequate supplies and potential technological gains mean greater efficiencies and more competition. According to the prevailing views of American democratic capitalism, markets are better suited than governments to order supplies, demands, and prices in a competitive environment. As a matter of allocative efficiency then, FERC's regulatory gamble is that price and allocation controls for natural gas and electricity should move outside the hearing rooms of the FERC, and into the government markets proposed by these rulemakings.

E. ELECTRICITY AND THE ENVIRONMENT

Environmental issues abound in the electricity fuel cycle. Depending on the natural resource used to generate the electricity, there are different environmental concerns. As examples, the construction of a hydroelectric facility may adversely affect sensitive ecosystems, and the mining and milling of uranium present radiological hazards. The most significant and complex environmental hazard arises with the burning of fossil fuels, principally coal, to generate electricity.

For over a decade, Congress debated making significant amendments to the Clean Air Act. Those amendments were signed into law by President Bush on November 15, 1990. Title IV of the Clean Air Act Amendments of 1990, Pub.L. No. 101–549, 104 Stat. 2399, directly affects electric utilities by addressing the problem of "acid deposition," also known as acid rain. Congress found that acid rain threatens natural resources and ecosystems and that the principal source was the burning of fossil fuels. The 1990 Amendments propose to reduce the annual emission of sulfur dioxide (SO_2) by 10 million tons from the 1980 emission level, and to reduce nitrogen oxide (NO) two million tons from the 1980 level. The reduction is to be accomplished through various techniques:

(1) Specified utility plants must meet emission limitations by certain deadlines;

(2) Alternative compliance can be made through an emission allocation and transfer system, more popularly known as emission trading; and,

(3) An incentive system is established for conservation, renewable and clean alternative technologies, and pollution prevention.

The Amendments set out annual allowances for SO_2 emissions for existing and new units. In order to facilitate compliance, the allowances may be traded among units. Under Phase I, units designated in the act must attain specific SO_2 reductions by January 1, 1995. Allowance requirements can be adjusted for utilities that use qualified conservation measures or qualified renewable resources. Phase II SO_2 reductions are scheduled for January 1, 2000, and are to be completed by the end of 2009. Nitrogen oxide emission reductions are also to be accomplished by emissions limitations through regulations promulgated by the EPA.

The emissions reduction program will be implemented through a system of fees and permits, monitoring and reporting, fines and penalties, and through some technology forcing provisions. The Amendments encourage "repowering," in which an existing utility can receive an extension on the deadline for emissions limitations if it uses an approved clean coal (i.e., low sulfur) technology.

III. PUBLIC UTILITY REGULATION

The public utility is the dominant mechanism for converting natural resources to useful energy and for distributing that energy to consumers. Public utilities have been regulated for over 100 years and, although this chapter concentrates on natural gas and electricity, public utility regulation also involves such goods as telephone, water, and cable television.

Government regulation of public utilities is based on two ideas. The first is economic—public utilities are natural monopolies that require public regulation. The second is more political—the utility being regulated is "affected with a public interest." A utility has a public interest dimension because public policy assumes that natural gas and electricity should be made widely and readily available at a reasonably low cost. These two ideas mean that utility regulation is based on what is called the regulatory compact. In exchange for an exclusive service territory (a monopoly), a utility agrees to let a government agency set its prices. In effect, the benefits of a government protected monopoly are exchanged for the ability of government to set the monopoly's prices.

As a result of the regulatory compact, the utility has a "service obligation," which means that it must serve customers in its service territory and must price its goods fairly and nondiscriminatorily. Also, the utility can only incur "prudent" costs. On the other hand, the government is obligated to reimburse a utility for its prudently incurred costs and to provide the utility with a fair rate of return on its capital expenditures. These obligations are described in more detail below, after discussion of the economic rationale behind the regulatory compact.

A. THE THEORY OF NATURAL MONOPOLY

Some public utilities, most of which are privately owned, deal in commodities and services such as natural gas, electricity, water, and telephone. These utilities are often referred to as "natural monopolies." They are seen as "natural" because of their structure—large and capital intensive, and their product—a social necessity.

A natural monopoly occurs when a firm is able to grow larger and reduce prices simultaneously until it is the only firm in a market. For example, once a natural gas company lays a pipeline or an electricity utility erects a transmission line, there is no good economic reason to lay another pipeline or transmission line. The additional lines are duplicative and wasteful. In order to eliminate such waste and to avoid the sins of misused market power caused by monopolistic pricing, government and utilities enter the regulatory compact. This regulatory compact is justified because: (1) through ratemaking, necessary utility services are provided in the public interest; (2) monopoly power is controlled; (3) waste is avoided; and (4) the distribution of wealth is managed.

B. RATEMAKING GOALS

Ratemaking is economic because it attempts to set prices at efficient (nonmonopolistic) levels. Ratemaking is political because the product is determined to be a social necessity and rates must be fair. Although it can be said that all regulation is a combination of politics and economics, sight of that combination is frequently lost in an arena as technical as ratemaking.

Ratemaking has five functions:

(1) Capital–Attraction;

(2) Low Cost Energy;

(3) Efficiency Incentive;

(4) Demand–Control or Consumer–Rationing; and

(5) Compensatory Income–Income Transfer. See generally J. Bonbright, A. Danielson & D. Kamerschen, Principles of Public Utility Rates (2nd ed. 1988).

While these regulatory goals (both political and economic) can conflict, they attempt to serve the several interests of the utility, its shareholders, consumers, and the public interest generally.

1. Capital–Attraction Function

Because of the regulatory compact and because of constitutional requirements, government must assure private firms that a fair revenue is available. Regulators ensure that the regulated utility does not gouge the customer by charging a monopolistic price. However, regulators cannot, either constitutionally or economically, keep prices so low that it simply is not worth it economically to stay in the public utility business. Therefore, regulated firms must be able to set rates which keep them competitive. Firms are allowed to charge "reasonable rates," which are rates that allow them to encourage people to invest in utility stocks and bonds as they would in comparatively risky private industries.

In addition to covering operating costs and expenses, rate-making has been structured to allow a firm to expand plant and production. The capital-attraction function is another way of saying that rates should be set which allow utilities to seek investment capital for growth. Rates are set at a level to attract investors. Traditionally, investment in public utilities has been very safe, promising a steady return. Because of the expansion and growth of the industry, together with the belief in an energy-economic growth link, utilities were seen as a steady growth industry. Hence, utilities were a prudent investment for portfolio managers and individual investors. Any diversified investment portfolio would certainly have its share of utilities whose dividends were almost certain. The return to shareholders has been a little lower than that of private industry, but that is because utility stocks and bonds have been perceived to be a much less risky investment.

2. The Low Cost Energy Function

Utilities found themselves in a financially risky environment after the 1970s. During this decade, resource prices were often controlled by international cartels, and there were increased costs, soaring domestic inflation, and a political climate which stressed conservation. By the beginning of the 1980s, the traditional assumption that utility stocks were relatively risk free was being challenged. Public utilities began to compete harder for investment capital, and rate setting agencies had to pay closer attention to the ability of a utility to find capital in the market. The direct consequence of such increased financial pressure on utilities was a demand by the utilities for higher rates. In no small measure, public utility commissions (PUCs) granted the requests for rate increases until there was a public backlash over escalating utility prices, sometimes referred to as rate shock.

As noted in Chapter Nine, one element of the nation's general energy policy is low cost energy. High utility rates are inconsistent with this policy, and, therefore, utility commissions took a much harder look at the requests by utilities for rate increases. The consumer pressure to reduce rates, and the reluctance on the part of PUCs to raise rates, have resulted in an era of greater competition in the electricity and natural gas industries. In the electricity industry, greater competition comes in the form of new producers. In the natural gas industry, greater competition was spawned by an increased supply of natural gas.

3. The Efficiency–Incentive Function

What is an efficient price? While economists will continue to debate this intractable question, under classic demand-supply theory, as the demand increases so does the price, until other competitors can attract customers with lower prices. The firm that can set prices low enough to attract the most customers, and stay in business, can be said to have reached the efficient price. Thus, efficient pricing is a function of competition. In a regulated industry, however, there is no competition so the rate must be set to promote the more abstract concept of an efficient price. For regulated utilities, an efficient price is one which is designed to yield revenues to cover costs plus a "fair rate of return" for the investors. Regulators approximate this price by paying attention to what costs are incurred by the utility, and what costs the utility attempts to pass on to its ratepayers. Costs allowed in the rate level are those which, in a PUC's view, are proper operating expenses and overhead. The resulting rate of return must be one which keeps the utility competitive compared with firms with similar financial risks. Contrariwise, costs are disallowed which are promotive of waste or imprudence, or costs that are not distributable to customer service.

4. The Demand–Control or Consumer Rationing Function

Another aspect of classic supply-demand theory is that price affects supply. The lower the price the more people will buy. A single firm can encourage people to purchase more of a service by lowering its prices. Likewise, a price increase should decrease demand.

Until the mid–1970s, utility rates reflected this theory by being set according to a declining block method. This rate structure is graphically depicted below:

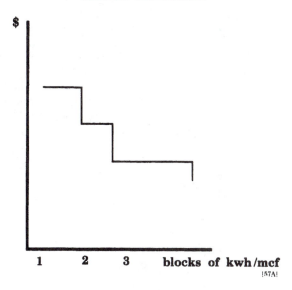

According to the above diagram, the price of electricity or natural gas declines as more is consumed. In other words, the cost of the product or the rate in block one is higher than that in block three. Such a rate design promotes consumption because people will consume more as prices fall. If the block were inverted so that prices increased as consumption increased, then conservation is promoted because people buy less as prices rise.

Ratemaking thus affects supply. If rates are set below their "true cost," then consumption will increase. Similarly, as rates rise, demand will fall off. The rate of the decline in demand depends on price elasticity. The 1970s demonstrated that the price elasticity of oil and electricity, as well as natural gas, was more elastic than once believed. One can now assume that if energy prices rise, consumers will buy less energy. Therefore, if conservation is seen as a desirable goal, regulators can promote conservation by letting prices rise so as to reflect the "true cost" of the product.

5. The Income–Distributive Function

At the most general level, ratemaking distributes wealth from consumers to utility owners. As prices are charged for the use of a service (e.g., electricity), income is distributed (actually redistributed) from consumers (ratepayers) to owners (shareholders). Thus, one function of ratemaking is to affect the amount of money that is transferred from ratepayers to the shareholders that own the utility.

Ratemaking also involves more subtle redistributions of wealth, sometimes called subsidies, among (and within) classes of customers. Utility customers generally can be grouped in three categories—residential, industrial, and commercial. Each group can be further subdivided. Residential customers, for example, can be classified by income level, or as owners of primary residences or vacation homes.

Each of the general categories has different costs associated with it. A large aluminum plant, for example, consumes large amounts of electricity but does not require equally costly transmission or customer service. Individual residential customers, though, consume quite a bit less electricity, yet they require an electric line into each residence which incurs relatively high service costs. One way to lower the cost of electricity to residential consumers is to set slightly higher rates for industrial customers, thus resulting in the subsidization of residential customers by industrial customers. These redistributions fall under the heading of rate design.

The ability of a utility to discriminate in the pricing of the product is not without an economic explanation or justification. Different consumers have different demand elasticities. As the price of electricity rises, industrial consumers will find it easier than residential consumers to use other forms of energy. Compared to industrial consumers, residential customers have a greater demand inelasticity. Consequently, their "willingness to pay" is higher than that of industrial customers, and differential rates can reflect that "willingness."

C. THE RATE FORMULA

The traditional rate formula is designed to produce a utility's revenue requirement. The formula is simple to state:

$$R = O + (V - D)r$$

The elements of the traditional rate formula are defined below:

R is the utility's total revenue requirement or rate level. This is the total amount of money a PUC allows a utility to earn.
O is the utility's operating expenses.
V is the gross value of the utility's tangible and intangible property.
D is the utility's accrued depreciation. Combined $(V - D)$ constitute the utility's *rate base*, also known as its capital investment.
r is the rate of return a utility is allowed to earn on its capital investment or on its rate base.

Defining the variables is simple, but determining their content and application is more difficult.

1. Operating Expenses

A firm's operating expenses, such as wages, salaries, supplies, maintenance, and research and development, must be recouped if the utility is to stay operational. Operating costs are most often the largest component of the revenue requirement (commonly three-fourths to four-fifths), and the easiest to determine. The determination of what constitutes operating expenses has generally been left to the management of the utility under the theory that these are essentially business decisions which will not be second guessed by a PUC or a court. Managerial good faith is presumed. Although both PUCs and courts have the legal authority to supervise the utility's management, they will not substitute their judgment unless there is an abuse of managerial discretion. State of Missouri ex rel. Southwestern Bell Tel. Co. v. Public Service Com'n of Missouri (1923). Hence, litigation involving operating expense issues has been light.

The PUC decides which items are to be included as expenses, and they examine the amount of the expenses. The following operating expense items have caught the attention of supervisory agencies and courts: automatic fuel costs, Re New England Power Co. (1972); Re Arizona Pub. Serv. Co. (1986); rate case and regulation expenses, Re Hudson Water Co. (1979); salaries, wages, and benefits, Re Ohio Power Co. (1986); Re Arizona Pub. Serv. Co. (1986); LaFourche Tel. Co., Inc. v. Louisiana Public Service Commission (1979); advertising and public relations fees, Illinois Bell Tel. Co. v. Illinois Commerce Com'n (1973); Central Hudson Gas & Elec. Corp. v. Public Service Com'n of New York (1980); and charitable contributions, Re El Paso Nat. Gas Co. (1971); Re Pacific Tel. & Tel. Co. (1964).

2. Rate Base

The next step in determining the rate level is to ascertain the net amount of capital investment that the company has made. This net or depreciated value includes tangible and intangible property. The rate base has been the subject of much litigation. The determination of what constitutes the rate base also forms the basis for the constitutional standard for judging whether or not rates are confiscatory. Tangible property includes plant and equipment used to provide the utility's service. Intangible property would include such items as working capital, leases, and franchises.

Valuation methods vary. In a period of static costs, an original cost valuation may be sufficient. With a period of high inflation, a rate base which values plant and equipment at original cost substantially shrinks the purchasing power of the dollar. In these circumstances, utilities argue in favor of reproduction cost valuations. In either case, depreciation on plant and equipment is subtracted from the rate base and carried as an operating expense. The theory behind including depreciation as an expense is that capital may be accumulated for further expansion and growth. With inflationary trends, utilities are seeking to use accelerated depreciation techniques to accumulate capital more quickly in the hope of beating inflation. Accelerated depreciation is the exception rather than the rule, but the trend persists.

Rates cannot be set so low as to be confiscatory, in which case they violate the Takings Clause of the Fifth Amendment to the Constitution. Early on in the history of ratemaking the legislature set the standard for what constituted a confiscatory rate. Munn v. Illinois (1876). Later, legislative standard setting gave way to the judiciary. In Smyth v. Ames (1898) and later in Bluefield Water Works & Imp. Co. v. Public Service Commission (1923), the Supreme Court listed factors that PUCs should consider in evaluating a company's property, and in determining a rate of return to which a company is entitled. If the factors were applied by PUCs in a manner acceptable to the courts, then the PUCs' decisions would not be disturbed. If not, then the PUCs could expect that their decisions would be overturned by the courts.

In 1944, the Supreme Court ushered in the era of deference to administrative agencies in their ratemaking decisions in Federal Power Com'n v. Hope Natural Gas Co. (1944). The *Hope* case established the principle that the Court would defer to FPC determinations as long as the "end result" was fair or reasonable. The end result test still survives. See Jersey Central Power & Light Co. v. FERC (1987).

The traditional rate formula encourages capital investment because it gives a rate of return on the rate base. In other words, the more a utility expends, the more money it earns. Where the economy is growing, capital expansion is productive. Economic waste results when the economy is shrinking because plant expansion simply contributes to unused capacity. In such circumstances, PUCs examine more closely the utility's inclusion of capital investment in the rate base.

In the late 1960s and early 1970s, several electric utilities planned their construction of new plants based on an average growth in demand at seven percent per year. The construction period for a utility plant can last from 8–14 years, depending on the type of plant being built. Coal plants can be built in about eight years and nuclear plants take about 12–15 years to construct. In the late 1960s and early 1970s, utilities that based expansion on the historic seven percent growth rate in demand were wrong. The growth rate was far less. This miscalculation resulted in capital investment in unnecessary power plants because growth in demand fell drastically. The electricity industry and its regulators were placed in an awkward and expensive predicament of having to decide how to allocate the costs associated with unnecessary plants.

Rate base issues were caught between an historic formula that encouraged capital investment and a dramatically changed economic climate. PUCs had to decide whether to allow a present cash flow to utilities with plants under construction, or force them to wait until the new plant was operating. Mid–Tex Elec. Co-op., Inc. v. FERC (1985) (partial cash flow allowed). State and federal commissions also had to decide how to treat excess capacity caused by the unused plant. Gulf Power Co. v. Florida Public Service Com'n (1984) (excess capacity disallowed).

A major issue that contributed to the downfall of the nuclear power industry was how to treat canceled plants. Dusquesne Light Co. v. Barasch (1989) (a state statute denying recovery costs expended on canceled nuclear power plants is not a taking). Some courts held that investment in canceled plants could not be recovered from ratepayers because the plant was not "used or useful." Jersey Central Power & Light Co. v. FERC (1985); Citizens Action Coalition of Indiana, Inc. v. Northern Indiana Public Service Co. (1985). Other states allowed the utility to recover prudently incurred expenses of canceled plants.

3. Rate of Return

Finally, a fair rate of return (expressed as a percentage) must be determined. Because there are different classes of owners—e.g., bondholders (debt), and preferred shareholders and common shareholders (equity)—each class must be taken into account. In effect, the rate of return reflects profit, interest on debt, and dividends. The final percentage is intended to reflect the return necessary to attract investment from each class of investor. In case of liquidation, holders of equity securities will be paid off before debt holders, and preferred shareholders will be paid off before common shareholders. In order of risk, the classes are bondholders, preferred, and common shareholders. The rate of return to attract these various investors must reflect the varying risks.

The rate of return can also be used as an incentive mechanism to reward utilities for desirable behavior. PUCs may choose to reward conservation or greater economic efficiency by awarding a higher rate of return to the utilities that achieve gains in these areas. Naturally, the rate cannot be so high as to cause injury to customers. Thus, the rate of return occurs within a zone of reasonableness. Federal Power Com'n v. Natural Gas Pipeline Co. (1942).

D. CONTEMPORARY RATEMAKING ISSUES

The traditional ratemaking formula fosters capital spending. When costs are declining, capital spending works to add needed production capacity. When costs are rising, however, a regulatory scheme which encourages capital spending has the undesirable effect of contributing to overinvestment of capital and to excess capacity. The tendency of the traditional ratemaking formula to encourage overinvestment is known as the Averch–Johnson effect. When demand for electricity began to level off in the late 1970s, the country found itself with excess electric capacity.

The traditional formula is cost based and works well with an expanding market. It works less well with either a contracting market or a stable market. Where the traditional formula promotes capital growth and consumption, in the contemporary market conservation and the reduction of excess capacity are seen as desirable goals. In order to promote these goals, regulatory authorities have concentrated on marginal cost pricing.

1. Marginal Cost Pricing

First adopted by the Wisconsin Utility Commission in In Re Madison Gas & Electric Co. (1974), the idea directly borrows the economic concept of marginal cost pricing previously explained in Chapter One. Prior to *Madison Gas & Electric*, rates were set based on historic cost. A PUC gathered financial data from the utility for a historic test year, usually the year just previous to the rate hearing, then set rates roughly by apportioning costs based on kilowatt hours (kwh) of electricity or thousands of cubic feet (mcf) of natural gas sold. This method had the effect of charging customers the average cost of their utility product. Marginal cost, however, is not based on historic cost. Instead, marginal cost is based on the total cost of producing the next increment (kwh or mcf) of a utility's service. If a utility is operating at 100% of its capacity, then the next customer that requires service literally forces the utility to add capacity. The cost of the necessary additional capacity is the true cost of production because resources are being allocated to produce that next incremental unit. In a sense, the traditional formula reflects cost of service, while marginal cost rates reflect value of service.

Proponents of marginal cost ratemaking argue that marginal cost pricing better reflects the true cost of a utility's product than does historic or average cost ratemaking. In fact, if utility rates were actually based on their true marginal cost, users would pay the exact value of the product at the exact time of use. Therefore, it is argued, if the electric market is to operate more efficiently, then users should pay rates calculated on current production costs. This theory has resulted in PUCs trying to set rates based on peak pricing. When electricity demand is high (e.g., during peak periods), the cost of producing that electricity is correspondingly high. During heat waves the use of air conditioners increases demand. Similarly, commercial users place a high demand on electricity consumption during office hours. Consequently, time-of-day or time of season rates (as examples of marginal rates) should reflect those costs.

2. Incentive Rates

There is evidence that electricity can be produced more efficiently and at a lower cost than it is being produced by large utilities. Large industrial users, for example can be self-generators or take advantage of co-generation to reduce their electric bills. Similarly, small power producers might be able to generate electricity at a cost lower than that of large public utilities.

This potential increased presence of competition means that a rate formula based on a specific utility's historic costs is inaccurate. The rate formula can be used to increase the efficiency of utilities, or rates can be based more on a market model by pegging rates not to a utility's historic costs, but to the costs of electricity in the market. Market-based rates are sometimes referred to as the avoided cost of electricity. The utility's rate is set at the price it would have to pay for a unit of electricity in the newly developing market, rather than that based on the utility's cost.

Incentives can be used in other ways. An example of an economic incentive is the establishment of a hypothetical optimum rate of return based on some market model, and the rewarding of utilities which approach that optimum return. Social incentives include rewarding with slightly higher rates of return utilities which promote conservation or meet or exceed certain environmental or efficiency performance standards. On the contrary, utilities which fail to meet such standards are "penalized" by lowering their rate of return.

3. New Utility Markets

Since the beginning of the 1980s, energy markets have moved toward equilibrium, thus reducing the need for radical executive and congressional intervention. Instead, day-to-day regulation takes place away from the more political branches and is accomplished through state PUCs, state and federal administrative agencies, and the court system. Contemporary federal regulation of the natural gas and electric industries is occurring most noticeably at the Federal Energy Regulatory Commission (FERC), the primary innovator in the developing area of government markets.

The simple theme for FERC regulation is competition. From the FERC's energy policy perspective, relative energy resource abundance and low prices indicate increasing competition in the natural gas and electricity industries. The FERC is trying to move the pricing and allocation decision of both industries toward market-based mechanisms and away from administrative law judges. The FERC's market based initiatives described earlier in this chapter are free market alternatives to traditional regulatory ratemaking.

INDEX

†